THE ACTS OF
THE APOSTLES

14 - 28

CALVIN'S COMMENTARIES

CALVIN'S COMMENTARIES

THE ACTS OF
THE APOSTLES

14 - 28

Translator

JOHN W. FRASER

Editors
DAVID W. TORRANCE
THOMAS F. TORRANCE

THE SAINT ANDREW PRESS
EDINBURGH

PUBLISHED . . . 1966

Published in Great Britain by Oliver and Boyd, Edinburgh

Translation © 1966 Oliver and Boyd Ltd.

PRINTED IN GREAT BRITAIN BY
ROBERT CUNNINGHAM AND SONS LTD., ALVA

INTRODUCTION

THE SECOND PART of John Calvin's *Commentary on the Acts of the Apostles* first appeared in 1554, two years after the First Part. It was dedicated to Frederick, son of the King of Denmark, and 'King-Elect'. The Dedicatory Epistle is given at the beginning of Volume I of the present translation, together with the Dedicatory Epistle to Nicolas Radzivil in the Second Edition of both Parts, which was published in 1560. Details of the various editions are given at the beginning of Volume I.

The translation of this Volume, like the First, has been made from the Latin texts of C.R. and Tholuck, and checked at various places from the French of Blanchier's edition, printed at Geneva, 1563, from the copy in the National Library of Scotland, Edinburgh. Professor T. F. Torrance translated chapter fourteen.

Other details given in the Introduction to Volume I apply also to this Volume.

When Calvin issued his Second Edition he made many additions. A few of these seem to have been done hurriedly, for the connexion is not smooth or clear; one at least is wrong (p. 205), and one redundant (p. 449). I have felt it necessary to draw attention to four of these additions in this Volume.

Manse of Farnell,   JOHN W. FRASER
Brechin, Angus.
Easter 1965.

CHAPTER FOURTEEN

And it came to pass in Iconium, that they entered together into the synagogue of the Jews, and so spake, that a great multitude both of Jews and of Greeks believed. But the Jews that were disobedient stirred up the souls of the Gentiles, and made them evil affected against the brethren. Long time therefore they tarried there speaking boldly in the Lord, which bare witness unto the word of his grace, granting signs and wonders to be done by their hands. But the multitude of the city was divided; and part held with the Jews, and part with the apostles. (1-4)

In the last chapter Luke declared how Paul and Barnabas set about their mission to the Gentiles. But, it might seem to be an unhappy and unfortunate beginning, in that they were not only expelled from Antioch, but also compelled by the obstinate wickedness of certain men to shake off the dust from their feet. But, however harshly they were received in one place, they do not give up, for they consider that they had been called by the Lord to exercise their ministry throughout the world, and specifically in face of the opposition of Satan. We see, therefore, that they came, not only prepared to teach, but armed for the struggle, going on undaunted to proclaim the Gospel in the midst of conflict.

There is a saying of Jeremiah that surely applies to all God's prophets and ministers, 'They shall fight against thee, but they shall not prevail' (Jer. 1.19). Now, wherever they are driven in their flight, they carry with them the same resolution, which shows that they were prepared not only for one combat, but for continual warfare, as Luke now goes on to relate. He tells us first that they came to Iconium, and adds that they did not look for some refuge there, where they might get some quiet and rest, but entered into the synagogue, as if they had met with no trouble.

The expression κατὰ τὸ αὐτό, which means 'together' or 'at the same time' in Greek, I take to apply to the Jews, rather than to Paul and Barnabas. Hence I interpret it to say, not that they both went in together, but that they followed the crowd at their regular and fixed time of assembly. We gather from this that they did not speak secretly with a few men, but in a great concourse of people, and that far from avoiding hostility or fearing danger, they showed confidence, eagerness and zeal.

That a great multitude believed. As Luke had earlier pointed out the

1

power of the Spirit in Paul and Barnabas, so now he lauds another
grace of God in the favourable results which they experienced, for the
single sermon they delivered was not without fruit, but produced many
sons for God from both Jews and Gentiles. If one or two, or a few,
had believed, they would not have been displeased with the reward
of their efforts at that point, but the Lord gives them greater encouragement, when, in a short time, they gather such an abundance
of fruit from their teaching. For they knew that it was not so much by
their own words, as by the power of the Spirit, that the hearts of so
many men were converted to believe. They were also able to conclude
from this that they were protected by the outstretched hand of God,
and that could increase their confidence a great deal.

2. *But the Jews that were disobedient.* Fresh persecution now overtakes them, and from the Jews at that, for they were like torches to inflame the minds of the Gentiles. Doubtless the Gentiles would have
borne the preaching of the Gospel with indifference had they not been
incited by those firebrands to resist. κακῶσαι I interpret here as 'to
infect with malice' or 'to urge on to do harm'. Under the name
brethren Luke includes, I think, all the godly, i.e. those who on embracing the Gospel had been troubled, as if some pernicious sect had
arisen to spread discord, to destroy the peace of the city, to disturb the
public order; but I do not object very much if anyone prefers to
restrict the term to Paul and Barnabas.

3. *Long time therefore.* Luke relates here that Paul and Barnabas did
not leave the city as soon as they saw some people opposed to them.
For when he says that they acted *boldly* he indicates that they had cause
for fear. From that we gather that they remained intrepid, and indeed
with extraordinary greatness of spirit counted all the hazards as nothing, until they were compelled by violence to move on to another
place.

The expression ἐπὶ κυρίῳ can be expounded differently, either that
they acted bravely in the Lord's cause, or that they took courage from
relying on His grace. I have followed the usual interpretation, that
they acted confidently and boldly in the Lord, being helped not by
their own strength but by His grace. Luke goes on to point out how
they were encouraged in the Lord, in that He was showing His
approval of their teaching by signs and wonders. Recognizing from
those that the Lord was with them, and that His hand was near to help
them, they were justly stimulated to vigorous activity. But in noting
one, he did not exclude other means, for the Lord encouraged and
established them in constancy in other ways. Yet Luke seems to have
spoken particularly about miracles, because in them the Lord was
manifesting His power openly before all the people. Accordingly

2

Paul and Barnabas were not a little assured, when the Lord delivered their teaching from contempt in this way.

Further, let us note what is said here, that the Lord bore witness to the Gospel in miracles, for it teaches us what the true use of miracles is. Their primary purpose is indeed to show us the power and grace of God, but since we are bad and perverse interpreters of them, God hardly ever allows them to be detached from His Word, lest they should be drawn into abuse and corruption. If miracles have at any time been wrought apart from His Word, in the first place it was a rare occurrence, and secondly a very meagre result followed from them. For the most part, however, God has wrought miracles, so that by them the world might know Him, not simply or in His bare majesty but in the Word. Hence Luke says at this point that the Gospel was established by miracles, not that some confused religion might possess the minds of men, but that through the teaching of Paul they might be brought to the pure worship of God. From this we may readily gather how foolishly the Papists act when they try to lead the world away from the reverence of God and the Gospel by bare miracles. We must keep to the principle that the miracles that come from God have never any other purpose than the establishing of the Gospel in its full and genuine authority.

Now we must see whether the Gospel commands us to invoke the dead, to burn incense to idols, to transfer the grace of Christ to alleged saints, to undertake votive pilgrimages, to devise profane acts of worship, of which there is never a mention in the Word of God. Yet there is nothing less consonant with the Gospel than that these super-stitions should have place. It follows from that that it is out of the supports of the Gospel that the Papists falsely construct the machines with which to attack it. Luke's statement that the Lord granted miracles to be done by the hands of His servants has the same end in view. By these words he is warning us that the only ministers were those who showed themselves obedient to the Lord, and that the real Author was He who used their hand and activity. Properly speaking, therefore, we are not to say that the miracles were Paul's or Barnabas', but were God's alone, who works through men in such a way that He does not wish His own glory to be obscured by their ministry.

Moreover, let us note the description which Luke gives to the Gospel here, in order to make us love it better. For in calling it *the Word of grace* he makes it taste very sweet to us, since in it salvation is offered to the world through Christ; and besides it is to be understood as the antithesis of the Law in which only a curse is set before us. Therefore let us remember that God speaks to us in the Gospel in order that He may reconcile Himself to us and testify that He is ready to forgive. This does not prevent it from being a *savour of death unto death* to the reprobate (II Cor. 2.16), because they do not alter its nature through their own depravity.

Concerning *signs and wonders* read what we have said in the second chapter.

4. *The multitude was divided.* Disaster now follows, for the city was divided into two factions, and in the end Paul and Barnabas are forced by the popular riot to depart elsewhere. If the source of the division is sought, it is certain that it originated from the Gospel, although there is nothing more contrary to it than the stirring up of discord. But the depravity of men causes the Gospel, which ought to be the bond of unity, to be the occasion for riots as soon as it appears on the scene. For this reason, whenever any schism arises, before we condemn those who seem to be the instigators we ought to consider wisely to whom the blame is to be attributed. Here we hear of one city rent by schism, out of which a part was led to Christ. This is declared by the Spirit of God to the praise, and not to the shame, of Paul and Barnabas. We must observe the same rule today, lest the Gospel be falsely charged with odium, if it does not bring all men to God in the same way, but the wicked riot against it. How wretched it is to see men divided from one another; but just as the unity that divides us all from God is accursed, so it is a hundred times better for a few to leave the world altogether and return to a state of grace with God, than to obtain peace with the world by being eternally separated from Him.

And when there was made an onset both of the Gentiles and of the Jews with their rulers, to entreat them shamefully, and to stone them, they became aware of it, and fled unto the cities of Lycaonia, Lystra and Derbe, and the region round about: and there they preached the gospel. And at Lystra there sat a certain man, impotent in his feet, a cripple from his mother's womb, who never had walked. The same heard Paul speaking: who, fastening his eyes upon him, and seeing that he had faith to be made whole, said with a loud voice, Stand upright on thy feet. And he leaped up and walked. (5–10)

5. Note how long the holy champions of Christ held out. They are not put to flight by the mere opposition of enemies; but when the sedition comes to boiling point, and the danger of being stoned is threatening, although many favour their teaching, they do not persist any further, but, remembering the saying of Christ in which He warned the faithful to possess their souls in patience, they avoid the fury of the enemy. And although they do flee, so as not to plunge rashly into death, yet their constancy in preaching the Gospel makes it clear that they had no fear of danger. For Luke adds that they preached

the Gospel in other places also. That is the proper kind of fear, when the servants of Christ do not run wilfully into the hands of their enemies to be cut down by them, and yet do not desist from their duty; nor does fear prevent them from obeying God, when He calls, and so, if the need arises, they will even go through death itself in the fulfilment of their ministry.

8. *And at Lystra there sat a certain man.* Luke refers to one miracle, which was probably one of many, but mention is made of it alone because of a memorable event. We shall soon see what happened. Luke recounts the circumstances which show the divine power all the clearer. when he says that the man had never walked, and had been a cripple from his mother s womb, that he was suddenly healed before the eyes of all by the voice of Paul alone, and that movement and agility came into his dead legs so that he leapt up without any difficulty.

9. *The same heard Paul speaking.* Hearing is given first place so that we may know that the faith which Luke is soon to commend was conceived through Paul's teaching. As soon as he heard Paul he hoped for healing. But the question is, whether this had been specially promised to him, for God does not command us to hope for anything we like on the spot, while He is offering to us eternal salvation in the Gospel. I reply that this was a unique and extraordinary movement of the Spirit in the cripple, as it was on the other hand in Paul when he recognized the man's faith solely through looking at him. It may well be possible for many to receive the Gospel, and yet not to be cured of the diseases from which they suffer. But since God determined to provide evidence of His grace in the cripple, He prepared his mind beforehand and made him capable of this new experience. Hence this must not be made into a common rule, because the cripple believed that he would be healed, but the preparation to receive the gift of healing was peculiar to him. And besides, this special kind of faith which makes room for miracles is not one that most of God's children have, although they are endowed with the Spirit of adoption all the same.

Who fastening his eyes upon him. We know how unreliable and deceptive a man's face is. From it one could not therefore be certain about a person's faith, which has God only to attest it, but, as I have already noted, the cripple's faith was revealed to Paul by the secret inspiration of the Spirit, as He was the one Guide and Teacher the apostles had for working miracles.

10. *Said with a loud voice.* Many old and very trustworthy manuscripts add, 'I say to thee in the name of Jesus Christ'; and certainly we see how anxious the apostles were to honour the name of Christ in all miracles. And so it seems very likely to me that this was ex-

pressed by Luke, although it is not commonly found now in our printed copies. Luke's subsequent statement that the lame man leapt up, not only serves to commend God's power, but such instant readiness to obey also indicates that he was duly prepared by the Lord, so that he was already walking in spirit when his feet were still dead. Although his quickness in rising made the power of God more conspicuous, Paul also deliberately raised his voice so that the sudden change might move the crowd all the more.

And when the multitudes saw what Paul had done, they lifted up their voice, saying in the speech of Lycaonia, The gods are come down to us in the likeness of men. And they called Barnabas, Jupiter; and Paul, Mercury, because he was the chief speaker. And the priest of Jupiter whose temple was before the city, brought oxen and garlands unto the gates, and would have done sacrifice with the multitudes. (11-13).

11. *And when the multitudes.* This story is ample testimony as to how prone men are to vanity. Paul did not utter the word *Arise* abruptly, but brought it in as a conclusion to his sermon about Christ. The people however ascribe the glory of the miracle to their idols, as if they had not heard a word about Christ. Indeed it is no wonder that, at the sudden sight of the miracle, the barbarous men lapsed into the superstition which they had imbibed from their childhood. But everywhere this is too common a fault, and is so inbred in us that we are naturally bad interpreters of God's works. From that arise such crass and crazy superstitions in the Papacy, for, snatching rashly at miracles, they give no ear to doctrine. Accordingly we must be all the more attentive and sober, lest we should happen to corrupt, by the carnal perception to which we are so inclined, the very power of God which is manifested for our salvation. And indeed it is not surprising that the Lord would have only a few miracles wrought, and for a short time at that, lest, through men's carnal desires, they should be directed into an entirely contrary end. For it is not right for Him to subject His name to the mockery of the world, and that is bound to happen when what is proper to Him is transferred to idols, or when unbelievers pervert His works in devising corrupt cults, as they set aside His Word and snatch at some deity invented by themselves.

Gods in the likeness of men. This was an idea taken from ancient myths, which nevertheless took their rise from an element of truth. The books of the poets are packed full of this nonsense, that the gods were often seen on earth in the form of men. Doubtless these were not invented out of nothing, for it is more likely that profane men turned into myths what the holy fathers had long ago handed down about angels. And it may well be that Satan made men foolish, and led them astray through his deceptions. It is certainly true that whatever came from God was corrupted by their wicked inventions as soon as it was transmitted to the heathen. And we must think of the sacrifices in the same way, for through them God trained His faithful people from the beginning, supplying their love and duty toward God, and their worship of Him, with external symbols. But after unbelievers invented strange deities for themselves, they corrupted the sacrifices for their own sacrilegious cult.

On seeing unaccustomed power in the healed cripple the men of Lycaonia decide that it is a work of God, and they are right so far. But then they go wrong, because, in keeping with habitual error, they make false gods for themselves in Paul and Barnabas. For what leads them to prefer Barnabas to Paul, except their following the childish fancy about Mercury as the interpreter of the gods, something with which they had long been imbued? We are warned by this example of how evil it is to be habituated to errors in our tender years, because it is by no means easy for them to be eradicated from our minds, so that they tend to become more hardened through the very works of God, by which they ought to have been corrected.

13. *And the priest of Jupiter.* Although Luke does not say what moved the priest to be so diligent, yet it is probable that he was driven by greed, since hope of great gain was offered. His future was bright with the hope of wealth if a rumour could be spread all round that Jupiter had appeared there. For it would have been immediately followed by the idea that Jupiter favoured the temple of Lystra more than any other. Now, when such a superstition has filled the minds of men, no expense is spared in the offering of gifts. Certainly this is the sort of thing that the world tends to do of its own accord, but then the sacrificing priests come on the scene to spur them on. There is also no doubt that ambition drove on the whole multitude, making them so eager in their desire to offer sacrifices to Paul under the name of Jupiter, in order that their city might be the more illustrious in fame and renown. As a result, while the priests are out to net their profits, and the people are truly delighted to be confirmed in their errors, Satan has such freedom to deceive.

But when the apostles, Barnabas and Paul, heard of it, they rent their garments, and sprang forth among the multitude, crying out and saying, Sirs, why do ye these things? We also are men of like passions with you, and bring you good tidings, that ye should turn from these vain things unto the living God, who made the heaven and the earth and the sea, and all that in them is: who in the generations gone by suffered all the

7

nations to walk in their own ways. And yet he left not himself without witness, in that he did good, and gave you from heaven rains and fruitful seasons, filling your hearts with food and gladness. And with these sayings scarce restrained they the multitudes from doing sacrifice unto them. (14-18)

14. *When the apostles heard of it.* By rending their garments and leaping into the midst of the crowd Paul and Barnabas show how great was their burning zeal for the glory of God. Not being content with words they do all they can to throw the preparations for the sacrifice into confusion. It does indeed happen sometimes that even hypocrites refuse excessive honour, but actually their assumed modesty gives more encouragement to the simple to give it to them. There was nothing of this in Paul and Barnabas, for both by words and their whole physical attitude they show openly, that, far from being pleased with the act of worship, which the men of Lystra were offering, they find it quite abominable. This is holy anger, by which the servants of God ought to be inflamed, whenever they see His glory outraged and discredited by the sacrilege of men. Certainly no one can be a sincere and *bona fide* servant of God, unless he has assumed that attitude of jealousy, of which Paul speaks in the Second Epistle to the Corinthians (11.2), when he writes that those, to whom the Lord has committed the care of His Church, are to be no less spirited and active in asserting the glory of their Lord, than a husband is eager and anxious to defend his wife's chastity.

Hence we must take good care that we allow no honour to be given to us, which may detract from the glory of God. On the contrary as soon as there appears to be any profaning of God's glory, let fervour burst out such as is exemplified for us in the case of Paul and Barnabas. Now, although the teachers of the Church especially ought to be endowed with this zeal, yet every one of the faithful ought to burn passionately, when he sees the worship of God polluted or transferred to another, for it is written of all, 'The zeal of thine house hath eaten me up, and the reproaches of them that reproach thee are fallen upon me' (Ps. 69.9). Now, if the saints abominated idolatry so much when they were still clothed in the flesh, how do we think they feel now that they have put off all carnal feelings? When the world abuses their names and persons for its own superstitious ends, it is convinced that it does them a favour, but it is greatly deceived. For they will be the first to stand up against their worshippers and will in fact make it known that nothing ever mattered more to them than that their own worship should remain wholly for God alone. In addition no greater injury can be done to the saints than when honour is taken away from

God and transferred to them, and that is bound to happen as soon as some divine attribute is ascribed to them.

As to what Luke relates about Paul and Barnabas *rending their garments*, it is quite clear from other passages of Scripture that this was a custom and rite commonly used by Easterners, whenever they wished to express, by an outward gesture, either great sorrow or detestation.

When Luke calls Barnabas an apostle along with Paul, he is extending the meaning of the term beyond the primary order (*longius quam ad primarium ordinem*), which Christ has instituted in His Church, just as Paul makes Andronicus and Junias 'men of note among the apostles' (Rom. 16.7). Properly speaking, however, evangelists were not apostles; unless perhaps, because Barnabas was joined to Paul as a colleague, we place them both on the same official level, and in that case the title of apostle will really be appropriate for him.

15. *Sirs, why do ye do these things?* They begin by a reproof, as the situation demanded, and then explain why they were sent. They then go on to preach about the one God and point out that He was unknown to the world. Finally, in order that they may the more powerfully eradicate the deceptions of the devil from their hearts, they teach that this ignorance is without excuse. Therefore the first part of their sermon is a rebuke, condemning the men of Lystra for their preposterous act in worshipping mortal men instead of God. However the reason they adduce does not appear to have much point, for one could easily conclude from it that it is not wrong to worship those whom death has freed from human misery. In this way the superstitions of all the Gentiles would remain untouched, for they were accustomed to reckon among the gods only men who were dead. The Papists have also tarred their idolatry with the same brush, worshipping dead men's bones, wood and stones, rather than living, breathing men. I answer that Paul and Barnabas drew this argument from the circumstances in which they found themselves, 'We too are miserable men, and therefore you are absurdly mistaken in imagining us to be gods, and in worshipping us as such.'

If consideration is given to idolatry in general, this will always be the grounds for condemning it, and in itself will be more than sufficient, that the entire devotion of piety is due to God alone, and that it is profaned as soon as it is ascribed in any degree to creatures, whether they are angels or men or stars. But an occasion will often permit many things to be said against one kind of idolatry which may not apply to others, and yet be of great value for the matter in hand, just as, by confessing themselves to be mortal men, subject to various needs, Paul and Barnabas had a reason suitable for reproving the madness of the people.

And bring you good tidings. This is an argument from contraries. For here they show that the purpose of their coming was for quite the opposite reason, namely to abolish the superstitions that had hitherto preyed upon men. What they said amounts to this: 'Does the miracle move and affect you? Then believe our words. And indeed the point of our mission is the destruction and elimination of all the fictitious deities with which the world has been deluded up till now.' But this is teaching of a general kind, by which they not only check the present madness, but censure every kind of superstition and everything that was utterly contrary to the true rule of godliness. Without any doubt they denounce as vanity all that men had devised for themselves out of their own minds. This is a definition to be noted, that all religion is vain that departs and degenerates from the pure and simple Word of God. Indeed, no express mention is made of the Word of God, since they were preaching to the Gentiles, but because God is worshipped rightly in no other way than according to His appointment, it follows from Paul's words that as soon as men depart from the worship that God has commanded and approves, they foolishly weary themselves with empty and useless labour. For there is no truth or genuineness about a religion, except one in which God alone is pre-eminent.

Hence it has come about that the sincere and sound worship of God (*pietas*) has never flourished in the greater part of the world. For men have laboured only to the extent of abolishing ancient idolatry, but at the same time they have certainly neglected the other side, to rally themselves to God alone, after they have abandoned their idols. Sometimes they did indeed change the name of the idol into the name of God, but under that very pretext they were still cherishing the old errors, which they ought to have taken pains to correct. Thus the Galli, the priests of the great Cybele, introduced (*genuerunt*) celibacy; nuns were substituted for the vestal virgins; 'All Saints' (*Pantagion*) succeeded 'All gods' (*Pantheon*); and ceremonies were replaced by others that were not unlike them. Finally a host of deities was brought in, which they thought would be legitimate if they were masked with the titles of saints. In this way corruptions are not purged, and stables full of filth are not converted into temples of God; but the name of God is mixed up with profanity and filth, and God Himself brought into a foul stall. Accordingly let us remember that the apostles were not only bent on overthrowing the idolatry, which had insidiously beset the world in past ages, but also that, when all vile errors were overthrown, they afterwards took care that pure religion should flourish.

Who made the heaven. We know that in teaching the right order requires a beginning to be made from things that are better known.

Since Paul and Barnabas were preaching to Gentiles, it would have been useless for them to attempt to bring them to Christ at once. Therefore they had to begin from some other point, not so remote from common understanding, so that, when assent was given to that, they could then pass over to Christ. The minds of the men of Lystra were possessed by the error that there are many gods. Paul and Barnabas show, on the other hand, that there is one Creator of the world. With the removal of that fictitious crowd of deities the way was open for the second step, to teach them what that God, the Creator of heaven and earth, was like. Our argument with the Papists today is a different one. They confess the unity of God, and they give admittance to Scripture. Therefore it remains for us to prove to them out of the Scripture what God is like, and the kind of worship He desires of men.

16. *Who in the generations gone by.* Because the men of Lystra could object that God had been unknown until then, Paul and Barnabas anticipate them, and show that all men, indeed, had wandered astray in darkness, and that the whole human race had been smitten with blindness, but they deny that the perverse ignorance of the world offers any ground for their presupposition. There were two great obstacles to unbelievers, the long stretch of antiquity, and the agreement of almost all nations. Both of these Paul and Barnabas demolish here, saying, 'If the error has been in existence for many ages, and if the world has strayed without understanding and discernment, that is no reason for God's truth to have less weight with you when it does appear. For since it is eternal and does not change, it is not right that the prescription of long years should be set against it.' They contend that there is no more value in pleading the number of men involved. 'Even the agreement of the whole world', they say, 'is no reason to keep you from the right way. Blindness has prevailed among all peoples, but God is now giving you light. Therefore your eyes must be opened, and you must not be impotent in the darkness, even although all peoples have been submerged in it until now.'

In their own ways. If he had only said that up to that time men wandered into deception by divine permission, we might now easily conclude from that that all men can do nothing but err, as long as they are not ruled by God. However he speaks much more explicitly in calling the errors the *ways* of men. For from this we clearly learn how effective the wisdom and understanding of the human mind are in keeping the way of salvation. 'All peoples', he says, 'have walked in their own ways, that is, have wandered in darkness and death.' It is just as if he were saying that not a single spark of true reason remains in the whole world.

Accordingly there is one rule of true godliness, that believers cast away all confidence in their own natural powers, and submit themselves wholly to God. For the ways of men are no different now from what they were in the past, and the examples of all periods of time teach how miserably blind are those, who are not enlightened by the Word of God, even if they think that they surpass the rest in perspicacity. Immediately after the beginning of the world, the greater part of mankind lapsed into various superstitions and depraved cults. How did that come about except that men chose to follow their own imaginations? Even when the world might appear to have been cleansed by the flood, it lapsed back right away into the same vices. Therefore there is nothing more deadly than reliance on our own wisdom.

On the other hand, however, no reason is offered by Paul and Barnabas as to why God allowed the world to wander astray for so long, and surely the will of God alone must be regarded by us as nothing else but the supreme law of equity. God has always the best of reasons for His acts, but because it is often hidden from us, we, for our part, have to be reverent, and marvel at His secret counsels. We must indeed confess that the world deserved such destruction, but no reason can be adduced as to why God had mercy on one age rather than others, except that it seemed good to Him to do so. Accordingly Paul calls the time divinely appointed for the proclamation of the Gospel 'the fulness of time' (Gal. 4.4), so that some other favourable time might not be looked for. And we must not forget what we found in the first chapter that it is not for us 'to know the times and seasons which the Father has set within His own authority' (1.7). Thus the cavil of the Papists is refuted, when they contend that it is not possible for God to have allowed His Church to be in error for so long. For where, I ask, did the nations spring from but from the ark of Noah, where the Church had a certain extraordinary purity? Even the posterity of holy Shem degenerated along with the rest. Yes, Israel too, God's chosen, peculiar people, was itself abandoned for a long time. For this reason it is not surprising that God avenged contempt of His Word with the same punishment of blindness under the reign of His Son as He did in ancient times.

17. *And yet he left not himself without witness.* Here Paul and Barnabas deprive the Gentiles of an excuse for their ignorance. For however pleased men are with their own inventions, when they are at last convicted of error, they take refuge in the excuse that no blame ought to be laid on them, but rather that God was cruel when He did not think it worth while to give even a whistle to call back those whom He saw to be perishing. Paul and Barnabas anticipate this frivolous

objection, when they teach that God lay hidden in such a way that all along He was giving evidence of Himself and His divinity. Nevertheless, we must see how these two things fit together, for if God did bear witness to Himself, then He did not allow the world to wander in error, as far as He was concerned. I reply that while the kind of witness mentioned deprived men of excuse, it was, nevertheless, not sufficient for salvation. For the word of the apostle is true, that it is 'by faith that we understand the worlds to have been framed by the Word of God' (Heb. 11.3). But faith is not conceived by the bare observation of heaven and earth, but by the hearing of the Word (*ex verbi auditu*). It follows from that that men cannot be brought to the saving knowledge of God except by the direction of the Word. Yet this does not prevent them being rendered inexcusable even without the Word, for, even if they are naturally deprived of light, they are nevertheless blind through their own malice, as Paul teaches in the first chapter of his Epistle to the Romans (v. 20).

And gave you from heaven rains and fruitful seasons. From the beginning God has indeed made Himself known to all mankind through the Word. But Paul and Barnabas show that there was no age on which God did not bestow His blessings, which could testify that the world is ruled by His power. However, because the light of doctrine had been buried for many generations, it is for that reason that they only say that God was manifested by natural evidences. That apart, it is probable that they praised the magnificence of God's works with fitting eulogies, but it was enough for Luke to touch upon the main points. On the other hand, I do not understand this to mean that they offered a closely reasoned discourse in the philosophical manner about the secrets of nature, for they were addressing uninstructed, ordinary people. And so they had to set forth in simple words what was known by all the uneducated. Nevertheless they assume this principle that in the order of nature there is a certain and clear manifestation of God. Because the earth is watered by rain, because the heat of the sun quickens its growth, because fruits in such great abundance are produced year by year, we may surely gather from these things that there is some God who governs all things. For the heaven and the earth are not moved by their own power, much less even by chance. Therefore the conclusion is that this amazing ingenuity of nature plainly points to the providence of God, and that those who have said that the world is eternal have not spoken according to the understanding of their minds, but have tried through spiteful and barbarous ingratitude to obliterate the glory of God, and in doing so have betrayed their own impudence.

Filling your hearts with food and gladness. The impiety of men is

13

brought home all the more if they refuse to acknowledge God, when He not only sets before their eyes testimonies to His glory in His works, but also appoints all things for them to use. For why do the sun and stars shine in the heavens except to be of service to men? Why does rain fall from heaven and why does the earth bring forth its fruits, if it is not to provide men with food to eat? Therefore God did not place man on the earth that he may idly contemplate His works as if in a theatre, but that, while enjoying the riches of heaven and earth, he may exercise himself in praising the bounty of God. Now, is it not worse than foul depravity that he is unmoved by such divine bounty in providing benefits in liberal abundance? To *fill hearts with food* simply means to bestow food that may satisfy the desires of men. By the word *gladness* Paul and Barnabas mean that out of His infinite indulgence God lavishes more on men than their need requires, as though it had been said that men are given meat not only to renew their strength, but also to gladden their hearts.

If anyone objects that very often it happens that men groan from hunger rather than rejoice from plenty, I answer that this is contrary to the order of nature (*praeter naturae ordinem*), namely, when God withholds His hand because of men's sins. For the liberality of God would flow to us freely and continuously, as Paul and Barnabas proclaim here, if the obstacles of our vices were not standing in the way. And yet never did such great barrenness exist that the blessing of God in feeding men dried up altogether. Indeed it was well said by the prophet, 'Open thy mouth wide and I will fill it' (Ps. 81.10), that we may know that we go hungry through our own fault, when we do not admit the beneficence of heaven. But however mean we may be, the fatherly love of God still breaks through even to the unworthy. In particular mankind as a whole is evidence that the benefits of God, in which He is seen to be our Father, never cease.

18. *And with these sayings.* Luke had already said that not only did they use words, but also rushed impetuously into the midst of the crowd. Now he adds that the fury of the people was hardly restrained by their vehemence, from which it appears how insane and untamed is the world's passion for idolatry. For if they believe them to be gods, why do they not have faith in their words declining false honour? But all idolaters suffer from this disease, that they are prepared to throw off the yoke of religion at once, if it does not serve their own good pleasure. Accordingly it is not surprising that the prophets should constantly remind us that men are carried away into the blind passion of superstition just as animals are driven to their lust.

But there came Jews thither from Antioch and Iconium: and having

persuaded the multitudes, they stoned Paul, and dragged him out of the
city, supposing that he was dead. But as the disciples stood round about
him, he rose up, and entered into the city: and on the morrow he went
forth with Barnabas to Derbe. And when they had preached the gospel
to that city, and had made many disciples, they returned to Lystra, and
to Iconium, and to Antioch, confirming the souls of the disciples, exhort-
ing them to continue in the faith, and that through many tribulations we
must enter into the kingdom of God. (19-22)

19. *But there came thither.* It is with difficulty that Paul and Barnabas
restrain the people from offering a sacrifice; on the other hand some
idle rascals have no difficulty in persuading them at once to stone
Paul whom they were recently treating as a god. It is apparent from
that how much more prone to superstition the world is than to
genuine obedience toward God, and how arrogant superstition is, for
it always wishes to play the chief part in ordering the worship of God.
The servants of the Lord seek nothing else but to bring men into His
obedience, and that is the only salvation and blessedness there is.
They do not lay claim to any lordship for themselves, they do not
chase after gain, and yet the world cannot tolerate them. For almost
all men cry out against them, and from time to time even riots break
out. Those who are so very unyielding toward God show that they
are exceedingly credulous to imposters and eagerly submit themselves
to their tyranny. Thus the Pope has been allowed to play his own
game as he liked, not only pressing wretched souls into slavery, but
also torturing them cruelly. Whatever he prescribed was obediently
accepted; and even today no matter how impossible are the laws he
makes, yet no one dares to murmur a complaint. At the same time
a few do acknowledge that Christ's yoke is agreeable (*suave*).

Accordingly, in this story we are given a graphic account of the
world's depravity. Paul could have reigned under the title of Mercury
to the applause of all, but he does not wish to be a god; because he
serves Christ faithfully, he is stoned. But his endurance is commended
that we may imitate it. He was wonderfully saved by the Lord,
indeed, but as far as he himself was concerned, he submitted to a very
cruel sort of death. Therefore this stoning must be regarded in the
same way as he himself describes it in his Second Epistle to the Corinthians (11.25), as if he had been slain on that occasion. Moreover there
is no doubt that the common people rose up in a riot against him. So,
whatever violence the ungodly inflict on the servants of Christ, no
investigation is made, the laws are silent, the courts are idle, the magistrate does nothing, defence is completely withdrawn.

20. *But as the disciples stood round about him.* Although no one de-

fended Paul, yet Luke shows that the believers were anxious about his
life, but that they held themselves in check so as not to attempt anything involving great danger to no purpose, seeing that they could
offer no help unless it was done in secret. And surely we must always
pay attention to what the Lord has put within our power. If from the
shore I see a shipwrecked man in deep water, and I cannot stretch out
my hand to help him, what is there left for me to do but to commend
him to the Lord? But of course if there is any hope of saving him
then I must run the risk. We shall not say, therefore, that Paul was
abandoned by the disciples because of cowardice, since it was not in
their power to help him at all. But they give evidence of their love
and care, when they stand round him lying stretched out there.

They went forth to Derbe. From this it is quite clear that Paul was
saved only by a miracle, for on the very day after he had been thrown
out for dead, he took to the road like a man fresh and vigorous. And
from that we also gather what an indomitable spirit he had in the face
of all evils. Nor did he seek some retreat where he might enjoy his
ease like a veteran soldier, but actually goes back to the places where,
a short while ago, he had been badly treated. However Luke first
relates that the Church was planted among the people of Derbe. He
then adds that Paul and Barnabas returned to the churches they had
established, in order to confirm the disciples. By this he means that the
use of the Word does not consist in mere instruction, by which the
hearer is only taught, but that it also avails for the confirmation of
faith, in warning, exhorting and convicting (*coarguendo*). Indeed
Christ commands His ministers not only to teach but to exhort, and
Paul also declares that Scripture is useful not only for teaching but
also for exhortation (II Tim. 3.16). Accordingly pastors are not to think
that they have fulfilled their ministry when they have properly imbued their people with the right knowledge, unless they also devote
themselves to this task. On the other hand believers are not to neglect
the Word of God, as if the reading and preaching of it were superfluous,
for there is no one who does not need constant confirmation.

22. *And exhorting.* This was the principal method of confirmation,
using exhortation to encourage the disciples, who had already embraced
and professed the Gospel, to continue. For we are far from being
ready and active, as we ought to be, in doing our duty. For that
reason our sloth needs goads, and our coldness needs to be warmed up.
But, because God wants His people to be disciplined through various
struggles, Paul and Barnabas warn the disciples to be prepared to endure tribulations. It is a very necessary warning that, if we are to live
devoted and holy lives, we have to engage in warfare in this world.
If the flesh would cause us no trouble, if Satan would not scheme

against us, if the wicked would not confuse us with stumbling-blocks, perseverance would not be so irksome, since it would be a pleasant walk along an easy and delightful road. But it is because innumerable provocations arise on every side and at every single moment, and tempt us to give up, that difficulty springs up, and that is why the power of perseverance is so rare. Therefore in order to persist right to the end, we must be prepared for warfare.

Apart from that, Luke does not only have in mind here persecutions, which the enemy brings upon us with drawn swords and flaming fires, but under *tribulations* he includes all the troubles to which the lives of the godly are liable; not because believers alone are miserable, but because this is the common condition of the good and the bad. And from that arises the celebrated proverb, 'the best thing is not to be born; the next best is surely to die as soon as possible'. But since God often spares the ungodly and fattens them with prosperity, He is austerer and harder in His dealings with His own children, for, apart from common troubles, they are particularly hard pressed by many misfortunes; and the Lord humbles them with these experiences, keeping their flesh under the rod, lest it should break out into lasciviousness, and He keeps them alert, lest they should lie asleep on the ground. Then there are in addition the reproaches and slanders of the wicked, for believers must be, as it were, the scum of the earth. Their simplicity is laughed at, but they are particularly annoyed by the impious jests against God. Finally, the passion of the wicked breaks out into open violence. Thus they have of necessity to contend with many tribulations, and it is inevitable that, among so many enemies, the whole of their life should be disturbed and troubled. But this is the best consolation, one abundantly capable of confirming their minds, that it is by such a way, difficult and hard though it is, that they pass into the Kingdom of God. For from this we gather that the miseries of the godly are more blessed than all the delights of the world may be.

Let us remember, then first of all, this law that is laid down for us, that we are to suffer many tribulations, but at the same time let us also add this, to mitigate the bitterness, that it is through them that we are brought into God's Kingdom. Moreover, those, who derive from this passage the idea that patience is a work meriting eternal salvation, are simply talking futile nonsense, for what is discussed here is not the cause of salvation, but the way in which God always treats His own in the world. And, on the other hand, the comfort is added, not to extol the worthiness or merit of works, but only to encourage believers not to give way under the weight of the cross. As it has already been said, all members of the human race without exception are subject to many ills. However for the reprobate their afflictions are nothing else than the prelude to hell, but for the saints their sufferings lead to a favourable and joyful end, and, besides, they assist their salvation because they share them with Christ (cf. II Cor. 1.5). It is to be noted that Paul and Barnabas, not content with the plural expressly mention *many tribulations* lest anyone, after suffering one or two, or a few at least, thinking himself finished, may finally give up. Therefore let believers make up their minds that they must persevere through many distresses, and then let them be prepared not only for one kind of persecution, but for different sorts. For although God deals more gently with certain people, yet He is not so lenient or indulgent to any one of His own, that he is altogether immune from tribulations.

And when they had appointed for them elders in every church, and had prayed with fasting, they commended them to the Lord, on whom they had believed. And they passed through Pisidia, and came to Pamphylia. And when they had spoken the word in Perga, they went down to Attalia; and thence they sailed to Antioch, from whence they had been committed to the grace of God for the work which they had fulfilled. And when they were come, and had gathered the church together, they rehearsed all things that God had done with them, and how that he had opened a door of faith unto the Gentiles. And they tarried no little time with the disciples. (23-28)

23. *When they had appointed elders (presbyteros).* It is apparent from this that it is not enough for men once to have been instructed aright in godly doctrine, and to hold the substance of the faith, if they do not make continual progress. That is why Christ not only sent apostles to spread the Gospel, but also commanded pastors to be appointed, so that the proclamation of the Gospel might be perpetual and in daily practice. Paul and Barnabas observe this order laid down by Christ, when they assign pastors to individual churches, so that after their departure teaching may not cease and fall silent. Moreover, this passage teaches us that the Church cannot be without the ordinary ministry, and it is only those who are willing disciples through the whole course of life, who are considered Christians in the eyes of God. I interpret *presbyters (presbyteros)* here as those on whom the office of teaching had been enjoined, for it is evident from what Paul says (I Tim. 5.17) that some were only censors of morals (*morum censores*). Now when Luke says that they were set over every church, a distinction is drawn from that between their office and that of the apostles. For the apostles did not have a definite station anywhere, but they moved about here and there, continually founding new churches. On the other hand pastors were appointed individually to their own

churches, and were placed, so to speak, in charge (*quasi locati ad prae-sidium*).

They had appointed (them) by votes (suffragiis creassent). The Greek word χειροτονεῖν means to determine something by raising hands, as is usually done in the assemblies of the people. However, ecclesiastical writers often employ the noun χειροτονία in another sense, namely, for the solemn rite of ordination, which in Scripture is called the imposition of hands. Moreover, by this way of speaking, the lawful way of ordaining pastors is very well described. Paul and Barnabas are said to *appoint presbyters*. Are they acting alone, by virtue of the office peculiar to them? On the contrary they allow it to take place by the votes of all. Hence in ordaining pastors the people had a free election; but in case there might be any disorder Paul and Barnabas preside like moderators. This is the way in which we are to understand the decision of the Council of Laodicea, which forbids election to be left to the common people.

And had prayed with fasting. They had a twofold purpose and reason for praying. The first was that God would direct them with the Spirit of wisdom and discretion to choose all the best and most suitable men. For they knew that they were not endowed with such great wisdom that they could not be deceived, nor did they put so much trust in their own diligence, that they did not know that the chief emphasis is laid on the blessing of God. Thus we see daily that men's judgments err where no heavenly direction is present, and that all their labours come to nothing if the hand of God is not with them. These are the true auspices of the godly, the invoking of the Spirit of God that He may preside over their counsels. And if this is the rule to be observed in all our affairs, then as often as we are concerned with the government of the Church, which depends wholly on His will, we must take good care to attempt nothing except with Him as Leader and Presider.

Now, their second purpose in praying was that God might endow with the necessary gifts those elected to be pastors. For the fulfilling of this office as faithfully as it ought to be is a more arduous business than human strength is fit for. Therefore they implore God's help in this connexion also, with Paul and Barnabas taking the lead (*auctoribus*).

Fasts are added as helps to stir up the fervour of their prayers, for we know what our coldness is like otherwise. This does not mean that it may always be necessary to add fasting to our prayers, since God invites even those who are satisfied to give thanks, but when some need makes it urgent for us to pray more fervently than usual, this is a very useful incitement. Now we have already explained how serious a matter the election of pastors is, for the preservation of the health of the Church is clearly involved in it. Hence it is not surprising if Luke writes that extraordinary prayers were introduced. And it is worth while noting this and other uses of fasting so that we may not imagine like the Papists that it is a meritorious work, or that we may not consider it to be in itself a worshipping of God, since it is nothing in itself, and does not have any importance with God, except in so far as it has reference to something else.

They commended them to the Lord. From this we learn, in the first place, how much Paul and Barnabas cared for the salvation of those who had been converted to the Lord through their own care and labour. They also testify to the fact that men are exposed, in this weak flesh, to too many dangers for their faith to continue to be stable in its own power. Therefore the only remedy is this, if the Lord continually guards those whom He has once received. Finally, Luke's statement that they were commended to God *on whom they had believed*, gives great confidence to us, because he assigns to God as His own office, the saving and keeping of all those who, by true faith, have embraced His Word.

24. *And they passed through Pisidia.* We have already said that Paul and Barnabas came to Antioch in Pisidia. Now, being about to return to Antioch in Syria, from where they had been sent out, they pass through Pamphylia, which was a region in between, facing Mount Taurus. Now, Perga and Attalia are adjacent cities. However, when Luke relates that they preached the Word in one only, we may deduce from that, that the opportunity of teaching, which they were not in the habit of neglecting or letting pass anywhere, was not presented to them in every place.

26. *From whence they had been committed.* Luke could have said that it was there that they had been appointed the apostles to the Gentiles, but by employing a circumlocution he expresses more clearly the fact that they had not been sent out by men, and that they had not attempted anything relying on their own strength, but that the whole expedition, with its success, had been entrusted to God (*Deo permissam*) as its Promoter. Their preaching, therefore, was not the work of man, but a work of divine grace. And the word *grace* refers as much to the power and efficacy of the Spirit, as to the other signs of divine favour, for all the gifts that God confers upon His servants are of grace (*gratuitum est*). And so the sentence can be interpreted to mean that they prayed God to bestow His grace to further the labours of His servants.

27. *And when they had gathered the church together, they narrated.* As ambassadors returning from a mission usually give an account of their acts, so Paul and Barnabas give to the Church a complete account of

their travels, in order to show how faithfully they carried out their ministry, and at the same time to encourage the believers to give thanks to God, for the actual situation was affording ample grounds for doing so. Accordingly Luke does not say that they extolled their own deeds, but all the things that the Lord had carried out through them. Literally it reads 'with them' (*cum ipsis*), but according to the Hebrew idiom it amounts to much the same thing as if there had been put, 'in them' (*in illis*), or 'by means of them' (*per illos*) or 'toward them' (*erga illos*), or the simple dative, 'to them'. Therefore Luke does not say σὺν αὐτοῖς but μετ' αὐτῶν. The reason why I say this is so that no ignorant person may ascribe a share of the praise to Paul and Barnabas, as if they had been God's partners in the work, whereas they rather make God the one and only Author of all the things that they had done effectively.

Luke adds immediately after that the Lord had opened *a door of faith* to the Gentiles. For even although they had been sent to the Gentiles, yet the novelty of the situation did not fail to surprise. And the sudden change was not the only thing that astonished the Jews. But because it was a monstrous thing to them that those who were unclean and alienated from the Kingdom of God should be united (*misceri*) with the holy seed of Abraham, so that together they might constitute the one Church of God, they are now taught by the actual result that the apostles had not been given to them for nothing. Moreover it is said that the door was opened for the Gentiles to believe, not only because the Gospel was preached to them by the outward voice, but because they were effectually called to faith by the illumination of the Spirit. The Kingdom of Heaven is indeed opened to us by the external preaching of the Gospel, but no one enters into it unless God reaches out His hand to him; no one draws near unless he is drawn inwardly by the Spirit. Therefore Paul and Barnabas show by the results that their calling was approved and ratified by God, for the faith of the Gentiles was just as if a seal had been imprinted by the hand of God, in order to confirm it, as Paul says in the Epistle to the Romans (16.25), and in Second Corinthians (3.7).[1]

[1] These references are given in both C.R. and Tholuck but hardly seem relevant. Tr.

CHAPTER FIFTEEN

And certain men came down from Judaea and taught the brethren, saying, Except ye be circumcised after the custom of Moses, ye cannot be saved. And when Paul and Barnabas had no small dissension and questioning with them, the brethren appointed that Paul and Barnabas, and certain other of them, should go up to Jerusalem unto the apostles and elders about this question. They therefore, being brought on their way by the church, passed through both Phoenicia and Samaria, declaring the conversion of the Gentiles: and they caused great joy unto all the brethren. And when they were come to Jerusalem, they were received of the church and the apostles and the elders, and they rehearsed all things that God had done with them. But there rose up certain of the sect of the Pharisees who believed, saying, It is needful to circumcise them, and to charge them to keep the law of Moses. (1-5)

1. Luke now begins to narrate that, when Paul and Barnabas were discharged from a variety of strenuous battles with professed enemies of the Gospel, they were tried by domestic war. Thus their doctrine and ministry had to be put to the test in every possible way, in order that it might be all the more evident that they were provided with divine help against all the onslaughts of Satan and the world. For it is no ordinary confirmation of their teaching that, when it was battered by so many instruments of war, it nevertheless stood firm, and its advance could not be interrupted by so many obstructions. Therefore, that is why Paul makes the proud boast that he experienced 'fightings without and fears within' (II Cor. 7.5).

This narrative is particularly well worth noting, for although we naturally dread the cross and persecution of any sort, yet greater danger comes from internal divisions, lest they should break our spirit or weaken us. When tyrants attack with all their force, the flesh is certainly afraid, and all who are not endowed with the spirit of fortitude tremble to the core of their being, but no temptation is really touching their consciences in those circumstances; a situation in fact recognized as fatal for the Church. But when it comes to the brethren being in conflict with each other, and the Church being in a state of internal upheaval, weak minds will inevitably be confused, and may even give way, and especially when the controversy is over doctrine, which alone is the sacred bond of fraternal unity (*quae una sacrum est vinculum fraternae unitatis*). Finally, there is nothing that damages the Gospel more than internal discords, for they not only discourage weak consciences, but provide the ungodly with an opportunity to speak evil of it.

Accordingly, let us take careful note of this narrative, so that we may know that it is not something without precedent, if controversies over doctrine still arise among those who profess the same Gospel, when conceited men cannot get the name, which they madly desire, in any other way than by introducing their own fancies. It is certain, indeed, that as God is one, so is His truth one. Therefore when Paul wishes to urge believers to mutual agreement, he makes use of this argument, 'One God, one faith, one baptism' etc. (Eph. 4.5f.). But when we see ungodly men emerge, trying to rend the Church with their factions, and either corrupting the very Gospel with their spurious fabrications or bringing it under suspicion, we ought to be aware of the trickery of Satan. For that reason Paul elsewhere speaks of heresies emerging into the open that those 'who are approved may be made manifest' (I Cor. 11.19). And the Lord certainly frustrates the subtlety of Satan for a wonderful purpose, because He tests the faith of His own people by such trials, He honours His Word with a glorious victory, and He makes the truth, which the wicked have tried to obscure, shine out all the more brightly. But it is proper to consider all the circumstances of this story, as they are noted by Luke.

Came down from Judaea. This pretext had considerable effect in deceiving even good men on that occasion. Jerusalem was not without cause held in the highest honour among all the churches, for they cherished and reverenced it even as their mother. For it was from that fountain that the Gospel had, as it were, been channelled out. Those imposters came; they make pretence of apostolic sanction; they boast that they bring nothing except what they have learnt from them. Anyhow, with this smoke they obscure the vision of the inexperienced; on the other hand those who are fickle and ungodly snatch greedily at the excuse that is offered. The disturbance of the Church, like a tempest, shakes those who are otherwise good and moderate, so that they are forced to falter. Therefore we must note this trick of Satan's, in misusing the names of the saints in order to deceive the simple, who, engrossed by reverence for the men, do not venture to make inquiry about the truth of the matter. Luke, indeed, does not say what it was that drove those knaves on, yet it is likely that κακοζηλία or perverted zeal caused them to oppose Paul and Barnabas, for there are certain peevish natures who are pleased with nothing except what is their own. They had seen that circumcision and other rites of the Law were observed at Jerusalem; wherever they appear they can tolerate nothing that is new or different, as if the example of that one

23

church binds all the rest with a fixed law. But although such men are moved by a perverted zeal to provoke disturbances, yet inwardly their own ambition incites them, and a certain arrogance spurs them on. At the same time Satan has what he wants, for the minds of the godly are so confused by the appearance of the smoke-screen, that they can scarcely discern black from white.

First, then, let us beware of this pest, so that some may not make their own customs into a law for others, and that the example of one church may not be the precedent for a universal rule. Secondly, we must take further care that personalities do not hinder or obscure inquiry into the matter or the cause. For if Satan transforms himself 'into an angel of light' (II Cor. 11.14), and if he often usurps the holy name of God with sacrilegious audacity, why should we be surprised if with the same wickedness he practises deception under the names of saintly men? The final result will show that the very last thing the apostles had in mind was to impose the yoke of the Law upon the Gentiles, yet it was by this trick that Satan sought to steal on them. So it very often happens that those who oppose the doctrine of Christ worm their way in under the title of His servants. There is only one remedy, therefore, to initiate an unprejudiced (*integris iudiciis*) inquiry into the truth of the matter. It is also incumbent upon us to obviate scandal, so as not to think that the faithful servants of God are fighting among themselves, because Satan makes false use of their names, making some of them indulge in shadow-boxing in order to alarm the simple.

2. *When dissension had arisen.* It was no trivial test for Paul and Barnabas to have been drawn into a stormy struggle. The dissension alone was bad enough already; but the evil is much blacker when the contention begins to boil up to the point that they are forced to fight with brethren like enemies. Also, take into account the bad reputation with which they saw themselves saddled among the ignorant and simple, as if they were disturbing the peace of the Church by their obstinacy. For so it usually happens, that after the servants of Christ have been unjustly tormented, and have performed faithful work in the defence of a good cause, in the end, on top of all the vexations, they suffer all the odium. They must therefore be endowed with an invincible and great courage, in order to despise the adverse rumours that are spread about concerning them. Accordingly Paul glories elsewhere that he made progress through seditions (II Cor. 6.5).[1] Yet the servants of Christ must observe such moderation that, as far as it is in their power, they may shrink from all discord; if at any time Satan stirs up disturbances and contentions let them try to settle them; and

[1] *Per seditiones.* Vulg.: *in seditionibus.* EVV, 'tumults'. Tr.

finally let them take positive action to foster unity. But on the other hand when the truth of God is being attacked, let them not avoid any battle for its defence; and let them not hesitate to be courageous in their opposition, even if heaven and earth come together.

For ourselves, having been surely warned by this example, as often as disturbances break out in the Church let us wisely learn to discern who is to blame for the thing happening, so that we may not rashly condemn faithful ministers of Christ, when we ought, rather, to be praising their strength (*gravitas*), because they sustain, undaunted, such violent assaults of Satan. Secondly, let us recall that Satan was restrained by the wonderful providence of God, so as not to destroy Paul's teaching. For if he had been allowed to do as much harm as he wished, the faith of the Gentiles would have been subverted and destroyed, the Gospel preached by Paul would have fallen to the ground, and the door would have been closed for the calling of the Gentiles. Thirdly, let us learn that disagreements, no matter what they are, must be resisted at an early stage, so that they may not burst out into the flame of contentions, because all that Satan is after with the fans of dissensions is to kindle just so many fires. But on the other hand when we see that the first Church was in an uproar, and that all the best ministers of Christ were busily engaged in quarrels, if the same thing happens to us today, let us not be alarmed, as if we were involved in something new and unexpected; but, seeking from God a solution like the one He gave on that occasion, let us carry on through stormy disturbances with the same tenor of faith.

Unless ye be circumcised. With these words Luke gives a brief definition of the main question at issue, namely that those impostors wished to bind consciences with the necessity of keeping the Law. Circumcision is certainly the only thing mentioned here, but it is quite clear from the context that they raised the controversy about the keeping of the whole Law. But because circumcision was, as it were, the solemn initiation into all the other rites of the Law, therefore, by synecdoche, the whole Law is included under one part. Those enemies of Paul were not denying that Christ is the Messiah, but while giving their allegiance to Him, they were still retaining the old ceremonies of the Law.

At first glance the error could have given the appearance of being a tolerable one. Why then does Paul not keep quiet, at least for a short time, so as not to shake the Church with conflict, for the dispute was about external things, about which Paul himself elsewhere forbids too much bitter quarrelling? In fact there were three important reasons, which forced him to protest. For if the keeping of the Law is a necessary thing, the salvation of men is bound to works, whereas it must be founded only on the grace of Christ, for faith to be peaceful and untroubled. Therefore when Paul saw the cult of the Law being set over against the free righteousness of faith, it was not right for him to be silent, unless he wished to abandon Christ. For when his adversaries denied that anyone will be saved, unless he keeps the Law of Moses, in this way they snatched away the glory of salvation from Christ, and were transferring it to works; and they were troubling and disquieting miserable souls by shaking their confidence. In the second place, it was not a matter of trifling importance to strip faithful souls of the liberty acquired by the blood of Christ. Even if the inward liberty of the Spirit was something common to the fathers and us, we know, however, what Paul says, viz. that they were confined under the childish custody of the Law, so that they were scarcely different from slaves (Gal. 4.1, 2); but that, after the manifestation of Christ, we have been set free from the custodianship (*paedagogia*) of the Law, to act with more freedom, as if our time for being protected has come to an end (Gal. 3.23f). The third fault of this teaching was that it poured out darkness on the light of the Gospel, or at least interposed something like dark clouds, so that Christ the Sun of Righteousness might not send out His full splendour. In short, it would have been all over with Christianity in a short time if Paul had yielded to such principles (*initiis*). He therefore took up the fight not on behalf of the external uncircumcision of the flesh, but for the salvation of men by grace; secondly, to set godly consciences free from the curse of the Law and the guilt of eternal death; and finally that, with the removal of all obstacles, the splendour of the grace of Christ might shine out again as though in a clear and serene sky. Also take into account the fact that those rascals were doing serious harm to the Law in impiously corrupting the proper use of it. The proper function of the Law was, like a custodian (*paedagogi instar*), to lead boys by the hand to Christ. Therefore it could not be worse adulterated than when it was being used as a pretext to diminish the power and grace of Christ.

The underlying sources (*fontes*) of all questions must be examined by us in this way, so that by our silence we may not betray the truth of God, whenever we see it directly attacked by the stratagems of Satan. And our minds are not to be turned aside by any dangers, or softened by insults and calumnies, because the pure religion must be constantly defended, even if heaven is bound to be united to the earth. Certainly Christ's servants 'must not be quarrelsome' (II Tim. 2.24). Therefore if any contention arises, they will make an effort to settle and compose it by their own moderation, rather than sound the trumpet straight away. Secondly they will be on unremitting guard against unnecessary and useless disputes; and they will not stir up controversies of little importance. But when they see the insolence of Satan increasing to the extent that religion can no longer remain unimpaired, unless he is faced, they must of necessity recover their courage and rise up to resist; and they are not to hesitate about engaging in battles, no matter how unpleasant. 'Peace' is certainly a pleasing word; but cursed is the peace that is obtained at so great a cost that there is lost to us the doctrine of Christ, by which alone we grow together into a godly and holy unity.

Today the Papists stir up much ill-will against us, as if the destructive tumults, by which the world is shaken, have been summoned up by us. But we have a ready defence, that the blasphemies against God, which we have taken pains to refute, were too atrocious for it to have been right for us to keep quiet; and equally that we are not to be blamed because we have joined issue with men on account of that cause, on behalf of which a war would have had to be waged with the very angels. Let them shout to their hearts' content! Paul's example is enough for us, so that we may not be frigid or slow about defending the doctrine of godliness, when the servants of Satan are destroying it with all their might; for their savage and outrageous conduct ought not to outstrip the perseverance of the servants of God. When Paul hotly opposed the false apostles, dissension finally blazed out from the clash; and yet the Spirit of God does not belabour him (*sugillat*) because of it; on the contrary, He honours with due praise the courage which He had conferred on the holy man.

They appointed ... to go up. The Spirit of God suggested this remedy for pacifying the disturbance, which otherwise could have gone further with quite disastrous effects. We are also taught from that that fit and appropriate methods must always be sought for settling discords. Because God commends peace so highly let believers show in very truth that it is not their fault that the Church is not at peace. Indeed the truth will always have the priority among them; and in order to protect it they will not be afraid of any disturbance. Nevertheless they will temper their fervour so as not to reject any method of honourable agreement; what is more, let them devise whatever ways they can on their own initiative; and let them use their heads in looking for them. Therefore we must preserve this moderation, so that we are not carried away by an excess of vehement zeal and swept beyond proper limits. For we ought to be courageous in the defence of true doctrine, neither inflexible nor rash. Let us therefore learn to combine those two virtues which the Spirit of God commends in Paul. When he is forcibly drawn into the arena by the ungodly he does not hesitate to present his case wisely (*cordate se offerre*), but calmly accepting the remedy proposed, he makes it quite clear that he has no desire to fight. For otherwise he could have boasted that he had no regard for the apostles, and obstinately persisted in that attitude; but concern for peace did not allow him evade their judgment. In addition the ignorant and weak would have got hold of the wrong idea if they had seen precisely two men separated from all the servants of Christ. But this particular way of fostering faith must not be neglected by godly teachers, that they show that they are in agreement with the Church.

Paul certainly was not at the apostles' beck and call, so that he would change his opinion if he were to find out that they were against him; for he would not have given way even to angels, as he boasts in the first chapter of Galatians (v. 8). But so that the ungodly might not misrepresent him as a man who was too proud and wrapped up in himself, and suiting himself with a shameful contempt for everyone else, he presents himself to give an account of his teaching, a proper thing to do, and something beneficial for the whole Church. Secondly, he was standing[1] in the presence of the apostles, with sure confidence in victory, because he well knew what sort of decision they would come to, for they were certainly governed by the same Spirit. However, it may well be asked with what intention the men of Antioch sent Paul and Barnabas to the rest of the apostles. For if their respect for those men had such a grip on them that they were in a state of indecision, until they had made a pronouncement on one side or another, their faith had been vanishing, even become completely non-existent, by this time. But the answer is easy. Since they knew that all the apostles were equally sent by the one Christ with the same commands, and that they were endowed with the same Spirit, they were quite convinced about the outcome. There is no doubt that this plan originated with upright and prudent men, who were not unaware that the scoundrels were making false pretence to the name of Peter and James. Accordingly all they were looking for was for the apostles to support the good cause with their favourable decision (*suffragio*).

All the holy synods have been convened from the beginning for the same purpose, that men who are eminent and well-versed in the Word of God might put an end to controversies, not in accordance with their own opinion, but in conformity with the will of God. It is worth while noting this so that the Papists may not discourage anyone by their empty clamours, for, in order to abolish Christ and His Gospel with Him, and to extinguish the light of godliness completely, they thrust Councils[2] on us, as if any decision of men at all is to be regarded as a heavenly oracle. Yet if the holy Fathers held their

---

[1] Reading *sistebat* with Tholuck for C.R. *resistebat*. Tr.
[2] Reading *concilia* with Tholuck for C.R. *consilia*. Tr.

assemblies today they would with one voice proclaim that they had
no right, or even no intention, to propound anything except the
words first given them by Christ (*nisi Christo verba praeeunte*), who
was their only Teacher, as He is also ours. I pass over the fact that the
Papists rely so much on abortive Councils, which breathe nothing
but crass ignorance and stupidity. But all the best and choicest of
them must of necessity be confined to that classification, that they are
subject to the Word of the Lord. There is a severe complaint of
Gregory of Nazianzus that no Council ever had a good result. It
cannot be denied that whatever excellence ever flourished and was
vigorous in the Church began to perish after a hundred years. Therefore if that holy man were alive now how angrily would he reject
the triflings (*nenias*) of the Papists, who without any shame bring in
deceiving masquerades (*larvarum praestigias*) for the legitimate Councils;
and indeed do so in order that the Word of God may take its departure, as soon as a few dull and stupid men have defined what suited
themselves.

3. *Being brought on their way by the church.* The fact that companions
were associated with Paul and Barnabas by the common consent of
the church, in order to escort them for courtesy's sake, allows us to
conclude that all the godly were on their side, and that they had no
other thought but that they had common cause with them. Accordingly they decided on the departure of Paul and Barnabas with the
same purpose as it was undertaken by them, viz. to suppress those
turbulent spirits who were falsely boasting of the apostles. His next
statement, that on the journeys they gave an account to the brethren
of the wonderful conversion of the Gentiles is evidence that they did
not come timidly to Jerusalem, but that even on that occasion they
fearlessly declared what they had taught before. Therefore they did
not come as men going to plead their cause before their judges, but to
establish, with a decision agreeable to both sides, what God had
commanded about the abrogating of ceremonies. For although they
were not spurning the judgment of the apostles, yet, because they
knew that neither they themselves nor the apostles were permitted to
come to different decisions about the cause, it was not fitting for them
to be made defendants. That is why they are confident and joyful.
In addition to that is the joy of the godly, because they subscribe both
to the teaching of Paul and the call of the Gentiles.

4. *They were received of the church.* By the word *Church* he means
the people themselves (*plebem ipsam*), and the whole body. He then
assigns a special place to the apostles and presbyters, by whom, in
particular, Paul and Barnabas were received. Moreover, since the
apostles did not have a fixed station at Jerusalem, but used to travel

continually hither and thither, wherever occasion called them, the
church there had its own presbyters, to whom the ordinary government of the church had been committed. But I have explained elsewhere how the one office differs from the other (on chapter 14.23).
Yet it is evident how brotherly and humane a spirit there was among
the apostles and presbyters, because, not only do they receive Paul and
Barnabas courteously, but they extol the grace of God, after they have
heard about the success of their work. Luke again repeats the mode
of expression which we found in the last chapter, when he says that
they 'gave an account of all the things that God had done with them'
(14.27). Along with that we must remember what I have said before,
that God is not to be thought of as a fellow-worker, but the whole
glory of the work is ascribed to Him alone. He is therefore said to
have *done with* Paul and Barnabas what He did through them. In the
same way He is said to deal mercifully with us, when He helps us in
our afflictions.

5. *Certain of the sect of the Pharisees.* It is not for nothing that Luke
describes the kind of men who tried to embarrass and impede Paul even
at Jerusalem. But it is probable that the evil sprang from that fountain;
and now Luke brings it out more clearly that from the same sect,
from which the perverse originators of that dissension had come forth,
agitators (*flabella*) now also burst on the scene. For even if they had
given their allegiance to Christ, yet vestiges of their former nature
were remaining. We know how proud, how confident, how super-
cilious the Pharisees were; and they would have forgotten all these
things if they had truly put on Christ; just as there was nothing of
Pharisaism left in Paul. But the majority had acquired the habit of
obstinacy from long usage, and it was not so easy for them to get rid
of it all at once. Since hypocrisy held sway among them to a very
great extent, they were too much intent on external rites which
provide cover for vices. They were also puffed up with pride, so that
they were tyrannical in their eagerness to subject everybody else to
their own principles. It is well enough known how violently monks
suffer from both diseases. That is also the reason why nothing is too
savage for them for the crushing of the Church, nothing is too outrageous or impudent for the spurning of the Word of God. Yes
indeed, we see that many have given up the cowl and come out of those
dens, and yet never forget the customs which they imbibed there.

*And the apostles and the elders were gathered together to consider of this
matter. And when there had been much questioning, Peter rose up, and
said unto them, Brethren, ye know how that a good while ago, God made
choice among you, that by my mouth the Gentiles should hear the word*

of the gospel, and believe. And God, which knoweth the heart, bare them witness, giving them the Holy Ghost, even as he did unto us; and he made no distinction between us and them, cleansing their hearts by faith. Now therefore why tempt ye God, that ye should put a yoke upon the neck of the disciples, which neither our fathers nor we were able to bear? But we believe that we shall be saved through the grace of the Lord Jesus, in like manner as they. (6-11)

6. *The apostles and the elders were gathered together.* Luke does not say that the whole church gathered together, but those who were powerful in doctrine and judgment, and who, by virtue of their office, were legitimate judges of this matter. It is certainly possible that the disputation was held in the presence of the people. But so that no one might imagine that the ordinary people were allowed to deal with the matter indiscriminately, Luke expressly mentions the apostles and presbyters, as they were more capable judges. Finally, let us realize that here a form and order is prescribed by God in convening synods, when any controversy has arisen which cannot be resolved in any other way. For when many were rising up daily against Paul, this single dispute, which carried the dangerous threat of a large-scale catastrophe, and which had already advanced to the point of bitter quarrels, drew him irresistibly to Jerusalem.

7. *But when there had been much questioning.* Although eminent men, the public teachers of the Church, were chosen, not even they could agree among themselves at once. It is clear from that how even at that time the Lord troubled the Church by the weakness of men, so that it might humbly learn to be wise. In addition He allowed the main principle of Christian doctrine to be turned over in different ways in that assembly over which He presided, so that we may not be surprised if it ever happens that otherwise godly and learned men fall into error through ignorance. For some of them were not so acute as to perceive the magnitude of the matter. So, when they are carried away by an unthinking zeal for the Law, and decide that the Law must be kept, they do not see into how dense a labyrinth they are hurling other men's consciences as well as their own. They were thinking that circumcision was an eternal and inviolable symbol of the divine covenant, and held the same opinion about the whole Law. Therefore Peter dwells most particularly on this, so as to indicate the main point at issue, for most of them were ignorant of it.

Now, his speech has two parts. For, first of all, in line with God's decision, he is vigorous in his contention that the Gentiles are not to be forced to keep the Law. In the second place he teaches that the whole salvation of men is overthrown if this snare has been laid for

31

consciences. Therefore the tenor of the first part, in which he repeats that he was sent by God to teach the Gentiles, and that the Holy Spirit had fallen on them, is this, that the ceremonies of the Law were not rashly abrogated by men, but that God is responsible for that abrogation. But when the authority of God is placed in the centre all doubt is removed, because the whole of our wisdom consists in acquiescing in the command of God, and in esteeming His will more highly than all arguments. It is now appropriate to ponder the words of Peter by which he proves that God allowed the Gentiles to be free from the yoke of the Law.

You know. He calls them as witnesses, so that no one might think that he is going to speak about an obscure or ambiguous matter. The story was known to all of them. As far as the rest is concerned, he shows that they are blind in broad daylight, because they are not paying proper attention to the work of God, and indeed, because they had not grasped long ago what had been plainly shown. He calls the beginning of the preaching of the Gospel, 'the old days', as if he meant 'long ago' (*pridem*), from the very beginning of the Church, as it were, after Christ began to gather some people to Himself.

God made choice among us.[1] The verb 'to choose' means to resolve and determine. However Peter is including at the same time both the gracious election of God, and the choice by which He admitted Gentiles into His own people. 'He therefore chose, that is, with the choice made, He wished them to hear the teaching of the Gospel from my lips, in order to provide evidence of free adoption among the Gentiles.' The phrase *in us* is the equivalent of 'in our sight', or 'with us as eye-witnesses', or 'in the midst of us'. For he means that he is only telling what was familiar and well-known to them, seeing that it had been done before their very eyes. The idiom is common enough in both Greek and Hebrew. Of course one may perhaps be disposed, along with others, to resolve it as, 'He chose me out of this assembly of ours'.

And believe. This was the seal for ratifying the call of the Gentiles. The task of teaching was imposed upon Peter by an oracle, but the fruit, which his teaching yielded, gives renown to his ministry, and makes it authentic, as the saying goes. For, seeing that the elect are enlightened to faith by the special grace of the Spirit, teaching will have no effect, except in so far as the Lord puts forth His power in ministers, in inwardly instructing the minds of those who hear, and in inwardly drawing their hearts. Therefore, since God ordered the teaching of the Gospel to be brought to the Gentiles, He consecrated them to Himself so that they might be no longer profane. But the

[1] Greek: ἐν ὑμῖν, followed by R.V. Calvin: *in nobis.* Tr.

solemn consecration was completed in all respects only when He engraved the mark of His adoption on their hearts by faith.

The sentence which follows immediately after must be taken as explanatory. Peter connects the visible graces of the Spirit, which he mentions, to faith, as they were assuredly nothing else but the accession to it. Therefore when the Gentiles were ingrafted into the people of God without circumcision or ceremonies Peter concludes that it is wrong for the need to keep the Law to be imposed upon them. However, it seems that the evidence of election, that the Holy Spirit fell on them, is not altogether convincing (*minus firmum*). For the gifts were of such a kind that one could not infer from them that those men were to be reckoned in the class of the godly. But it is the Spirit of regeneration alone who distinguishes the sons of God from outsiders (*alienis*). I reply that, despite the fact that men, who were frauds (*vani*) in other respects, might have been endowed with the gift of tongues and similar things; yet Peter takes it for granted that it was known that God sealed His gracious adoption in Cornelius and his relatives with the visible grace of the Spirit, as if he were pointing to His sons with a finger.

8. *The knower of hearts.* He makes this description apply to God in the circumstances of the case under review. And there is an underlying tacit contrast, that men are rather devoted to external purity, because they judge according to their dull, earthly understanding; God, on the other hand, looks into hearts. Peter therefore warns that a perverted judgment is being made in this matter out of human understanding, since only the inner purity of hearts must be evaluated here, and that is hidden from us. And in this way he puts a bridle on our rashness, so that, by taking more on ourselves than is proper, we may not make loud protest against the judgment of God. It is as if he said: 'If the nature of the testimony, which God gave to them, is not apparent to you (*tibi*), think how great is the difference between you and Him. For outward splendour holds you back on account of your dull mental outlook, but that splendour must be past and done with, when one comes to the judgment-seat of heaven, where a spiritual examination of hearts is made.' Finally, a general doctrine must be held in the meantime, that the eyes of the Lord do not look to the showy parades of works, but on the integrity of the heart, as is held in Jeremiah (5.3).

The translation of the Vulgate[1] and Erasmus, that God knows the hearts, does not sufficiently bring out what Luke is saying in Greek. For in calling God καρδιογνώστην he is contrasting Him with men, who usually judge rather by the outward appearance, and therefore

---

[1] Vulg.: *Et qui novit corda Deus etc.* Calvin: *Et qui cordium cognitor est Deus etc.* Tr.

can be called προσωπογνῶσται, 'face-knowers', if they are compared with God.

9. *And he made no distinction.* Indeed there was a distinction, because the Gentiles had been suddenly admitted from uncircumcision to the covenant of eternal life, whereas the Jews had been prepared for faith by circumcision. But Peter means that both were equally drawn by God into the hope of the same inheritance, and that they were raised to an equal level of honour, to be sons of God and members of Christ, and, finally, the holy seed of Abraham, and a priestly and royal people (*genus*). From that it follows that it can only be sacrilege to regard them as unclean after God has chosen them for His own private property, and has consecrated them holy vessels of His temple. For with the destruction of the wall, by which they had been separated from each other, He joined the Gentiles to the Jews, to grow together into one body; and, if I may put it like this, he has joined circumcision to uncircumcision, so that both the members of the household and outsiders may be one in Christ, and form one Church; and that there may no longer be Jew or Greek.

Since he had purified by faith. This phrase corresponds to the description which he applied to God previously (v. 8); as if he said that God, who is the knower of hearts, cleansed the Gentiles inwardly, when He thought them worthy of His adoption, so that they might be endowed with spiritual cleanness. But he adds, moreover, that this purity depends on faith. He therefore teaches, first of all, that true holiness, which is to be sufficient before the judgment-seat of God, exists for the Gentiles without ceremonies; secondly, he teaches that this holiness is obtained by faith, and flows from it. In the same way Paul concludes that uncircumcision does not prevent a man being reckoned righteous and holy in God's sight, because in the case of Abraham circumcision followed righteousness and came later in time (Rom. 4.10).

But at this point the question is asked, 'Was the purity of the patriarchs of long ago different from that which God now conferred on the Gentiles? For Peter clearly seems to separate the Gentiles from the Jews by this distinguishing feature, that, content with the purity of the heart alone, they need no support from the Law.' I reply that they do differ from each other, not in substance, but only in form. For God always looked to the inner cleanliness of the heart. Ceremonies were given to the people of old only in order to help their faith. So cleanness, related to forms and practices (*quoad figuras et exercitia*), was temporary until the coming of Christ, and there is now no place for it among us; for just as the true, that is, spiritual worship of God remains the same from the very beginning of the world right to the end, there is nevertheless a great difference in the visible form. Now

34

we see that the fathers obtained righteousness, or were pure, in the sight of God, not by ceremonies, but by cleanness of heart. For ceremonies in themselves were of no importance for justifying them, but were mere supports, which cleansed accidentally, if I may say so, so that the truth was still the same for the men of old and for us. Now with the coming of Christ everything accidental has vanished; and therefore, with the scattering of the shadows, purity of heart survives in its bare simplicity.

In this way a difficulty that the Jews think is inexplicable is easily solved. Circumcision is called the eternal or everlasting covenant (Gen. 17.13). They therefore deny that it had to be abolished. If anyone objects that this does not refer to the visible symbol but rather to the thing signified, he will have answered correctly. But there is another solution, which I have mentioned, that since the rule of Christ was a kind of renewing of the world, there is nothing absurd about His having put an end to all the shadows of the Law, seeing that the perpetuity of the Law is founded on Christ.

I come now to the second phrase, in which Peter establishes the cleanness of the Gentiles on *faith*. Why does he not say, 'by perfection of virtues', or 'by sanctity of life', except that righteousness comes to men from another person than themselves? For if men were to acquire righteousness for themselves by living justly and properly, or were clean by nature, in the sight of God, this sentence of Peter's would fall to the ground. Therefore the Spirit plainly announces by these words that the whole human race is polluted and defiled with filth; secondly, that the filth cannot be removed in any other way than by the grace of Christ. For since faith is the remedy by which God helps us out of favour, it is set in opposition both to the common nature of all, and to each person's particular merits. When I say that the whole human race is convicted of pollution, I mean that we take nothing from the womb except genuine filth, and that there is no uprightness in our nature which may procure the favour of God for us. The soul of man was indeed furnished with excellent gifts at its very beginning, but all its parts are so currupted by sin, that not even a drop of purity remains in it any longer. Cleanness must therefore be sought outside ourselves. For if anyone takes up the point that it can be recovered by meritorious works, there is no greater absurdity than imagining a perverse nature being capable of being worthy. The result is that men are to seek elsewhere for what they will never find within themselves. And it is certainly the function of faith to transfer to us what belongs to Christ, and to make it ours by imparting it freely; thus there is a mutual relation between faith and the grace of Chrst; for faith does not cleanse us as a virtue or quality poured into our souls, but because

35

it receives the cleanness offered in Christ. We must also note the
expression, *God cleansed their hearts,* by which Luke both makes God
the creator of faith, and teaches that cleanness is a blessing from Him.
In short, he points out that what men cannot give themselves, is conferred on them by the grace of God. But since it has been said that
faith transfers to us what it takes from Christ, we must now see how
the grace of Christ purifies us, so that we may be pleasing to God.
Now the method of cleansing is twofold, first, that Christ, by daily
destroying our sins, for which He once made atonement by His blood,
offers and presents us, pure and righteous, in the sight of the Father;
and, secondly, that mortifying the desires of the flesh by His Spirit
He reforms us in sanctity. I willingly understand both by these words,
because Luke does not refer to one kind of cleansing only, but teaches
that it stands in all its perfection independent of the ceremonies of the
Law.

10. *Now therefore why do you tempt.* This is the second part of the
speech, in which Peter points out how deadly is that teaching, which
the enemies of Paul wished to force on them, for it would overwhelm
all godly souls in despair. He infers and concludes from the previous
sentence that God is *tempted* if the Gentiles are forced into the necessity
of keeping the Law; but he probes deeper and penetrates to the very
root of the matter. For up to now he has been arguing that harm is
being caused to the Gentiles if more is demanded from them than God
wishes; and that when He has made them equal to the holy people,
and thought them worthy of the honour of adoption, it is a shameful
and absurd thing for them to be rejected, and His generosity thus
checked; and finally, that faith alone is enough for them, lacking ceremonies though they may be. He now brings forward a profounder
principle indeed, that those who bind the salvation of men to the
works of the Law leave them with nothing good to hope for; but on
the contrary that the whole world is being rushed into horrible destruction, if it can obtain salvation by no other means than by keeping the
Law. We shall soon see, in their proper place, what arguments he
uses to prove this. As far as the words are concerned, seeing that
Scripture says that God is *tempted* in various ways, in this context
Peter means that God is being challenged, deliberately as it were,
when there is placed on men a burden greater than they can bear; and
that His power is restricted when the yoke, which He Himself relaxes,
is tightened. And that is nothing else but, by fighting against nature,
trying to be like the giants, as the saying goes.

That a yoke be placed on the necks. The meaning of the words is
plain: that God is tempted when a greater burden is laid on consciences
than they can bear; and when this happens the salvation of souls

receives a mortal wound, seeing that they are bound to be over-whelmed with despair in this way, and that can only bring destruction. But no more must there be tolerated the wrong that is done to God, when His prerogative (*ius*) is snatched away from Him, so that He is not free to set us free. Leaving that aside, it is easy to gather from the actual situation that he is not speaking about ceremonies alone. The servitude of the old custodianship (*paedagogiae*) was, I grant, hard and laborious, but it would be extremely absurd for the yoke to be called insupportable; and we do know that not only holy men, but also a great many hypocrites acquitted themselves correctly and punctiliously in the outward observation of the rites. Yes, and what is more, it would not be such a difficult thing to satisfy the moral law, if it were satisfied with bodily obedience only, and did not demand spiritual righteousness. For it is given to many to control their hands and feet, but it is really extremely hard to manage all the affections, so that perfect self-restraint and purity reign in the soul as well as in the body. Accordingly it is ridiculous for people to limit Peter's word to cere-monies, which express the powerlessness of men to show righteous-ness of the heart, something which is not only far beyond their strength, but completely contrary to their nature. Those who think like that have of course been misled by the single argument that the question had been raised about ceremonies only; but it has not entered their heads that Peter properly considered with more attention and prudence what sort of labyrinth an error, to all appearances trivial, was bringing along with it. For the false apostles were denying that anyone could obtain salvation unless he kept the ceremonies. If the salvation of men is bound to works, it will be founded on the grace of Christ no longer; and so reconciliation by grace will fall to the ground. Now, since human strength is not able to cope with the keeping of the Law, the curse, which God announces in it for transgressors, falls on all; and so despair will grip all when they see themselves condemned to eternal death by the Law. Perhaps the false apostles were shrewdly keeping those things back. But Peter penetrates to the very source, in order to bring the deadly poison of that doctrine into the light of day; and we must do the same as often as Satan covertly insinuates impious errors.

Today we appear to be extremely contentious to some people, since we contend so much that prayers must not be made for the dead. For apart from being a very ancient custom, there does not appear to be much in the way of danger, even if unnecessary prayers are poured out. Yes, and what is more, it is a plausible doctrine, because it has a show of human piety. Moreover, ignorant men think like that, be-cause they do not look for the source itself. For if we admit that prayers must be made for the dead at the same time it will have to be accepted that they are now suffering punishment by the judgment of God, because they made no amends for their sins in this life. Now in this way the virtue of the atonement completed by Christ is transferred to the works of men. Secondly the rule for praying properly is overthrown, if men are allowed to pray haphazardly without the Word of God. This absurdity is even too great to be bound to be disregarded. In short a proper decision will never be made about any question unless all the consequences, which a doctrine brings along with it, when it becomes controversial, have been deduced, and the source has been thoroughly examined. It is therefore no wonder if, in order to drag the false apostles out of their hiding-places, Peter deals in a general way with the whole Law, because he lays bare nothing but the truth itself, which was hidden from the simple, so that all may see how deadly is a doctrine which both abolishes the graces of Christ, and plunges souls into the abyss of fearful despair.

Neither we nor our fathers. Peter is discussing not only what men have done, but what they could have done by work alone; and he is speaking not only about the great mass of men, but about the holy patriarchs. When he says that they were unable to bear the yoke of the Law, it is established that it is impossible to keep the Law. I know that that statement of Jerome's has been accepted so universally as to be almost a fixed axiom, 'If anyone has said that it is impossible to keep the Law, let him be accursed'. But we must not listen to any human voice that is in opposition to the judgment of the Spirit of God. We hear what the Spirit pronounces here through the lips of Peter, not about the will and works of men, but about their ability and power. And Paul agrees, maintaining that it has been impossible for the Law to confer life on us, seeing that it was weak through the flesh (Rom. 8.3). Certainly if anyone could fulfil the Law, he will obtain the life promised in it. But since Paul denies that life can be obtained from the Law, it follows that in it a higher righteousness is required than men can achieve. I certainly admit that Jerome does not grant the ability to fulfil the Law to natural powers completely, but also gives a part to the grace of God; just as he later explains that a believing man, helped by the grace of the Spirit, may be said to be able to fulfil the Law. But that mitigation is not true. For if we consider only natural powers, men will not only be unequal to bearing the yoke of the Law, but will not be able to move even one finger to fulfil the least part of the Law. And certainly if all these are true, that the thoughts of the human mind are evil from childhood (Gen. 8.21); that all the inclinations (*sensus*) of the flesh are hostile to God (Rom. 8.7); and that there is no one who seeks after God (Ps. 14.2); and things in the same vein which occur frequently in Scripture, particularly those which Paul lists in the third chapter of Romans (v. 11ff); then man's ability to fulfil the Law will not only be weak and impaired, but he will be quite incapable of beginning. It must therefore be concluded that even believers, after they have been born again by the Spirit of God, and are eager for the righteousness of the Law, yet fulfil the half of it, and even far less than half, not the whole. For Peter is not speaking here about Epicurus or worldly men, but of Abraham, Moses and the other holy fathers, all the very best of men (*perfectissimi*) who ever were in the world. And yet he says that they succumbed to the burden of the Law, because it overwhelmed their strength.

The odious objection is made that the Spirit of God is being insulted, when the power of fulfilling the Law is taken away from His grace and help. But there is an easy explanation, that we are not dealing with what the grace of the Spirit is capable of doing, but with what the measure of grace, which God distributes to each of His own in this life, is able to do. For it is always proper to think over what God promises that He will do, and it is not for us to ask if something can happen, which He himself declares will never be, and He does not wish to happen. He promises the grace and help of the Spirit to the faithful so that they may fight against the desires of the flesh and subdue them; but yet not[1] utterly destroy them. He promises grace by which they may walk in newness of life, yet not run with as much haste as the Law requires. For He wishes them to be answerable to Himself for the whole of their lives, so that they may have recourse to asking for pardon. If it is not permitted to separate the purpose of God and the order laid down by Him from His power, it is a foolish and futile cavil with which our adversaries are trying to burden us, when they claim that we detract from the power of God. Rather are they themselves transforming God, when they contend that His purpose can be changed. Long ago the Pelagians heaped the same calumny on Augustine also. He replies that even if it is possible for the Law to be fulfilled, yet it is enough for him that Scripture testifies that nobody has ever fulfilled it, and that it is not going to be fulfilled right to the end of the world. With these words he extricates himself from their troublesome subtlety. But there was no reason for him to be hesitant about conceding, freely and clearly, that it was possible with the Holy Spirit as the Performer (*autore*); for the grace

---

[1] Following Tholuck: *non tamen penitus aboleant. Promittit gratiam qua ambulent in vitae novitate, non tamen currant tanta celeritate quantam Lex postulat.* C.R. omits all the words between the first and second *non tamen*. The French supports Tholuck. Tr.

of the Spirit must be put within limits, in order to conform to the promises. Furthermore we have already shown how far the promises extend themselves. Certainly there is no question in anybody's mind as to whether God can, if He wishes, make men perfect; but all who separate His power from His purpose, of which they have clear evidence in Scripture, are impious and raving. What God wishes and what He has determined to do, He shows plainly a hundred times; to go beyond that is sacrilege. A philosophical argument drove Jerome to hurl the thunderbolt of his curse at Peter and Paul, viz. that laws ought to be tempered to the ability of those for whom they are produced. And although I admit that there is room for that in human laws, yet I deny its validity as far as the Law of God is concerned, for in its demand for righteousness it does not look to what man is able to do, but what he ought to do.

However a more difficult question suggests itself here: 'Has the Law not been given for the purpose of forcing men to obey God? Now there would have been no point in that happening, unless the Spirit of God were guiding the faithful in the keeping of it. And that solemn testimony of Moses seems to remove any doubt, when he warns that he is giving precepts to the Jews, not for them to read, but to fulfil in action (Deut. 30.12ff). And we gather from that that a yoke was placed on the Jews, when the Law was given, because it made them subject to God, so that they would not live according to their own will.' I reply that the Law is thought of as a yoke in two ways. For seeing that it bridles the desires of the flesh and provides a standard for leading godly and upright lives, it is right for the sons of God to submit their necks to this yoke. But seeing that it lays down precisely what we owe to God, and promises life only on the added condition of perfect obedience, and, on the other hand, promises a curse if men have wandered from it in any respect, it is an intolerable yoke. I shall make this a little clearer. The simple doctrine of leading a good life, by which God calls us to Himself, is a yoke to which all ought to be willing to submit. For there is nothing more absurd than for God not to be ruling over the life of men, but for them to be wandering about as they like without any bridle. Therefore the yoke of the Law must not be rejected if consideration is given to the simple teaching of it. But these sentences, if I may use the expression, qualify the Law with a different aspect (*aliter qualificant*): 'He who does these things shall live in them' (Lev. 18.5); again, 'Everyone is accursed who does not abide in all the things that are written' (Deut. 27.26); with the result that the yoke begins to be insupportable. For as long as salvation is promised only for perfect obedience of the Law, and any transgression at all is called to judgment, the human race is absolutely done for. Following this reasoning Peter asserts that God is being tempted when men in their arrogance lay the burden of the Law on consciences. For he does not mean to deny that men must be governed by the teaching of the Law, and so he concedes that they are under the yoke; but because it is the function of the Law not simply to teach, but also to humble men with the condemnation of eternal death, and when he considers that property annexed to the teaching, he contends that the souls of the godly ought not to be bound by the yoke of the Law, because in this way they are bound to be plunged into eternal destruction. Finally, when we have the present help not only of the grace of the Holy Spirit, to direct us, but also of the free forgiveness of sins, to deliver and absolve us from the curse of the Law, then that word of Moses is fulfilled, 'The commandment is not beyond you' (Deut. 30.11). Then we also realize how agreeable Christ's yoke is, and how light His burden (Matt. 11.30). For we know that by the indulgence of God we are forgiven what we fail in because of the weakness of the flesh, and because of that we undertake what He enjoins eagerly and without arrogance. Accordingly, provided that the rigour of the Law is removed, the teaching of the Law will not only be tolerable, but also pleasing and agreeable; and we must not refuse the bridle which restrains us gently, but does not drive us further than is expedient.

11. *Through the grace of the Lord Jesus.* Peter compares these two things with each other as opposites: to have hope of salvation in the grace of Christ, and to be under the yoke of the Law. And this comparison makes the justification of Christ stand out in a very clear light, inasmuch as we gather from it that those who, independently of and free from the yoke of the Law, seek salvation in the grace of Christ, are justified by faith. Moreover I have already said that the yoke of the Law is a combination of two strands. The first is: 'He who does these things, shall live in them' (Lev. 18.5); the second is 'Everyone is accursed who does not persevere in all the precepts' (Deut. 27.26). Let us return to the opposite position: if we obtain salvation by the grace of Christ, just as if the yoke of the Law were out of the way, it follows that salvation for us does not depend on keeping the Law, and all who believe in Christ are not liable to the curse of the Law. For if a man who is still gripped by the yoke of the Law could be saved by grace, Peter's argument would be absurd, for it is established that it is based on contradictory things, in this sense, 'We look for salvation by the grace of Christ, therefore we are not subject to the yoke of the Law.' Peter would be deceiving us unless there was a cleavage between the grace of Christ and the yoke of the Law (*eius iugum*). Accordingly all who desire to obtain life in Christ must depart from the righteous-

ness of the Law. For this contradiction does not refer to doctrine but to the cause of justification.

This also refutes the fabrication of those who state that we are justified by the grace of Christ, in that He regenerates us by His Spirit, and gives us the power to fulfil the Law. For although those who imagine this seem to be relaxing the yoke of the Law a little, yet they are keeping souls bound by both its strands. For this promise will always be in force, 'He who does these things, will live in them'. On the other hand the curse will fall on all who have not fulfilled the Law exactly. Accordingly the grace of Christ, on which the assurance of salvation rests, must be defined quite differently from what these men dream of, viz. that it is the free reconciliation procured by the sacrifice of His death; or, what amounts to the same thing, the free forgiveness of sins, which, by appeasing God, makes of an enemy, or a severe and implacable judge, a Father favourable to us. I certainly admit that we are regenerated to newness of life by the grace of Christ, but when it is a question of the assurance of salvation, we ought to be thinking about free adoption alone, which is bound up with the expiation and pardon of sins. For if works come into the reckoning, to procure righteousness for us in some degree at least, the yoke of the Law will not be broken; and so Peter's antithesis will collapse or be removed.

In like manner as they. Here Peter is testifying that even if the servitude of the Law had been imposed on the fathers, as far as the outward form was concerned, yet their consciences were unfettered and free. And that disposes of an absurdity which otherwise could have troubled godly minds a good deal. For since the covenant of life which God made with His servants from the beginning right to the end of the world, is eternal and the same, it would be absurd and intolerable for there to be taught today another and different way of obtaining salvation than the one the fathers had long ago. Therefore Peter affirms that we are completely at one with the fathers, because they, no less than we, placed the hope of salvation on the grace of Christ. And so, making the Law and the Gospel one, because he bears in mind the object of teaching (*quod ad finem doctrinae spectat*), he removes from the Jews the stumbling-block, which they were imagining for themselves on account of the disagreement.

It is apparent from that that the Law was not given to the fathers so that they might obtain salvation from it, and that the ceremonies were not added so that they might acquire righteousness by observing them, but that the whole Law had one single aim, that, having cast away reliance on works, they might transfer all their hopes to the grace of Christ. This also clearly refutes the nonsense of those who think that the people of old were content with earthly blessings, and gave no thought to the life of heaven. But Peter makes the fathers sharers of the same faith with us, and assigns a common salvation to both. And yet there are those whom the fanatical fellow, Servetus, pleases with such abominable sacrileges. Furthermore we must note what Peter teaches, that the faith of the men of old was always founded on Christ, seeing that life could never be found in any other source, and there was no other means by which men might come to God. Therefore this verse agrees with that saying of the apostle, 'Christ yesterday, and today, and for ever' (Heb. 13.8).

And all the multitude kept silence; and they hearkened unto Barnabas and Paul rehearsing what signs and wonders God had wrought among the Gentiles by them. And after they had held their peace, James answered, saying, Brethren, hearken unto me: Symeon hath rehearsed how first God did visit the Gentiles, to take out of them a people for his name. And to this agree the words of the prophets; as it is written, After these things I will return, And I will build again the tabernacle of David, which is fallen; And I will build again the ruins thereof, And I will set it up: That the residue of men may seek after the Lord, And all the Gentiles, upon whom my name is called, Saith the Lord, who maketh these things known from the beginning of the world. (12-18)

12. *All the multitude kept silence.* Luke means by these words that the Spirit of God reigned in that assembly in such a way that they yielded to the argument straight away. Earlier they were engaging in a heated discussion; now, after Peter has explained the purpose of God, and dealt with the actual question at issue, according to the teaching of the Gospel, all the uproar immediately comes to an end, and the men who were recently hotly defending an error are quiet and silent. This is the living image of a proper Council, where the truth of God puts an end to all controversies as soon as it has appeared on the scene. And certainly when the Spirit presides He is effectual enough to put an end to all disagreement; because here, again, He is a Guide capable of directing the tongues of those who ought to be leading the way for others, as well as urging the rest to obedience, so that they might not be too devoted to themselves, but lay aside their obstinacy, and show themselves obedient to God. And there is no doubt that a certain few remained inflexible as usually happens in a great crowd; yet the truth of God prevailed so that the silence, which Luke mentions, was clear evidence of a common obedience. On the other hand it was no ordinary moderation that Peter showed, for he allowed individuals to state publicly whatever they had in mind, and

deferred his own opinion, in case it might be prejudicial to others, until they had discussed the matter backwards and forwards.

They hearkened unto Barnabas and Paul. From these words one may gather that they were not heard in silence before. For since the majority had been convinced that profane Gentiles had been wrongly admitted into the Church by those men, nothing that they would have said would have fallen on sympathetic ears, unless that false opinion had been corrected, but everything would have been seized upon in an unfavourable sense. We see how venemous a thing aversion is, when it is conceived for no reason, for it takes possession of the mind of men so as to block every entrance to the truth. From this we learn how true is the word in Titus 1.15, 'To the sound all things are sound' (*omnia sana sanis*). For there is nothing so wholesome that corrupt attitudes of mind may not turn into something harmful. Finally, in their account Paul and Barnabas aim at showing that their apostleship among the Gentiles was approved by God; seeing that it had been confirmed and ratified by miracles, which are, as it were, the seals of it.

13. *James answered, saying.* Very many of the ancient ecclesiastical writers think that this James was one of the disciples, named 'The Just' and 'Oblias', whose shameful death Josephus reports in the twentieth book of the *Antiquities.* But I wish that those men of long ago had taken pains to identify the man, rather than to celebrate the sanctity of an unknown man with fabulous praises. Their statement that only he was allowed to go into the holy of holies is a childish fabrication. For if any religious rite (*religio*) underlay that entry, then he, who was not the high priest, would have been doing it against the Law of God. Secondly it was a superstitious thing to encourage the shadowy worship of the temple in this way. I omit other and similar trifling things. But they are very much mistaken in denying that he was one of the twelve apostles. For they are forced to admit that it is he whom Paul honours so highly as to assign to him the leading place among the three pillars of the Church (Gal. 2.9). Certainly someone who was inferior in rank would never have excelled over the apostles like that; for Paul honours him with the title of 'apostle'. And Jerome's view that the word[1] is used in a general sense there, does not deserve attention, since it is the dignity of the order (*dignitas ordinis*) that is being deliberately dealt with, seeing that Christ placed the apostles before the other teachers of the Church.

Besides, it is easy to gather from this verse that he was held in unusually high regard, seeing that he confirms Peter's words, with his own approbation, so that all go over to his opinion. And in chap-

[1] i.e. pillar. Tr.

44

ter 21 we shall see again how powerful his authority was at Jerusalem. The ancient writers think that that happened because he was the Bishop of the place. But it is not likely that, of their own free-will, the faithful changed the order established by Christ. Accordingly I have no doubt that he was the son of Alphaeus, and a blood-relation (*consanguineus*) of Christ's and in that sense he is also called His brother. I leave it an open question whether he was the Bishop of Jerusalem or not, and it is not very relevant, except that the impudence of the Pope is clearly refuted by the fact that the decree of the Council is determined by the authority of James rather than of Peter. And Eusebius in the beginning of the second book (of his *Church History*) certainly does not hesitate to call James, whoever he was in the end, the Bishop of the Apostles. Let the men of Rome now go and boast that the Pope is the head of the Universal Church, because he is the successor of Peter, who allowed another to be over him, if Eusebius is to be believed.

14. *Brethren, hearken unto me.* James' speech consists of two main parts. For he first confirms the call of the Gentiles by the testimony of the prophet Amos; he then suggests what is a helpful thing to do to foster peace and concord among the faithful, so that liberty might still remain unimpaired for the Gentiles, and the grace of Christ might not be obscured. As to Peter being called *Simeon*, it is possible that this name was pronounced in different ways at that time. In saying that God visited to take a people out of the Gentiles, a reference is being made to the mercy of God, by which He deigned to admit outsiders to His family. Indeed it is an awkward expression, but one that contains useful doctrine, because he is making God responsible for the call of the Gentiles, and makes known that it is His favour that they begin to be reckoned among His people, when he says that they were taken by Him. But he goes further in saying 'He visited to take'. For the meaning is that when the Gentiles were alienated from God, He looked upon them with indulgence; because we can do nothing else but go farther and farther away from Him, until He looks at us in His fatherly way, and steps in before us, without being asked.

In His name (*in nomine suo*). The Vulgate has 'for His name' (*nomini suo*), which means almost the same thing; although the preposition ἐπί[1] can be translated in other ways viz. 'on account of His name' (*propter nomen suum*) or 'upon His name' (*super nomine suo*). And the meaning will suit quite well that the salvation of the Gentiles is founded on the name or power of God, and that in calling them God had nothing else in mind than His own glory. However I have retained the more usual interpretation, viz. that in including them with

[1] There is no preposition in the Greek, τῷ ὀνόματι αὐτοῦ. Tr.

45

His people He wished them to be known by His Name, just as it will be said a little later that His Name is invoked upon all whom He gathers into His Church. The adverb of time, πρῶτον, can be explained in two ways. If you read *primum*, 'first of all', along with Erasmus and the Vulgate, the meaning will be that Cornelius and the others were, so to speak, the firstfruits, by whom God began the call of the Gentiles. But it can also be taken in a comparative sense, that He had already produced evidence of the adoption of the Gentiles in Cornelius and his relatives, before Barnabas and Paul were making the Gospel known to the Gentiles. And this latter meaning is more pleasing to me.

15. *And to this agree the words of the prophets.* We now see that the apostles took nothing on themselves imperiously, but reverently followed what was laid down by the Word of God. And they did not feel it an irksome thing, or consider it out of keeping with their dignity, to profess themselves students of Scripture. We must also note from this that the use of prophetic teaching is still held in esteem, whereas certain lunatics would like to drive it out of the Church. By appealing to the evidence of the prophets in the plural, while quoting only one passage, he means that there was such agreement among them, that what is said by one is the common testimony of all, because they all speak with one mouth, and individually speak as if in the person of all, or rather the Spirit of God speaks in all of them. In addition the oracles of all the prophets were collected together to form a single corpus. Accordingly what was taken from some part of a collective book could justifiably and properly be ascribed to the prophets in common.

16. *After these things I will return.* Because the passage is not quoted word for word as it appears in the writings of the prophet we must see what difference there is; although there is no need carefully to examine what difference there is in the words, so long as it is clear that the prophecy fits in well with the situation under review. After God has promised the restoration of the tabernacle of David, He adds that He will also cause the Jews to possess the remnant of Edom (Amos 9.11f). In the whole of that context nothing as yet appears from which the call of the Gentiles can be elicited. But what follows immediately after in the writing of the prophet about the remnant of the nations, upon whom the name of God will be invoked, plainly shows that there will be one Church of Jews and Gentiles, because what particularly belonged to the Jews alone at that time is given to both in common. For God places the Gentiles on the same level of honour as the Jews, when He wishes His name to be invoked upon them. The Idumeans and neighbouring peoples were once made subject to the

Jews under David; but although they were tributaries to the people of God, they were nevertheless outside the Church. Therefore it was a new and unaccustomed thing that God adds them to His holy people, so that He may equally be called the God of all, inasmuch as it is certain that they are all made equal in honour among themselves in this way. From that it is quite evident how well the prophet's testimony suits the present purpose. For God promises the restoration of the tabernacle that had fallen in ruins, that in it the Gentiles may be subject to the Kingdom of David, not merely to pay tribute, or to take arms at the king's command, but to have a common God and be His one family.

However the question can be raised why he preferred to quote this prophecy rather than many others which contain clearer proof of the question at issue, when Paul cites many of this kind (Rom. 15.9ff). I reply first of all that the apostles were not ambitious about collecting Scripture passages, but that they were simply intent on this one thing, that was more than enough for them, viz. to prove that their own doctrine was taken from the Word of God. In the second place I maintain that this prophecy of Amos' is clearer than is commonly thought. It concerns the restoration of a house that had collapsed, and the prophet describes its wretched and ruinous state. Therefore the promise that follows immediately after, that the throne is to be set up again, from which kings, the descendants of David, may rule over the Gentiles, strictly refers to Christ. Therefore when the Kingdom of Christ has been set up, what the prophet says at the same time is bound to follow, that the name of God must be invoked upon the Gentiles. We now see that James did not select this passage at random. For if the Kingdom of Christ can only be established if God is invoked everywhere throughout the whole world, and the Gentiles united into His holy people, then it is absurd for them to be kept back from the hope of salvation; and the middle wall, by which they had been separated from each other under the Law, must fall down. Among other things ceremonies served the purpose of distinguishing the holy people of God from the profane Gentiles. Since the distinction has now been removed, it is proper for ceremonies also to be abrogated. The prophet does not have the first verb, *I will return*, but the change of circumstances, which he announces is very well brought out in this way.

The tabernacle of David which is fallen. That ugly devastation and ruin of the royal house is set before our eyes by the prophet to good purpose. For unless the godly were convinced that, despite the fact that the kingdom of David was reduced to nothing, Christ would yet come, not only to restore ruinous things to their original order, but to raise up even to the heavens the glory of the kingdom with incomparable success, they would have despaired a hundred times every day. When they had returned from the exile in Babylon, they had been reduced almost to destruction by incessant and innumerable disasters. Afterwards the remainder was cut down by degrees by internal dissensions. Yes, and what is more, when God came to their rescue in their wretched circumstances, the kind of help which He brought was a certain source of despair. For the sovereignty, which the Maccabees assumed for themselves, was taken away from the tribe of Judah at that time. For those reasons the Spirit of God carefully impresses through the prophet that Christ would not come until the kingdom of David has perished, in case they might despair of salvation when they were in discouraging situations. Thus Isaiah announces that a shoot will spring forth from a despised and ignoble trunk (11.1). And let us also remember that in restoring the Church God has the wonderful method of building it out of ruins.

Moreover this verse teaches what the true and proper constitution of the Church is, viz. when the throne of David is raised up on high, and Christ alone is prominent, so that all may unite in obeying Him. Although the Pope has crushed the Church with his sacrilegious tyranny, yet he vaunts himself with the title of the Church. On the contrary he is causing deception through the empty title of the Church, in order to put out the light of sound doctrine. But yet if it comes to a proper examination, it is easy to refute such gross mockery, because Christ has been set aside and he himself alone seizes supreme power. Indeed he makes the verbal admission that he is the vicar of Christ, but in actual fact he banishes Christ to heaven for a specious exile, and appropriates all His power to himself. For the only way that Christ reigns is by the teaching of the Gospel, which is abominably trodden under foot by this accursed idol. Let us be sure to remember that the proper state of the Church among us would be this, if all to a man were subject to Christ, the King supreme, so that there may be one sheepfold and one Shepherd.

17. *That those who remain may seek.* By way of explanation James has added that *seek*, for it is not included in the prophet's statement. And yet it is not superfluous, because, so that we may be counted in the people of God, and He may acknowledge us as His own, we, for our part, ought to be disposed to seek Him. And it is likely that Luke briefly summarised what James had discussed with the Jews in their native language, with the result that the explanation of the matter was mingled with the words of the prophet. For 'the residue of the nations' which Amos puts, Luke, following the more familiar Greek translation, has substituted *the residue of men*, with the same meaning,

48

viz. that a pruning would precede the purging of the filth of the world, as actually did happen. And this teaching must also be applied to our own time, for, seeing that the corruption of the world is too bad for the whole of it to yield obedience to Christ, He scatters the refuse and darnel with the fans of various tribulations, so that in the end He may gather to Himself the residue that will remain.

18. *Those things known from the beginning of the world.* This is an anticipation to remove the odium of newness. For the sudden change could have been suspect, and was disturbing weak minds on that occasion. Therefore James counteracts it, pointing out that this was no new thing for God, even if it did happen suddenly and in a way different from what men supposed, since God had foreseen before the creation of the world what He was going to do, and the call of the Gentiles had been hidden in His secret purpose. The result is that that call must not be appraised according to human understanding. Moreover, James is looking to the words of the prophet, when he asserts that God, who was to do all those things, was also the Author of the prophecy. The meaning therefore is: when God speaks through the prophet He foresaw, certainly then, but, what is more, from the farthest limit of eternity, that neither uncircumcision nor anything else would prevent Him electing the Gentiles into His family. At the same time there is an underlying general exhortation in case men may judge the works of God by the measure of their own natural ability, when the reason for them is often known only to Himself. On the contrary let them cry out with amazement that His ways are unsearchable, and His judgments too profound an abyss (Rom. 11.33).

Wherefore my judgment is, that we trouble not them which from among the Gentiles turn to God; but that we write unto them, that they abstain from the pollutions of idols, and from fornication, and from what is strangled, and from blood. For Moses from generations of old hath in every city them that preach him, being read in the synagogues every sabbath. (19-21)

19. *We must not trouble them.* He says that the Gentiles are not to be kept out of the Church by the disagreement about ceremonies, for they had been admitted by God. Yet he seems to contradict himself when he says that they must cause them no trouble, and yet lays down certain definite rules. There is an easy solution, which I shall go on to deal with rather fully. In the first place he exacts nothing from them, which they did not owe to brotherly concord. Secondly, these precepts could cause no trouble or uneasiness to their consciences, after they realized that they were free in the sight of God, and after that spurious and perverted religion, which the false prophets had

tried to bring in, had been removed. It is now asked why James enjoins only these four things on the Gentiles. Some teach that it was derived from the ancient custom of the fathers, who were not in the habit of making a covenant with any people, whom they could not compel to obey them except under this stipulation. But because no reputable author is cited for that account, I leave it in doubt and un-decided. Apart from that, a probable reason appears why they gave particular instructions about things offered to idols (idolothytis), blood and what is strangled. Certainly these things were neutral in them-selves, but they did have something special, more than the other rules of the Law. We know how strictly the Lord commands the avoidance of those things which are in conflict with the outward profession of the faith, and which contain any appearance or suspicion of idolatry. Therefore, so that no stigma of superstition might cling to the Gentiles, and so that the Jews might not see in them anything out of keeping with the pure worship of God, it is no wonder if, for the sake of guarding against a stumbling-block, they are commanded to abstain from things offered to idols (idolothytis).

The word which Luke uses, ἀλίσγημα, means any sort of profanation. Accordingly I have not changed the usual translation, which has 'filthy things' (inquinamenta). But sometimes it is taken for sacrifices, and that meaning would fit in well with James' purpose, and it will perhaps be simpler and more realistic to use that explanation in the present verse, because, when, a little later (v. 29), Luke mentions the same decree again, he puts 'things sacrificed to idols' (εἰδολόθυτα; idolothyta).

As far as blood and what is strangled are concerned, it was not only the Jews who were prohibited from eating them by the Law of Moses (Deut. 12.23), but this law had been given to the whole world imme-diately after the flood (Gen. 9.4). As a result those who were not utterly degenerate had an aversion to blood; I mean not the Jews only, but many of the Gentiles. I do acknowledge indeed that that precept was also temporary, but that it nevertheless extended far beyond one people. It is no wonder therefore if there could have arisen from it a major stumbling-block, which it seemed proper to the apostles to remedy.

But a more difficult question arises about fornication, because James seems to include it along with neutral things, which have to be avoided only from the point of view of being a stumbling-block. But there was another reason why he referred fornication to the class of those things which were not in themselves unlawful. It is well enough known that the licence to fornicate raged everywhere without re-straint. Especially was this disease far too prevalent among Orientals, as they are more prone to lust. Certainly the faithfulness and chastity of marriage were nowhere else less conscientiously respected. Moreover, to my mind, it is not a question here of any kind of fornication without distinction, such as adultery, and wandering and uncontrolled passion, by which all chastity is publicly outraged and corrupted, but I think that concubinage, as it is called, is meant, for the Gentiles had become so accustomed to it, that it was almost like a law. Therefore there is nothing absurd about James including a common corruption with things that are not bad in themselves, provided that we realize that he had no intention at all of placing in the same class things which differ widely from each other. For it is easy to refute the way that impure men snatch at this as an excuse for their filthiness. They say, 'James links the eating of blood with fornication.' But does he compare them with each other as things that are similar, or, at least, have no difference? On the contrary, he is considering only a depraved and corrupt custom of men, which had departed from the first law of nature and the order established by God. As far as the judgment of God is concerned, knowledge of that must be sought from the permanent teaching of Scripture. But there is no ambiguity about what Scripture proclaims, viz. that fornication is an accursed thing in God's sight, and that the soul of man is made filthy by it, that the body, the holy temple of God, is polluted, and that Christ is torn to pieces; that daily God inflicts punishments on fornicators, and one day will be an awful avenger. Certainly the filthiness of fornication, condemned so severely by the heavenly Judge, will be defended by no alluring words from its advocates, no matter how clever and eloquent they may be.

21. *For Moses hath.* In my opinion this verse has been badly explained, and made to yield the opposite sense. For commentators think that it was added by James because it would be superfluous to lay down anything for the Jews, to whom the teaching of the Law was familiar, and was read every sabbath. And they draw out this meaning: 'Let us be content to exact these few things from the Gentiles, who are not accustomed to bearing the yoke of the Law. As for the Jews they have Moses, from whom they may learn more.' Some even deduce from this verse that circumcision, and all that goes with it, should be observed by the Jews today as well. But they are making a silly inference, even if that explanation, which I have mentioned, were true. But in fact James had something quite different in mind. He warns that it is not possible for the ceremonies to be abolished so quickly, as if at one fell swoop, because the Jews had already been accustomed to the teaching of the Law for many generations, and Moses had his preachers; that agreement therefore must be gained for

a short time until the freedom, procured by Christ, should gradually be more clearly understood; in other words, as the common saying goes, that the ceremonies had to be buried with some decency.

Those who are experienced in translating Greek will know that the phrase, 'since he is read in the synagogues every sabbath' has been deliberately changed by me,[1] to avoid ambiguity.

Then it seemed good to the apostles and the elders, with the whole church, to choose men out of their company, and send them to Antioch with Paul and Barnabas; namely, Judas called Barsabbas, and Silas, chief men among the brethren: and they wrote thus[2] by them. The apostles and the elder brethren[3] unto the brethren which are of the Gentiles in Antioch and Syria and Cilicia, greeting: Forasmuch as we have heard that certain which went out from us have troubled you with words, subverting your souls[4]; to whom we gave no commandment; it seemed good unto us, having come to one accord, to choose out men and send them unto you with our beloved Barnabas and Paul, men that have hazarded their lives for the name of our Lord Jesus Christ. We have sent therefore Judas and Silas, who themselves also shall tell you the same things by word of mouth. For it seemed good to the Holy Ghost, and to us, to lay upon you no greater burden than these necessary things; that ye abstain from things sacrificed to idols, and from blood, and from things strangled, and from fornication; from which if ye keep yourselves, it shall be well with you. Fare ye well. (22-29)

22. *It seemed good to the apostles.* The storm was made to subside, but not without the grace of God, so that when the matter had been properly discussed, they all came down in agreement of the true teaching. And besides, one gathers from this how modest the people were, because, after entrusting the decision to the apostles and the rest of the teachers, they now also subscribe to their decree. On the other hand the apostles also gave evidence of their fairness, because they determined nothing concerning the common cause of all the godly, without consulting the people. For surely this is a tyranny born of the pride of the pastors, that things which belong to the common circumstances of the whole Church are submitted to the judgment, not to speak of the caprice, of a few, to the exclusion of the people. Indeed

---

[1] Calvin: *quum in synagogis per omne sabbatum legitur.* Vulg.: *in synagogis, ubi per omne sabbatum legitur.* Greek: ἐν ταῖς συναγωγαῖς κατὰ πᾶν σάββατον ἀναγινωσκόμενος.

[2] Calvin, with RV margin and AV reads *a letter after this manner.*

[3] Calvin, as AV, RV margin reads *and elders and brethren.*

[4] Calvin follows this Western reading, with AV, RV margin, with the addition, *saying, Ye must be circumcised amd keep the law.* Tr.

the apostles and presbyters wisely resolved to send Judas and Silas, so that the matter might be above suspicion. We know how difficult it is to check the calumnies of the ungodly, to satisfy very many who are too fastidious, to keep the unreliable and ignorant in check, to banish conceived errors, to cure grudges, to allay controversies, and to kill false rumours. The enemies of Paul and Barnabas perhaps might have said that they obtained the letter by flatteries; they might have thought up some new cavil; the ignorant and the weak might have been immediately perturbed. But when leading men appear with the letter, to speak seriously and to their face about the matter, every sinister suspicion is removed.

24. *Certain who went out from us.* We see that the holy men were no respecters of persons, an attitude that always spoils sound and proper judgments. They admit that they were worthless fellows out of their own flock; and yet they do not make allowances for them, or tend, with misguided favour, to cover their error. On the contrary, by freely condemning them they do not even spare themselves. And, first of all, they take away from them that mask which they had wrongly used to deceive. They were boasting that they knew the mind of the apostles. The apostles expose their vanity in that deceitful pretence, when they deny that they commanded anything of the sort. Secondly they accuse them, far more severely and sternly, of disturbing the Church and destroying souls. For in this way they make them odious and detestable to all the godly, because their admission can only lead to destruction. Finally, false teachers are said to destroy souls, whereas the truth of God builds them up. And so that expression contains the general doctrine that, if we do not of ourselves wish our souls to be dragged headlong, so that they are no longer the temples of the Holy Spirit, and if we do not desire their ruin, we must be very much on our guard against those who endeavour to lead us away from the pure Gospel. Although what they say about the keeping of the Law refers only to ceremonies, yet we must always remember that ceremonies were dealt with in such a way that both the righteousness and salvation of men turned on that point. For the false apostles were ordering their observance, as if the Law conferred righteousness, and salvation depended on works.

25, 26. *With our beloved Barnabas and Paul.* Those praises they set over against the calumnies, which the false apostles tried to fasten upon Paul and Barnabas. And in the first place in order to remove the impression of disagreement that had taken possession of the minds of many, they make known that they are in agreement. In the second place they commend Paul and Barnabas, because of their fervent zeal, and their extreme manliness and greatness, because they did not hesitate to endanger their lives for Christ's sake. And in a minister of the Gospel it is an excellent virtue, and a most praiseworthy one, if he has been not only diligent and indefatigable in pursuing the task of teaching, but has also been ready to undergo the danger of death for the defence of the doctrine. As the Lord proves the faithfulness and constancy of His own by instances such as these, so He makes them conspicuous, as it were, by the badges of virtue, so that they may be distinguished in His Church. Therefore Paul holds forth the marks of Christ, which he bore in his body (Gal. 6.17) like shields to drive back the worthless fellows, who were causing trouble for his teaching. But even although it does not fall to the lot of the majority of vigorous and whole-hearted teachers of the Gospel, to fight for the Gospel to the point where their lives are in danger, because their circumstances do not demand it, yet that does not prevent Christ providing power (*autoritatem*) for His witnesses, as often as He leads them forth into memorable conflicts. At the same time let those, for whom there is no need to fight, be ready to shed their blood if ever it seems good to God for them to do so.

Finally, the apostles commend the bravery of Paul and Barnabas only in a good cause, because if it were enough to undergo dangers undaunted, Christ's witnesses would be no different from trouble-makers and fanatics, no different from gladiators. Therefore Paul and Barnabas are praised, not simply because they exposed themselves to danger, but because they did not avoid death for the name of Christ. Perhaps the apostles also intended indirectly to reprove those rascals who had never suffered anything for the sake of Christ, and came out of their delightful seclusion to disturb the churches, which had meant so much to the undaunted soldiers of Christ.

28, 29. *It seemed good to the Holy Spirit and to us.* When the apostles and presbyters link themselves as associates to the Holy Spirit, they do not attribute anything to themselves independently, but this expression amounts to the same thing as their saying that the Spirit was their leader and director, and that it was by His dictation that they came to a decision about what they are writing. For this way of speaking is common enough in Scripture, that after mentioning the Name of God it also subordinates ministers to the second place. When the people are said to have believed in God and His servant Moses (Exod. 14.31), their faith is not being torn apart, as if it gave itself partly to God and partly to a mortal man. What then? Obviously when the people had God as the one and only Creator of their faith, they put their faith in His minister, who was inseparable from Him. And the truth is that they could not believe in God in any other way than by accepting the teaching given to them by Moses, just as previously they had shaken off the yoke of God by repudiating and rejecting Moses. And that also rebuts the audacity of those who impudently boast of faith, and despise the ministry of the Church with irreverence as well as pride. For just as it would be a sacrilegious separation, if faith were to rest, even in the slightest degree, on a man on his own, so those who neglect the ministers through whom God speaks, and pretend that they are taking Him as their Teacher, are openly making a laughing-stock of God. Therefore the apostles deny that the decree which they are transmitting to the Gentiles was a fabrication of their own brains, but maintain that they were merely the ministers of the Spirit, so that with the authority of God they are commanding something that originated with Him, and which they are faithfully handing on. So when Paul speaks of 'his Gospel' (Gal. 1.11), he is not introducing a new Gospel, which he himself has made up, but he is preaching what has been committed to him by Christ.

The Papists are truly absurd in wishing to prove from these words that some sort of special authority remains with the Church; yes, and what is more, they are plainly contradicting themselves. For on what pretext do they contend that the Church cannot err, except that it is governed directly by the Holy Spirit? That is why they noisily boast that the things, that we expose as their own fabrications, are oracles of the Spirit. Therefore they stupidly put too much weight on the phrase *it seemed good to us*. Because, if the apostles resolved anything independently of the Spirit, this basic principle will collapse, that nothing is determined by Councils except the things declared by the Spirit.

Than these necessary things. Using this phrase as a pretext the Papists are proud and triumphant, as if it is permissible for men to introduce laws which may bind consciences with necessity. They say that whatever the Church enjoins or commands must be observed under pain of mortal sin, because the apostles assert that what they decree must necessarily be kept. But there is an easy answer to such a worthless cavil. For there was no further point to this necessity than the danger there was of destroying unity. So, properly speaking, that necessity was accidental or extrinsic, that is to say, it did not depend on the substance, but only on avoiding a stumbling-block. And that is seen more clearly from the immediate abrogation of the decree. For laws about things necessary in themselves are bound to be permanent. But we know that, as soon as the uproar and contention had ceased, this law was abolished by Paul, when he teaches that nothing is unclean, and gives freedom and permission to eat any foods at all, even those that had been sacrificed to idols (Rom. 14.14; I Cor. 10.25). Accordingly they are snatching at an empty pretext for binding consciences out of this phrase, since the necessity, which is the question now at issue, had only to do with men's outward behaviour, so that no scandal might arise from it, but that their liberty might remain intact in the sight of God.

It is also in vain for them to try to deduce from the whole of this verse that the power has been given to the Church to decide anything that is contrary to the Word of God. The Pope has made laws just as he liked, contrary to the Word of God, with which to govern the Church, and he has produced not ten or twenty of them, but an immense pile, so that they not only oppress souls tyrannically but they are also dreadful tortures for tormenting them. In order to excuse cruelty of that sort, the Pope's hired pettifoggers object that the apostles also forbade the Gentiles what was not forbidden by the Word of God. But I deny that the apostles added anything to the Word of God; and that will be quite clear if only we are willing to pay attention to their purpose. I have just pointed out that the last thing they had in mind was to establish a permanent law with which to bind believers. What then? They are employing a remedy which was suitable for promoting brotherly peace and concord among the churches, so that in time the Gentiles may accommodate themselves to the Jews. But, if anything else, we shall certainly admit that it is in accordance with the Word of God for love (*caritas*) to bear rule among us in neutral things, that is, that the external practice of those things, which are in themselves under no restriction, be directed according to the rule of love. To sum up, if love is the bond of perfection and the end of the Law, if God's command is for the faithful to strive after mutual unity, and for each one to serve his neighbours for their edification, nobody is so ignorant as not to see that what the apostles enjoin here is contained in the Word of God; only they adapt the general rule to their own time.

Moreover let what I touched on previously be called to mind, that it was a politic law, in order to provide no snare for consciences, and introduce no fictitious worship of God; two faults in human traditions which are condemned all through Scripture. And even if we grant something that is nevertheless groundless, that what was decreed in that Council was not according to the Word of God, yet that gives no support to the Papists. It may be lawful for Councils to decree something contrary to the express Word of God, according to the revelation of the Spirit; and of course this authority will have to be given only to legitimate Councils. Therefore let them prove the piety and holiness of the Councils, to the decrees of which they wish to subject us. But I shall not pursue this aspect further now, since it was dealt with at the beginning of the chapter. Let readers grasp what suffices abundantly for the present verse, that the apostles do not go beyond the limits of the Word of God, when they propose an external law, according to the circumstances of the time, by which they may reconcile the churches with each other.

So they, when they were dismissed, came down to Antioch; and having gathered the multitude together, they delivered the epistle. And when they had read it, they rejoiced for the consolation. And Judas and Silas, being themselves also prophets, exhorted the brethren with many words, and confirmed them. And after they had spent some time there, they were dismissed in peace from the brethren unto those that had sent them forth.[1] (But it seemed good unto Silas to abide there.[2]) But Paul and Barnabas tarried in Antioch, teaching and preaching the word of the Lord, with many others also. (30-35)

30. *When the multitude was gathered.* It was the proper thing to do. to bring in the whole of the people to hear the reading of the letter, For if any controversy has arisen in the teaching of the faith, it is right that the decision be left to the learned, who are both experienced and versed in the Scripture, and, in particular, to the duly ordained pastors. However, because it is of equal concern to all to know what they ought to hold with certainty, the teachers for their part ought to share, in a brotherly manner, with the whole Church, what they have decided from the Word of God. For there is nothing less consistent with holy and Christian order than the exclusion of the body of the people from the common doctrine, as if they were a herd of pigs, as usually happens under the tyranny of the Papacy. For because the Pope and the horned bishops were not expecting the people ever to be obedient enough, until they were reduced to crass ignorance, they supposed that the best summary of the faith is by knowing nothing to depend on their opinions. On the contrary a middle position must in fact be preserved, so that governing authorities (*praefecturae*) may continue undisturbed, and, on the other hand, the people may have their liberty maintained, so that they are not oppressed like slaves.

31. *They rejoiced over the consolation.* Since the letter is so short, and contains nothing except a bare account, what sort of consolation could the faithful have derived from it? But we must note that there were great grounds for consolation in it, because, when they knew of the agreement of the apostles, not only were individuals pacified, but also they all returned to good relations from disagreement. Since a false rumour had been spread abroad that all the apostles were in opposition to Paul and Barnabas, it had disturbed some who were too credulous; many were vacillating with their minds in doubt; the ungodly took advantage of this opportunity for slander; curiosity and the love of

---

[1] Calvin reads, with RV margin, *to the apostles*. Tr.

[2] Calvin retains v. 34; omitted by RV but noted in margin. Tr.

novelty tickled others; and they were also divided from each other. Now, when they see that the judgment of the first church agrees with the teaching of Paul and Barnabas, they obtain what is most desirable for the sons of God, that, established in the right faith, and sharing unanimity, they may with quiet minds cultivate peace with one another.

32. *And Judas and Silas.* Those two brethren were sent for the specific purpose of also adding their spoken testimony to the letter. Otherwise the apostles would not have sent such a short and concise letter about a matter of such importance, and would have mentioned something about the mysteries of the faith, and would have given an exhortation at greater length for devotion to godliness. Luke then relates something else that they did, viz. that, being endowed with the gift of prophecy, they edified the Church in a general way; as if he said that not only did they faithfully carry out their duty in the immediate situation, but also by teaching and exhorting they did a useful service for the Church. But we must note that he says that they exhorted the Church because they were *prophets*, for it is not given to all to discharge such a distinguished function. Therefore care must be taken that no one rashly oversteps his limits, just as Paul teaches (I Cor. 7.20; Eph. 4.1) that individuals are to confine themselves within the measure of grace received. Accordingly it is not for nothing that Luke mentions that the task of teaching is a special one, so that nobody who wishes to come on the scene, either out of ambition unaccompanied by ability, or thoughtless zeal, or other stupid desire, may disturb the order of the Church.

They were prophets. Although the word has various meanings it is not taken in this verse for seers, to whom it was given to predict future events, because this phrase would have been inserted quite inappropriately when another situation is being dealt with. But Luke means that Judas and Silas were endowed with an exceptional understanding of the mysteries of God so that they were excellent interpreters of God; just as Paul in I Cor. 14.3, when he is dealing with prophecy, and prefers it to all other gifts, does not put prophecies or predictions in the centre, but commends it on account of this result, that it builds up the Church by teaching, exhortation and consolation. In this way Luke assigns exhortation to the prophets as if it were the principal duty of their office.

33, 34, 35. *They were dismissed in peace.* That is, when they left, the brethren, in saying good-bye to them, wished them well, as usually happens among friends. But there is synecdoche in this phrase, because only one of the two men returned to Jerusalem. And a correction is immediately added in the text, that 'it seemed good to Silas to remain there'. But when Luke connects them both together he only wishes to teach that the Church was at peace before they thought about their return.

He finally adds that as long as Paul and Barnabas were at Antioch they were intent on teaching, and were constantly engaged in this task, and yet they allowed a place for many others at the same time. From that it is apparent that they all had the same devotion, without jealousy, and that they combined their efforts in public in order to be effective. However mention seems to have been made of *many others* deliberately, so that we may not imagine that that Church was deserted after the departure of Paul and Barnabas, when it flourished with an abundance of teachers. In addition, the blessing of God soon began to flourish again, and once more to be honoured in that Church, in which Satan had recently attempted the most melancholy destruction through his men.

And after some days Paul said unto Barnabas, Let us return now and visit the brethren in every city wherein we proclaimed the word of the Lord, and see how they fare. And Barnabas was minded to take with them John also, who was called Mark. But Paul thought not good to take with them him who withdrew from them from Pamphylia, and went not with them to the work. And there arose a sharp contention, so that they parted asunder one from the other, and Barnabas took Mark with him, and sailed away unto Cyprus; but Paul chose Silas, and went forth, being commended by the brethren to the grace of the Lord. And he went through Syria and Cilicia, confirming the churches. (36-41)

36. *Let us visit our brethren.* We must first of all note in this narrative how assiduous Paul was in his solicitude for the churches which he founded. He is certainly doing useful work at Antioch; but because he remembers that God ordained him as an apostle, and not merely as the pastor of one place, he holds to the course of his calling. In the second place, just as it was not fitting for him to be tied down to one place, so he considers that he is under an obligation to all whom he begot in the Lord. Therefore he does not wish to deprive them of his services. In addition the work begun in those places could not be neglected without fading away soon afterwards. Yet it is easy to deduce that Paul stayed on in the Church at Antioch until he saw its circumstances in proper order, and concord established. For we know from experience how much influence principal churches have in preserving other, lesser ones. If any tumult arises, or if any cause of offence occurs, in an out-of-the-way district, news of it is not spread so far, and neighbours are not moved so very much. But if any place

is notable, it will never tumble without great ruin, or at least without shaking smaller buildings far and wide. Therefore in staying at Antioch for the time being Paul did have a concern for the other churches. And so in this example we should pay heed to his prudence as well as his zealousness, because the excessive fervour of pastors in fussing about, often does as much harm as their doing nothing.

How they fare. Paul knew that if anything has been properly established among men, it rarely remains stable and enduring, when the fickleness of men is so great, and considering the proneness of their nature to faults, and indeed he was especially aware that churches easily collapse and degenerate if they are not constantly looked after. Indeed nothing under heaven ought to have been as firm as the spiritual building of faith, seeing that its stability is founded in heaven itself, but there are few in whose souls the word of the Lord strikes deep and living roots; therefore stability in men is a rare thing. Secondly, even those who have their anchor grounded in the truth of God, do not however cease to be liable to be tossed about in different ways, and even if their faith is not overthrown yet it needs confirming to strengthen it. In addition, we see the engines with which Satan makes his attacks, and the artifices with which he secretly tries to destroy now whole churches, now every single one of the faithful. Paul has therefore good reason for being anxious and apprehensive about his disciples, lest they may behave differently than is to be desired, and therefore if anything troublesome has arisen, he desires to counteract it promptly; and that cannot be done without investigation.

37. *But Barnabas made up his mind.* Luke gives an account of this melancholy disagreement, and it is one that ought justifiably to strike terror in all the godly. The partnership of Paul and Barnabas had been consecrated by a heavenly oracle. They had laboured for a long time in harmony under this yoke to which the Lord had bound them; they had experienced many instances of the remarkable favour of God. Furthermore that wonderful success, which Luke mentioned previously, was clearly a blessing of God. Although they had so often been nearly overwhelmed by so many stormy persecutions, and innumerable enemies had repeatedly pressed on them so sharply, although even local insurrection was inflamed against them everywhere, far from being estranged, their unanimity had then been demonstrated in the highest degree. Now, over a trivial matter, and one that could have been disposed of with no difficulty, they burst that sacred bond of the divine calling. This certainly could not have taken place without disturbing all the godly very greatly. When the dispute was so passionate and violent between these two holy men, who for many years had accustomed themselves to putting up with all circumstances, what will

happen to us whose desires have not been brought into obedience to God in that way, and repeatedly run wanton without control? When a trivial occasion tore apart men who had conscientiously cultivated unity in the midst of so many hostile attacks, how easily Satan will have access to separate those whose desire to foster peace is either non-existent or cold? Considering that there was no greater honour for Barnabas than to be the companion of Paul, so as to conduct himself like a son toward a father, what great pride caused him to reject his plan so firmly? On the other hand some might perhaps find Paul lacking in kindliness because he did not pardon a faithful assistant this mistake. We are therefore warned by this example that, unless the servants of Christ are intent on keeping a sharp look-out, many chinks are open to Satan, by which he may steal in to disturb the harmony among them.

But now we must discuss the cause itself. For there are those who lay the blame for the dispute on Paul's excessive rigidity; and, at a first hearing, the reasons which they bring forward are probable. John Mark is rejected because he had withdrawn himself from the company of Paul; but he had not severed himself from Christ. Being young, and not yet accustomed to bearing the cross, he had returned home from the journey. Some allowance had to be made for his age. As a recruit he had given in to troubles at the beginning; but that did not mean that he was going to be a cowardly soldier all his life. Now when his return to Paul is clear evidence of his penitence, it seems in-human to reject him. For those who voluntarily accept the punish-ment for their own wrongs must be dealt with more leniently. There were also other reasons which ought to have moved Paul to clemency. The home of John Mark was a renowned place of hospitality for the Church. In the severest persecution his mother had taken in the faith-ful; when Herod was raging, and all the people were in a fury, they were in the habit of holding their sacred meetings there, as Luke has already reported (Acts 12.12). Surely such a holy and good-hearted woman ought to have been spared, so that excessive rigour might not alienate her. She wished her son to be devoted to preaching the Gospel; how very bitter a thing could it have been to her that his services are now rejected on account of one trivial mistake? Now when John Mark not only deprecates his fault, but actually makes amends, Barnabas has a plausible excuse for forgiving him.

However one may gather from the context that Paul's decision was pleasing to the Church. For Barnabas hurries off and sails with his companion for Cyprus. No mention is made of the brethren, as if he had gone away in secret, without greeting them. But the brethren commend Paul to the grace of God by their prayers; which makes it evident that the Church stood by his side. In the second place, because God puts forth the power of His Spirit in blessing Paul, and pursues his labours with the favourable success of His grace, and in fact leaves Barnabas as if he were buried, one can draw the probable conclusion from that that God intended such an example of severity to be made. And the sin of John Mark was certainly far more serious than is commonly supposed. Indeed he had not defected from the faith of Christ; yet he was a deserter and apostate from his calling. Therefore, if, having withdrawn from the calling, he had been taken back again into it soon afterwards, it would have provided a very bad example. He had devoted his services to Christ on this condition, that no longer would he be free or his own master. It was no more permissible for him to break the promise given in this connexion, than it is lawful for a wife to leave her husband or a son his father. And weakness certainly does not excuse the perfidy by which the sanctity of the call had been violated. And we must note that he was not absolutely rejected by Paul. He was regarding him as a brother, provided that he would be content with the ordinary standing (*plebeio ordine*). He was refusing to admit him to the public office of teaching, of which he had been shamefully deprived by his own fault. But it makes a great deal of difference whether a man, who has sinned, is absolutely debarred from pardon, or is merely denied public office. However it is possible that both men went beyond the score, as things that are non-essential may often spoil an otherwise good situation. Paul was correct and duly acting in accordance with disciplinary authority in being unwilling to accept the companion, whose unreliability he had once experienced; but when he saw Barnabas insisting more stubbornly he could have given into his request. The truth certainly ought to mean more to us than the favour of the whole world, but it is proper to give wise consideration to how important is the matter, which is under discussion. For if, in a matter of no importance, or one that has nothing edifying about it, a man boasts of his constancy, stirs himself up for a fight, and, once he has come to a decision does not cease to defend it to the end, this will be foolish and perverse obstinacy. There was also another middle course by which Paul might have yielded to some extent to the importunities of his colleague, and yet not turn aside from the truth. He was not bound to flatter Mark, or make excuses for his sin, but, after freely expressing his own point of view, no religious scruple prevented him from nevertheless allowing himself to be the loser in that matter, which was not carrying with itself the loss of either sound doctrine or the salvation of men. And I make that suggestion for this reason, that we may learn to temper our zeal even in the best of causes, so that it may not boil over uncontrolled.

CHAPTER SIXTEEN

And he came also to Derbe and to Lystra: and behold, a certain disciple was there, named Timothy, the son of a Jewess which believed; but his father was a Greek. The same was well reported of by the brethren that were at Lystra and Iconium. Him would Paul have to go forth with him; and he took and circumcised him because of the Jews that were in those parts: for they all knew that his father was a Greek. And as they went on their way through the cities, they delivered them the decrees for to keep, which had been ordained of the apostles and elders that were at Jerusalem. So the churches were strengthened in the faith, and increased in number daily. (1-5)

1. Luke now begins to narrate the sort of progress made by Paul after his separation from Barnabas. And in the very first place he reports that at Lystra he adopted Timothy as his companion. But so that we may know that Paul did nothing rashly, or without consideration, Luke clearly states that Timothy was approved of by the brethren, and his godliness was borne witness to by them, for that is exactly how he expresses it. And so Paul himself is now observing the selectiveness which elsewhere he orders to be kept in the election of ministers (cf. I Tim. 3). For although Paul says elsewhere (I Tim. 1.18) that the Spirit marked out Timothy by prophecies, it is not likely that they had already been uttered at that time. But there seems to be some difference in the fact that Luke says that Timothy had a good reputation among the *brethren*, whereas Paul wishes a man, who is chosen to be a bishop, to be well thought of by outsiders (I Tim. 3.7). I reply that the judgment of the godly must be especially respected, as they alone are suitable witnesses, and they alone distinguish correctly and wisely by the Holy Spirit; but no more deference must be paid to the ungodly than to the blind. It is therefore evident that the estimation of godliness and a holy life ought to be made according to the judgment and approbation of the saints, so that the man, whom they commend with their reports may be regarded as fit to be a bishop. However I admit that it is also required in the second place that unbelievers be forced to praise him also, so that the Church of God may not be exposed to their reproaches and slander, if it allows itself to be ruled by men of scandalous reputation.

3. *He circumcised him because of the Jews.* Luke makes it quite clear that Timothy was not circumcised because it was necessary, or because

the religion of that sign still continued in existence, but so that Paul might avoid a scandal. Therefore regard was paid to men, although there was freedom in the matter in the sight of God. Accordingly the circumcision of Timothy was not a sacrament, such as had been given to Abraham and his descendants, but a neutral and indifferent ceremony, which was of use only for the fostering of love, and not for the exercise of godliness. It is now asked whether Paul had the right to usurp the use of an empty sign, the meaning and force of which had been abolished. For it seems to be an ineffective thing when it is separated from the institution of God. But at any rate circumcision had been commanded by God only until the coming of Christ. To this question I reply that circumcision ceased at the coming of Christ in the sense that its use was not completely abolished all at once; but it remained free until, with the light of the Gospel being seen more clearly, all might know that Christ is the end of the Law.

And at this point we must notice three stages. The first is that the ceremonies of the Law were so abrogated by the revelation of Christ that they pertained to the worship of God no longer, they were not figures of spiritual realities, and there was no necessity to make use of any one of them. The second is surely that their use was free until the truth of the Gospel would become more clearly known. The third is that the faithful were not permitted to retain them, except in so far as their use would make for edification, and no superstition would be encouraged by them. However there was an exception to that power to use them freely, of which I have spoken. For circumcision was not in the same position as the sacrifices which had been ordained for the expiation of sins. Accordingly it was legitimate for Paul to circumcise Timothy; but it would not have been lawful to offer a sacrifice for sin. This is indeed a general principle, that the whole of the worship of the Law, because it was a temporary thing, came to an end at the advent of Christ, as far as faith and conscience were concerned. But as to use, we must hold this view, that[1] it was left neutral and in the freedom of the godly,[2] in so far as it was not contrary to the confession of the faith. We must pay attention to the short period of time of which I speak, viz. until the clear manifestation of the Gospel, because certain learned men are confused and wandering in this respect, for to them circumcision seems still to have a place among the Jews, whereas Paul teaches that it is superfluous when we are buried with Christ through baptism (Col. 2.11, 12; Gal. 2.3). It has been expressed more correctly in the old proverb, that the synagogue is to be buried with honour.

[1] French adds, 'for a very short time'. Tr.
[2] Reading *in piorum libertate* with C.R. for Tholuck's *impiorum libertati*. Tr.

Now it remains to say to what extent the use of circumcision was indifferent. That will easily appear from the principle (*ratione*) of liberty. Because the call of the Gentiles had not yet become known everywhere, some prerogative had to be granted to the Jews. Therefore until it would be better known that adoption has been transferred from the descendants of Abraham to all nations, it was permissible, as edification required, to retain the differentiating sign. For since Paul did not wish to circumcise Titus and states that that course of action was correct (Gal. 2.3), it follows that this ceremony was free, but not without discrimination or selectiveness. Therefore attention had to be paid to edification and the common well-being of the Church. Because he was not able to circumcise Titus without abandoning the pure teaching of the Gospel, and exposing himself to the calumnies of enemies, he abstained from the free use of the ceremony, which he allowed himself in the case of Timothy, when he saw that it was beneficial to the Church. It is easily seen from this how horrible confusion rages in the Papacy. An immense heap of ceremonies exists there. Why is that, except that instead of the one veil of the old temple, they may obtain a hundred? God has abrogated the ceremonies which He had enjoined so that the truth of the Gospel might shine more brightly. Men have dared to introduce new ones, and indeed without keeping to any limit. Then the perverse fiction was added that they are all of value for the worship of God. Finally the diabolical assurance of merit followed. Now, since it is plain enough that such ceremonies are neither veils nor sepulchres by which Christ is hidden, but rather stinking dunghills, by which sincere faith and religion are buried, those, who make free and indiscriminate use of them, arrogate far more to the Pope than God grants to His Law. There is no point in speaking about the Mass and similar filthy things, which manifestly contain idolatry in themselves.

For they all knew. Luke advises us that it was Paul's intention to give Timothy a way of making an approach to the Jews, so that they would not shrink from him as from a profane man. He says, 'They all knew that his father was a Greek'. Therefore because mothers had no power over children, they had been quite convinced that he was not circumcised. In passing let readers observe how wretched was the servitude of the people of God at that time. Eunice, the mother of Timothy, belonged to the tiny remnant, which even the Jews themselves regarded as a monstrosity, and yet, being married to an unbeliever she did not dare to dedicate her children to God, at any rate to give them the external mark of grace. And yet she did not cease on that account to be conscientious in bringing up her son from boyhood in the fear of God and in the true worship; an example that

surely ought to be imitated by women who are prevented by the
tyrannous authority of their husbands from keeping the children and
family purely in true godliness. Here, *Greek* is used for 'Gentile'
according to the common custom of Scripture.

4. *They delivered the decrees to be kept.* Luke is pointing out with
these words how eager Paul was for peace. At that time the best bond
for fostering concord among the churches was to observe what had
been settled by the apostles. While Paul is diligent in that, he is
conscientiously on his guard lest any disturbances arise through his
fault. But let us remember that that was temporary, because when he
sees the danger of a stumbling-block coming to an end, he relieves
the churches completely, and, setting the decree aside, he makes free
what the apostles had forbidden in it. Yet, by that abrogation, he
does not rescind and violate what the apostles had resolved, or condemn the authors themselves; because they had had no intention of
establishing a permanent law, but only of mitigating for a short time
what could have wounded weak consciences, as I have dealt with
more fully in the previous chapter.

But that makes the foolishness of the Papists quite clear, when they
seriously accuse us of being greatly different from Paul, because
despising the decrees of the Church, as they talk of, we wish the
consciences of the godly to be ruled by the Word of God alone, but
not to be subjected to the opinion of men. But as I have already said,
the last thing that Paul had in mind was to put the snare of necessity
on consciences. For he is not inconsistent with himself, since he declares elsewhere, 'To the pure all things are pure' (Titus 1.15); again,
'He who is strong eats whatever things he likes' (Rom. 14.2); again,
'The Kingdom of God is not food and drink' (ib. v. 17); again, 'Food
does not commend us to God' (I Cor. 8.8); again, 'Eat all that is sold
in the meat-market, asking no question on account of conscience'
(I Cor 10.25). But with one word he reconciles things which could
otherwise appear to agree very little, when he directs them to abstain
from meats sacrificed to idols for the sake of another man's conscience.
At the same time he takes very good care not to bind pious souls
with the laws of men. Therefore we today are attempting nothing
different from Paul.

But the Papists are making too gross a violation when they compare
their laws with the decrees of the apostles. The apostles had invented
no new worship of God, they had set up no new spiritual regime, but
because of their eagerness for peace, they had strongly urged the
Gentiles to concede something to the Jews. For the Pope to excuse
his laws on that pretext, it will be necessary for the whole of them to
be changed first. But since the Papists base their spiritual worship of

God on the inventions of men, and they transfer to men the authority
(*ius*) that is God's alone, so that they may domineer over souls, we, for
our part, are forced to resist them courageously, if we do not wish,
by the silence of treachery, to surrender the grace procured by the
blood of Christ. Now, what similarity is there between three decrees
made to sustain the weak, and an immense pile of laws, which not only
crushes wretched souls by its weight, but devours faith? The complaint
of Augustine to Januarius is well known, that already at that time the
Church was wrongly burdened with too great a load of traditions.
Would he put up, I ask you, with the servitude of the present day,
which is almost a hundred times harder?

5. *The churches were confirmed.* We gather from this that what
Luke mentions about the apostles' decrees was like a so-called added
ornament and accessory. For he commends quite a different effect and
result of Paul's teaching, when he says that *the churches were strengthened
in the faith.* Therefore Paul ordered external things in such a way that
he was giving his main attention to the Kingdom of God, which rests
upon the teaching of the Gospel, and is higher and greater than external
order. Therefore mention was made of those decrees inasmuch as
they were of importance for agreement, so that we might know that
it mattered to the holy man. But religion and godliness are put on a
higher level, and faith is the one and only foundation of these. In its
turn faith itself rests on the pure Word of God, and does not depend
on the laws of men. Now by this example Luke urges us on to continuous advances in faith, so that at the beginning laziness or neglect
to derive advantage, may not steal upon us. The method of increasing
faith is also described, viz. when the Lord rouses us by the work of
His servants, as at that time He made use of the labour of Paul and his
companions.

When he goes on at once to say that they were also *increased in
number,* he is certainly commending another of the results of preaching;
however at the same time he makes the suggestion that in so far as
those who have been called to Christ first make progress in the faith,
they lead more men to Christ, as if faith spread wider to others by
propagation.

*And they went through the region of Phrygia and Galatia, having been
forbidden of the Holy Ghost to speak the word in Asia; and when they
were come over against Mysia, they assayed to go into Bithynia; and
the Spirit of Jesus[1] suffered them not; and passing by Mysia, they came
down to Troas. And a vision appeared to Paul in the night; There
was a man of Macedonia standing, beseeching him, and saying, Come*

[1] Calvin omits *of Jesus,* a reading of later MSS also followed by AV. Tr.

over into Macedonia, and help us. And when he had seen the vision,
straightway we sought to go forth into Macedonia, concluding that God
had called us for to preach the gospel unto them. (6-10)

6. *When they had gone through Pamphylia.* Here Luke recounts how
diligently and actively Paul and his companions devoted themselves
to the office of teaching. For he says that they journeyed through
various regions of Asia Minor for the sake of spreading the Gospel.
But he records one thing deserving particular mention, that they were
forbidden by the Spirit of God to speak about Christ in certain places.
That is most valuable for commending the apostleship of Paul; just
as there is no doubt that he himself was encouraged in no ordinary
way to carry on when he knew that he had the Spirit of God as the
guide of his life and actions. But in preparing themselves to teach
wherever they came to, without any distinction, they were doing that
by virtue of their calling, and in accordance with the commandment
of God. For they had been sent to publish the Gospel among the
nations without any exception. But the Lord disclosed His intention,
which had previously been hidden, in directing their journey at
appropriate moments (*in ipsis temporum articuis*).

However the question is asked, 'If Paul did not teach anywhere
except by the guidance of the Spirit, what sort of certainty of their
calling will the ministers of the Church have today, who have no
oracles to make them more certain as to when they are to speak or keep
quiet?' I reply that since Paul's province was so wide and extensive,
he needed the extraordinary direction of the Spirit. He had not been
appointed the apostle of one place or of a few cities. But he had
received a mandate to publish the Gospel through Asia and Europe,
and that meant sailing in a very vast sea. Accordingly there is no
reason for us to wonder that, in the confusion of that wide area, God
gave him a sign, as if with outstretched hand, as to what place He
wished him to make for, and how far to proceed.

But here another and more difficult question is raised, 'Why did
the Lord forbid Paul to speak in Asia, and did not allow him to come
into Bithynia?' For if the answer has been given that those Gentiles
there were not worthy of the teaching of salvation, on the other hand
it will be in order to object, 'Why was Macedonia more worthy?'
Those who strive to be exceedingly wise attribute the causes of this
discrimination among men to the fact that the Lord considers worthy
of His Gospel such (*quosque*) as He sees disposed to the obedience of
faith. But He Himself reveals something far different, viz. that He
has appeared openly to those by whom He was not sought, and that
He has spoken to those who were not asking questions about Him.

For where do docility and a submissive mind come from except from His Spirit? Therefore it is certain that some are not preferred to others by their own merit, since all are quite equally hostile to faith by nature. Therefore there is nothing better than to leave God the freedom and power to deem those, whom He pleases, worthy of His grace, or deprive them of it. And certainly since His eternal election is of grace, so must the calling, which flows from it, be considered of grace, and it is not founded on men, since it owes nothing to anyone. Accordingly let us realize that the Gospel comes forth to us from the one fountain of pure grace. However God does not lack a legitimate reason why He offers His Gospel to certain ones, but passes others by; but I maintain that that reason is hidden in His secret purpose. In the meantime let believers know that they have been called gratuitously when others have been neglected, so that they may not ascribe to themselves what belongs to the mercy of God alone. On the other hand as for the rest whom God rejects for no apparent reason, let them learn to wonder at the profound abyss of His judgment, into which it is not permitted to pry.

Finally, the name *Asia* is taken here for that part, which is properly so called. When Luke says that Paul and his companions tried to go *into Bithynia*, until they were prevented by the Spirit, he is showing that they were directed by oracles only when it was necessary, as the Lord is usually near His own in situations of doubt and confusion.

9. *A vision in the night.* The Lord did not wish Paul to put off any more time in Asia, because His purpose was to bring him to Macedonia. But Luke describes the way he was led there, that *a man of Macedonia* appeared to him by night. We must observe from that, that the Lord does not always keep to the same method of revelation, because differet kinds are better suited for confirmation. But this vision is not said to have been presented by a dream, but only, at night; for there are certain night visions which appear to men when they are awake.

Help us. This expression gives commendation to the ministry which had been imposed upon Paul. For since the Gospel is the power of God unto salvation, his ministers are said to bring help to those who are perishing, so that they may snatch them away from death, and bring them into the inheritance of eternal life (Rom. 1.16). And it ought to be a considerable incentive for stimulating the zeal and eagerness of godly teachers, when they hear that they are recalling miserable souls from destruction, and are helping those who otherwise are lost, so that they may be saved. Again, all the people to whom the Gospel is brought are taught to love and reverence its ministers as if they were liberators, if they do not wish to reject the grace of God by their own bad grace (*maligne*). Nevertheless this description is not transferred to men so that God is deprived of even the smallest part of His glory, because even if He does confer salvation by means of ministers, yet He alone is responsible for it, as if He were stretching out His hands to bring help.

10. *Being fully convinced.* We gather from this that it was not a bare vision, but one backed up by the testimony of the Spirit. For Satan also often makes use of apparitions and appearances for his own deceptive tricks, to make fools of those who do not believe. The result is that the bare vision leaves a man's mind in a state of suspense. But the Spirit seals those which truly come from God with a sure mark, so that those whom God wishes to have truly devoted to Himself may not waver or hesitate. An evil spirit appeared to Brutus, luring him to that calamitous battle which brought about his death at Philippi, the very place, of course, to which Paul was later called. But as there was a great difference in the causes, so the Lord dealt quite differently with His servant, so that he freed him of all anxiety, but did not leave him struck dumb with fear. Now in the case of Paul and his companions certainty was quickly followed by eagerness to obey. For as soon as they grasp that they are summoned by the Lord, they get ready to set out.

The participle used here has an active ending ($\sigma \upsilon \mu \beta \iota \beta \acute{\alpha} \zeta o \nu \tau \epsilon \varsigma$). But although it has many meanings, I have no doubt that in this verse Luke means that, when Paul and the others connected this vision to previous oracles, they were convinced, without the shadow of a doubt, that they were being called into Macedonia by God.

Setting sail therefore from Troas, we made a straight course to Samothrace, and the day following to Neapolis; and from thence to Philippi, which is a city of Macedonia, the first of the district, a Roman colony: and we were in this city tarrying certain days. And on the sabbath day we went forth without the gate[1] by a river side, where we supposed there was a place of prayer[2]; and we sat down, and spake unto the women which were come together. And a certain woman named Lydia, a seller of purple, of the city of Thyatira, one that worshipped God, heard us: whose heart the Lord opened, to give heed unto the things which were spoken by Paul. And when she was baptized, and her household, she besought us, saying, If ye have judged me to be faithful to the Lord, come into my house, and abide there. And she constrained us. (11-15)

11, 12. This story shows, as if in a mirror, how sharply the Lord exercised the faith and patience of His men, presenting arduous difficulties, which only extraordinary steadfastness could be a match to

---

[1] Calvin, as AV, reads *the city*. Tr.
[2] Calvin, as AV and later MSS, reads *where prayer was wont to be made*. Tr.

overcoming. For Paul's introduction to Macedonia is described as such as could have taken away confidence in the vision. Abandoning the work that they had in hand, the holy men quickly cross the sea, as if the whole Macedonian nation was going to come and meet them, eager to ask for help. Now the outcome corresponds to their expectation so little that nearly all doors are closed for them to speak. Having entered the principal city they find nobody there to whom to give their services. Therefore they are forced to go out into the open country, to speak in an unfrequented and out-of-the-way spot. There they cannot meet with even a single man, to listen to their teaching. They only obtain one woman as a disciple for Christ, and a foreigner at that. Who would not have said that this journey had been undertaken foolishly, and most inauspiciously, when it was turning out to be so unfruitful? But the Lord carries through His works under a humble and weak appearance like that, so that His power may in the end shine out more clearly. In particular it was necessary for the beginnings of the Kingdom of Christ to be ordered in this way, so that they might taste the humility of the cross. But we must observe the perseverance of Paul and his companions, who are not discouraged by such unfavourable beginnings, but nevertheless try if any, even the slightest, opportunity may present itself beyond their expectation. And the servants of Christ must certainly struggle against all sorts of obstacles, and not give way to difficulties, but continue tomorrow, if no result appears from their labour today. For there is no reason for them to ask to be more successful than Paul.

When Luke says that *they were tarrying in that city* (διατρίβοντες) some prefer 'they conferred' or 'disputed'. But the other translation is simpler, and the context draws us to it, because a little later Luke will show that Lydia was the firstfruits of the Church. And it is easy to conclude that the apostles went outside, because no door in the city had been opened to them.

13. *On the sabbath day.* There is no doubt that the Jews sought a solitary place, when they wished to pray, because everywhere at that time their religion was regarded with the greatest odium. But God wished to teach us by their example how highly we ought to prize the profession of faith, certainly that we are not to abandon it from fear of unpopularity or danger. Of course they used to have synagogues in many places, but at Philippi, which was a Roman colony, it was illegal to hold public meetings. Therefore they have recourse to a remote corner, so that they might pray to God well away from onlookers. Yet even this was not free from the ill-will which could create trouble and danger for them; but they prefer the worship of God to their own comfort and convenience. Moreover one gathers

from the word 'Sabbath' that Luke is speaking about Jews. In the second place since he commends the piety of Lydia, she must have been a Jewess. And in fact there is no need of a long argument, since we know that it was a capital offence for Greeks and Romans to celebrate the Sabbath, or practise Jewish rites. Now we understand that it was not on account of superstition that the Jews chose the river-bank as a place of prayer, but that they avoided crowds of gazing people. If anyone makes the objection, 'Why did each man not pray privately at home?' there is an easy reply, that this rite of praying was customary for demonstrating piety, and so that, clear of the superstitions of the Gentiles, they might encourage each other in the worship of the one God, and foster among themselves the religion received from the fathers. As for Paul and his companions, who were unaccustomed visitors, one may well believe that they came there, not so much for the sake of praying, as that they were looking for some success. For it was a suitable place for teaching, being far away from noise, and it was proper for those who had gathered there for prayer to be more attentive to the Word of God.

Luke has put 'the day of the Sabbaths' for 'the Sabbath'. Where, following Erasmus, I have translated 'prayer was accustomed', the Vulgate has 'seemed'.[1] And the verb νομίζεσθαι means both in Greek. However the meaning, 'prayer was held there according to custom' suits the present verse better.

We spoke to the women. Either that place was intended for the meeting of women only, or religion was coldly received among the men, as they were slower to appear at any rate. Be that as it may, we do see that the holy men neglect no opportunity, because they have no reluctance about presenting the Gospel to women alone. Moreover since it is likely to me that prayer was shared by men and women in that place, I think that Luke made no mention of men, because either they were unwilling to listen, or they got no benefit out of what they heard.

14. *A woman named Lydia.* If they had been heard by a few women, it was still like penetrating through a narrow crack. Now when in fact only one hears attentively and effectively, could it not have appeared that the way was blocked for Christ to make an entry? But afterwards from that frail shoot a famous church sprang up, whose praises Paul sings in splendid terms. Yet it is possible that Lydia had some companions, of whom no mention is made, because she herself far surpassed them. Yet Luke does not attribute the cause for this one woman having shown herself docile, to the fact that she was sharper-

[1] Calvin: *ubi solebat esse precatio.* Vulg.: *ubi videbatur oratio esse.* Greek: οὗ ἐνομίζομεν προσευχὴν εἶναι. Tr.

witted than the others, or that she had some preparation by herself, but says that the Lord opened her heart, so that she gave heed to Paul's words. He had just praised her piety; and yet he shows that she could not understand the teaching of the Gospel without the illumination of the Spirit. Accordingly we see that not only faith, but also all understanding of spiritual things, is a special gift of God, and that ministers do not accomplish anything by speaking, unless the inward calling of God is added at the same time.

By the word *heart* Scripture sometimes means the mind, as when Moses says (Deut. 29.4), 'until now the Lord has not given you a heart to understand'. So also in this verse Luke means not only that Lydia was moved by the inspiration of the Holy Spirit to embrace the Gospel with a feeling of the heart, but that her mind was illuminated to understand. We may learn from this that such is the dullness, such the blindness of men, that in hearing they do not hear, or seeing they do not see, until God forms new ears and new eyes for them. But we must note the expression that *the heart of Lydia was opened* so that she paid attention to the external voice of a teacher. For as preaching on its own is nothing else but a dead letter, so, on the other hand, we must beware lest a false imagination, or the semblance of secret illumination, leads us away from the Word upon which faith depends, and on which it rests. For in order to increase the grace of the Spirit, many invent for themselves vague inspirations (ἐνθουσιασμοὺς) so that no use is left for the external Word. But the Scripture does not allow such a separation to be made, for it unites the ministry of men with the secret inspiration of the Spirit. If the mind of Lydia had not been opened, the preaching of Paul would have been mere words (*literalis*); yet God inspires her not only with mere revelations but with reverence for His Word, so that the voice of a man, which otherwise would have vanished into thin air, penetrates a mind that has received the gift of heavenly light. Therefore let us hear no more of the fanatics who make the excuse of the Spirit to reject external teaching. For we must preserve the balance which Luke establishes here, that we obtain nothing from the hearing of the Word alone, without the grace of the Spirit, and that the Spirit is conferred on us not that He may produce contempt of the Word, but rather to instil confidence in it in our minds and write it on our hearts. Now if someone asks the reason why God opened the heart of only one woman it is necessary to revert to that principle that as many as are preordained to life believe. For the fear of God, which in Lydia had preceded the plain and explicit knowledge of Christ, was itself the product of gracious election.

Geographers teach that *Thyatira* is a city of Lydia, situated on the bank of the river Hermus, and was at one time called Pelopia. However, some assign it to Phrygia, others to Mysia.

15. *When she was baptized.* It is clear from this how in a short space of time God had been effectively at work in Lydia. For there is no doubt that she genuinely embraced the faith of Christ, and gave her allegiance to Him, before Paul admitted her to baptism. This was an example of real promptitude; also, her holy zeal and piety reveal themselves in the fact that she dedicates her household to God at the same time. And it certainly ought to be the common desire of all the godly to have their relations, who are under their charge, of the same faith. For any man who wishes to rule over wife, children, and men and women servants in his home, and will not trouble himself about giving any place to Christ, does not deserve to be counted among the sons of God, and to be set over others with authority. Therefore let every one of the faithful take pains to organize his home so that it is an image of the Church. I admit that Lydia did not have the hearts of all her people in her power, to turn whomever she liked to Christ at her own bidding, but the Lord blessed her godly devotion, so that she had the members of her household obedient. As I have already said all the godly ought to be exerting themselves to keep superstitions of every kind away from their homes; and secondly not to have families that are profane, but to keep them under the fear of the Lord. Thus Abraham, the father of the faithful, was commanded to circumcise all his servants along with himself, and he is commended for the care with which he organized his house. Moreover if this duty is demanded of the head of a household, it is required much more of a prince, not to allow, as far as he can help it, the name of God to be profaned in his domain.

She besought, saying. Her words, *If you have judged me faithful*, have the force of an oath. It is as if she said, 'I implore you by the faith, which you have confirmed by the sign of baptism, not to refuse my hospitality.' Apart from that, Lydia certainly testified by such an ardent wish how passionate and serious she was in her love for the Gospel. At the same time there is no doubt that the Lord granted her such an attitude of mind that Paul might be all the more encouraged to carry on, not so much because he saw himself being generously and kindly received, as because he could form an opinion from that about the success of his teaching. Therefore that invitation to detain Paul and his companions was not only the woman's but also God's. And the same thing also applies to what follows, that Lydia *constrained* them; it is as if God laid His hand on them by the agency of the woman.

And it came to pass, as we were going to the place of prayer, that a

*certain maid having a spirit of divination met us, which brought her
masters much gain by soothsaying. The same following after Paul and
us cried out, saying, These men are servants of the Most High God,
which proclaim unto you the way of salvation. And this she did for
many days. But Paul, being sore troubled, turned and said to the spirit,
I charge thee in the name of Jesus Christ to come out of her. And it
came out that very hour. But when her masters saw that the hope of their
gain was gone, they laid hold on Paul and Silas, and dragged them into
the market place before the rulers, and when they had brought them unto
the magistrates, they said, These men being Jews, do exceedingly
trouble our city, and set forth customs which it is not lawful for us to
receive, or to observe, being Romans. And the multitude rose up together against them: and the magistrates rent their garments off them,
and commanded to beat them with rods.* (16-22)

16. Luke carries on with the increases of the Church. For even if
he does not expressly mention it, yet it is easily gathered from the
context that a great many were led to the faith, or at least that the
Church was increased by a considerable number; and Paul's frequent-
ing of the assemblies at the hour of prayer was certainly not in vain.
Yet at the same time Luke reports that this course was broken by
Satan; namely, that after the apostles had been beaten with rods, and
cast into prison, they were finally forced to depart from the city. Yet
whatever Satan contrived, we shall see at the end of the chapter that,
before they left, a considerable body of the Church was gathered
together.

Having a spirit of divination (pythonis). The poets have told the fable
that the serpent, Python by name, was killed by the arrows of Apollo
(*Phoebi*). From this fiction there arose another, that they said that those
possessed were filled by the spirit of Python; also inspired women
(*Phoebades*) were perhaps so called in honour of Apollo. And Luke
follows the accepted way of speaking, because he records the error of
the common people, but not what inspired the girl to prophesy. For
it is certain that the devil masqueraded as Apollo to deceive, as all
idolatries and artifices are forged in his workshop. But someone
might be wondering that the devil, at whose instigation the girl was
shouting out, was the author of such an honourable commendation,
as the one by which she was extolling Paul and Silas and the others.
For since he is the 'father of lies' how could the truth come forth from
him? Secondly, how did it come about that of his own accord he
gave place to the servants of Christ, by whom his kingdom was being
destroyed? How consistent is it of him to prepare the minds of the
people to hear the Gospel of which he is such a deadly enemy? There

is certainly nothing more appropriate for him than to turn the world away from the Word of God, for which he is now procuring a hearing. What brings about such a sudden change and unaccustomed development? But the devil is in fact the 'father of lies' in this way, that he conceals himself with a deceitful display of the truth. Therefore with craft and cunning he played a different part than the one that naturally belonged to him, so that by penetrating in secret he might do more harm. And therefore, it is not right to interpret his description as the 'father of lies' as if he always lies openly and without deceiving. On the contrary we must be on our guard against his indirect and crafty devices, so that by pleading the excuse of the truth, he may not deceive us with an empty show. We also see that he uses similar cunning every day. For what is more plausible than the titles of the Pope, by which he boasts that he is not the adversary but the vicar of Christ? What is more plausible than that solemn preface, 'In the name of the Lord, Amen'? Yet when the truth is alleged by the counterfeit ministers of Satan like that, we know that it is corrupted and infected by a deadly plague. While Satan has a twofold method of opposing the Gospel, viz. that sometimes he attacks in an open way, sometimes he in fact worms his way in with lies, he also has two kinds of lying, either when he overthrows the Word of God with false doctrines and gross superstitions, or when he astutely pretends that he is a friend of the Word, as if he creeps in by underground passages; yes, and what is more, he is never a more harmful enemy than when he transforms himself into an angel of light. Now we understand what was the object of such a splendid description, by which he exalted Paul and his companions, viz. because it was not so advantageous for him to wage open war on the Gospel, he tried to destroy confidence in it by secret stratagems. For if Paul had acceded to that testimony, there would have been no longer any difference between the saving doctrine of Christ and the mockeries of Satan. The splendour of the Gospel would have been enveloped in the darkness of falsehood, and so would have been extinguished.

But it is asked why God gives so much licence to Satan that he also deceives and bewitches miserable men with true predictions. For setting aside the penetrating arguments, which several raise about his perspicacity, I take it for granted that it is only by the permission of God that he produces prophecies about secret or future things. But in this way God seems to be exposing improvident men to his deceptions, so that they cannot be on their guard. For since prophecies manifest the power of God, as often as they appear among men their minds must of necessity be moved with reverence, if they do not hold God in contempt. I reply, that God never permits so much to Satan, except in order that punishment may be inflicted on an ungrateful world, which strains so passionately after falsehood, that of its own accord it prefers to be deceived rather than obey the truth. For it is a universal evil of which Paul complains in the first chapter of Romans (v. 21) that men do not glorify God who is known naturally from the handiwork of the world,[1] and unjustifiably suppress the truth. It is a just reward for such great ingratitude that Satan is given free rein to use various tricks to bring down in ruin those who turn away with a bad grace from the light of God. Therefore, as often as you read of Satan's predictions, reflect upon the just vengeance of God.

Now, if God punishes contempt of His light so severely in the case of the profane pagans (*gentibus*), whose only teacher is heaven and earth, how much harsher a punishment do those deserve, who knowingly and willingly stifle the pure teaching of salvation laid open for them in the Law and the Gospel? Accordingly it is no wonder if Satan has so freely deluded the world by his stratagems throughout so many generations, because the truth of the Gospel, which had become clearly known, has been wickedly despised.

But again it is objected that none are free from danger, when false predictions fly about like that. For even the good as well as the bad appear to be exposed to the snares of Satan when the truth is darkened. The answer is easy, that, even if Satan lays traps for all indiscriminately, yet the godly are preserved by the grace of God, so as not to be caught along with the rest. An even clearer distinction is taught in Scripture, that in this way the Lord tests the faith and godliness of His own, but makes the reprobate blind so that they may perish as they deserve. Therefore Paul plainly states that Satan is only allowed to have success with his error in the case of those who refuse to obey God and embrace the truth (II Thess. 2.11).

And that is also sufficient to expose the wickedness and ungodliness of those who find an excuse for the profane contempt of all doctrine on this pretext, saying, 'Where shall we turn to, seeing that Satan has the power to deceive with so many and such a variety of stratagems? It is therefore better to live free of all religion, rather than to bring down destruction on ourselves by religious zeal.' And in fact they are not serious in pleading this fear. But since all they desire is to wander about unconcernedly, without any fear of God, like the beasts, they welcome any sort of way out, so that no religion may keep them tied down. Of course I admit that Satan is every bit as cunning as wicked in abusing the name of God in innumerable ways, and that

[1] Calvin generally understands this verse in this sense, rather than 'since the creation of the world'; see his Commentary *ad loc.* and also his Commentary on I Cor. 13.12. Tr.

proverb, which the Papacy has made a reality for us, is all too true,
'All evil begins in the name of the Lord'. But since the Lord declares
that He is the teacher of the humble (cf. Ps. 25.9); and has promised
that He will be near to the upright in heart; since Paul teaches (Eph.
6.17) that 'the Word of God is the sword of the Spirit'; since he testifies that those who are properly founded on the faith of the Gospel
are no longer exposed to the impostures of men (cf. Eph. 4.14); since
Peter calls the Scripture 'a lamp shining in a dark place' (II Pet. 1.19);
since that generous invitation of Christ's cannot disappoint us, 'Seek
and you shall find; knock and it shall be opened unto you' (Matt. 7.7);
whatever Satan endeavours to do, and whatever darkness false prophets
try to spread, we must not be afraid of being abandoned by the Spirit
of wisdom and discernment, who curbs Satan by His power, and
makes us triumph over him through confidence in His Word.

18. *Paul being sore troubled.* It is possible that at the beginning Paul
took no notice of the girl's shouting, because he was hopeful that it
would be regarded as unimportant, and he would have preferred it
to disappear on its own. But the constant repetition finally wearies
him, because he could not suppress his feelings any longer, without
Satan becoming more insolent by his silence and patience. Secondly,
he was duty bound not to burst out with this prohibition rashly, until
he knew for certain that he was provided with the power of God.
For without the authority of God Paul's imprecation would have been
futile and ineffectual. And we must take note of that in case anyone
ventures to condemn Paul for being in too much of a hurry, because
he engaged with the unclean spirit so impetuously. For he harboured
no annoyance and indignation until he saw the cunning of Satan pre-
dominating, if he did not resist it quickly: and he attempted nothing
without the instigation of the Spirit, and joined battle only when he
was equipped with heavenly power. Yet he does not seem to be consistent, when he asserts elsewhere (Phil. 1.18) that he rejoices when
he sees the Gospel advanced by any means whatever, even by insincere
men, and men who deliberately desired to cover him with odium. I
reply that there was a different reason here, because all would have
thought that the girl's evil spirit was in collusion with Paul. In this
way the teaching of the Gospel would not only have been suspect,
but also would have become a pure laughing-stock. It was also for
this reason that Christ ordered the evil spirit to be silent (Mark 1.25);
while at other times, however, He allowed His name to be praised by
unworthy men (Luke 4.36).

I charge thee in the name. We must take note of the form of his
speech. For just as the miracle had a twofold use, viz. that the power
of Christ might be made known, and, secondly, that it might be made

plain that he had nothing to do with the deceitful tricks of Satan, so, in yielding the authority and power to Christ alone, Paul declares that he is only a minister, and, secondly, he openly sets Christ in opposition to the evil spirit, so that all may know from the conflict that they are at daggers drawn with each other. For it was a beneficial thing that many who had been subjected to such gross deception, be wakened up, so that being thoroughly cleansed they might yield to the sound faith.

19. *But when her masters saw.* The same devil that was recently trying to catch Paul with its flattering and enticing words through the mouth of the girl, now whips up her masters into a fury, to drag him off to death. In this way, having clearly assumed a fresh role, he acts a tragedy, because the previous play met with no success. But even if the passionate zeal, with which Paul had burned, raised a hurricane of persecution, yet he must not be considered at fault on that account, and indeed Paul himself had no regret about the miracle, to wish that what had been done were undone, because he was well aware by what influence he had driven the devil out of the girl. That teaches us that we are not to condemn things that have been done properly, even if it is something that has been undertaken by the commandment of God, although an unfortunate result follows, because God is then testing the perseverance of His people, until a happier and more favourable outcome dispels all sadness.

As far as the men are concerned, Luke explains the reason why they were so mad against Paul, viz. that the expectation of their discreditable gain had vanished. But although it was avarice alone that roused them to hatred of the Gospel and its ministers, yet they plead the fine excuse that they are grieved that the public order is being convulsed, the customary laws are being violated, and the peace disturbed. Thus although the enemies of Christ behave themselves impudently and badly, they always think up some other causes of wrong-doing. Yes, and even if their vicious cupidity is plain to see, yet with faces like iron they always bring in something to cover their own filthy ways. So today all the Papists who are the most violent zealots for their own law, are nevertheless thinking about nothing else except their own gain or domination. Let them swear by all the sacred things they can, that they are driven by a godly motive, yet the actual situation betrays[1] that their zeal is kindled from a cold kitchen, and is fanned by ambition. For they are either famished dogs which are driven on by ravenousness, or fierce lions, which breathe out nothing but cruelty.

20. *These men trouble our city.* This accusation was cunningly con-

---

[1] Reading *clamitat* with Tholuck for C.R.'s *clamavit.* Tr.

cocted to aggravate the situation of the servants of Christ. For on the one hand they claim the name of the *Romans,* and there was nothing more in favour than that; on the other hand they stir up ill-will against them with the name of the *Jews,* which had a bad reputation at that time; for as far as religion was concerned the Romans had greater affinity with all the rest of the nations put together than with the Jews. For a Roman was allowed to perform sacred rites in Greece, or in Asia and other regions, wherever both idols and superstitions were flourishing. Of course it was easy for Satan to be self-consistent although he assumed a variety of forms; but the Romans regarded as a detestable thing the only religion that was in the world. They produce a third false charge out of the offence of sedition, for they allege that the public peace was disturbed by Paul and his companions. Christ was brought into disgrace and odium by the same allegation (Luke 23.5). And now the Papists have nothing more plausible for bringing hatred down on us than by loudly crying out that our teaching aims at nothing else but fomenting disturbances, so that all things may finally end up in horrible confusion. But we ought to follow the example of Christ and Paul, and be courageous in rejecting this false and evil report, until the Lord brings the malice of our enemies to light, and refutes their impudence.

21. *Customs which it is not lawful.* They rely on precedent, so that there may be no argument about the matter; just as the Papists also deal with us today, saying, 'This has been decreed in a General Council'; 'An opinion is too well accepted for it to be right to question it'; 'Long usage has given approval to this'; 'This has been established by consent for more than a thousand years *(saeculorum)*'. But what is the point of all these things except to leave no authority to the Word of God? They boast of the opinions of men, but at the same time not even the lowest place is conceded to the laws of God. We may determine from the present verse how much force these precedents ought to have. The Roman laws were splendid, but religion depends on nothing else than the Word of God alone. Therefore in this matter we must always carefully see to it that, with men reduced to order, only the authority of God prevails, and that He brings into subjection to Himself all that is excellent in the world.

22. *The multitude ran together.* When Luke tells that, as soon as a few worthless men, that is to say money-making impostors, pretty well known for their sordid ways, caused a disturbance, a concourse of people took place, he is warning how uncontrolled the world's behaviour is when it is driven to resist Christ. And indeed foolishness and fickleness are common and almost perpetual faults with all peoples. But the extraordinary power of Satan betrays itself in the way that

men, who in other matters are modest and quiet, suddenly boil up for no reason, and link themselves, as allies, to all the most worthless characters, when the truth of God is to be resisted. There was no more moderation in the very judges, if we only reflect upon what their precise duties were. For, with their authority, they ought to have checked the fury of the people, and sharply resisted their violence. They ought to have protected the innocent with their help. But in fact they lay hold of them in the midst of the confusion (*tumultuose*), and, after their clothes have been stripped off, they order them to be beaten with rods, naked and without a hearing. Certainly the perverseness of men is to be deplored, for it has caused almost all the judgment-seats of the world, which ought to have been the sanctuaries of justice, to be discredited by impious and sacrilegious attacks on the Gospel.

However it is asked why they were cast into *prison*, since punishment had already been inflicted on them; for prison has been set up as a place of confinement. Obviously they made use of this kind of correction until they might make further inquiries. And so we see that the servants of Christ are treated more inhumanly than adulterers, robbers and all sorts of other criminals. That makes us see more clearly that power of Satan's in moving the minds of men to have no respect for any semblance of a judicial investigation in the persecution of the Gospel. But even if the circumstances of the godly in the defence of the truth of Christ are harder than those of the ungodly in their crimes, yet it goes well with them, because in all the injuries which they suffer, they triumph gloriously in the sight of God and the angels. They endure insults and ignominies, but because they know that the marks of Christ have more value and merit in heaven than the empty and fading shows of earth, the more unjustly and abusively the world torments them, the richer grounds they have for glorifying. For if secular writers honoured Themistocles so much that they preferred his prison to the judgment-seat and court of the judges, how much more respect ought we to feel for the Son of God, whose cause is on trial as often as the faithful suffer persecution for the sake of the Gospel? Therefore even if the Lord allowed injuries to be inflicted on Paul and Silas by unjust judges, yet He did not allow them to be branded with any disgrace which would not result in greater glory. For since all the persecutions that we must suffer for the testimony of the Gospel are what is left of the sufferings of Christ (cf. Col. 1.24), just as our Head turned the cross, accursed as it was, into a triumphal chariot, so He will also honour the prisons and gibbets (*patibula*) of His own, so that there they may triumph over Satan and all the ungodly.

Their clothes having been torn off. Because the Vulgate had translated
it properly, Erasmus was wrong in changing it to, 'the magistrates
tore their own clothes'. For Luke meant only this, that, with the
lawful proceedings of a judicial inquiry set aside, the holy men were
knocked about in the confusion, and hands were laid on them with
such violence that their clothing was stripped off. On the other hand
it would have been quite out of keeping with Roman custom for the
judges to tear their own clothing publicly in the market-place, especially since it was an inquiry about an unknown religion, about
which they did not particularly care. But I do not wish to argue any
longer about something that is settled.

*And when they had laid many stripes upon them, they cast them into
prison, charging the jailor to keep them safely: who, having received
such a charge, cast them into the inner prison, and made their feet fast in
the stocks. But about midnight Paul and Silas were praying and singing
hymns unto God, and the prisoners were listening to them; and suddenly
there was a great earthquake, so that the foundations of the prison-house
were shaken: and immediately all the doors were opened; and every
one's bands were loosed. And the jailor being roused out of sleep, and
seeing the prison doors open, drew his sword, and was about to kill
himself, supposing that the prisoners had escaped. But Paul cried with
a loud voice, saying, Do thyself no harm: for we are all here. (23-28)*

23. *To keep them safely.* When the magistrates gave such strict
instructions for Paul and Silas to be kept unharmed, they did so in
order that they might make further inquiries about the case. For they
had beaten them with rods for the sake of quietening the tumult. And
it is true what I have just said, that the world rages against the ministers
of the Gospel with such blind fury that it does not observe any proper
measure in its severity.

Apart from that, as it is exceedingly beneficial[1] for us to know, by
way of example, the harsh ways in which the witnesses of Christ were
treated long ago, so it is no less useful to know what Luke goes on
at once to record about their courage and endurance. For although
their feet were bound in fetters, he says that they praised God in
prayer; which makes it plain that neither the abuse which had been
inflicted on them, nor the wounds which made their flesh inflamed,
nor the stench from the depths of the prison, nor the danger of death
which was threatening them, prevented them from giving thanks to
God with eager and joyful hearts. Indeed we must observe the
general rule that we cannot pray properly as we ought, without

[1] Reading *prodest* with C.R. for Tholuck's *potest*. French: 'il profite grande-
ment'. Tr.

praising God at the same time. For even if the desire to pray is born from an awareness of our need or troubles, and therefore is usually connected with sorrow and mental anxiety, yet believers ought to control their feelings so that they do not cry out against God. So the proper method of prayer unites two apparently opposite moods, anxiety and sorrow from a sense of need, which overwhelms us, and joyfulness from the obedience, with which we submit ourselves to God, and from the hope, which, by showing us a haven close at hand, revives us in the very process of shipwreck. Paul prescribes such a form for us in Phil. 4.6, when he says, 'Let your requests be made known to God with an act of thanksgiving'. But in this incident the circumstances must be noted. For although the pain of their wounds was sharp, although the prison was irksome, although the danger was grave, since Paul and Silas do not cease praising God, we gather from that how they were constantly encouraged to bear the cross. In the same way Luke reported previously that the apostles 'rejoiced, because they were counted worthy to suffer dishonour for the Name' of the Lord (5.41).

25. *Were listening to them.* We must realize that Paul and Silas raised their voices when they prayed, in order to bear witness to the confidence of a good conscience to the others, who were imprisoned along with them. For they could either have made their prayers with the silent sighing of the heart, as they were accustomed to doing; or prayed to the Lord in whispers. Why therefore do they raise their voices? They certainly do not do it out of ostentation, but to make open confession that, relying on the goodness of their cause, they take refuge in God undaunted. Therefore their prayers included a confession of faith, which had the effect of being a public example, and prepared the jailer's (*insularii*) household, as well as the criminals, to pay attention to the miracle.

26. *There was an earthquake.* In producing this visible sign, the Lord first of all intended to have regard to His servants, so that they might know more plainly that their prayers were heard; yet He was also concerned about the others. He could have taken Paul and Silas out of their fetters, and opened the doors, without an earthquake. But the addition of it was very effective for encouraging them, seeing that for their sakes God shook the air and the earth. Secondly, it was necessary for the keeper of the prison, and the others, to be aware of the presence of God, so that they might not think that the miracle happened by chance. And indeed there is no doubt that at that time the Lord produced an example of His power, which would be beneficial for all generations, so that the faithful may be quite convinced that He will be near them, as often as they will have to undergo

struggles and dangers for the defence of the Gospel. All the same He does not always keep to the same course, so as to demonstrate His presence by clear signs; and it is not right to prescribe a principle for Him. For He also helped His own men at that time for this reason, that we today may be content with His secret grace. I have said more about this matter in the second chapter.

27, 28. *The keeper of the prison having been roused.* He was intending to kill himself, thus anticipating punishment; for it would have been ridiculous to defend himself by saying that the doors of the prison were opened by themselves. But it can be asked, 'Since Paul sees that the hope of escape depends on him, if he kills himself, why does he prevent him? For in this way he seems to be rejecting a God-given deliverance. Yes, and what is more, it seems to have been pure ludicrousness for God to wish the keeper to be aroused, so that there would not be any benefit from the miracle.' I reply that here attention must be paid to His purpose. For He did not free Paul, Silas, and the rest from their fetters, and did not open the doors in order to send them out of there as free men immediately, but, by disclosing the power of His hand, to set a seal upon the faith of Paul and Silas, and to make the name of Christ truly illustrious among the others. Therefore He answers the prayers of Paul and Silas in this way, to show that He is powerful enough to set them free as often as it will please Him, and that nothing at all can prevent Him from penetrating not only into prisons, but also into tombs to snatch away His own from death. He opened prison gates for Peter for another purpose, as we saw in chapter 12. But now when a different method was available to Him for saving Paul and Silas, He intended not so much to bring them out by a miracle at the present time, as to encourage them for the future. Again what I have just said must be recalled to mind, that the opening of the prison concerned others, so that it might be known to many eye-witnesses that God approves the teaching, which had already been loaded with unjustified prejudice. There is no doubt that Paul realized this, and therefore, when he was freed from his chains, he did not stir a foot from the spot. The way was open for him to escape. Why does he stay? Is it because he values the grace of God lightly, or because he may be willing to make the miracle useless by his own laziness? Neither of these is likely. We conclude from that, that he was divinely held back, in the way that the Lord usually guides the minds of His own in situations of perplexity, so that they may pursue, sometimes with knowledge, sometimes in ignorance, what is the best thing to do, and not miss their own goals.

And he called for lights, and sprang in, and, trembling for fear, fell down[1] before Paul and Silas, and brought them out, and said, Sirs, what must I do to be saved? And they said, Believe on the Lord Jesus, and thou shalt be saved, thou and thy house. And they spake the word of the Lord unto him, with all that were in his house. And he took them the same hour of the night, and washed their stripes; and was baptized, he and all his, immediately. And he brought them up into his house, and set meat before them, and rejoiced greatly, with all his house, having believed in God. (29-34)

29. *Trembling for fear fell down.* As well as being prepared by the miracle this keeper was constrained by fear to show obedience to God. From this it is apparent how beneficial it is for men to be stripped of their pride in order to learn to submit themselves to God. He had become hardened in his superstitions, and would therefore have shown high-minded contempt for anything that Paul and Silas would have said, particularly when he had disgracefully thrust them into the place in the prison for closer confinement. Fear now makes him docile and obedient. Therefore as often as the Lord smites us or affects us with any consternation, let us realize that it happens so that instead of being too high and mighty we may be forced into our proper place.

But it is strange that he is not rebuked because he fell down at their feet. For how does it happen that Paul takes no notice of something that Peter did not tolerate in the case of Cornelius, as Luke reported earlier (Acts 10.26)? I reply that Paul lets the keeper off because he knows that he has been induced to humble himself in this way not from superstition, but from fear of divine judgment. Veneration of this kind was common enough, and indeed it was particularly customary for the Romans, when they wished to ask for something humbly, or to beg for forgiveness, to fall down at the knees of those, whom they were supplicating. Therefore there was no reason why Paul should be incensed against a man, who was simply humbled by God. For if anything that was contrary to the glory of God had been given entry, he had not forgotten the zeal which he had shown earlier among the men of Lycaonia. We therefore conclude from his silence that in this kind of adoration there was nothing contrary to godliness or the glory of God.

30. *Sirs what must I do?* He asks advice in such a way that he demonstrates at the same time that he will be obedient. We see from this that he was seriously impressed, so that he was prepared to carry out the instructions of the men, whom he had cruelly fettered a few hours earlier. Often when the ungodly witness miracles, even al-

[1] Calvin has the Western reading *fell down at the feet of Paul and Silas.* Tr.

though they are momentarily terrified, yet the immediate effect is that they are made more obstinate, as happened to Pharaoh; at any rate they are not subdued so as to submit themselves to God. But this keeper, recognizing the power of God, was not terrified merely for a short time, soon afterwards to return to his former cruelty, but shows himself obedient to God, and eager for sound teaching. He asks about the way to obtain salvation, and that makes it all the plainer that he was not suddenly shaken, merely by a vanishing fear of God, but that he was truly humbled to present himself as a pupil to His ministers. For he knew that they had been thrown into prison for no other reason except that they were overthrowing the normal, established religion. Now he is ready to attend to their teaching, which he had previously despised.

31, 32. *Believe on the Lord Jesus.* This definition of salvation, that one is to believe in Christ, is short and meagre in appearance, but yet it is ample. For Christ alone has all the elements of blessedness and eternal life included in Himself. He offers them to us through the Gospel, but we receive them by faith, as I have argued in chapter 15 (v. 9). But two things must be noted here. The first is that Christ is the one and only goal of faith (*unicum fidei scopum*); and that accordingly when the minds of men turn away from Him they do nothing else but wander. Therefore it is no wonder if the whole theology of the Papacy is a vast chaos and a horrible labyrinth, because, with Christ neglected, they give themselves up to vain and windy speculations. In the second place we must observe that after we have embraced Christ by faith, that alone suffices for salvation. But the sentence which Luke adds immediately after gives a better description of the nature of faith. Paul and Silas tell the keeper of the prison to believe on the Son of God. Do they come to a stop with that one utterance? Of course not, for it follows in Luke's context that they proclaimed the Word of the Lord. Therefore we see that faith is not a trivial or arid opinion about unknown things, but a clear and distinct knowledge of Christ derived from the Gospel. On the other hand take away the preaching of the Gospel, and no faith will remain. In a word, Luke links faith with preaching and teaching and after he has spoken briefly about faith, he gives an explanatory account of the true and proper way of believing. Therefore instead of the fiction of implicit faith (*implicitae fidei*) about which the Papists babble, let us keep the faith that is united (*fidem implicitam*) to the Word of God, so that it may unfold the power of Christ to us.

33. *He was baptized, he and all who belonged to his household.* Luke again commends the godly zeal of the keeper, because he dedicated his whole household to God. The grace of God is also reflected in

that, because He suddenly brought a whole family to godly unanimity. At the same time the extraordinary change must truly be observed. Not long before he intended to kill himself, because he thought that Paul and the others had fled; now, having got rid of his fear, he willingly takes them home. So we see that faith gives a disposition for prompt action to those who previously had no feeling. And certainly when fear and doubt make us do nothing, there is no better source of confidence, than being able to cast all our cares on the bosom of God, so that no danger may deter us from performing our duty, while we may expect an advantageous outcome from God, for He Himself will see to it that it will be so.

34. *He rejoiced because he had believed.* The outward proclamation of faith, on the part of the keeper, has already been praised; now the inward result of faith is described. When he received the apostles hospitably, and had no dread of punishment, but treated them kindly in his home, contrary to the instructions he had received from the magistrate, he testified that his faith was not useless. On the other hand, the joy, of which Luke speaks here, is a singular blessing, which individuals derive from their faith. No torture is more grievous than a bad conscience; for even if unbelievers try by all means to make themselves insensitive, yet, because they do not have peace with God, they are bound to be agitated. But if they do not undergo torments at the present time, if, on the contrary, they indulge in revels with wild and unbridled licence, yet they are never at peace, and do not obtain unclouded joy. Therefore genuine and enduring joy comes only from faith, when we enjoy the favour of God. In this way Zechariah says (9.9), 'Rejoice and exult, O daughter of Zion, behold thy King comes'. Yes, and what is more, all through Scripture this effect is attributed to faith, that it makes hearts rejoice. Therefore let us realize that faith is no empty or dead figment of the imagination, but a lively awareness of the grace of God, which brings genuine joy from the certainty of salvation. It is right that the ungodly have no share in that joy, for they both flee from the God of peace, and throw all righteousness into confusion.

But when it was day, the magistrates sent the serjeants, saying, Let those men go. And the jailor reported the words to Paul, saying, The magistrates have sent to let you go: now therefore come forth, and go in peace. But Paul said unto them, They have beaten us publicly, un-condemned, men that are Romans, and have cast us into prison; and do they now cast us out privily? nay verily; but let them come themselves and bring us out. And the serjeants reported these words unto the magistrates: and they feared, when they heard that they were Romans; and they came and besought them; and when they had brought them out, they asked them to go away from the city. And they went out of the prison, and entered into the house of Lydia: and when they had seen the brethren, they comforted them, and departed. (35-40)

35. *When it was day.* The question is asked: 'What caused the judges to change their plan so suddenly? The previous day they had ordered Paul and Silas to be bound with fetters, as if they were going to inflict severe punishment on them; now they allow them to go away unpunished. At any rate if they had heard them, knowledge of the case could have restored them to clemency and a proper attitude of mind. But it is apparent, since the circumstances of the case were still the same, that they were brought to a change of mind of their own accord.' I reply that here there is narrated nothing else than what usually happens once sedition is set in motion. For not only do the minds of the common people boil over, but the disturbance carries off the rulers also; which is certainly a wrong thing. For what Virgil says is well known:

'And as often happens in a great multitude, when sedition has broken out, when the minds of the base-born crowd seethe with fury; and firebrands and stones are already flying, and madness supplies weapons; then if perchance they have descried any man, venerable because of his dutifulness and his services, they fall silent, and stand, all ears. With his words he sways their minds and soothes their feelings.' (*Aeneid* 1.148f.)

Accordingly there is nothing less fitting than for the judges to burn along with the people in the heat of the tumult; but it usually happens like that. Therefore when those ruling citizens (*decuriones*) saw the people in revolt they thought that it provided sufficient grounds for them to beat the apostles with rods. But now they are forced to suffer the punishment of their carelessness with shame and the brand of disgrace. Also, when they make inquiries about the origin of the tumult perhaps they discover that agitators (*circulatores*) are to blame; therefore, having been assured of the innocence of Paul and Silas too late, they set them free. All who bear rule are warned by this example how much excessive haste is to be avoided. Again we see how unconcernedly the magistrates condone their own faults, although quite well aware of them, especially when they are dealing with unknown and obscure men. When those men allow Paul and Silas to leave in freedom, they are not ignorant that they had previously been wronged; yet they think it sufficient if they do not continue to be unjust and cruel to them right to the bitter end.

The public officers (*apparitores*) are called ῥαβδοῦχοι from the staffs which they carried; while the lictors' badges of office were axes bound round with rods.

37. *They have beaten us publicly.* There are two grounds of defence, first, that violence was done to the person of a man who was a Roman, secondly, that it was done contrary to the order of the law. We shall see later that Paul was a Roman citizen. But it was strictly decreed by the law of Porcius, by the laws of Sempronius, and many others besides that no man, but only the people, had power of life and death over a Roman citizen. Nevertheless it might appear strange that Paul did not claim his right before he was beaten with rods; for the judges could have honestly pled his silence by way of excuse for themselves. But it is probable that he was not heard in the midst of the heat of the tumult. If anyone objects that he is now seeking a late and untimely remedy, further, that he is snatching at a foolish and useless means of relief, in asking that the magistrates come themselves, there is also an easy answer to that. Certainly Paul's situation was not going to be any better because of that, but we must note that the last thing that was in his mind was to have regard to his own private advantage, but to obtain some relief for all the godly in the future, so that the magistrates might not venture to proceed with so much licence against good and innocent brethren. Because he now held them in his power, he used his own right to help the brethren, so that no harm might come to them. That was the reason for his complaint. And so Paul made wise use of the opportunity presented to him; just as we must neglect nothing that is of value for restraining enemies, so that they may not assume too much licence for themselves in oppressing and harassing the innocent, since it is not for nothing that the Lord puts helps of that kind within our grasp. However let us remember, if men hurt us on any account, that we must not retaliate with injuries, but we must only take pains to restrain their passion, so that they may not harm others in the same way.

38. *They were afraid because they were Romans.* They are not influenced by the other point, that they had wrongly vented their rage on innocent men, without bringing in an inquiry; and yet that charge was the graver one. But because they had no fear of any human avenger, they were not disturbed by the judgment of God. That is why they unconcernedly take no notice of the objection made about injustice. They are only afraid of the Roman axes for themselves, because of the violation of liberty in the person of a citizen. They knew that this was a capital offence for the highest governors; what therefore would befall the ruling citizens of one colony? The fear of the ungodly is like that; because their consciences are dull before God,

they indulge themselves copiously in all sins, until the vengeance of men threatens them.

40. *When they had seen the brethren.* They had been asked to leave at once; yet they had to be concerned about the brethren, so that the still tender seed of the Gospel might not perish. And there is no doubt that they would have stayed longer, if permission had been given them; but the requests of the magistrates were imperious and backed by arms, and they are forced to obey them. All the same they do not neglect a necessary duty, but encourage the brethren to be steadfast. But because they went straight to Lydia's house, it is proof that, although the Church had been increased, even in a great number that woman held the leading place, as far as zeal in carrying out the duties of piety was concerned; and that is made all the clearer by the fact that all the godly met in her house.

CHAPTER SEVENTEEN

Now when they had passed through Amphipolis and Apollonia, they came to Thessalonica, where was a synagogue of the Jews: and Paul, as his custom was, went in unto them, and for three sabbath days reasoned with them from the scriptures, opening and alleging, that it behoved the Christ to suffer, and to rise again from the dead; and that this Jesus, whom, said he, I proclaim unto you, is the Christ. And some of them were persuaded, and consorted with Paul and Silas; and of the devout Greeks a great multitude, and of the chief women not a few. (1-4)

1. *They came to Thessalonica.* We are not certain why Paul attempted nothing at Amphipolis and Apollonia, for they were not obscure cities by any means, as Pliny establishes, except that he followed the guidance of the Spirit of God, and also he decided whether to speak or be silent from the actual situation, as opportunity presented itself. And perhaps he did also try to be of use there but, because there was no success, Luke therefore passes it over in silence.

But it is evident from his preaching Christ at Thessalonica, after having been beaten and hardly escaping from great danger at Philippi, how unbroken he was in his determination to hold to the course of his calling, and how undaunted he was to meet new dangers continually. Such unconquerable mental courage and indefatigable endurance of the cross are enough to show that Paul did not labour in human fashion, but that he was equipped with the heavenly power of the Spirit. And it was also wonderful patience on his part that, notwithstanding the fact that he had so often experienced the ungovernable obstinacy of the Jews, he did go in among them, and continued to be concerned about their salvation. But because he realized that Christ was given to the Jews for salvation, and that he himself had been made an apostle on this condition, that he should preach repentance and faith first to the Jews and secondly to the Gentiles, he commits the outcome of his labour to the Lord, and obeys His commandment, although with no great hope of success. Indeed he did appear to have said a final farewell to the Jews previously (13.46), when he said, 'It was certainly right to make the Kingdom of God known to you in the first place, but because you do not accept it, behold, we are turned to the Gentiles.' But that rather severe sentence ought to be confined to that company, who had impiously rejected the Gospel offered to them, and had made themselves unworthy of the grace of God. Towards the nation itself Paul certainly does not cease to discharge the ambassadorship committed to him. We are taught by that example that the call of God ought to be of such importance to us that no men may prevent us, by their ingratitude, from continuing to care for their salvation, as long as the Lord appoints us ministers to them. But one may believe that straight away on that first sabbath there were already some who refused the sound doctrine, but their perverseness did not prevent him from coming back on other sabbaths.

2. *He reasoned from the scriptures.* In the first place Luke records the substance of the argument, viz. that Jesus, the Son of Mary, is the Christ promised in time past in the Law and the Prophets, who made atonement for the sins of the world by the sacrifice of His death, and brought righteousness and life by His resurrection; in the second place he reports the way in which he proved what he was teaching. Let us take first his handling of the second aspect. Luke says that he argued from the Scriptures; therefore proofs of the faith are only to be sought from the mouth of God. If there is a discussion about human affairs, then human reasons may have their place, but in the teaching of the faith, the authority of God alone ought to be sovereign, and we ought to be dependent upon it. Certainly all admit this, that assent must be given to God alone, but at the same time there are few who hear Him speaking in the Scriptures. And if that principle has influence among us, that Scripture originated from God, the rule of either teaching or learning was bound to be derived from no other source. That is why it is also apparent how the Papists are driven by a diabolical madness, when they deny that any certainty can be acquired from the Scriptures, and therefore maintain that they must depend on the opinions of men. For I ask whether the method of arguing, to which Paul adhered, was legitimate or not. At least let them be ashamed that more reverence was held for the Word of the Lord in an unbelieving nation than obtains among them today. The Jews admit Paul and bear with him as he argues from the Scriptures; the Pope and all his people look upon it as a mere laughing-stock when Scripture is quoted in public, as if God speaks ambiguously in it, and mocks with meaningless obscurities. In addition to that, today more light appears in the Scriptures, and the truth of God shines out more clearly in them than in the Law and the Prophets. For in the Gospel Christ, the Sun of Righteousness, shines upon us with full splendour, so that it is an intolerable blasphemy when the Papists take certitude away from the Word of God. But let us, for our part, realize that as faith can be founded nowhere else than on the Word of the Lord, so in all controversies we must take our stand only on its evidence.

3. *Opening*. Here he describes the substance or the subject, as men say, of the disputation, and posits two statements about the Christ; that it was necessary for Him to die and rise again, and that He is the Son of Mary who had been crucified. When there is a dispute about the Christ three questions arise, whether He does exist, who He is, and what is His nature. If Paul had been dealing with Gentiles it would have been necessary for him to start further back, because they had heard nothing about the Christ; and profane men do not think that they need any mediator. But there was no doubt about that point among Jews, to whom a Mediator had been promised. Therefore Paul omits as superfluous what all of them accepted with common consent.

However, because there was nothing more difficult than for Jews to acknowledge the crucified Jesus as Redeemer, Paul therefore begins from this aspect, that it was necessary for the Christ to die, and he does so in order to remove from the scene the stumbling-block of the cross. Yet we must not think that he told the bare story, but he adopts the undoubted principle that there were obvious reasons why Christ had to suffer and rise again, because, of course, he spoke publicly about the ruin of the human race, about sin and its punishment, about the judgment of God, and the eternal curse in which we are all involved. For Scripture also recalls us to these things when it foretells the death of Christ. For instance Isaiah does not simply say that the Christ will die, but, plainly stating that we have all erred and every one has turned aside into his own way, he assigns the cause of His death, that God laid on Him the iniquities of us all, that the chastisement of our peace is upon Him, so that we may be healed by His stripes (*livore*), that by expiating our sins He has obtained righteousness for us (Isa. 53.5, 6). So also Daniel tells of the meaning and effect of His death in chapter 9 (v. 24), when he says that a seal must be put on sin in order that everlasting righteousness may take its place. And surely there is no more appropriate or effective way to prove the function of Christ, than when men have been humbled by an awareness of their misfortunes, and see that there is no hope left unless they are reconciled by the sacrifice of Christ. Then, laying aside their pride, they humbly embrace His cross, which formerly they used to loathe, and of which they were ashamed. It is therefore right for us today to come to the same fountains from which Paul drew the proof of the death and resurrection of Christ.

Now that explanation has brought a very great deal of light to the second point. It was not so easy for Paul to succeed in proving, and concluding with certainty, that the Son of Mary is the Christ, if the Jews had not been previously informed what sort of redeemer was to be expected. When that is in fact established it only remains to apply to Christ the things that Scripture attributes to the Mediator.

Finally, this is the substance of our faith, that we know that the Son of Mary is the Christ and that Mediator whom God promised from the beginning; secondly, that we understand why He died and rose again, so that we may not invent some earthly king for ourselves, but may seek spiritual righteousness and all aspects of our salvation in Him. Because Paul is said to have proved both from the Scriptures we must realize that the Jews were not yet as dull, and were not possessed of such great impudence as they are today. From the sacrifices and the whole cult of the Law, Paul could have drawn arguments which today the Jews snap at like dogs. It is well enough known how shamefully they mangle and tear to pieces other Scripture passages. At that time they certainly had some honourableness left them, and they also possessed some reverence for Scripture, so that they were not completely unteachable. Today a veil is placed over their hearts (II Cor. 3.15), so that in broad daylight they see no more than moles.

4. *Some of them believed.* Here we see the result of Paul's disputation. He certainly proved openly to all that Jesus is the Christ, who reconciled the Father to us by His death, and whose resurrection is the life of the world. Yet only some of the Jews believe; the rest are blind in broad daylight, and with deaf ears reject the certain and manifest truth. It is also worth noting that while a few of the Jews believed, a great multitude of the Greeks, who were far more remote, gave their assent to the faith. Why do you say that they were trained in the doctrine of the Law from childhood, only to be more hostile to God Himself? Therefore God was now beginning to bring out in them examples of that blindness, with which the prophets rather frequently threaten them. However He declares that His covenant is not invalid, inasmuch as He gathers at least some of that people to Himself, so that glimmers of the election may shine in a remnant saved by grace. Luke also informs us, not that they had faith in Paul's words only to the extent that they agreed with cool assent, but that they gave evidence of serious intention by associating with Paul and Silas as companions. And by their frank profession of the Gospel they called down on themselves the animosities of their own nation. For what does this association mean for them except that they acknowledge that they approve of the teaching, that he was giving, and that they take their stand by his side? For there is nothing more damaging to faith than if, when we recognize the truth of God, we still remain undecided and on the fence (*suspensi et medii*). If anyone prefers the explanation that they adhered to Paul and Silas because of their eagerness to learn, so that they could be taught more intimately at home, the lively glow of

their faith is also evident from that. And it always remains a fixed principle that nobody really believes in Christ, unless he yields himself to Him, and freely takes his stand under His standard.

Of the devout Greeks a multitude. Because these had imbibed the rudiments of piety they were nearer to the Kingdom of God than the others who had always lain in the filth of superstitions. However the question is asked how religion came to the Greeks, for they were bewitched by ungodly errors and fancies, and were completely without God, as Paul teaches in Eph. 2.12. But one must realize that, wherever the Jews had been driven in exile, some seed of piety was scattered, and that the fragrance of the purer teaching was diffused. For by the wonderful plan of God their wretched dispersal was turned to the opposite purpose, so that it gathered those wandering and lost in errors to the right faith. But even although religion was also spoiled by many vicious fabrications in their midst, yet, because very many of the Gentiles were weary of their folly, they were being attracted to Judaism by this summary, that there is nothing that gives more security than the worship of the one God. Therefore understand by the *devout Greeks* those who had some taste of the true and legitimate worship of God, so that they were no longer devoted to crass idolatries. However, as I have said, it is probable that their taste was only vague and slight, so that it was far removed from true instruction. Accordingly Luke is wrong in giving them such an honourable title. But just as the Spirit of God sometimes thinks some rude first beginning, or the mere preparation of faith deserving of the name of 'faith', so here 'devout' is applied to those who had taken farewell of idols and were beginning to acknowledge the one God. But even if that confused or obscure persuasion does not deserve, by itself, to be regarded as religion, yet, because it is a step by which one draws nearer God, it takes the name of the consequent, as men say. Besides, blind and superstitious fear of God is sometimes called 'religion', not because it is, but, by misapplication ($\kappa\alpha\tau\alpha\chi\rho\eta\sigma\tau\iota\kappa\hat{\omega}s$), to point out the difference between any sort of worship of God, and gross and Epicurean contempt. At the same time let us realize that the truth and the sound teaching of the Word of God is the rule of piety, so that there may be no religion without the true light of understanding.

But the Jews,[1] being moved with jealousy, took unto them certain vile fellows of the rabble, and gathering a crowd, set the city on an uproar; and assaulting the house of Jason, they sought to bring them forth to the people. And when they found them not, they dragged Jason and certain brethren before the rulers of the city, crying, These that have turned the

[1] Calvin reads *unbelieving Jews*, with RV margin. Tr.

*world upside down are come hither also; whom Jason hath received: and
these all act contrary to the decrees of Caesar, saying that there is another
king, one Jesus. And they troubled the multitude and the rulers of the
city, when they heard these things. And when they had taken security
from Jason and the rest, they let them go. And the brethren immediately
sent away Paul and Silas by night unto Beroea: who when they were
come thither went into the synagogue of the Jews. (5-10)*

5. *But being moved with jealousy.* We see that Paul did not set up the
Kingdom of Christ anywhere without a struggle; for as soon as any
fruit of the teaching emerged persecutions arose. But because he
knew that he had to wage war with Satan and the perverseness of the
world, not only had he become hardened to all attacks, but he was
spurred on all the more to carry on with greater courage. In the same
way the servants of Christ ought to be content with his example
alone, if they see that their labour is not completely fruitless, so that they
may compensate all sorts of persecutions with this reward.

Apart from that this verse teaches that the burning zeal, which
drives unbelievers, is nothing else but a raving passion, because it is
not controlled by the prudence of the Spirit or even by rectitude or
fairness. But even if they themselves plead the name of God as an
excuse for their preposterous zeal, yet this story clearly demonstrates
that nothing but hypocrisy holds sway within, and that all the corners
of their hearts are full of poisonous malice. Those enemies of Paul
were boasting that they were the protectors of God's Law, and that
they were hostile to, or contending with Paul, only for the sake of its
defence. Why then do they arm all the ungodly, and conspire with
them to raise a tumult? Why also do they appear before a worldly
magistrate and load the Gospel with the same odium as could have
redounded on the Law? Such a faction clearly demonstrates that they
were not prompted by devotion for God at all, to have been inflamed
against Paul. For why do they besiege Jason's house and tumultuously
strive to drag Paul out of it, except to set him before the people to be
stoned? Let us therefore realize that the wicked zeal (*cacozeliam*), which
burns in superstitious men is always tinged with hypocrisy and malice.
It happens, as a result, that it bursts out in cruelty that knows no
bounds.

Took unto them certain frequenters of the market-place (circumforaneis).
The Greek word which Luke uses (*ἀγοραῖοι*) means idlers, and worthless
men, who have nothing to do or attend to at home, and wander all
over the market-place unemployed; or presumptuous starvelings who
are prepared to perjure themselves, to foment disturbances, and hire
out their services for any sort of crime. That makes it clear again that

those who, of their own accord, had recourse to the support of hopeless characters knew in themselves that they were in the wrong. For seeing that the magistrate was favourable to them, what impelled them to raise that disturbance except that they were not looking for any success unless things were thrown into confusion? Moreover Luke describes how sedition was whipped up by such fans, viz. that they stirred up the people in groups, and, as it were, made their poison go the rounds (*per circulos sparserint*) until there were enough men to take violent action. Cities that are liable to this disease know from experience that that is all too common a trick with insurrectionists.

6. *Those who have turned the world.* This is the lot of the Gospel, that the tumults which Satan stirs up in his attack on it are imputed to it. Here also is the badness of the enemies of Christ, in throwing the blame for disturbances, of which they are the instigators, on holy and modest teachers. Certainly the Gospel is not preached for the purpose of inciting men to fight with one another, but rather to keep them at peace as men reconciled to God. Since Christ kindly invites us in it to Himself, Satan and the ungodly are in an uproar. Paul and Silas therefore had a ready defence, but they had to submit to this false infamy for a time, and as long as they were not heard, to put up with it in silence. And the Lord has intended to warn us by their example not to give way to calumnies or harmful rumours, but to persist bravely in the defence of the truth, being prepared to hear evil in connexion with things well done. Accordingly let there be an end to the perverted wisdom of certain men who, in order to avoid a false accusation, do not hesitate to betray Christ and the Gospel by their treacherous moderation, as if their reputation were more precious than that of Paul and men like him; and even than the sacred name of God, which is not immune from blasphemies.

7. *These all act contrary to the decrees of Caesar.* The second point in the accusation is that they violate the majesty of the Roman empire; a serious and hateful crime, but one invented with too much impudence. Paul and Silas were striving to set up the Kingdom of Christ, which is spiritual. The Jews knew that this was being done without any harm to the Roman Empire. They knew that there was no question of those men intending to overthrow the public order, or snatch Caesar's authority away from him, but they maliciously plead this excuse for the sake of procuring ill-will. Religion, particularly the Jewish religion, did not matter so much to the Macedonians that they would rush unknown men to immediate execution for the sake of it. Therefore the Jews seize on the pretext of treason in order to cover innocent men with the odium of the offence alone. And today Satan does not cease to spread such smoke-screens to close men's eyes.

The Papists know very well, and in the sight of God they are refuted again and again, that there is absolutely no foundation to the charge they make against us, that we overthrow the political order, put an end to laws and judicial investigations, and subvert the power of kings. Yet in order to make the whole world hostile to us, they are not ashamed to tell the lie that we are enemies of public order. For we must note that the Jews invent the charge that the decrees of Caesar were violated, not only because Paul and Silas dared to make some change in religion, but because they said that there was another king. That charge was absolutely fictitious. Finally, if religion ever forces us to resist tyrannical edicts, which forbid giving due honour to Christ, and due worship to God, then we too may rightly testify that we do not violate the authority of kings. For they have not been lifted to such an exalted position, that, like the giants, they may endeavour to pull down God from His throne. Daniel's defence was true. 'I have done nothing wrong against the king', although he had nevertheless not obeyed the impious edict, for he had done no injury to a mortal man, because he had preferred God to him (Dan. 6.22). So let us, in good faith, pay to princes their proper dues, let us be ready for civil obedience of all kinds, but if they are not content with their own station, and wish to take away from us the fear and worship of God, there is no reason for anyone to say that they are despised by us, because the authority and majesty of God are of more importance to us.

8, 9. *They excited the multitude.* We see how unfairly the holy men were treated. Because they were given no opportunity of defending themselves, it was an easy matter for them to be crushed, although they were innocent. We also see that it is no new thing for the vehemence of the people, like a tempest, to sweep away the very magistrates as well, especially when the wrong affects unknown strangers, from whom they expect no reward, because they do not wish to run into danger for nothing. For under these circumstances no consideration is given to reason or equity, nor is a trial of the case undertaken, but the one urges on the other, with nobody protesting, and everything is conducted in confusion, as when men are running to some conflagration. But it came about by the extraordinary blessing of God that such great heat was quickly checked. For as soon as the magistrates declare that they will investigate the case, the crowd grows quiet, bail is accepted, and the affair finally dies down.

10. *They sent them away to Beroea.* From this it is evident that Paul's work bore fruit in a short time. For although the brethren send Silas and him away, yet by this service they are giving themselves, as voluntary associates, to their danger and cross. On the other hand,

Paul's persistence is incredible, because as often as he experienced the obstinacy and ill-will of his own nation, yet he never ceases to try whether he can lead some to Christ. Of course since he knew that he was under an obligation to both Jews and Gentiles, no injustice on the part of men could take him away from his calling. All the servants of Christ must struggle like that against the malice of the world, so that, whatever injuries may provoke them, they may not shake off the yoke.

Now these were more noble than those in Thessalonica, in that they received the word with all readiness of mind, examining the scriptures daily, whether these things were so. Many of them therefore believed; also of the Greek women of honourable estate, and of men, not a few. But when the Jews of Thessalonica had knowledge that the word of God was proclaimed of Paul at Beroea also, they came thither likewise, stirring up and troubling the multitudes. And then immediately the brethren sent forth Paul to go as far as to the sea[1]: and Silas and Timothy abode there still. But they that conducted Paul brought him as far as Athens: and receiving a commandment unto Silas and Timothy that they should come to him with all speed, they departed. (11-15)

11. *They were outstanding in nobility.* Luke returns once again to the men of Thessalonica.[2] The memory of Christ might have seemed to have been buried with the departure of Paul, and it is certainly wonderful that the little light, which had given scarcely a glimmer, was not extinguished, and that the seed of sound doctrine, which needed constant watering in order to grow, did not shrivel up. But after Paul left it was apparent how effectual and fruitful his preaching had been. For those who had tasted only the first principles of godliness, nevertheless make progress in his absence, and exercise themselves in constant reading of Scripture.

But Luke says, first of all, that they belonged to the chief families. For the *nobility*, which he mentions, refers not to the mind but to breed (*gentem*). Some are rather of the opinion that the men of Beroea are being compared with those of Thessalonica, because he uses εὐγενεστέροι, 'nobler', and not the superlative, εὐγενεστάτοι, 'noblest'. But I think that the idiom, which was rather harsh to Latin ears, was common and familiar to the Greeks. In addition he had said a little earlier that the chief women of Thessalonica believed, and it does not seem likely that the citizens of that city are esteemed less than those of Beroea.

[1] Calvin reads *as it were to the sea*, with later MSS, AV, RV margin. Tr.
[2] Calvin's text reads, *Hi autem nobilitate praestabant inter Thessalonicenses*, 'now these were outstanding in nobility among the Thessalonians'. Tr.

But there is a threefold reason why Luke mentions superiority of birth in their case. We know how reluctantly men come down from a high position, how rare it is for the great, who are prominent in the world, to lay aside their pride, and submit to the ignominy of the cross, and to glory in humiliation, as James enjoins (1.10). Therefore Luke commends the remarkable efficacy of the Spirit of God, when he says that the dignity of the flesh was no obstacle to those noblemen, but that having embraced the Gospel, they prepared themselves to bear the cross, and preferred the reproach of Christ to the glory of the world. In the second place Luke wished to make it plain to us that the grace of Christ is open to men of all ranks. That is what Paul means, when he says that God wishes all men to be saved (I Tim. 2.4); so that those who are poor, and of lowly birth, even although Christ did think them deserving of the first place, may not close the door to the rich. Therefore we see that noblemen and common men are gathered together, that men distinguished by a position of honour, and those who are despised, are growing together into the one body of the Church (*in unum Ecclesiae corpus coalescere*), so that all, without exception, may humble themselves and truly extol the grace of God. In the third place Luke seems to be pointing out the reason why so many were added, and why the Kingdom of Christ increased in such a short time at Thessalonica, viz. because it was no ordinary help that the leading men, and those distinguished by birth, showed the way to others, because the common people are usually influenced by authority. And even if this was by no means a fitting support for faith and piety, yet it is no unusual thing for God to lead unbelievers, who are still wandering in error, to Himself by indirect ways.

They had received the word. The first thing for which he expressly praises the men of Thessalonica is that they were ready and eager in their desire to receive the Gospel; the second, that they strengthened their faith daily by a diligent inquiry. So their piety and faith is praised on account of its readiness at the start, and on account of their constancy and fervent desire to make progress as they went on. And certainly this is the way to enter into the faith first of all, that we are ready to follow, and, having renounced our own fleshly understanding, we show ourselves docile and obedient to Christ. In also honouring the Thessalonians with this description Paul gives his support to Luke's account (I Thess. 2.13). As far as the second aspect is concerned, this earnestness is not a virtue to be despised, for Luke says that in consequence of it the believers were intent on strengthening their faith. For many who show enthusiasm at the start immediately fall into lazy ways, and so long as they are touched by no concern to make progress, they lose any seed of faith they may have.

But two absurd objections can be made here. For it seems to smack of arrogance that they make an investigation in order to come to a decision, and it seems very much out of keeping with the readiness which he has just mentioned. Secondly, since investigation is a sign of doubt, it follows that they were previously endowed with none of the faith, to which conviction (πληροφορία) and certitude are always linked. To the first objection I reply that Luke's words ought not to be read as if the Thessalonians took judgment upon themselves, or debated whether the truth of God should be received. They were merely examining Paul's teaching according to the rule of Scripture, just as gold is tested by fire. For Scripture is the true touchstone by which all doctrines must be tested. If anyone objects that this kind of examination will be ambiguous, since Scripture is often obscure, and twisted to yield different meanings, I say that we must at the same time bring in the judgment of the Spirit, who is not called the Spirit of discernment without good reason. But with the Spirit as leader and director, believers will form a judgment about any doctrine at all from no other source than the Scriptures. And in this way that sacrilegious assertion of the Papists is refuted, that, because nothing certain can be derived from Scripture, faith depends only on what the Church decides. For since the Spirit of God commends the Thessalonians, in their example He lays down a rule for us. But an inquiry from the Scriptures would be useless, if they did not have sufficient light to teach us. Therefore let this firm axiom stand, that no doctrine is worth believing except such as we perceive to be based on the Scriptures. The Pope wishes all to accept without questioning, whatever he has blabbed out according to his own fancy. But will he be regarded as superior to Paul, into whose teaching learners were allowed to make inquiries? And let us note that this is not said about some masquerading (larvato) Council, but of a small company of men, which makes it all the clearer that individuals are called to read Scripture. In this way also inquiry is not in conflict with readiness of faith. For as soon as anyone listens, and in his eagerness to learn shows himself attentive, he is already well-disposed and docile, even if he does not give his assent openly and at once. For instance: an unknown teacher will profess that he is bringing the true teaching; I shall come to him, ready to listen, and my mind will be disposed to obey the truth; nevertheless at the same time I shall ponder what sort of teaching it is, and I shall only embrace what I recognize to be the certain truth. And the best disposition is this, when, held fast by reverence for God, we gladly and quietly hear what is placed before us, as proceeding from Him. Yet at the same time we are on our guard against the impostures of men, and our minds do not rush, with the blind impetuosity of the fickle, to believe anything without thinking. Therefore the investigation, which Luke mentions, does not have as its object that we be slow and difficult to believe; but rather readiness, with judgment, is considered the mean between levity and obstinacy.

The second objection must now be removed. Faith is contrary to doubt; the inquirer is a doubter; therefore it follows that the Thessalonians, since they make inquiries about Paul's teaching, are still without faith. But the certitude of faith does not debar confirmation. I mean by 'confirmation', when the truth of God, which was however not in doubt before, is being sealed on our hearts more and more. For instance, I shall hear from the Gospel that I am reconciled to God by the grace of Christ, and that my sins are expiated by His sacred blood; evidence will be produced which makes me believe. If afterwards I examine the Scriptures more thoroughly, other testimonies will repeatedly present themselves, and these will not only help my faith, but increase and establish it, so that greater certitude may come. Similarly as far as understanding is concerned, faith makes progress from the reading of Scripture. If anyone objects, again, that little authority is being assigned to the teaching of Paul by those who inquire diligently from Scripture whether it accords with the truth (*an ita res habeat*), I reply that the effects of faith are such that sometimes they search the Scriptures for something, about which they have already been persuaded by God, and have the testimony of the Spirit within. And Luke does not state that faith was complete in all its aspects among the Thessalonians, but he only relates how they were initiated into Christ, and what sort of advances they made in faith, until the complete building of godliness would exist in their midst.

12. *And many did indeed believe.* This has no reference to the previous sentence, as if a selection had been made from those whom he mentioned, and they began to believe; for that would be absurd. But Luke means that the Church was increased in that city, because many were added through their example. And so far indeed Luke has recorded the beginnings of the Church at Thessalonica, so that nobody might think that with Paul's sudden and violent departure his efforts came to nothing, for unless I am very much mistaken it was for that purpose that he interposed the fruit, which his preaching had produced at the other city, before he came to the banishment at Beroea.

13. *When the Jews knew.* We see how implacably hatred of the Gospel hurried the Jews hither and thither. For not only do they madly drive Christ out, when He is presented to them, face to face, at home, but when they hear that He is being preached elsewhere, they fly there like men driven by avenging spirits. But here we must not pay attention to the fury of one nation so much, as to the desperate ill-will of

Satan, who incites his men to throw the Kingdom of Christ into confusion, and destroy the salvation of men, and uses them like fans to
raise disturbances. Accordingly, today when so many furious enemies
set themselves in opposition to the faithful ministers of Christ, let us
realize that it is not men who cause the war, but that Satan, the father
of lies, contrives all these things in order to overthrow the Kingdom
of Christ. But if the method of fighting will not always be the same,
yet Satan will never cease tormenting those, whom he knows to be
serving Christ faithfully, either with open war or by insidious means,
or even with domestic struggles.

*Now while Paul waited for them at Athens, his spirit was provoked
within him, as he beheld the city full of idols. So he reasoned in the
synagogue with the Jews and the devout persons, and in the marketplace
every day with them that met with him. And certain also of the Epicurean and Stoic philosophers encountered him. And some said, What
would this babbler say? other some, He seemeth to be a setter forth of
strange gods: because he preached Jesus and the resurrection. And they
took hold of him, and brought him unto the Areopagus, saying, May
we know what this new teaching is, which is spoken by thee? For thou
bringest certain strange things to our ears: we would know therefore what
these things mean. (Now all the Athenians and the strangers sojourning
there spent their time in nothing else, but either to tell or to hear some
new thing.) (16-21)*

16. *His spirit was burning.* Although, wherever he went, Paul
strenuously carried out the office of teaching, that he knew had been
laid upon him, yet Luke records that at Athens he was more incensed
because he saw idolatry had a greater grip on it than on other places
generally. Indeed the whole world was full of idols at that time;
the pure worship of God existed nowhere; and in fact there were
countless monstrous superstitions everywhere. But Satan had bewitched Athens more than other cities, so that the men were driven
with greater madness to their impious and perverted rites. And this
is an example that is worth noting, that the city, which was the abode
and seat of wisdom, the fount of all the arts, the mother of humanity,
surpassed all the others in blindness and madness. We know how intelligent and learned men were unanimous in praising and honouring
it. And she herself flattered herself to the extent that she considered
all, whom she had not refined, barbarians. But the Holy Spirit,
convicting the whole world of ignorance and stupidity, says that all
the teachers of liberal science were spell-bound by an unusual madness; and from that we gather what use human shrewdness is in the

things of God. And there is no doubt that God allowed the Athenians to fall into extreme folly, so that they might be a warning to all generations that all the acuteness of the human mind, aided by learning and teaching, is nothing but foolishness, when it comes to the Kingdom of God. Undoubtedly they had their pretexts, to excuse their fictitious cults, no matter how preposterous and corrupt they were. And yet it is certain not only that they were toying with childish and frivolous trifles, but also that they were deceived by gross and filthy illusions, in a shameful manner just as if they were deprived of common sense, and were absolutely stupid and unreasonable. But just as we know what sort of religion springs from the human understanding, and that human wisdom is nothing else but a factory of all the errors, so let us realize that the Athenians, being intoxicated by their own pride, wandered from the truth more shamefully than the rest. The antiquity, amenity, and beauty of the city went to their heads, so that they boasted that the gods sprang from it. Therefore when they dragged God out of heaven, to make Him belong to their city, it was only right for them to be plunged into the lowest depths. Be that as it may, the vanity of human wisdom is here branded by the Spirit with eternal dishonour, because in the place it had its chief seat, there darkness was thicker, idolatry was most rampant, and Satan had more freedom to drive the minds of men in circles with his capers.

Now let us turn to Paul. Luke says that when he saw the city so devoted to idolatry, his spirit was incensed. In saying so he does not attribute simple indignation to him, and does not merely say that he was offended by such a spectacle, but he is describing the unusual heat of righteous and holy anger, which whetted his zeal, so that he prepared himself more fervently for the work.

Now two things must be observed here. For when Paul grew hot at the sight of the impious profanation of the name of God, and the corruption of His pure worship, he made it plain in that way that nothing was more precious to him than the glory of God. And this zeal ought to have been more lively among us, as, for example, it is described in Ps. 69.9, 'The zeal of thine house hath eaten me up'. For it is a common rule of all the godly that, as often as they see infamy directed against their heavenly Father, they are violently disturbed; just as Peter teaches that the godly man, Lot, tormented his soul because he could not correct the most abominable enormities (II Pet. 2.8). But teachers must be more inflamed than others, as Paul says that he himself is jealous to preserve the Church in pure chastity (II Cor 11.2). Indeed those who are not affected by the abuses of God, and not only unconcernedly pretend that they are not abuses at all, but also ignore them completely, do not deserve to be reckoned among

His sons, for they do not even give Him as much honour as they do to an earthly father.

In the second place we must note that he was not so inflamed that he gave in, broken by despair after the manner of a great many of whom we are aware; for, if they ever see the glory of God impiously violated, they are so far from becoming heated, that, while making a show of sorrow and grief, they nevertheless become profane along with the rest, rather than attempt to correct them. At the same time they make the plausible excuse for their inactivity, that they are not willing to cause a disturbance for no result. For they think that their efforts will have no effect, if they struggle against the violent conspiracy of the people. Certainly not only does Paul not become broken by weariness, or succumb to difficulty, so that he gives up the task of teaching, but he is driven by a sharper goad to defend the faith.

17. *With the Jews and the devout persons.* Wherever the Jews had synagogues it was Paul's normal practice to make a beginning in them, and offer Christ to his own nation. After that the next step was to Gentiles, who had experienced the teaching of the Law, and, although they were not yet properly imbued with true godliness, were nevertheless worshipping the God of Israel, and, being eager to learn, did not reject the things that they knew to be taken from Moses and the prophets. But because such docility was an entrance to faith, and indeed, a kind of beginning of faith, the Spirit thought worthy of a title of honour those, who, with but a slight smattering of first principles, had drawn nearer to the true God, for they are called *devout* (*religiosi*). But let us remember that they are distinguished from others by this mark, so that the whole of the world's religion might be reduced to nothing. Those who gave their allegiance to the God of Israel are specifically[1] called 'worshippers of God'; religion is attributed only to them. Therefore there is nothing left for the rest except the ignominy of atheism, no matter how anxiously they torture themselves in superstitions. And that is justified, for whatever splendour idolaters may boast of, if their inner attitude is examined, nothing will be found there except a horrible contempt of God, and it will be clear that their pretence of fawning upon idols is merely an excuse.

18. *Debated with him.* Luke now adds that Paul had a contest with the philosophers; not that he approached them deliberately, since he knew that they were born only for disputes and sophistries, but he was dragged into such a conflict against his will and judgment; just as Paul himself orders godly teachers to be equipped with spiritual arms, with which they may bravely defend the truth if any enemies set themselves in opposition (Titus 1.9). For it is not always in our

[1] C R., *specialiter*. Tholuck reads *spiritualiter*. French: 'specialement'. Tr.

control to choose with whom we are to deal, but the Lord often allows inflexible and persistent men to arise, in order to vex us, and so that the truth may stand in a clearer light through their contradiction. And there is no doubt that the Epicureans, in accordance with their customary impudence, annoyed the holy man; also that the Stoics, relying on their subtle and fallacious arguments stubbornly insulted him. Yet the outcome will show that he did not dispute sophistically, and that he was not dragged into useless contentions about words (λογομαχίας), but preserved the moderation which he enjoins elsewhere. And generally we must so act, that by refuting futile and subtle arguments in a moderate and dignified way, we may bring out the truth, and we must always avoid the danger that ambition, or eagerness to show off our talents, may involve us in unnecessary and worldly controversies.

Moreover Luke mentions two schools, which, although they were diametrically opposed to each other, yet laboured under opposite faults. The *Epicureans* not only used to despise good and liberal arts, but openly hated them. Their philosophy was to think that the sun is two feet wide, that the world was constructed out of atoms, and, by trifling like that, to destroy the wonderful craftsmanship that is seen in the fabric of the world. If they were refuted a hundred times, they had no more sense of shame than dogs. Although, briefly, they admitted that there were gods, yet they imagined them to be idle in heaven, and to be devoting themselves to living on a magnificent scale, and that their blessing consisted in idleness alone. As they used to deny that the world was divinely created, as I have just said, so they supposed that human affairs are turned by chance, and are not governed by the providence of heaven. To them the greatest good was pleasure, not obscene and unbridled pleasure indeed, but yet such as by its attractions more and more ruined men already naturally inclined to the indulgence of the flesh. The immortality of souls was like a fairytale to them, so that the result was that they freely allowed the indulgence of their bodies.

Although the *Stoics* said that the world is under the providence of God, yet they later spoiled that principle of their teaching with an absurd fiction or rather fantasy. For they did not acknowledge that God rules the world by His purpose, justice and power, but they constructed a labyrinth out of a complicated system (*complexu*) of causes, so that God Himself was bound by the necessity of fate, and was violently swept along with the heavenly machine, just as the poets bind their Jupiter with golden fetters, because the fates govern, while he is doing something else. Although they placed the highest good in virtue, they did not grasp what true virtue was. And they inflated men with proud confidence so that they adorned themselves with the things they stripped off God. For although the grace of the Holy Spirit was made powerless by all, yet the boasting of no school was haughtier. Courage to them was nothing else but hard-hearted cruelty. Paul therefore was possessed of the wonderful vigour of the Spirit, when, surrounded by such beasts, who tried to pull him this way and that, he stood firm in the genuine sincerity of the Gospel; and, holding his ground, withstood the dog-like impudence of the first school, as well as the pride and cunning sophistries of the second. Finally, we see still more clearly from this how ill the sagacity of the flesh agrees with the wisdom of the Spirit. For although the whole crowd was hostile to the Gospel, yet the philosophers were the leaders and standard-bearers in the fight against it. For there was particularly evident in them what Paul himself asserts about the wisdom of the flesh, that it is hostile to the cross of Christ (I Cor. 1.21), so that no one can be fit to learn the first principles of the Gospel, except the man who has first renounced that wisdom.

Others said. Luke places two kinds of men before us; both are indeed far removed from godliness, yet one of them is far worse than the other. Take those who once more desire to hear what they call 'something new'. In the first place they are not moved by a proper desire to learn, but by empty curiosity. Secondly they do not feel enough respect for the Word of God, for they treat it just like a profane novelty. Yet because they do listen, and are indeed open-minded until they would find out more about the matter, they are not absolutely hopeless. The others, however, by proudly rejecting what is offered, and, what is more, by insolently condemning it, close the gate of salvation for themselves. For the insult, 'What does this charlatan[1] mean?' bursts out from prodigious pride, because they think that Paul does not deserve a hearing, and insolently repudiate him, as if he were any ordinary babbler. In addition they do not shrink from his teaching from thoughtless zeal, but openly spurn what is brought to them about religion, although it is still unknown to them, because they are men who had previously boasted that they were the teachers of the whole world, and are ashamed to learn anything from an obscure man.

A setter forth of strange gods (daemoniorum). They do not use demons *(daemonia)* in a bad sense, as Scripture usually does, but for lesser gods, or genii, whom they thought of as being mediators *(medios)* between the most high God and men. Plato makes much and repeated mention of them. As far as the substance of the matter is concerned, we must note that the things Paul had said about Christ and the resurrection

---

[1] Adopting the apposite N.E.B. translation of σπερμολόγος which Calvin has transliterated. Tr.

seem to them to be new gods (*daemonia*). From that we gather that our faith is chiefly distinguished from the superstitions of the Gentiles by these features, that it sets forth Christ as the one Mediator; that it teaches that salvation must be sought from Him alone; that it bids us seek the expiation, by which we may be reconciled to God, in His death; that it teaches that men, who had previously been unclean and in the grip of sin, are restored and renewed by His Spirit, to begin to live righteous and holy lives; lastly, that, from such beginnings, which make it clear that the Kingdom of God is spiritual, it finally lifts our minds to the hope of the future resurrection. For even if the philosophers had not dealt properly with other matters, yet they do make some mention of them. Yes, and what is more, they have a lot to say about eternal life and the immortality of the soul. But about faith, which reveals the gracious reconciliation in Christ, and regeneration by which the Holy Spirit restores the image of God in us, about the invocation of God and resurrection at the last, there is complete silence.

19. *They brought him to the street of Mars* (*ad Martium vicum*). Although it was a public place for administering justice, yet Luke does not mean that Paul was hauled to court to plead his case before the members of the Court of the Areopagus, but that he was led to that place where a greater throng of people was in the habit of meeting, so that a serious public debate might be held in the famous court of justice. And while we may grant that Paul was led to a judgment-seat, yet the outcome shows that he was not brought before the judges, but that he spoke freely as if before an assembly. Finally, what is added just afterwards about the nature and customs of the Athenians, makes it plain enough, that their curiosity was the reason why they gave such a hearing to Paul, why such a famous place was open to him for preaching Christ, why so many hurried there. For otherwise it would have been a capital offence to gather the people together and address them in the market-place or in a public place. But because pedlars of trifles were granted licence to speak in that place, on account of their excessive desire for novelty, Paul was given freedom, and requested, to speak about the mysteries of the faith.

21. *Spent their time on nothing else.* The two faults which Luke mentions nearly always go together. For it rarely happens that the same men who are eager for new things are not garrulous also. For what Horace says is very true, 'Avoid the inquiring man, for he is also a prattler'. And surely we see that curious men are like leaking barrels. Furthermore both faults were born of idleness, not only because the philosophers spent the whole of their days in arguing, but because the common people themselves were far too ready for new things; and in

that city there was not a workman so menial that he did not take it upon himself to set the affairs of Greece in order. And certainly nearly all the Greek and Latin writers are unanimous in confirming what Luke says here, that there were none more passionately eager, or more fickle, or more forward than that people. That is why a settled government could never be established in that city, despite the fact that it was the mistress of all the sciences. Therefore though they gained the peak of political power (*in summa potentia*), nevertheless they did not have independence for long; and they were continually involved in trouble and confusion until they destroyed themselves and the whole of Greece. Even when the state collapsed, they did not give up their audacity. Therefore Cicero laughs at their foolishness, because in his day they were issuing their decrees just as insolently as when they were masters of the realm of Greece. Now even if there was slender hope of success among curious men, yet Paul did not neglect the opportunity, if perhaps he could win some, out of a great crowd, for Christ. And indeed it was no ordinary glory that belonged to the Gospel, in the most famous place in the city, and, as it were, in a public theatre, to rebut and openly prove to be wrong all the fictitious cults, which had held sway in that place to that very day.

And Paul stood in the midst of the Areopagus, and said, Ye men of Athens, in all things I perceive that ye are somewhat superstitious. For as I passed along, and observed the objects of your worship, I found also an altar with this inscription, TO AN UNKNOWN GOD. What therefore ye worship in ignorance, this set I forth unto you. The God that made the world and all things therein, he, being Lord of heaven and earth, dwelleth not in temples made with hands; neither is he served[1] by men's hands, as though he needed anything, seeing he himself giveth to all life, and breath, and[2] all things. (22-25)

22. *Ye men of Athens.* One may divide this speech of Paul's into five parts. For although Luke only briefly mentions the things that Paul discussed at length, yet I have no doubt that he included the substance, so that he omitted none of the main points. First Paul charges the Athenians with superstition because their worship of their own gods is a haphazard affair. Secondly he shows by arguments from nature who God is, what He is like, and how He is to be worshipped properly. In the third place he inveighs against the stupidity of men, who, although they were created for the purpose of knowing their Maker and Creator yet wander about in the darkness like blind men. In the fourth place he warns that there is nothing more absurd than making

---

[1] Calvin reads with AV and RV margin, *worshipped.* Tr.
[2] Calvin reads, *through all things.* Tr.

statues or pictures of God, since the mind of man is the true image of Him. Finally, in the fifth place, he passes on to Christ and the resurrection of the dead. For it was worth while dealing with those four points in a general way, before he came down to the faith of the Gospel.

As it were, rather superstitious. δεισιδαιμονία is often used in a good sense in Greek. However it sometimes means the excessive fear with which superstitious men anxiously torment themselves, when they make up empty scruples for themselves. But the meaning here in this verse seems to be that the Athenians go to extremes in the worship of God, or that they do not grasp how beneficial moderation would be; as if he said that they do not use their heads about what they are doing, because they are tiring themselves out by taking indirect and roundabout ways. So much for the word!

This is what we must grasp about the subject-matter. He proves that all the cults of the Athenians are corrupt on the single ground that, being uncertain what gods they ought to worship, they take up various rites haphazardly and at random, and indeed without any limits. For the fact that they had set up an altar to unknown gods (*ignotis diis*) was a sign that they had no certainty at all. Certainly they used to have a huge host of gods, about whom they told many tales, but when they mix up unknown gods with them they are admitting by this very fact that they have learnt nothing about the true God. Moreover whoever worships God without any certitude is merely worshipping his own fabrications in the place of God. No matter how pleased credulous men are with themselves, yet no religion is either pleasing to God or ought to be regarded as holy and legitimate if it lacks knowledge and truth. No indeed, and however much they boast, yet because they continue to be perplexed in their consciences, they are bound to be held convicted by their own judgment of themselves. For superstition is always in an agitated state, and continually turning out something new. Therefore, we see how wretched is the lot of those who do not possess the certain light of the truth, because they are always restless in themselves, and labour in vain in the sight of God. Yet we must note that, so long as unbelievers now blind themselves with self-willed stubbornness, and now are swept into the midst of a great many different uncertainties,[1] they are fighting against themselves. They are often not only deceiving themselves,[2] but, if anyone dares to whisper against their absurdities, they turn on him savagely. In this way the devil bewitches them so that they think that there is nothing better than what is pleasing to themselves. At

---

[1] *aestus.* French: 'doubts and disturbances of conscience'. Tr.

[2] *sibi delicias faciunt.* French: 'make believe that they are doing well, and get satisfaction out of it'. Tr.

the same time if any scruple is put in the way, if any impostor arises, if any new and crazy thing comes on the scene, not only do they swither in doubt, but they are quite willing to offer themselves to be swept this way and that. That makes it plain that they do not acquiesce, either with judgment or a calm state of mind, in the usual custom of worshipping God, but are as stupid as drunkards. But anxiety, which does not allow unbelievers to plume their feathers, is more tolerable than such stupidity. Finally, although superstition is not always full of fear, yet, entangled with a variety of errors as it is, it disturbs minds and harasses them with the tortures of uncertainty. That was why it came about that the Athenians mixed up unknown gods with their own domestic gods, who, they thought, were known to themselves, because they had formed them out of their own imagination. For their restlessness is apparent from the fact that they admit that they have not yet discharged their duty, when they have sacrificed to the popular gods, who had been handed down to them by their ancestors, and whom they called patrons (*indigetas*) and native deities. Therefore in order to destroy all the false opinions that were implanted in their minds, Paul takes it as axiomatic, that they do not know what they are worshipping, and do not have any definite deity. For if they had known any god at all, they would have been content with him and never been reduced to 'unknown gods'; since the knowledge of the true God is indeed sufficient in itself for the destruction of all idols.

23. *To the unknown God.* I readily admit that this altar was dedicated to all foreign gods, but I do not agree with what Jerome says, that Paul, by sanctified trickery, ascribed to the one God what had been written about many gods. For since the inscription was a common one everywhere, there was surely no cause for cunning. Why then did he change the plural? Certainly not in order to deceive the Athenians, but, because the situation so demanded, he said that he was bringing teaching about a particular, unknown God. But after his introductory remarks that they were mistaken because they did not know what God should be worshipped, and they did not have any definite deity among the great host of gods, he now introduces himself, and procures good-will for his teaching, because it was unfair to despise and reject what was being publicly presented about the new God, to whom they already gave their devotion, and because it would be far better to have knowledge of Him rather than worship Him blindly (*temere*). In this way Paul once again returns to that principle that God cannot be worshipped in a proper and devout manner until He has been made known.

But here the question can be asked, 'How does he say that God was worshipped at Athens, the God who rejects all cults different from what His Law lays down, and also makes it known that whatever men invent without His Word is idolatry? If God regards no worship as valid except what is agreeable to His Word, how does Paul give, to men whose silliness knew no bounds, this commendation, that they worshipped God? For in His censure of the Samaritans Christ rests on, and is content with, this one principle, that they worship God without knowledge (John 4.22); yet they used to boast that they worshipped the God of Abraham. What therefore will have to be said about the Athenians, who killed and buried the memory of the true God, and in His place substituted Jove, Mercury, Pallas and all that filthy crew?' I reply that here Paul is not praising what the Athenians had done, but takes free material for teaching from their attitude, corrupt though it was.

24. *The God that made the world.* Paul's intention is to teach what the nature of God is. Moreover, because he is dealing in debate with profane men, he takes his proof from nature itself, for he would have wasted his time in contending with them by citing scriptural proof-texts. I have said that the holy apostle's intention was to bring the Athenians to the true God. For they were convinced that there was some divinity; their perverted religion was merely requiring to be corrected. From that we conclude that the world wanders through ever-changing, roundabout ways, one should rather say, is involved in a labyrinth, as long as confused opinion about the nature of God holds sway. For the true rule of godliness is precisely this, to have a clear grasp of who the God is, whom we worship. If anyone wishes to discuss religion in general this will be the first point, that there is some deity to whom worship is due from men. But because there was no dispute about that, Paul passes on to the second point, that the true God ought to be distinguished from all fabrications. So he makes a beginning with a definition of God, so that he may prove from that how He ought to be worshipped, because the one thing depends on the other. For what gave rise to such perverted cults and such great hastiness in adding to them continually, except that men[1] fashioned God for themselves according to their own opinion? But there is nothing easier than to adulterate the pure worship of God, when men measure God according to their own inclination and understanding. Accordingly there is no way better designed to destroy all corrupt cults than to begin with what the nature of God is like. In this way Christ also reasons in John 4.24, 'God is Spirit; therefore the only worshippers He approves of are those who worship Him spiritually'. And he (Paul) certainly does not deal in a subtle way with the secret

[1] Reading *homines* with C.R. for Tholuck's *omnes*. Tr.

essence of God, but shows from His works what profitable knowledge of Him is. But what conclusion does Paul come to from the fact that God is the source, Creator, and Lord of the world? It is this, that 'He does not dwell in temples made with hands'. For since it is evident from the creation of the world that the righteousness, wisdom, goodness and power of God are diffused beyond the limits of heaven and earth, it follows that He cannot be confined within any spatial localities.

Yet this demonstration seems to have been superfluous, because it was easy to object that statues and images are placed in temples to testify to the presence of God, and indeed no one was so stupid that he did not know that God fills all things. I reply that what I suggested a little earlier is true, that idolatry is self-contradictory. Unbelievers used to say that they were calling on the gods at their images, but if they had not bound the will (*numen*) and power of God (*Dei*) to the images, would they have expected help from them, or would they have directed their prayers and requests to those images? That was how it came about that one temple was more sacred than others. They used to run to Delphi, to seek for the oracles of Apollo there. Minerva used to have her seat and dwelling at Athens. Now we see that Paul's words were censuring the false opinion by which men have been nearly always deluded, because they used to conceive of a carnal God.

The first approach to proper knowledge of God is this, if we go out of ourselves and do not measure Him by our own mental capacity, and, what is more, do not form any mental pictures of Him according to our carnal understanding, but set Him above the world, and distinguish Him from created things. The whole world has always been far removed from such a sober outlook, because there is always this perversity innate in men, to spoil the glory of God with the things that they have made. For as they are carnal and earthy they wish to have one who corresponds to their own nature. Secondly, in conformity with their audacity they make Him of such a nature as they can grasp. By such fabrications the genuine and clear knowledge of God is spoiled; yes, and furthermore, as Paul says, 'His truth is turned into a lie' (Rom. 1.25). For the man who does not ascend above the world grasps empty shadows and appearances instead of God. Moreover unless we are lifted up to heaven with the wings of faith, we must necessarily die away in our own thoughts. And it is no wonder that the Gentiles were deceived by those stupid illusions, so that they dragged God off His heavenly throne, and made Him part and parcel with the elements of the world, seeing that the same thing happened to the Jews, to whom God had, nevertheless, revealed His spiritual glory. For it is not for nothing that Isaiah rebukes them because they confine Him within the walls of the temple (Isa. 66.1). And from

Stephen's speech, which Luke has reported in chapter 7 (vv. 49, 51), we gather that that fault was rampant among them in every generation. If anyone would have asked the Jews, whose denseness the Holy Spirit censures, whether they thought that God was shut up in their temple, they would have strongly denied that they were in the grip of such a stupid error. But because their minds used to rise no higher than what they saw of the temple with their eyes, and because, putting their trust in the temple, they were boasting that God was, so to speak, bound to them, the Spirit is justified in reproving them, because they tie Him to the temple just like a mortal man. For my previous statement is true that superstition is inconsistent with itself, and that it melts away into various figments of the imagination. And indeed today no other defence is available for the Papists than the one with which the Gentiles and the Jews long ago tried to camouflage or hide their errors somehow or other. In a word superstition supposes that God 'dwells in temples made with hands'. It is not that it intends to hold Him captive as if in penitentiaries, but, because dreaming of a carnal God, they link the divine power (*numen*) to idols, and transfer the glory of God to outward forms.

But yet, if God 'does not dwell in temples made with hands' why has God testified in so many passages of Scripture that He sits amid the cherubim, and that the temple is His eternal resting-place (II Kings 19.15; Ps. 80.1; 132.14)? I reply that as He was not tied to one place, so the last thing He intended was to tie down His people to earthly symbols. On the contrary He comes down to them, in order to lift them up on high to Himself. Accordingly the temple and the ark were so sadly abused by men, who were so possessed by respect for those things, that they remained earthbound, and departed from the spiritual worship of God. We see from this that there was a great difference between the symbols of God's presence, which men thoughtlessly devised for themselves, and those which God ordained, because men always incline downwards to understand God in a carnal way, but God raises them up on high by the guidance of His Word. He merely uses symbols as intermediaries with which to introduce Himself in a familiar way to slow men, until, step by step, they ascend to heaven.

25. *Neither by men's hands.* The same question, which has just been dealt with about the temple, can now be raised about ceremonies. For it seems that what Paul condemns in the rites of the Gentiles can be made to apply to the cults of the Mosaic Law. But the answer is not difficult, that the faithful never based the worship of God strictly on ceremonies, but thought of them merely as aids, with which to discipline themselves on account of their weakness. When they sacrificed

animals, offered bread and libations, lit lamps, they knew that piety did not depend on those things, but, while being assisted by such rudiments, they always had regard to the spiritual worship of God, and considered that alone as of value. And God clearly proclaims in many passages that He has no time for anything external or visible, that ceremonies in themselves must be regarded as of no importance, and that the only way He is worshipped is by faith, a pure conscience, prayers and gratitude. What then of the Gentiles? Of course when they erected statues, burnt incense, performed plays, and spread their couches for idols, they thought that they discharged the duties of piety very well. Indeed not only the philosophers, but also the poets, sometimes jeer at the absurdities of the common people, because they wrongly make the worship of God consist in the ostentation and splendour of ceremonies. While I pass over countless testimonies, this one of Persius' is well known (*Sat.* II. 69ff).

'Tell me, high priests, what is the value of gold in the temples? Obviously, it is just as much use as the dolls a virgin gives to Venus. Why do we not give to the gods what the half-blind breed of the great Messalla could not give out of their vast charger, well-ordered justice and fair-mindedness, sacred secrets of the soul, and a breast filled with the virtue of generosity? These I am going to bring to the temples, and the grain I offer will be accepted.'[1]

There is no doubt that God uttered these words by profane men so that the words might remove the pretext of ignorance. But it is quite clear that those who spoke in that way fell back immediately into the general folly; and, furthermore, that what this meant for themselves never penetrated into their minds. For even if those, who are far more discerning than the common people, are forced to admit that bare ceremonies are valueless, yet they are never shaken in this conviction, but persuade themselves that these are a part of divine worship. Accordingly they are quite sure that, the more diligently they devote themselves to such shows, they are properly discharging the duties of piety. Therefore because all mortals, from the highest to the lowest, suppose that God is appeased with ceremonies and other external things, and wish to discharge their obligations towards Him with their own works, Paul refutes that. A reason is also added, that since He is Lord of heaven and earth, there is nothing that He needs; that since He bestows life and breath on men, He, in turn, can receive nothing from them. For what may men bring of their own, when they lack all good things, and have nothing except from His gracious kindness;

[1] The French version is quoted in C.R., and has been used in this translation along with the Latin. Tr.

yes, and who are nothing, except by His sheer grace, for they must soon be reduced to nothing, if He withdraws the Spirit by whom they live? From that it follows that they are not only thoughtless, but too proud, if they bring themselves to worship God with the works of their own hands. For his statement that alms and loving services are sweet-smelling sacrifices (cf. Phil. 4.18) ought to be distinguished from the present situation, where it is merely a question of ceremonies, which unbelievers plead by way of excuse for the spiritual worship of God.

By *life and breath* is meant the life depending on what men call the breath or air.[1]

In regard to the last phrase of the sentence, even if some present-day Greek manuscripts agree on this reading κατὰ πάντα, that is, 'through all things', yet it seems to me that the translation of the Vulgate is more appropriate, καὶ τὰ πάντα, 'and all things', because it is both clearer, and contains a richer doctrine; for it is easier to gather from that, that men have nothing of their own. And certain Greek copies also agree.

> *And he made of one[2] every nation of men for to dwell on all the face of the earth, having determined their appointed[3] seasons, and the bounds of their habitation; that they should seek God, if haply they might feel after him and find him, though he is not far from each one of us: for in him we live, and move, and have our being; as certain even of your own poets have said, For we are also his offspring. Being then the offspring of God, we ought not to think that the Godhead is like unto gold, or silver, or stone, graven by art and device of man. (26-29)*

26. *And he made of one blood.* Paul now warns the Athenians of the purpose for which the human race was created, so that in this way he may invite and encourage them to consider the purpose of their own life. It is certainly shameful ingratitude on the part of men, when all enjoy a common life, not to consider why God has given them life. But yet this brute-like stupidity has the majority in its grip, so that they do not reflect upon why they are placed in the world, and they do not give a thought to the Creator of heaven and earth, with whose good things they gorge themselves. Therefore, after Paul has discussed the nature of God, he opportunely introduces this admonition, that men ought to give careful consideration to the knowledge of God, because it was for this reason that they were made, and they were born for this end. For, briefly, he assigns to them this reason for living, to seek for

---

[1] *vita spiritualis vel animalis* with Tholuck, whose *spiritualis* is preferable to C.R.'s *spirabilis*. Tr.

[2] Calvin, with RV margin, has *one blood*. Tr.

[3] Calvin, with RV margin, has *before-appointed*. See p. 118. Tr.

God. Moreover, because a single religion was not flourishing in the world, but the nations were divided into various sects, he suggests that that variety is born of corruption. For in my opinion that is the import of his statement that 'all were created *of one blood*'. For blood-relationship and the same origin of birth ought to have been a bond of mutual agreement among them; but yet religion is the thing which most unites men or separates them. And from that it follows that those, who are so at variance in religion and the worship of God, have deviated from nature. Because from whatever place they have sprung, or whatever region of the world they inhabit, yet there is one Creator and Father of all, who must be sought by all with common consent. And certainly neither the distance between places, nor territorial boundaries, nor diversity of customs, nor any cause of separation among men, makes the slightest difference to God Himself. In a word, he wished to teach that the order of nature was violated when religion was torn to pieces among them, and that the dispersion, which is to be seen among themselves, is evidence of the overthrow of godliness, because they have broken loose from God, the common Father, from whom all blood-relationship is derived.

To dwell. In accordance with his custom Luke gives a summary of the substance of Paul's speech. But there is no doubt that Paul first of all showed that men are placed here, as in a theatre, to be spectators of the works of God, that he then spoke about the providence of God, that reveals itself in the whole government of the world. For when he says that God 'determines their previously-appointed seasons and the bounds of their habitation', he means that this world is ruled by His hand and purpose, and, on the other hand, that human affairs are not turned by chance, as profane men fondly suppose. And so we gather from Luke's few words that Paul embraced the most momentous subjects. For when he says that the seasons had been previously ordained by Him, he testifies that, before men were brought into existence, He determined what their future circumstances would be like. When we see various changes happening in the world, when the downfall of kingdoms, the alteration of territories, the destruction of cities, the overthrowing of nations occur, we foolishly imagine that either fate or fortune is in control of these events. But in this verse God testifies through Paul's lips that it was previously fixed by His purpose how long He wished each people to continue in existence, and by what boundaries He intended each one to be contained. But if He appointed a certain time for them, and fixed the boundaries of their territories, there is no doubt that He disposed the whole course of their life.

But it must be noted that Paul does not merely attribute to God bare

foreknowledge and cold speculation, as very many do in their ignorance, but he bases the course of the things that happen on His
purpose and will. For he does not say simply that the times were
foreseen but προτεταγμένα,[1] 'previously appointed', that is, disposed
with the order that seemed good to Him. But when he adds at the
same time that God set bounds from the beginning to the things that
He had previously ordained, the meaning is that by the power of His
hand He accomplishes the things that He decreed by His purpose, in
accordance with that word, 'Our God is in the heaven; He has done
everything that He intended' (Ps. 115.3). We now see that just as
there are in a camp, separate lines for each platoon and section, so
men are placed on the earth, so that each nation may be content with
its own boundaries, and that each man may live in his own dwelling-
house among his own people. Finally, although ambition has been
repeatedly rampant, and many, burning with a depraved greed, have
crossed over their own boundaries, yet the wilfulness of men has never
had the effect that God did not direct all events from His secret sanctuary. For even if by raising a tumult on the earth men seem to be
attacking heaven, in order to overthrow the providence of God, yet
they are being forced, whether they like it or not, rather to establish
it. Therefore let us realize that the world is turned through different
cycles of upheavals, so that God may at last restore everything to the
purpose that He has appointed.

27. *That they should seek God.* This sentence has two parts; viz. that
it is man's duty to seek God, and, secondly, that God Himself comes
to meet us, and makes Himself conspicuous by such clear signs, that
there is no excuse for our ignorance. Therefore let us remember that
all those who do not bend their energies to seeking God, are gravely
abusing this life, and do not deserve to dwell on the earth; as if the
separate kinds of brute beasts revolted from the inclination given them
by nature, and that would quite rightly be considered monstrous.
And there is certainly nothing more absurd than for men to be ignorant of their Creator, when they have been endowed with intelligence to be exercised most of all in this way. Indeed we must take
particular note of the goodness of God in that He makes Himself
known in such an intimate way that He can also be felt by the blind.
Accordingly the blindness of men is all the more shameful and intolerable, when, confronted by such a clear and obvious manifestation,
they are not moved by an awareness of the presence of God. Wherever
they turn their eyes, upwards or downwards, they are bound to fall
on living, and indeed countless, reminders (*imagines*) of God's power,

[1] The Greek is προστεταγμένους καιρὸυς i.e. 'appointed'. Calvin's text is *prae-
stituta tempora.* Tr.

wisdom, and goodness. For God has not given obscure hints of His glory in the handiwork of the world, but has engraved such plain marks everywhere, that they can be known also by touch by the blind. From that we gather that men are not only blind but stupid, when they are helped by such very clear proofs, but derive no benefit from them.

However this question arises, whether men can reach a genuine and clear knowledge of God by nature. For Paul means that it is only due to their own sloth that they do not feel the presence of God, because, even if they close their eyes, yet He Himself is, as it were, palpable. I reply that such perverseness is mingled with their ignorance and stupidity that, devoid of proper judgment, and with no true understanding, they disregard all the signs of the glory of God that plainly shine out in heaven and on earth. Yes, and since true knowledge of God is a special gift of His, and faith, by which He is properly known, proceeds only from the illumination of the Spirit, it follows that with nature alone as guide our minds cannot penetrate to Him (*illuc*). And of course Paul is not speaking here about the ability of men, but he is only warning that they are inexcusable, when they are blind in such a clear light; as he says in the first chapter of Romans (v. 20). Therefore, although the senses of men fail in the search after God, yet they have no excuse for their own failure, because, although He shows that He is to be felt after, they nevertheless remain in a state of stupor. I have said more about this matter in chapter 14 (v. 17).

Although he is not far from. In order to put a greater check on the perversity of men, He denies that God is to be sought by long roundabout ways, or a wearisome journey, because every man will find Him in himself, if only he is willing to pay attention. From that experience we are clearly shown that our dullness is not devoid of blame, even although we did contract it from the fall of Adam. For although there is no corner of the world without some evidence of the glory of God, yet there is no need to go outside ourselves to lay hold of Him. For He so influences every single one of us by His power within, that our stupidity is like a monster, because while feeling Him we do not feel Him. Certain of the philosophers called man a microcosm (μικρόκοσμος), because, above all the other creatures, he is a proof of the glory of God, full of countless miracles as he is.

28. *For in him.* I grant that the apostles, according to the Hebrew idiom, often use the preposition *in* instead of *per*, 'by'; but because the expression 'we live in God' is more emphatic and more expressive, I did not see fit to change it. For I have no doubt that Paul means that we are in some way contained in God, because He dwells in us by His power. And therefore God Himself distinguishes Himself from all

creatures so that we may realize that strictly speaking He alone is, and that we truly subsist in Him, seeing that He quickens and sustains us by His Spirit. For the power of the Spirit is diffused through all parts of the world, to keep them in their place; and to supply the energy to heaven and earth which we see, and also movement to living creatures. This does not mean the way that crazy men talk nonsense about all things being full of gods, and even the very stones being gods, but that by the wonderful activity and instigation of His Spirit God preserves all that He has created out of nothing. But here particular mention is made of men, because Paul has said that they have not to go far to look for God, when they have Him within.

Moreover since the life of men is far superior to movement, and movement surpasses existence, Paul has put the most important thing in the highest place, so as to pass down, step by step, to *being*; in this sense, 'Not only is there no *life* for us except in God, but there is not even *movement*, no, and what is more, there is no *being*, which is an inferior thing to both of them.' I say that life is superior in men, because not only do they have sensation and movement in common with the brute beasts, but they are endowed with reason and intelligence. Accordingly Scripture justifiably honours that unique gift, with which God has distinguished us, with a separate description of its own. So in John, when mention is made of the creation of all things, there is added separately and not without good reason, that 'the life was the light of men' (John 1.4).

Now we see that all who do not know God do not know themselves; because they have God present not only in the extraordinary gifts of their minds, but in their very being; because existence belongs only to God, all other things subsist in Him. This verse also teaches that the world was not created by God once, in such a way that afterwards He abandoned His work, but that it endures by His power, and that the same One who was once its Creator is its perpetual ruler. We must properly be meditating upon this constant quickening, so that God may come into our thoughts every single moment.

Certain of your own poets. He quotes a half-verse from Aratus, not so much for the sake of an authority, as to make the Athenians ashamed, for such sentences of the poets flowed from no other fountain than nature and universal reason. And it is indeed no wonder that Paul, who was speaking to men who were unbelievers and ignorant of true godliness, uses the testimony of a poet, in which there appeared the confession of that knowledge, which nature has put into human minds and engraved upon them. The method of the Papists is far different. For they are so dependent on the testimonies of men that they place them over against the oracles of God, and not only do they consider Jerome, or Ambrose and the rest of the holy Fathers teachers of the faith, but they wish to bind us by the rotten opinions of their Popes, just as if God had spoken. Yes, and what is more, they have not been afraid to give so much authority to Aristotle that, compared with him, the apostles and prophets were silent in the schools.

Now, to return to the present sentence there is no doubt that Aratus spoke about Jupiter; and yet when Paul adapts his clumsy statement about his Jupiter to the true God, he does not twist it into another meaning. For since men are imbued by nature with some knowledge of God, they draw true principles from that source. But despite the fact that as soon as thought of God steals upon their minds, they are soon in the midst of improper fabrications and die away, and so the pure seed degenerates into corruptions, yet the first general knowledge of God remains in them for a time. In this way nobody of sound mind may hesitate to transfer to the true God what Virgil holds about the fictitious Jupiter, that 'all things are full of Jupiter' (*Eclog*. III.60). One should rather say that, when Virgil wished to give expression to the power of God, he substituted the wrong name in error.

As far as the meaning of the words is concerned, it may be that Aratus imagined that some particle of divinity is in the minds of men, in the way that the Manichees fashioned souls out of something transferred from God (*ex Dei traduce*). So when Virgil says of the world, 'A spirit sustains within, and a mind, diffused through all the limbs, moves the mass' (*Aeneid* 6.726), he is philosophizing in the manner of Plato, rather than simply meaning that the world is sustained by the secret inspiration of God. But this fiction should not have prevented Paul from maintaining the true principle, corrupted though it was by men's fables, that men are *the off-spring of God*, because they reproduce something divine in the superiority of their nature. This is what Scripture teaches, that we are created in the image and likeness of God (Gen. 1.27). Certainly the same Scripture teaches in many places that we are made the sons of God by faith and gracious adoption, when we are engrafted into the Body of Christ, and having been reborn by the Spirit, we begin to be new creatures. But just as it gives various names to the Spirit Himself on account of His numerous graces, so it is no wonder that the word 'sons' is taken in different ways. All mortal men, without distinction, are called 'sons', because they resemble God in mind and intelligence, but since the image of God is almost obliterated in them, so that scarcely the faint outlines of it appear, this name is properly restricted to believers, who, having been endowed with the Spirit of adoption, reproduce the heavenly Father in the light of reason, righteousness and holiness.

29. *Therefore since we are the offspring.* He concludes that God cannot

be represented by a picture or sculpture, since He has intended His likeness to appear in us. For the soul, on which the image of God is properly engraved, cannot be painted; therefore it is all the more absurd to wish to paint God. Now we see how much harm is done to God by all those who make up a physical shape for God, seeing that the soul of man, which scarcely reproduces a tiny spark of the immense glory of God, does not permit anything of the sort.

Moreover, since it is certain that Paul is inveighing here against the common superstition of all the Gentiles, because they wished to worship God under corporeal figures, the general doctrine must be held that God is worshipped wrongly and irreverently, and His truth is turned into a lie as often as His majesty is represented by some visible form, as the same Paul teaches in the first chapter of Romans (v. 25). And even if the idolaters of all ages did not lack their excuses, yet it was not for nothing that the prophets always made the objection to them that Paul is now making, that God is made like wood and stone, or gold, when an image is made to Him out of dead and corruptible matter. The Gentiles used images so that, on account of their ignorance, they might better imagine God to be near them. But since God is by an immense distance far and away beyond the capacity of our minds, everyone who tries to grasp Him with his mind, disfigures His glory with a perverted and deceitful imagination. Accordingly it is sinful to devise anything concerning Him by our own understanding. Secondly, and what is worse, it is well enough known that men erect statues to God for no other reason than that they conceive something carnal concerning Him, in which dishonour is inflicted upon Him.

There is also no more excuse for the Papists today. For whatever excuses they bring forward to gloss over the images with which they try to portray God, yet because they are involved in the same error as the men of old, they are pressed by the testimonies of the prophets. But it is well enough known from the books of the heathen that long ago they put forward the same excuses as those with which the Papists try to protect themselves today. Therefore the prophets do not escape the derision of certain people, as if they groundlessly charge them with being extremely stupid, no, one should rather say, as if they heap false accusations upon them, but when everything has been properly considered, those who will judge rightly will find that, whatever evasions even all the most intelligent men have snatched at, they were nevertheless possessed by this folly, that proper and acceptable worship is made to God before images.

Where, with Erasmus, I have translated *Godhead* (*numen*), Luke has put the neuter τὸ θεῖον, for 'divinity' doubtless. When Paul says that God is not like gold, or silver, or stone, and then adds, *graven by art*

and device of man, he is ruling out matter and form, and at the same
time condemning all human fabrications whatever, which do damage
to the true nature of God.

> *The times of ignorance therefore God overlooked; but now he com-*
> *mandeth men that they should all everywhere repent: inasmuch as he*
> *hath appointed a day, in the which he will judge the world in righteous-*
> *ness by the man whom he hath ordained; whereof he hath given assurance*
> *unto all men, in that he hath raised him from the dead. Now when they*
> *heard of the resurrection of the dead, some mocked; but others said, We*
> *will hear thee concerning this yet again. Thus Paul went out from*
> *among them. But certain men clave unto him, and believed: among*
> *whom also was Dionysius the Areopagite, and a woman named Damaris,*
> *and others with them.* (30-34)

30. *And indeed the times of this ignorance.* Because it is commonly
believed that something that is both accepted by long usage, and
approved by universal consent, is right, the objection could have been
made to Paul, 'Why do you now overthrow things that have been
continuously accepted in the course of so many generations right from
the beginning of the world? And whom are you going to convince
that the whole world has been deceived for so long?' Similarly there
is no kind of abomination so vile that the Papists do not believe it well
protected by this shield. Paul anticipates this question, warning that
the reason why men have wandered from the truth for so long is that
God did not stretch forth His hand from heaven to lead them back
to the way. It may appear absurd for men endowed with reason
and judgment to err so stupidly and disgracefully in a matter of the
utmost importance. But Paul means that men will go on erring
endlessly until God comes to their aid.

Now, without a doubt he assigns no other reason why He did not
bring in a remedy sooner, than His good pleasure, as men say. And
certainly since we cannot understand the reason why God suddenly
kindled the light of His teaching, when He had allowed men to wander
in darkness for four thousand years; at any rate since Scripture is
silent about it, prudence is of more value here than preposterous
wisdom. For all who do not allow God to be silent or to speak as He
alone decides, are striving to reduce God to order, a thing that is intolerable in the extreme and contradictory to nature itself. Secondly
those who will not be content with His wisdom and secret purpose
are bound to raise their voices against Paul, who plainly teaches that
ignorance was rampant in the world, as long as it pleased God to take
no notice of it. Others have a different explanation, that God spared
ignorance, as if He were unwilling to punish it, and connived at it.

But such a fabrication is absolutely alien to Paul's thought and purpose, for his intention was not to lessen men's blame, but to magnify the grace of God, which had dawned unexpectedly. And it is shown to be false from other passages, because 'those who have sinned without the Law will notwithstanding perish without the Law' (Rom. 2.12). In short Paul's words mean nothing else to him than that men were given up to blindness until God revealed Himself to them; and that we are not to be too bold and inquisitive in probing into the reason why He did not scatter the darkness sooner, but whatever seemed good to Him ought to appear right and proper to us, without any question. For even if it is a harsh statement that men were miserably deceived for many generations by God's ignoring them (*dissimulante*), yet we ought to rest on His providence. But if ever there steals upon us the useless and perverse desire to know more than is allowable, let there immediately come to mind what Paul teaches in many passages, that the mystery was hidden for centuries, because the light of the Gospel suddenly shone on the Gentiles (Rom. 16.25; Eph. 3.9); and that this is a proof of the manifold wisdom of God, which devours all the senses of men. In the second place let us remember that men's blame is not lessened, because God did not wish to correct their errors, seeing that their own consciences will always hold them convicted, so that they may not escape a rightful condemnation. And Paul has said that the world wandered in error with the connivance of God, not to transfer the blame to God, but to deny the opportunity for curious and harmful questions. And we learn from this how reverently and modestly we must reflect upon the providence of God, viz. that no one may dare, in view of the pride of human nature, to demand from God a reason for His actions.

Moreover this warning is just as beneficial today as it was to the men of that generation. When the Gospel has revived, its enemies regard it as a great absurdity that God allowed men to wander in error for so long under the apostasy of the Pope, as if indeed, although no reason may be apparent, it has not been legitimate for Him to pay no attention to (*dissimulare*) the ignorance of men now, just as He did long ago. But we must pay especial attention to the purpose for which this is said, viz. that we may not be prevented by the ignorance of an earlier time from obeying God as soon as He speaks. Very many think that they have a plausible excuse for going wrong, provided that they have the fathers to support them, or they seize on the defence of long custom, yes, and what is more, they freely and eagerly snatch at this evasion so as not to obey the Word of God. But Paul denies that when God addresses us, an excuse is to be sought from the ignorance of the fathers; because even if they are not innocent in God's sight, yet our negligence is not to be tolerated, if we are blind in the full light of day, and lie deaf or asleep, while the Gospel trumpet is sounding.

Now he commands all. With these words Paul warns that we must listen to God as soon as He speaks, as it is written (Ps. 95.7), 'Today if you will hear His voice, harden not your hearts'. For there is no excuse for the obstinacy of those who let this opportunity pass, when God kindly invites them to Himself. At the same time, we gather from this verse, the purpose for which the Gospel is preached, viz. that God may gather us to Himself from the errors of our former life. Therefore as often as the voice of the Gospel sounds in our ears, let us realize that God is urging us to repent.

We must also note that he assigns the role of speaker to God, although He does it through men. For otherwise full authority, to the extent that the heavenly truth deserves, does not exist for the Gospel, except when our faith regards Him as the One directing the prophetic office, and hangs upon His words.

31. *Because he has appointed a day.* In addition he mentions the last judgment, to shake off torpor. For we know how difficult it is for men to deny themselves. Therefore violent action is needed to force them to repentance; and there can be no better way of doing that than when they are summoned to the judgment-seat of God, and that dreadful judgment is set before them, which one may not despise or escape. Therefore let us remember that the teaching of repentance flourishes only when men, who would naturally desire to delude themselves, are awakened by fear of God's judgment; and that the only proper teachers of the Gospel are those who are heralds or court officials of the supreme Judge, to bring the guilty to defend themselves, and to announce the punishment that threatens, just as if it were in their own hands. And the phrase *in righteousness*, or 'justly', is not added for nothing. For even if all men nominally acknowledge that God is a just Judge, yet we see how they usually play tricks on themselves (*quas sibi delitias faciant*),[1] for they do not allow God to exact an account beyond their own knowledge or understanding. Therefore Paul means that men gain nothing from empty flatteries, because in this way they will not prejudice the justice of God, which shows that what seems great to men is an abomination in the sight of God, because He will not follow the opinions of mortal men, but the method which He has prescribed.

By the man whom he hath ordained. There is no doubt that Paul said a good deal more about Christ, so that the Athenians might know that He is the Son of God, by whom salvation had been brought to the

---

[1] French: 'ils se flattent volontiers'. Tr.

world, and to whom all power in heaven and on earth had been given. Otherwise the speech, such as we read it here, would have been powerless to persuade. But Luke considered it sufficient to give a brief summary of the discourse. However it is likely that Paul first spoke about the grace of Christ, and proclaimed Him the Redeemer of men, before he made Him the Judge. But because Christ is often held in contempt, when He presents Himself as Redeemer, Paul now declares that one day He will avenge such impious contempt, because the whole world is to be judged by Him.

The verb ὁρίζειν can be referred to the secret purpose of God, as well as to the external manifestation. Yet because the first explanation is more customary, I gladly adopt it, namely, that by His eternal decree God has appointed His Son the Judge of the world, and He did so in order that the reprobate, who reject the sovereignty of Christ, may learn that it is useless for them to offer resistance to the inviolable decree of God.

Apart from that, because nothing is further from ordinary human understanding than that God will judge in the person of a man, Paul adds that this dignified office of Christ's, which might be difficult to believe in, was confirmed by His resurrection. Certainly the will of God alone ought to be esteemed with such reverence among us, that every single one of us may subscribe to His decrees without delay, but because the excuse of ignorance is often in the habit of being offered, Paul therefore clearly warns that by His resurrection Christ was openly shown to be the Judge of the world, and what God had previously decreed within Himself about Him, was revealed to the eyes of men. For Paul dealt at length with this fundamental principle of doctrine, which Luke briefly mentions with a few words. Not only did he briefly report that Christ rose from the dead, but at the same time he dealt with the power of the resurrection, as was proper. For why did Christ rise again, except that He might be the firstfruits of those rising again? (I Cor. 15.23). And why shall we rise again, except into life or death? From that it follows that Christ has been declared and proved the Judge of the world by His resurrection.

32. *Some mocked.* From this we see how heedless and unconcerned men are, for neither the judgment-seat of God nor the very majesty of the supreme Judge strikes them with any fear. We have certainly said that, when God's judgment is placed before the eyes of men, it is the sharpest goad for pricking their minds to fearing Him; but there is such iron hardness in despisers, that they have no hesitation about making a mockery of the statement about one day rendering an account of our lives, as if it were incredible. Yet there is no reason why the ministers of the Gospel should give up the proclaiming of

the judgment, with which they have been charged. Although the ungodly may laugh, yet this teaching, which they try to elude, will so bind them, that at last they may realize that they have struggled with their fetters in vain. And surely it is no wonder that this part of Paul's speech was scoffed at in Athens. For it is a mystery hidden from human minds, a mystery about which not an inkling ever entered the heads of even the greatest philosophers. And it can only be grasped by us when we lift up eyes of faith to the immense power of God. And yet Paul's speech was not fruitless, because there were some of the audience who desired to go further. For when they openly admit that they wish to hear him again, they mean that, although they are not yet fully convinced, they nevertheless have some taste, which makes them eager to learn more. Certainly this desire was a different thing altogether from scornful contempt (*fastidio*).

34. *Among whom also was Dionysius.* Since Luke names only one man and one woman, it appears that at the beginning the number of believers was small. For the *others*, whom he mentions, remain as it were on the fence (*medii*), because they were not rejecting Paul's teaching out of hand, but they had not been so seriously affected that they attached themselves to him as disciples. Luke names Dionysius before the others because he possessed no ordinary authority among his fellow-citizens; and in the same way it is very likely that Damaris was a woman of the first rank.

Apart from that, it is ridiculous that the Papists have made an astrologer out of a judge. But this must be put down, partly to their ignorance, partly to their presumption, for, since they did not know what the Areopagus was, they took the liberty for themselves of inventing whatever they liked. For those who ascribe to this Dionysius the books about *The Celestial* and *Ecclesiastical Hierarchies* and *The Divine Names*, are indeed extremely, crassly stupid. For *The Celestial Hierarchy* is not only stuffed full with many silly and monkish trivialities, but also abounds with many absurd fabrications, and impious speculations. On the other hand the books about *The Ecclesiastical Hierarchy* reveal that they were composed many centuries afterwards, when the purity of Christianity had now been adulterated by a mass of ceremonies. But although the book about *The Divine Names* contains certain things that must not be absolutely despised, yet it breathes subtlety rather than sound godliness.

CHAPTER EIGHTEEN

After these things he departed from Athens, and came to Corinth. And he found a certain Jew named Aquila, a man of Pontus by race, lately come from Italy, with his wife Priscilla, because Claudius had commanded all the Jews to depart from Rome: and he came unto them; and because he was of the same trade, he abode with them, and they wrought; for by their trade they were tentmakers. And he reasoned in the synagogue every sabbath, and persuaded Jews and Greeks. But when Silas and Timothy came down from Macedonia, Paul was constrained by the word,[1] testifying to the Jews that Jesus was the Christ. (1-5)

1. This story is indeed a memorable one for the single reason that it contains the beginnings of the Church in Corinth. While, on the one hand, that church was justly renowned, both on account of its great numbers of people, and on account of the extraordinary gifts with which they had been endowed, so, on the other, it was troubled by gross and disgraceful faults. Moreover Luke makes it plain here how great was the labour and how many were the dangers and difficulties by which Paul won them for Christ. It is well enough known how populous a city Corinth was, how rich it was on account of its fame as a trading-centre, and how devoted it was to pleasure. In fact the old proverb, 'It is not granted to everybody to go to Corinth', testifies that it was extravagant and full of debauchery. When Paul goes into it, what hope, I ask you, can he have in his mind? He is an unknown, little man, lacking eloquence or brilliance, making no show of wealth or power. From the fact that that huge whirlpool did not swallow up his confidence and his eagerness for spreading the Gospel, we gather that he was equipped with the extraordinary power of the Spirit of God, and at the same time that God operated through his agency in a heavenly, and in no human, fashion. Accordingly it is not for nothing that he boasts that the Corinthians are 'the seal of his apostleship' (I Cor. 9.2). For those, who do not recognize that the glory of God shone all the more clearly in such a humble and contemptible way of working, are doubly blind. And he himself gave a clear example of invincible steadfastness, when he was harassed by the mockeries of all, for to the proud he was an object of contempt, but yet relied on the help of God alone. But it is worth the trouble to note the individual circumstances, as Luke describes them in order.

[1] Calvin, with RV margin, reads *in spirit*; or, *by the Spirit*. Tr.

2. *A Jew named Aquila.* It was a severe test for Paul to find nobody at Corinth to give him hospitality except Aquila, an exile twice over. For although he was born in Pontis, he had left his native land and crossed the sea to live in Rome. Again, he had been forced to leave there by an edict of Claudius Caesar. Although, I say, the city was so commodious, its wealth was so great, its situation was so pleasant, and there were also so many Jews there, yet Paul found no more suitable host than a man, who was an exile both from his native land and a foreign country. If, with such a poor beginning, we compare the huge success that emerged as soon as he preached, the power of the Spirit of God will be made much clearer. We may also see how, by His extraordinary purpose, the Lord turns those things, which seem to the flesh, hostile and unpropitious, to His own glory and the salvation of the godly. Nothing is more wretched than exile according to the understanding of the flesh. But it was far more desirable for Aquila to become Paul's associate, than to assume all the high magistracies either at Rome or in his own country. Therefore that fortunate misfortune of Aquila's tells us that the Lord often has better regard for our welfare, when He inflicts us rather severely, than if He were to deal with us with the utmost indulgence, and when He makes us go through the hardships of exile in order to lead us to the peace of heaven.

All the Jews to depart from Rome. At that time that nation was in very bitter circumstances, so that it is a wonder that almost all of them did not give up the worship of God. But it is more wonderful that the religion, in which they had been brought up, prevailed against the tyranny of Caesar. But in fact when Christ, the Sun of Righteousness shone forth, few were turned to Him. And yet I have no doubt that the Lord deliberately allowed them to be driven this way and that through many different troubles, so that they might receive more willingly, one should rather say, more eagerly, the grace of proferred redemption. But the majority, as usually happens, were stupefied by their misfortunes; a few, like Aquila and his wife, proved themselves docile under the scourges of God. Yet if Suetonius is telling the truth, they were expelled out of hatred for the name of Christ (*Christiani nominis*). And so calamity could have irritated the majority all the more because they were falsely put in the position of guilty men, on account of the religion, to which they were hostile.

3. *They were of the same trade.* This verse informs us that before Paul came to Corinth he was accustomed to working with his hands, and he did so, not to amuse himself, but in order to make a living for himself by manual work. It is not known where he first learnt the craft; yet it is established from his own testimony that he laboured

at Corinth in particular. Indeed he gives the reason for it, that false apostles were teaching for nothing in order to worm their way in cunningly; therefore the holy man was unwilling to give way to them on that account, so that he might not bring reproach on the Gospel of Christ (I Cor. 4.12; 9.12, 15). But it is easy to gather from this verse that wherever he came to, and all the time he was busy in the unremitting labour of teaching, he practised his craft, in order to make his living from it. When Chrysostom teaches that Paul was a shoemaker he is not saying anything that is out of step with Luke, since at that time men were in the habit of making tents out of skins.

4, 5. *He reasoned in the synagogue.* It is strange where the common reading in the Latin manuscripts[1] crept in from, that 'Paul introduced the name of Christ', except that perhaps some reader wished to make good the weakness of a general sentence. For Luke clearly sets down two things here, viz. that Paul contended with the Jews, secondly, that after the arrival of Silas and Timothy he began to profess Christ more openly. But even if it is probable that he had something to say about Christ right from the start, because he could not omit the principal point of the heavenly teaching, yet that does not prevent a different method of argument having been open to him. Therefore I take πειθεῖν, that is, to *persuade*, in the sense of 'to introduce little by little'. For in my opinion Luke means that since the Jews discussed the Law coldly and half-heartedly, Paul spoke about the corrupt and ruined nature of man, about the necessity of grace, about the promised Redeemer, about the method of obtaining salvation, in order to waken them up; for that is an apt and suitable preparation for Christ. Secondly, when he adds that he was '*constrained* in the spirit' (*spiritu*) to teach that Jesus is the Christ, the meaning is that he was driven with greater vehemence to speak freely and openly of Christ. So we see that Paul did not bring everything forward at one and the same time, but that he regulated his teaching as the occasion demanded. And since that moderation is also beneficial today it is proper for faithful teachers to consider wisely where to make a start, so that an inopportune and confused argument might not impede the progress of the teaching itself. Moreover even if Paul had fervour enough, yet it is not inconsistent with that, that he was made bolder by the acquisition of fresh help, not because he took courage from respect for and confidence in his companions, but because he thought that these helpers were sent to him, as it were, from heaven.

[1] Vulg. (Clem) reads at v. 4, *Et disputabat in synagoga per omne sabbatum, interponens nomen Domini Jesu, suadebatque Judaeis et Graecis.* But see Vulg. (WW) for the variant readings of the Latin MSS. Tr.

But this *constraining* of the spirit[1] is not taken to mean a violent and, as men say, extrinsic pressure, in the way that the priestesses of Apollo (*Phoebades*) and inspired men were in the habit of being carried away with diabolical raving, but to the normal inspiration of the Spirit of God, which was vigorous in Paul, more ardour was added, so that he was driven by fresh power of God, and yet, of his own accord, followed the lead of the Spirit.

Paul's testimony that *Jesus is the Christ* I interpret in this way, that, when he had thoroughly taught the Jews about the office of the Redeemer, he made it plain, from the testimonies of Scripture, that this is He who was to be expected, because all the things that the Law and Prophets attribute to the Christ, apply appropriately to Him. Therefore he did not make a simple assertion, but, as if with the introduction of a solemn attestation, he carried his point that Jesus, the Son of Mary, is that Christ, who was to be the Mediator between God and men, in order to restore a ruined world to life.

And when they opposed themselves, and blasphemed, he shook out his raiment, and said unto them, Your blood be upon your own heads; I am clean: from henceforth I will go unto the Gentiles. And he departed thence, and went into the house of a certain man named Titus[2] Justus, one that worshipped God, whose house joined hard to the synagogue. And Crispus, the ruler of the synagogue, believed in the Lord with all his house; and many of the Corinthians hearing believed, and were baptized. And the Lord said unto Paul in the night by a vision, Be not afraid, but speak, and hold not thy peace: for I am with thee, and no man shall set on thee to harm thee: for I have much people in this city. And he dwelt there a year and six months, teaching the word of God among them. (6-11)

6. *When they contradicted.* The Jews put up with Paul, however, until he came to the clear preaching of Christ. At this point their fury, in fact, broke out. And we must note what is said, viz. that from contradiction straight away they burst out into blasphemies. For what usually happens when men allow themselves so much licence is this, that the devil gradually inflames them to greater madness. That is why we must be the more strictly on our guard so that no depraved passion may incite us to fight against the truth. In particular let that fearful judgment, with which the Holy Spirit thunders against all rebels through Paul's lips, strike terror into us. For the sign of cursing which Paul displayed by shaking out his garments was not human or private indignation, but zeal kindled by God in his heart; more than

---

[1] The majority and the best of the Greek MSS read συνείχετω τῷ λόγῳ, *was constrained by the word.* Tr.   [2] Calvin omits *Titus.* Tr.

that, God roused him to be a herald of His vengeance so that enemies
of the Word might know that they will not go unpunished for their
obstinacy. Something has been said about this sign of cursing in
chapter 13 (v. 51); and readers should make reference to it. The
point is this, that God is more gravely offended by contempt of His
Word than by any crimes; and certainly men are absolutely lost when
they tread under foot, or put far from them the one and only remedy
for all ills. Now just as rebellion against His Word is intolerable to
God, so it ought to grieve us very much. My meaning is this, that,
when the ungodly, so to speak, deliberately join battle with God, and,
as it were, arm themselves, to resist we are called to the conflict as if
by a heavenly trumpet; because there is nothing more disgraceful
than for the ungodly to scoff at God openly, indeed to the extent of
insults and blasphemies, while we do nothing.

Your blood. He announces the punishment of God to them, because
they are inexcusable. For they cannot transfer any part of the blame
to anyone else, after they have rejected God's invitation and tried to
extinguish the light of life. Therefore since they bear the blame for
their own destruction, he asserts that they will also suffer punishment.
Indeed in saying that he will be *clean*, he is testifying that he has discharged his duty. The warning which the Lord gives to all his ministers in the writings of Ezekiel (3.18) is well known, 'If you do not
warn the ungodly man to be converted, I shall require his blood at
your hand'. Therefore because it had not been Paul's fault that the
Jews did not come to their senses again, he confidently frees himself
of all guilt. But teachers are warned by these words, if they do not
wish to be guilty of blood in the sight of God, to make all the efforts
they can, to lead wanderers back to the way, and not allow anything to perish through ignorance.

I shall go to the Gentiles. No matter how teachable the Jews might
otherwise have been, Paul was nevertheless bound to devote his
labour to the teaching of the Gentiles, for whom he had been ordained
an apostle and minister. But here he refers to a transition by which
he was to remove himself completely from the obstinate Jews. For
the method of teaching for him was this, that, making a beginning
with the Jews, he might unite the Gentiles with them in the com-
munity of faith, and so from both, without distinction, form the one
body of the Church. When hope of success among the Jews was taken
away, only the Gentiles were left. Therefore the meaning is that they
must be stripped and deprived of their inheritance in order that it
might be transferred to the Gentiles, and that they are wounded in
this way, partly so that, smitten with fear, and perplexed into the
bargain, they might return to soundness of mind, partly so that

emulation of the Gentiles might stir them up to repent. But because
they are incurable, the only purpose that disgrace served was to rush
them into despair.

7. *He departed thence and went into.* Paul did not change the lodgings,
which he had with Priscilla and Aquila, because he was tired of living
with them, but in order to put himself on more intimate terms with
the Gentiles. For I suspect that this *Justus*, whom Luke mentions, was
a Gentile rather than a Jew. And the proximity of the synagogue does
not rule that out, for the Jews were dispersed, so that no definite area
of the city was allotted to them to dwell in. Moreover Paul seems to
have taken good care to choose a house close to the synagogue, in
order to spur on the Jews more readily. The description that is added
about Justus, viz. that he was a worshipper of God, confirms that
opinion. For even if sound religion did not flourish so well among
the Jews, yet because they all used to profess the worship of God, the
impression could have been given that piety commonly had a place
in the nation as a whole. But because it was a rare thing among the
Gentiles to worship God, if anyone had drawn closer to true godliness,
this remarkable testimony, which is set over against idolatry, is applied
to him. I also think that the *Corinthians*, whom Luke mentions a little
later, were Gentiles. However, so that we may not think that Paul's
work among the Jews bore no fruit at all, Luke names two of those
who believed, Crispus and Sosthenes, about whom Paul also speaks
in First Corinthians chapter 1. For in his salutation he associates
Sosthenes with himself as a colleague; and later he says that Crispus
was baptized by him (vv. 1, 14). I explain *ruler of the synagogue*, not in
the sense of one who would be in sole charge, because Sosthenes is also
honoured with the same title a little later, but as one of the chief men.

9. *And the Lord said.* Although the success of his teaching could
have justifiably encouraged Paul to be determined to carry on, since
he was winning some people for Christ every day, yet a heavenly
oracle is added to fortify him. We gather from that, that great
struggles were confronting him, and that he was severely troubled in
various ways. For the Lord never poured out His oracles haphazardly,
and it was not an everyday experience for Paul to have visions. But
the Lord used this kind of remedy, when necessity required it, and the
actual situation shows that the holy man was weighed down by a huge
mass of difficulties, under which he would not only sweat, but also
nearly faint, if he had not been encouraged and refreshed by new help.
And indeed it is not for nothing that he states that his coming was
contemptible, and that he stayed there in fear and trembling (I Cor.
2.3). Indeed my opinion is this, that the wonderful efficacy of the
Spirit, with which Paul had already been previously endowed, was

sustained by the oracle. Moreover, since Scripture distinguishes visions from dreams, as is plain from Numbers chapter 12 (v. 6), Luke means by the word *vision*, that, when Paul was transported into a trance, a definite shape (*speciem*) was presented to him, from which he recognized the presence of God. There is really no doubt that God appeared by some sign.

Be not afraid. This exhortation shows that Paul had some grounds for being afraid. For it would be superfluous to correct fear, when things were quiet and favourable, and especially in the case of a man so willing and eager. Moreover when, in order to have His servant carry out his task faithfully and strenuously, the Lord begins by checking fear, we gather from that, that nothing is more unfavourable to the pure and free preaching of the Gospel, than the perplexities of a petty spirit. And experience certainly shows that none of those, who are hindered by this fault, is a faithful and whole-hearted minister of the Word, and indeed that the only ones who are properly prepared for teaching are those, to whom it has been given to overcome any sort of danger with fortitude of mind. That is why he writes to Timothy that 'a spirit of timidity has not been given' to preachers of the Gospel, but one 'of power and love and self-control (*sobrietatis*)'. (II Tim. 1.7). Therefore we must note this connexion of the words, *Fear not but speak*, for it amounts to the same thing as if he said, 'Do not let fear keep you from speaking.' Finally, because timidity does not deprive us of speech altogether, but puts a restraint on us, so that we do not say what needs to be said, clearly and frankly, Christ mentioned both briefly, 'Speak', he says, 'and do not be silent', that is, 'Do not speak not just with half a mouth', as the common proverb goes. And, besides, in these words a general rule is prescribed for ministers of the Word, that they explain simply, and without pretence or deceit, whatever the Lord wishes to be known to His Church, yes, and that they do not conceal anything that is of value for the upbuilding or growth of faith.

10. *For I am with thee.* Here is the first reason why Paul ought to undertake his task quietly and undauntedly, with his fear subdued; he has God standing by his side. To that there corresponds David's glorious assertion, 'If I walk in the midst of the shadow of death, I shall fear no evil, because thou art with me' (Ps. 23.4); and, again, 'If tents are pitched round about me' etc. (Ps. 27.3). It is asked whether he had not also been aware of the presence of God elsewhere, as he had frequently experienced His help in various places. For the promise 'I am with you even to the consummation of the age' (Matt. 28.20), is general and enduring. And as often as we are obedient to His call, it is not right for us to doubt that He will be present with us. But it

is not unusual for the Lord to adapt what He has promised He will
do in all undertakings, to particular kinds, when the situation so
demands. And we know that, when we come to face a particular
situation, welcome help is bestowed upon us in a greater degree. In
addition these two phrases, *I am with thee*, and *Nobody will harm thee*,
are closely connected together. For it sometimes happens that God
may help us, and yet may be allowing us to appear to be overwhelmed,
just as He did not forsake Paul even when in the grip of death itself.
Here indeed He is promising the special protection of His hand, by
which he may be shielded from the attack of enemies.

But it is asked whether such confirmation was necessary for Paul,
who ought to have been willing to undergo all sorts of dangers. For
what if he might have had to die? Did that give him any right to
give way to fear? I reply, if God ever states that His servants will be
safe and unharmed for a time, that does not prevent them from
preparing themselves to meet death bravely. But just as we distinguish
between the useful and the necessary, so we must observe that if the
faithful are deprived of certain of the promises that exist, then they
must of necessity give up altogether; but that others are added as
extras, when it is expedient for that to be done, and the faith of the
godly does not collapse when they are taken away, because the grace
of God still remains firm. In this way Paul is ordered not to trouble
himself, because no enemies will touch him. Even if he had to be
overwhelmed by their violence at that time, he would not have given
way to trepidation. But God wished to increase his courage and
boldness from the fact that he was to be free from danger. If the Lord
is ever favourable to us to such an extent, we should not spurn such
comfort for our weakness. In the meantime let this one thing suffice
for us for the suppression of all the corrupt fears of the flesh, that we
cannot be forsaken by Him, as long as we wage war under Him. But
when He says, 'No one will rise up to hurt thee', the Lord does not
mean that the man, on whom the Jews made a deadly attack immediately afterwards, would be immune from violence and uproar, but
the meaning is that their efforts will be useless, because God had
determined to snatch him safely out of their hands. Therefore we must
fight with alacrity, in order to gain the victory.

Because I have people. The second reason for his taking courage is
that God wished to raise up a great church there, with many people.
However there is doubt as to whether this clause depends on the preceding one. For the connexion flows smoothly in this way, that,
since God decided to gather a great church by Paul's agency and effort,
He will not allow enemies to interrupt his work; as if He had said, 'I
shall help you, so that you may not fail my people, to whom I have

appointed you a minister.' But I readily adopt this explanation, that
different reasons are not being brought forward to be read separately,
but that they are kept distinct like this, although closely connected
with each other.

Moreover the Lord calls the people His own, for, even if they
could have been justifiably called outsiders at that time, yet they are
properly honoured with this title, because they were written in the
book of life, and must soon be admitted by election into the family.
For we know that many sheep wander outside the flock for a time, just
as many wolves are mixed up with the sheep. Therefore those whom
the Lord has decided to acquire for Himself soon afterwards, He already
acknowledges to be among His own people, because of their future
faith. But let us remember that those, who are engrafted into the body
of Christ, belong to it by the eternal adoption of God, as it is written,
'Thine they were, and Thou hast given them to me' (John 17.6).

11. *He dwelt there a year, etc.* We do not read that Paul voluntarily
delayed so long anywhere else, and yet it is apparent from his two
Epistles not only that he had to put up with innumerable troubles but
that he endured many intolerable things on account of the pride and
ingratitude of the people. So we see that there was no aspect of warfare in which the Lord did not discipline him in a wonderful way.
We also gather how difficult and laborious the building of the Church
is, when the most distinguished master-builder spent so much time
in laying the foundation of one. For he boasts not that the work was
completed by himself, but that others were put in his place by the
Lord to build on his foundation; as he says later that he certainly
planted, but Apollos watered (I Cor. 3.6).

> But when Gallio was proconsul of Achaia, the Jews with one accord rose
> up against Paul, and brought him before the judgment-seat, saying,
> This man persuadeth men to worship God contrary to the law. But
> when Paul was about to open his mouth, Gallio said unto the Jews, If
> indeed it were a matter of wrong or of wicked villany, O ye Jews,
> reason would that I should bear with you: but if they are questions
> about words and names and your own law, look to it yourselves; I am
> not minded to be a judge of these matters. And he drave them from the
> judgment-seat. And they[1] all laid hold on Sosthenes, the ruler of the
> synagogue, and beat him before the judgment-seat. And Gallio cared
> for none of these things. (12-17)

12-14. *When Gallio.* Either the change of proconsul encouraged
the Jews to grow more bold and insolent, as impious and impudent
men are in the habit of taking advantage of new things to stir up

---
[1] Calvin reads *all the Greeks.* Tr.

trouble; or, in the belief that the judge would be well-disposed towards them, they suddenly broke the peace and silence of a whole year. But the burden of the charge is that Paul is trying to introduce worship of God that is perverted and *contrary to the law*. The question is now asked whether they mean the Law of Moses, or the familiar rites of the Roman Empire. Because the latter seems flat and forced to me, I prefer to accept the former, that they charged Paul with the offence of violating the worship divinely laid down in the Law of God, and they did so with the intention of accusing him of innovation. And indeed Paul would have had to be justly condemned, if he had attempted anything of the sort. But since it is quite certain that the holy man was treacherously and wickedly misrepresented, they took pains to conceal bad grounds with a decent excuse. We know how strictly the Lord prescribes in the Law how He wishes to be worshipped by His own people. Therefore it is sacrilege to depart from that rule. But since it never entered Paul's head to add anything to the Law, or to take anything from it, he is dragged off to face this charge unjustly. From that we gather that no matter how uprightly and blamelessly believers conduct themselves, yet they do not avoid an undeserved bad reputation, until they are allowed to come and clear themselves.

Anyhow Paul was not only undeservedly and falsely disgraced by his opponents, but when he wished to speak to rebut their impudence, and remove their false reproaches, he was cut short by the proconsul. He was therefore forced to leave the judgment-seat, without defending himself at all. Indeed Gallio refuses to inquire into the case, not because of any grudge against Paul, but because it did not belong to the office of a governor to pronounce judgment on the religion of each province. For although the Romans could not force the nations, that were subject to them, into their own rites, yet, so that they might not appear to be approving what they tolerated, they forbade their magistrates to deal with this field of jurisdiction. We see from this what ignorance of true godliness does in the ordering of the affairs of each state or empire. All admit that it is of primary importance that religion thrive and flourish. Now when the true God is known, and the definite rule for worshipping Him is adhered to, there is nothing more reasonable than God's direction in His Law, viz. that those, who rule with power, maintain the pure worship of the true God, and abolish contrary superstitions. But since the Romans preserved their own rites only out of pride and obstinacy, and, on the other hand, since they had no certitude where there was no truth, they thought that it would be to their best advantage if they allowed those living in the provinces freedom in their way of life. But there is nothing more absurd than to surrender the worship of God to the opinion of men. Accordingly it is not without good reason that God commanded, by Moses, that the king should see that a special copy of the Law be written out for himself (Deut. 17.18), doubtless so that, having been properly instructed, and being more sure of his faith, he might undertake, with a stronger will, to maintain what he knew with certainty to be right.

15. *About words*[1] *and names.* Words are piled up, and arranged badly; but in this way Gallio speaks contemptuously of the Law of God, as if the Jewish religion consisted only of words and useless questions. And as the nation was contentious, there must be absolutely no doubt that many worked themselves and others into a state of agitation with unnecessary and trifling things. Yes, and what is more, Paul reproaches them in many passages, particularly in the Epistle to Titus (1.14; 3.9). Yet Gallio does not deserve to be excused for mocking at the sacred Law of God along with their curiosity. For just as he ought to have denied any opportunity for empty contentions about words, so, on the other hand, when it is a question of the worship of God, we must realize that this is no dispute about words, but that we are dealing with the most serious matter of all.

17. *All the Greeks apprehended Sosthenes.* This is the *Sosthenes* whom Paul honourably associates with himself at the beginning of the First Epistle to the Corinthians. But although no previous mention had been made of him among the believers, yet it is probable that at that time he was one of Paul's companions and assistants. But what madness drove the Greeks so that they all made a violent attack on him, apart from the fact that it is, so to speak, fated for the sons of God to have the world in opposition and hostile, for some unknown reason? (*causa incognito*) Accordingly there is no reason for us to be disturbed today by the indignity of seeing the wretched Church attacked everywhere. In addition the viciousness of human nature is painted for us, as if in a picture. Although we may grant that the Jews deserved to be objects of hate everywhere, yet why do the Greeks turn the violence of their anger on an unassuming man like Sosthenes, rather than on the men responsible for the tumult, who were, for no good reason, causing trouble for Paul? Of course the reason is this, that when men are not ruled by the Spirit of God, they are swept into evil as if by the secret instigation of nature. However, it is possible that they were so hostile to Sosthenes, because they believed that he offered hospitality to violent men for the purpose of raising sedition.

And Gallio cared for none of these things. Such non-interference ought to be attributed not so much to the sloth of the proconsul, as to hatred

---

[1] Calvin's text has *de sermone*. Greek, περὶ λόγου. Tr.

THE ACTS 18 [v. 17-18]

of the Jewish religion. The Romans would have wished for the memory of the true God to be buried; and so, since it was lawful for them to offer and pay vows to all the idols of Asia and Greece, it was a capital offence to perform religious rites to the God of Israel. In a word, when common licence was given to all superstitions, the only exception was the true religion. That is why it comes about that Gallio takes no notice of the injuries to Sosthenes. He had just acknowledged that he would avenge injuries if any were inflicted; now he allows an innocent man to be beaten before his judgment-seat. What gave rise to such tolerance, except that he wished all the Jews to perish from wounds they inflicted on each other, so that their religion might be destroyed along with them? But when, through the mouth of Luke, the Spirit condemns Gallio's negligence, because he does not assist and protect a man who is afflicted unjustly, let our own magistrates realize that there will be far less excuse for them, if they close[1] their eyes to injuries and wrongs, if they do not restrain the impudence of the wicked, if they do not reach out a hand to the oppressed. But if a just condemnation awaits the lazy and idle, how terrible is the judgment that threatens the treacherous and malicious, who countenance bad causes, and are indulgent to crimes, as if they are under a standard raised to impunity, and so are fans for encouraging men to be bold in inflicting injury.

And Paul, having tarried after this yet many days, took his leave of the brethren, and sailed thence for Syria, and with him Priscilla and Aquila; having shorn his head in Cenchreae: for he had a vow. And they[2] came to Ephesus, and he left them there: but he himself entered into the synagogue, and reasoned with the Jews. And when they asked him to abide a longer time, he consented not; but[3] taking his leave of them, and saying, I will return again unto you, if God will, he set sail from Ephesus. And when he had landed at Caesarea, he went up and saluted the church, and went down to Antioch. And having spent some time there, he departed, and went through the region of Galatia and Phrygia in order, stablishing all the disciples. (18-23)

18. *Having tarried many days.* Paul's firmness of character reveals itself in the fact that he is not driven away by fear, lest he might upset the disciples, who were still ignorant and weak, by a sudden and untimely departure. Quite often in other passages we read that he fled at once when persecutions were inflamed against him. Why then

[1] Reading *conniveant* with Tholuck, for C.R.'s *conveniant*. Tr.
[2] Calvin reads *he came.* Tr.
[3] Calvin reads, as AV, *but bade them farewell, saying I must by all means keep this feast that cometh in Jerusalem but I will return again etc.* Tr.

AOA K   139

does it come about that he stays on at Corinth? The answer is that when he saw enemies encouraged by his presence to vent their rage on the whole church, he did not hesitate to procure peace and quiet for the faithful by his departure; but now, on the other hand, when he sees a check put on their ill-will, so that they may do no harm to God's flock, he prefers to provoke them, than, by departing, to give them fresh opportunity to vent their rage.

To move on, this was the third time that Paul set out for Jerusalem. For on his departure from Damascus, he went up the first time to become known to the apostles (Gal. 1.18). On the other hand, he was sent, in the second place, with Barnabas, in order to settle the controversy about ceremonies. Luke does not tell the reason why he now undertook such a long and wearisome journey, from which he intended to return soon.

When he had shorn his head. It is not certain whether this is said about Aquila or Paul, and it does not matter very much. However I gladly take it to apply to Paul, because I think it likely that he conceded this to the Jews, to whom he was about to come. I certainly take it for granted that he did not take a ceremonial vow in a private capacity, to offer some worship to God. He knew that what God had commanded for the people of old under the Law was a temporary thing. Indeed we know how carefully he teaches that the Kingdom of God does not depend on those external elements, and how strongly he urges their abrogation. It would certainly have been absurd for him to bind his conscience with that scrupulousness (*religione*) from which he was setting all other men free. Therefore he shaved his head for no other purpose except to accommodate himself to the Jews, who were still ignorant, and not yet properly instructed; just as he testifies that, in order to win those who were under the Law, he voluntarily subjected himself to the Law, from which he was free (I Cor. 9.20). If anyone objects that he could not pretend to a vow which he had not conceived from the heart, there is an easy reply, that he did not falsify anything with respect to the substance of purification, indeed that he did not use this ceremony, which was still free, as if God demanded such worship, but to concede something to the ignorant.

Therefore the Papists are ridiculous when they draw out of this an example of making a vow. No religious scruple moved Paul to make a vow; those men in fact make a false worship of God rest on vows. The circumstances of the time were forcing Paul to keep the rites of the Law; those men accomplish nothing except to entangle the Christian Church in superstition, when its freedom has been established a long time ago. For it is quite a different matter to bring obsolete ceremonies back into use again, than still to tolerate those that survive, until they gradually fall into disuse. I pass over the fact that the Papists uselessly and foolishly compare their clerical tonsure with the symbol of purification that God had approved in the Law. But because no further refutation is necessary let this one thing suffice for us, that, in order to lead the weak to Christ, at any rate not to offend them, Paul bound himself with a vow, which he knew was of no consequence in the sight of God.

19, 20, 21. *Having entered into the synagogue.* This verse teaches us that, when Paul had shaken out his garments at Corinth as a sign of cursing, he did not do so because he was casting the whole nation aside, but those whom he had already experienced to be of incorrigible obstinacy. Now he makes a fresh approach to the Ephesians, to try whether he would find more obedience among them. Further, since it is apparent from Luke's account that he was given a quieter hearing in this synagogue than anywhere else, and was even asked to stay on, it is a strange thing that, nevertheless, he did not accede to their requests. It is surely easy to conjecture from that, what I have said already, that he had a strong reason for going up to Jerusalem quickly. He himself also makes it plain that he had to make haste, saying, 'I must keep the feast which is soon to take place at Jerusalem'. And there is no doubt that when he had diligently put their affairs in order, he departed with their good leave and favour; and one may gather from Luke's words that his excuse was accepted, so that his refusal did not offend them. Finally, it is worth while noting that, when there is a better hope of success than we have been used to, we are being drawn to different undertakings, as if by the hand of God, so that we may learn to yield ourselves to be ruled by His will.

The feast that approaches. What I have just said about the vow, also applies to the feast day. For Paul was not intending to perform a duty of piety towards God, but to take part in an assembly, in which he could do more good, than at other times of the year. Even the Epistle to the Galatians alone is witness enough as to what value he set on a distinction between days (Gal. 4.10).

Certainly we must note that he promises nothing about a return, without interposing the qualification, 'if it pleases the Lord'. Indeed we all confess that we cannot move even one finger without His leading. But because so much arrogance holds sway in men everywhere, that they venture to set God aside and settle anything, not just for the near future, but even for many years, we must often ponder over this religious reverence and prudence, so that we may learn to submit our purposes to the will and providence of God, lest, if we make plans, as men, who seem to themselves to have fortune in their control are in the habit of doing, we may suffer just punishment for our temerity. And even if there is not such religious force (*religio*) in words, that we are not free to say that we shall do this or that, it is nevertheless a useful thing to become used to forms of speech, which may remind us that all our steps are directed by God.

22. *When he had landed at Caesarea.* Although Luke briefly reports that Paul *saluted the church* at Jerusalem, it is certain, however, that he was drawn there by some great compulsion. And yet one may gather from the context, that he did not stay long at Jerusalem, perhaps because the outcome of the matters, in which he was engaged, did not match up to his expectation and wish.

He further declares that his return journey was neither unpleasant nor unprofitable, for he says that he confirmed all the disciples; no doubt with a great deal of trouble, because he was forced to turn aside and take many roundabout ways. For the adverb καθεξῆς[1] suggests a continuous sequence. I have already said elsewhere (Acts 9.36) why those who gave their allegiance to Christ, and professed the faith of the Gospel, are called *disciples*; it is because there is no godliness without proper instruction. Certainly those men had their own pastors, under whom they made progress. But because Paul had greater authority, and had the power that came from a superior spirit, they were greatly strengthened by him when he passed through; especially since he had been the principal master-builder in laying the foundations of all their churches.

> *Now a certain Jew named Apollos, an Alexandrian by race, a learned[2] man, came to Ephesus; and he was mighty in the scriptures. This man had been instructed in the way of the Lord; and being fervent in spirit, he spake and taught carefully[3] the things concerning Jesus, knowing only the baptism of John: and he began to speak boldly in the synagogue. But when Priscilla and Aquila heard him, they took him unto them, and expounded unto him the way of God more carefully. And when he was minded to pass over into Achaia, the brethren encouraged him, and wrote to the disciples to receive him: and when he was come, he helped them much which had believed through grace: for he powerfully confuted the Jews, and that publicly, shewing by the scriptures that Jesus was the Christ. (24-28)*

24. *A certain Jew.* It must really be attributed to the providence of God, that when Paul is forced to leave Ephesus, Apollos is sent in his place, to make good the loss caused by his absence. But it is important

---

[1] Greek is: διερχόμενος καθεξῆς τὴν Γαλατικὴν χώραν κ.τ.λ. Tr.
[2] Calvin, as AV, reads *eloquent*. Tr.
[3] Calvin, as AV, reads *diligently*. Tr.

to know what sort of origin this man had, since he was also Paul's successor among the Corinthians, and gave such an excellent account of himself, and did such faithful and strenuous work, that Paul praises and honours him, as if he were a unique colleague. He says, 'I planted, Apollos watered' (I Cor. 3.6), and again, 'I have figuratively applied these things to myself and Apollos' (I Cor. 4.6). But Luke first commends him with two descriptions, that 'he was eloquent and mighty in the Scriptures'; secondly he will add his zeal, faith and steadfastness. But even if Paul truly denies that the Kingdom of God depends upon speaking, and he himself lacked the commendation of eloquence, yet skill in discussion, such as Luke praises here, is not to be despised, especially when ostentatious display is not striven after with a splendour of words. But he who maintains the responsibility of teaching has enough to do to give a clear statement of the matter which is in question, without pretence or ambition, without bombastic words and cultivated artifice. Paul lacked eloquence; evidently the Lord intended the chief apostle to be without this virtue, so that the power of the Spirit might shine with greater brilliance in his clumsy and uncouth speech. And yet he was endowed with that ability of speaking, which sufficed to make the name of Christ renowned, and to declare the doctrine of salvation. Finally, as the gifts of the Spirit are distributed in numerous and varied ways, Paul's inability to speak, if one likes to use such an expression, did not prevent God from choosing fluent ministers for Himself. Moreover so that no one might think Apollos' eloquence was profane, or empty and futile, Luke says that it was united with a greater power, viz. that *he was mighty in the Scriptures*. I take that expression to mean, not only that he was well and soundly versed in the Scriptures, but that he had a grip of their power and efficacy, so that, armed with them, he was victorious in all contests. But in my opinion this praise is due to Scripture rather than to the man, because it is more than effective enough both for defending the truth, and for rebutting the stratagems of Satan.

25. *This man had been instructed.* Luke's subsequent statement that 'he knew only the baptism of John' seems to have little agreement with this description; but that later phrase was added by way of correction. All the same these two things agree easily with each other, that he understood the teaching of the Gospel, both because he knew that a Redeemer has been presented to the world, and because he had been properly and sincerely instructed about the grace of reconciliation; and that nevertheless he was imbued only with the rudiments of the Gospel, as far as John's instruction allowed. For we know that John was, so to speak, an intermediary between Christ and the prophets; and both his father, in his song, and the angel, using the prophecy of Malachi,

speak about his office (Luke 1.16ff; 76). Certainly since he went before, lighting the way for Christ, and gave a wonderful explanation of His power, his disciples are justifiably said to have had knowledge of Christ. In addition the statement that *he knew the baptism of John* deserves attention. For from that we gather what the true use of the sacraments is, viz. to initiate us into some particular kind of doctrine, or to establish the faith which we once embraced. It is certainly wrong and impious to separate them from teaching. Accordingly in order that the sacraments may be rightly administered, it is necessary that the accent of the heavenly teaching resound in them. For what is the baptism of John? Luke gathers up the whole of his ministry in this word, not only because doctrine is bound to baptism (*Baptismo annexa est doctrina*), but also because it is its foundation and head, without which it would be an empty and dead ceremony.

Being fervent in spirit. Here Apollos is given the further commendation that he was inflamed with a holy zeal for teaching. Teaching without zeal either is a sword in the hand of a madman, or lies cold and useless, or serves perverse ostentation. For we see that some learned men are lazy and inactive, that others, which is worse, are tormented by ambition, and that others, which is worst of all, disturb the Church with controversies and disputes. Therefore teaching in which zeal will not be vigorous will be flat. But let us keep in mind that Luke has put knowledge of Scripture first, so that it might have a moderating effect on zeal. For we know that many get heated up thoughtlessly, as the Jews were raging against the Gospel out of a perverse devotion to the Law. And today we see how the Papists are urged on by a rashly conceived opinion, and are agitated with furious violence. Therefore let knowledge be present as a moderating influence to control zeal.

Now, in fact, fervour is said to have been the cause of diligence, in that Apollos diligently devoted himself to teaching. But if that man, who was not yet accurately and completely instructed in the Gospel, preached Christ so diligently and freely, what excuse may men expect there to be for themselves, men who have come to clearer and fuller knowledge of what was still hidden from him, if they do not try to promote the Kingdom of Christ to the utmost of their ability? Therefore Luke attributes his fervour to the Spirit, because it is a rare and special gift; for I do not take him to mean that Apollos was urged on by the instigation of his own mind, but by the influence[1] of the Holy Spirit.

26. *But when they heard him.* Aquila and Priscilla are not devoted to themselves, with the result that they are not envious of another man's

---

[1] The first edition reads *grace*, according to C.R. margin. Tr.

ability. That is evident from the fact that they give private and intimate instruction to an eloquent man about the things, which he is to present in public afterwards. They were not strong in the same grace as he had, and perhaps they might have been treated with contempt in the assembly. Moreover they are eager to help a man, whom they see to be better equipped, both with eloquence and the use of the Scripture, on the condition that they themselves are to remain silent, while he alone is to speak. Again, Apollos was unusually modest, for he allowed himself to be taught and refined, not only by a manual worker, but also by a woman. For he was mighty in Scripture, and far superior to them; but those, who could have given the impression of being hardly suitable ministers, give him the finishing touches about what makes the Kingdom of Christ complete. We also see that at that time women were not so unacquainted with the Word of God as the Papists wish to have them, since we see that one of the chief teachers of the Church was taught by a woman. Yet we must remember what I said, that Priscilla carried out this instruction privately, within the walls of her own home, so that she might not destroy the order prescribed by God and by nature.

27. *When he wished ... into Achaia.* Luke does not say explicitly why Apollos wished to go to Achaia. However we gather from the context that he was not drawn by private advantage, but because a greater abundance of fruit might appear from the spreading of the Gospel there; and we do so because the brethren encouraged him further by their exhortation, and spurred a willing horse. And they would surely not have done that, if it was not for the common good of the Church. For it was absurd to send off elsewhere, with their good wishes, a man, who had benefited them by his faithful work, and whom, they knew, they would need in the future, unless something better presented itself by way of compensation. I understand that the brethren at Ephesus wrote to those at Achaia, not only to receive the man with hospitality, but to admit him to the office of teaching. It is truly a holy commendation when we take pains to lift up every good man with our testimony and our approval, so that gifts of the Holy Spirit, which He has entrusted to individuals for the upbuilding of the Church, may not lie buried.

When he had come. This had been foreseen by the brethren, who had already experienced it, when they encouraged him to undertake the journey, which he had planned. But his statement that he benefited the faithful can be taken in two ways. (1) He brought help to those who were less well equipped, and supported them in breaking down the stubbornness of enemies; for it did not belong just to anyone to have weapons ready for sustaining a difficult battle against experienced enemies, who would never have given in unless forced to do so. Or (2) he gave support to them so that their faith might not be struck down by the contradiction of enemies and collapse, as usually happens very often to the weak. I take it to mean that they were helped in both ways, so that having a skilled and experienced leader they might be victorious in the conflict; secondly, that their faith was established on a new base, so that it was no longer in danger of tottering.

Moreover Luke seems to hint that the brethren were helped by his activity and determination, when he mentions that he disputed publicly with the Jews. For it was a sign of zeal and confidence, not to avoid the public (*lucem*).

The closing phrase of the sentence, *through grace*, either is connected with the preceding words, *they believed*, or must be referred to the help that he brought to the brethren. The first interpretation has no difficulty; for the meaning will be that the believers were illuminated by the grace of God to believe. It is as though he had said, 'The brethren, who were already called to faith by the help of God, were led on to something better.' However connecting it in the other way seems to fit in better, that Apollos helped the brethren by sharing with them the grace with which he was endowed. In this way *through grace* will amount to much the same thing as 'according to the measure of grace received'.

28. *He confuted the Jews.* This makes it clear what purpose Apollos' ability, of being mighty in the Scriptures, served, viz. that powerful and effectual proof was available to him for refuting enemies. The main theme of the disputation is also briefly set down, that *Jesus was the Christ*. For there was no controversy among the Jews that Christ, the Deliverer, was promised, but it was not easy to persuade them that Jesus, the Son of Mary, was this Christ, through whom salvation had been offered. Therefore it was necessary for Apollos to deal with the office of Christ, so as to prove that the testimonies of Scripture have been fulfilled in the Son of Mary, and to deduce from that that He was the Christ.

Moreover this verse is evidence that Scripture is useful, not only for teaching, but also for breaking down the stubbornness of those who do not give their willing assent. For our faith would not be strong enough, if there did not exist in it a clear description of those things that we need to know for salvation. Certainly if the Law and the Prophets had so much light that Apollos proved clearly from them that Jesus was the Christ, as if he pointed out the fact with his finger, the addition of the Gospel ought to prove at least this, that the full knowledge of Christ is to be sought from the whole of Scripture. Accordingly the Papists' charge that Scripture is obscure and ambiguous is a detestable insult to God. For why would God have spoken, except that the clear and invincible truth might reveal itself in His words? And their cavil, which is an inference from that, that we must adhere to the authority of the Church, and that we must not use Scripture to dispute with heretics, is abundantly refuted by Luke. For since there were none more stubborn than the Jews, we must have no fear that the same weapons, which Apollos relied on to overcome them, may be sufficient for us against all heretics, since they give us victory against the devil, the prince of all errors.

CHAPTER NINETEEN

And it came to pass, that, while Apollos was at Corinth, Paul having passed through the upper country came to Ephesus, and found certain disciples: and he said unto them, Did ye receive the Holy Ghost when ye believed? And they said unto him, Nay, we did not so much as hear whether the Holy Ghost was given.[1] And he said, Into what then were ye baptized? And they said, Into John's baptism. And Paul said, John baptized with the baptism of repentance, saying unto the people, that they should believe on him which should come after him, that is, on Jesus. And when they heard this, they were baptized into the name of the Lord Jesus. And when Paul had laid his hands upon them, the Holy Ghost came on them; and they spake with tongues, and prophesied. And they were in all about twelve men. (1-7)

1. Here Luke records that on Paul's return the Church at Ephesus was not only confirmed and increased, but was also provided with a miracle, in that the visible graces of the Spirit were conferred on certain new and inexperienced disciples there. Again, it is not known whether they were residents of the city, or recent incomers (*hospites*), and it does not matter very much to us. But there is no doubt that they were Jews, because they had received the baptism of John. It is also probable that they did reside in Ephesus, seeing that Paul found them there.

2. *Did you receive the Holy Spirit?* The conclusion of the story shows that here Paul is not speaking about the Spirit of regeneration, but of the special gifts, which God distributed, at the beginning of the Gospel and in a variety of ways, on those whom He pleased, for the general edification of the Church. But now the question arises from Paul's inquiry, whether all, everywhere, had the Spirit in common at that time. For if He was being given to a certain few, why does he link Him with faith, as if the connexion was inseparable? Perhaps the men did not belong to the flock, or, because their number, twelve that is, was a modest one, Paul asks whether they are all without the gifts of the Spirit. However my own judgment is this, that so many Jews, and indeed disciples, that is, members of the flock of the faithful, were presented to the Gentiles' view at one time, not by chance, but by the purpose of God, to confess, nevertheless, that hitherto the supreme glory of the Gospel, which was conspicuous in spiritual gifts,

[1] Calvin, as Greek, reads, *whether the Holy Spirit is.* Tr.

148

had been unknown to them, so that lustre might be given to Paul's ministry through them. For it is not likely that so few disciples were left at Ephesus by Apollos; and they would have been instructed more correctly by him, seeing that he himself had learnt the way of the Lord precisely from Aquila and Priscilla. Yes, and what is more, I do not doubt that the brethren, whom Luke mentioned previously (18.27), were different from these particular men. To sum up, when Paul sees that these men are confessing the name of Christ, he asks whether they have received the Holy Spirit, in order to find out more precise information about their faith. For Paul himself makes it clear that this method was a sign of the grace of God, for establishing the trustworthiness of doctrine, 'I wish to know whether you received the Holy Spirit by works of the Law, or by the hearing of faith' (Gal. 3.2).

3. *We do not know whether there is a Holy Spirit.* How was it possible for men who were Jews to have heard nothing about the Spirit, about whom the Prophets everywhere proclaim, and with descriptions of whom Scripture is full? We certainly gather from this that Paul did not speak in general terms about the Spirit, and that those men, in accordance with the way they had been questioned, deny that they knew anything of those visible graces, with which God had furnished the Kingdom of His Son. They therefore confess that they do not know whether God bestows gifts of that kind. Therefore there is metonymy in the word *Spirit*. And this meaning is confirmed by the fact that, if they had completely denied that they knew anything about the Spirit of God, Paul would not have passed over in silence such a gross, even monstrous error. When he asks for what purpose, or in what way, they have therefore been baptized, he implies that, wherever Christ had been soundly preached, the visible graces also shone brightly, so that such splendour might be common to all the churches. Accordingly Paul has good reason for wondering that the faithful are ignorant of such glory of Christ as God was intending to be conspicuous everywhere at that time; and he is quick to add a corrective, warning them that they must not continue in those rudiments, which they had imbibed, because it had been John's function to prepare disciples for Christ.

4. *John indeed.* Paul's correction[1] has this end in view, that those men, having been convinced of their ignorance, might aspire to make further progress. He says that John proclaimed that Christ was coming. Therefore he sent disciples from the starting-lines so that, running in the race-course, they might aim for Christ, not yet made manifest.

---

[1] Reading *admonitio* for *admiratio* (C.R. and Tholuck). French: 'l'admonition'. Tr.

Accordingly, so that those men might not be satisfied with themselves, and scornfully refuse to progress further, he shows that they are still far from the goal. For the awareness of their deficiency encourages men to try to get what they lack. The substance of what Paul had been saying amounts to this, 'Before Christ was glorified, that power of His was not at work in the world; it was when He finally ascended into heaven that He intended His Kingdom to flourish in this way. Therefore the graces of the Spirit, which now testify that Christ is seated at the Father's right hand, were poured out far less when John was still acting as an ambassador, seeing that at that time He had not openly revealed Himself to the world as the Redeemer. Therefore realize that you must make further progress, because you are far away from the goal.' Therefore he clearly teaches that the faith of the godly, who had been taught by John, ought to have been looking to the Christ, who was to come, so that those men might not stick at first principles.

But we are also taught from this that the baptism of John was a sign of repentance and remission of sins, and that today there is no difference between it and our own baptism, except that Christ has been revealed, and in His death and resurrection all parts of our salvation have been completed. And so baptism was brought to its effect, both because repentance flows out of that fountain of death and resurrection, which I have mentioned, and faith is carried back to the same place, there to seek the righteousness of grace. To sum up, Paul clearly shows that it was a baptism of regeneration and renewal, as is ours. But because both cleansing and newness of life flow from Christ alone, he says that it has been founded on His faithfulness. We are also taught by these words that by faith in Christ we may lay hold of all that it figures; it being far from the case that the outward sign diminishes the grace of Christ in any way.

5. *When they heard these things they were baptized.* Since the opinion prevailed among the men of old that the baptisms of John and Christ were different, they did not think it absurd for those, who had only been prepared by the baptism of John, to be baptized again. But that their belief in that difference was false and wrong, is evident from this fact, that it was a token and pledge of the same adoption and the same newness of life, which we receive in our baptism today. Therefore we do not read that Christ baptized afresh those who came over to Him from John. In addition Christ received baptism in His own flesh, so that He might associate Himself with us by that visible symbol; but if that fictitious difference is admitted, there will vanish and be lost to us this unique favour, that we have a common baptism with the Son of God (*Baptismum habemus cum Filio Dei communem*). And indeed

there is no need of a long refutation, because in order that they may convince us that the baptisms are different, they must necessarily show, first of all, how the one differs from the other. But the resemblance and correspondence to each other is excellent, and there is a symmetry and similarity of all parts, which forces us to admit that it is the same baptism.

But now the question is asked whether it was right to repeat it. And fanatical men of our day, relying on this evidence, have tried to introduce Anabaptism. Some take the word baptism for new instruction; and I do not agree with them for the reason that their explanation, forced as it is, smacks of evasion. Others deny that baptism was repeated, because they had been baptized wrongly by some foolish imitator of John. But because their conjecture has no substance, and, what is more, because Paul's words suggest that they were true and genuine disciples of John, and Luke does them the honour of calling them disciples of Christ, I do not subscribe to this opinion also; and yet I do deny that the baptism of water was repeated, because Luke's words imply nothing else but that they were baptized with the Spirit. In the first place it is no new thing for the name of baptism to be transferred to the gifts of the Spirit, as we have seen in chapters 1 and 11 (1.5; 11.16). There Luke said that, when Christ promised that the Spirit would be sent in visible form to the disciples, He called it 'baptism'; and again, that when the Spirit descended on Cornelius, Peter remembered the words of the Lord, 'You will be baptized with the Holy Spirit'. Secondly, we see that those visible gifts are expressly mentioned here, and that they are given along with baptism. But I understand the statement that follows immediately afterwards, that the Spirit came when *he laid his hands upon them*, to have been added by way of explanation. For it is a frequent and habitual mode of expression in Scripture, to set something down briefly, and then to state it in a clearer way. Therefore in saying that the Spirit was given to them by the laying on of hands, Luke expresses better, and explains more fully, something that was rather obscure on account of its brevity. If anyone objects that when the word baptism is used for the gifts of the Spirit it is not being taken in its simple form, but with an added overtone, I reply that Luke's thought is plain enough from the context, and, secondly, that Luke is alluding to the baptism that he has mentioned.[1] And certainly, if you take it to mean the external symbol, it will be absurd that it was given to them without the introduction of any fuller (*meliore*) teaching. If however you take it metaphorically for instruction (*institutione*), the expression will be harsher still, and the report that the Holy Spirit des-

[1] i.e. in chapters 1 and 11. Tr.

cended on them after they had been instructed, would not be suitable.

Further, while I admit that this laying on of hands was a sacrament, I maintain that those who have prolonged it, imitating it perpetually, have fallen into ignorance. For when all agree that it was a temporary grace, that was exhibited by that symbol, it is perverse and ridiculous to retain a sign, when the reality has been removed. Baptism and the Supper are a different matter altogether; for the Lord testifies that with them there are presented to us those gifts, which the Church will continue to enjoy right to the end of the world. Accordingly we must carefully and wisely distinguish perpetual sacraments from temporary ones, so that worthless and ludicrous counterfeits (*larvae*) may not find a place among the sacraments. I do not condemn the use of the laying on of hands by the men of old to confirm adults in the profession of the faith, so long as no one thinks that the grace of the Spirit is tied to such a ceremony, as Jerome asserts against the Luciferians. But the Papists do not deserve to be pardoned, for, not being content with the ancient rite, they have dared to obtrude disgusting anointing, to be not only a confirmation of baptism, but also a sacrament of greater worth, by which they imagine believers, who were previously only half complete, are made perfect, and by which those, who had only had their sins forgiven before, are armed for the fight. For they have not hesitated to spew out these detestable blasphemies.

And he entered into the synagogue, and spake boldly for the space of three months, reasoning and persuading as to the things concerning the kingdom of God. But when some were hardened and disobedient, speaking evil of the Way before the multitude, he departed from them, and separated the disciples, reasoning daily in the school of Tyrannus. And this continued for the space of two years; so that all they which dwelt in Asia heard the word of the Lord, both Jews and Greeks. And God wrought special miracles[1] by the hands of Paul: insomuch that unto the sick were carried away from his body handkerchiefs or aprons, and the diseases departed from them, and the evil spirits went out. (8-12)*

8. *Having entered the synagogue.* We gather from this that Paul began with the company of the godly who had already given their allegiance to Christ, and that he then entered the synagogue in order to gather into the one body of the Church the rest of the Jews, who had not yet come to know Christ, or at any rate had not yet accepted Him.

He says that Paul *spoke boldly*, so that we may know that he was

---

[1] Calvin reads, as RV margin, *no common powers.* Tr.

heard for the continuous period of three months, not because he cunningly concealed the teaching of the Gospel, or wormed his way in by obscure and roundabout ways. Also Luke goes on at once to give evidence of his confidence, when he reports that he disputed and persuaded concerning the *Kingdom of God*. And we know that by this name is often meant that renewal which had been promised to the fathers, and was to be made manifest at the coming of Christ. For since, apart from Christ, everything is in unseemly and confused disarray, the Prophets quite rightly attributed it to the coming Messiah that He would establish the Kingdom of God in the world. Now, indeed, because this Kingdom brings us back from rebellion to be under obedience to God, and makes sons out of enemies, it consists, first of all, of the free forgiveness of sins, by which God reconciles us to Himself, and brings us into His people by adoption, and, secondly, of the renewal of life, by which He fashions us according to His own image.

He says that *he disputed and persuaded*, meaning that Paul argued in such a way, that he used sound reasons to prove the things that he was asserting in public; and, secondly, that, in addition, he used godly exhortations on his hearers as incentives, to open up an entrance for the Kingdom of God. For no subtleties of speech will make us obedient to God, if we are not moved by godly admonitions.

9. *When they were hardened.* We do not read that Paul was heard by Jews anywhere so quietly and with such forbearance as he was, when he first came to Ephesus. For while others raised an uproar and drove him out, he was asked by them to stay longer. Now, after he has tried for three months to set up the Kingdom of God among them, the ungodliness and stubbornness of many reveals itself. For Luke says that *they were hardened*. And the heavenly doctrine has this particular power, that it either turns the reprobate into a fury, or makes them more obstinate; and it does so, not because of its own nature, but accidentally, as men say, because, when the truth presses hard upon them, their hidden venom breaks out.

Luke adds that they *spoke evil of the Way before the multitude.* For those who despise the Gospel at last degrade themselves to this extent, that they make a hostile attack in the presence of others on what they are unwilling to embrace; and they do so for no other purpose, except that they desire, if possible, to have all men share in the same impiety.

It is well enough known that by the word *way* is meant any sort of way of life, but here it is applied to the Gospel of Christ.

Luke now says that Paul *departed from them and separated the disciples.* We are warned by this example that when we experience hopeless and incurable obstinacy, we must not waste our efforts any longer. For that reason Paul himself advises Titus (3.10) to avoid a heretical man after one or two admonitions. For the Word of God has shameful insult inflicted upon it, if it is prostituted to pigs and dogs. At the same time it is also proper to have regard for the weak, so that their piety may not be shaken by vicious disparagements and mis-representations of sound doctrine. Therefore Paul *separated* the dis-ciples, so that the goats might not infect the flock of sheep with their filthy smell; and secondly, so that profession of the faith might flourish freely among the pure worshippers of God.

Reasoning daily. This verse shows how unremitting and zealous Paul was in teaching; and that those who are overtaken at once by the irksomeness of learning are too capricious or pleasure-loving. For we are aware how few there are who are burning with a readiness and inclination to hear every day. On the other hand even if he had a particular concern for his own personal flock, which he had gathered, as it were, into a sheepfold, yet he does not deprive those outside of his attention, but maintaining the course of discussion, he makes the attempt to find out whether there are any that are teachable.

He calls it *the school of Tyrannus*, not meaning a man who possessed sovereign power at that time,[1] for the Romans held sway in the whole of Asia, but one may well believe that it was a gymnasium formerly erected at the expense of a man called Tyrannus, and given to the city. Therefore the faithful used a public place, which bore the name of its founder, for holding their meetings.

10. *All who were dwelling.* Luke does not mean that the men of Asia came there to hear Paul, but that the whole of Asia was pervaded by the odour of his preaching, and the seed was scattered far and wide, so that his labour was fruitful not only for one city, but also for distant places. And it often happens that when the truth of God is preached in one place, and has been spread far and wide, it echoes where the voice of the minister himself cannot be heard, because it is passed on from person to person, and men teach each other. For one man would not be enough, unless each man were intent on propagating the faith according to his ability.

11, 12. *No common powers.* He calls *miracles*, 'powers', as Scripture frequently does, for they were proofs of God's extraordinary power. But he records that Paul's apostleship was distinguished by these signs, in order that the authority of his teaching might be more certain. For it is a common saying, that signs are produced through the agency of a man. In this way the glory of them is ascribed to God as the only Author; on the other hand the man is put in his proper place as a

---

[1] Latin *tyrannus* = ruler. Tr.

minister. And in order to amplify the miracles further, he says that *handkerchiefs and aprons (sudaria et semicinctia)* were brought to the sick, who were healed by touching them. It is quite clear why this ability was given to Paul, viz. to prove himself a true apostle of Christ, to win men's confidence for the Gospel, and to confirm his ministry. And here it is appropriate to call to mind what we have said previously about the proper use of miracles. Also, what God did in healing the sick with Paul's handkerchiefs had this as its object, that those who had never seen the man, might reverently embrace his teaching, even although he was not on the spot. That is why the Papists are all the more absurd when they twist this verse in favour of their relics, as if Paul in fact sent his handkerchiefs so that men might venerate and kiss them in his honour, as in the Papacy men reverence Francis' shoes and breeches, Rose's girdle, Saint Margaret's comb, and similar trifles. No, one should rather say that he chose the cheapest of things, so that no superstition might develop out of value or splendour. For it was his intention to claim the glory, wholly and completely, for Christ.

But certain also of the strolling Jews, exorcists, took upon them to name over them which had the evil spirits the name of the Lord Jesus, saying, I adjure you by Jesus whom Paul preacheth. And there were seven sons of one Sceva, a Jew, a chief priest, which did this. And the evil spirit answered and said unto them, Jesus I know, and Paul I know; but who are ye? And the man in whom the evil spirit was leaped on them, and mastered both of them, and prevailed against them, so that they fled out of that house naked and wounded. And this became known to all, both Jews and Greeks, that dwelt at Ephesus; and fear fell upon them all, and the name of the Lord Jesus was magnified. (13-17)

13. So that it might be seen more clearly that Paul's apostleship was confirmed by those miracles, which have just been mentioned, Luke now shows that when certain men made false pretence to the name of Christ, such an abuse was severely punished. We learn from this that such powers were put out through the agency of Paul for no other purpose except that evidence might be given to all that he was faithfully preaching Christ as the power of God, since the Lord not only did not allow them to be separated from the pure teaching of the Gospel, but also punished so severely those who were irregularly appropriating them for their own exorcisms. Again we gather from that, that all miracles obscuring the Name of Christ are deceptions of the devil, and that those, who lay claim to genuine miracles of God for any other purpose than confirming the pure religion, are deceivers.

Certain exorcists. I have no doubt that this office sprang from foolish emulation. God was in the habit of exercising His power among the Jews in a variety of ways; and He had once used the Prophets as His agents for driving out demons. Using that as a pretext, they invented exorcisms for themselves, and in this way an extraordinary office was rashly set up without the commandment of God. It may even be that, with God so disposing, they accomplished something, not because He countenanced this irregularity, but so that they might be more willing to devote themselves to the religion of their fathers until the coming of Christ. Under the rule of Christ perverse ambition brought about a clash between Christians and Jews, for exorcists were created by the will of men. Afterwards, as superstition always tends to become worse, the Pope wished this to be something common to all his clerics, who were to be promoted to a higher office. For after they have been appointed Door-keepers, they are immediately commissioned with the conjuration of evil spirits; but in actual practice they make themselves quite ridiculous. For they are forced to admit that they are bestowing a title that is empty and noneffective. For where is the power by which they conjure devils? And Exorcists themselves lay themselves open to derision, by taking on an office which they never practise. But of course it is a just result for departing from the Word of God, that there is no end to errors.

As far as these particular men are concerned, we gather that they were unsettled vagrants, and frequenters of market-places, and many of that sort are seen in the Papacy today. For he says that they went round about (*circumivisse*) and by that word he means that they directed their steps this way or that, as opportunity for deceiving was presented.

We adjure you by Jesus. It is very likely that those impostors had recourse to the name of Christ in order to acquire the new power of which they had previously boasted falsely, or to obscure the Gospel, because the ability, with which they had been endowed, had ceased. But this invocation was defective in two ways. For although they do not understand Paul's teaching, without any faith they take advantage of it as a pretext for what amounts to magical incantations. In the second place, without God's call they appropriate for themselves something that is not in men's control. On the other hand the invocation of the name of God and Christ is legitimate, when it is directed by faith, and does not go beyond the limits of a man's calling. Accordingly we are warned by this example not to attempt anything without the previous enlightenment of the Word of God, so that we may not suffer similar punishment for sacrilege. The Lord Himself encourages us to pray. Let all those who have not been endowed with the gift of miracles, keep themselves within those limits. For when the apostles compelled unclean spirits to come out at their command, they regarded God as the responsible agent, and they knew that they were faithfully discharging a ministry, which He had laid upon them.

16. *The man leaping upon them.* The man is credited with what the devil did through him. For he would not have been equal to such great violence that he drove out seven robust young men, after wounding them and stripping them of their clothes. But one cannot define with certainty how the devil dwells in men, apart from the fact that it can be affirmed that there is opposition between the Spirit of God and the spirit of Satan. For just as Paul teaches that we are the temples of God, because the Spirit of God dwells in us, so on the other hand he says that Satan is effectually at work in all unbelievers (cf. I Cor. 3.16; II Cor. 6.14ff). However we must realize that here Luke is dealing with an extraordinary kind of indwelling, viz. when Satan is given free rein so that he takes possession of the whole man.

Further God wished to provide such an example to show that His power is not confined to the sound of a voice, and that He does not allow the Name of His Son to be appropriated for superstitions. On the other hand when He allows Satan to play with us let us realize that we are being punished more severely than if He wounded us in the flesh. For the false appearance of miracles is a horrible charm for deluding unbelievers, so that they are plunged into deeper darkness, because they rejected the light of God.

17. *Fear fell.* The result of that punishment which God had inflicted for the impious abuse of the name of Christ, is that all were infused with fear of God (*religio*), in case they might despise teaching, of which God had shown, by a remarkable example, that He would be a very sharp avenger, and that they were moved to reverence for Christ. For apart from the fact that God uses all His judgments to summon us to the point where they may strike fear of sinning into us, the Majesty of Christ has been particularly commended, and the power of the Gospel confirmed, in this instance. Because a severer punishment awaits impostors, who deliberately profane the name of Christ with their incantations, do not let them promise themselves impunity for such a great sacrilege.

His statement that it *became known to all* amounts to the same thing as 'generally' or 'everywhere'. For he means that the affair was made known as people talked with one another, and in this way the Name of Christ acquired fame among many.

Many also of them that had believed came, confessing, and declaring their deeds. And not a few of them that practised curious arts brought their books together, and burned them in the sight of all: and they

*counted the price of them, and found it fifty thousand pieces of silver.
So mightily grew the word of the Lord and prevailed. Now after these
things were ended, Paul purposed in the spirit, when he had passed
through Macedonia and Achaia, to go to Jerusalem, saying, After I have
been there, I must also see Rome. And having sent into Macedonia
two of them that ministered unto him, Timothy and Erastus, he himself
stayed in Asia for a while.* (18-22)

18. *Many who had believed.* Luke cites one proof of that fear of
which he has spoken. For those men gave real evidence that they
were deeply affected by serious fear of God, when they voluntarily
confessed the offences of their former life, lest, by concealing them
within themselves, they might foment the wrath of God. We know
how reluctant sinners are to have a genuine and frank confession
forced out of them. For since men regard nothing more precious
than their own reputation, disgrace always carries more weight with
them than truth, yes, and as far as it is in their power, they try to cover
up their shameful deeds. Therefore this voluntary confession was
evidence of repentance and fear. For nobody, unless thoroughly
moved by a sense of God's judgment, will subject himself to the insults
and disgrace inflicted by men, and of his own accord will submit to
judgment on earth, in order that he may be acquitted in heaven.

We gather from his use of the word *many* that all did not have the
same cause for coming; for it is possible that those men had festering
consciences for a long time, in the way that many are very often
troubled with hidden inner faults. Accordingly Luke does not lay
down a universal law, but offers an example which those, who have
need of similar medicine, may follow. For why did those men confess their deeds, except to give evidence of their repentance, and to
seek advice and relief from Paul? There was a different reason in the
case of those who also confessed their sins, when they approached
John for baptism. For in this way they were confessing that they
were being admitted to repentance without any deception on their
part. But here Luke shows by one instance how the faithful were
moved by reverence for God, when God presented them with an
example of His severity.

That is why the impudence of the Papists is all the greater, for they
bring this forward as an excuse for their tyranny. For what connexion
has their auricular confession with this example? In the first place
the faithful confessed how miserably they had been deceived by Satan
before they entered upon the faith; and produced some examples in
public. On the other hand by the Papal law an enumeration of all
deeds, sayings and thoughts is demanded. We read that those men

made confession once; the Pope's law orders it to be repeated, annually at least. Those men came forward of their own accord; the Pope binds all with necessity. Luke says that many, not all, came; there is no exception in the Pope's law. Those men humbled themselves before the assembly of believers; the Pope's commandment is quite different, that the sinner mutter secret whispers into the ear of his own priest. See how skilfully they adapt Scripture to prove their own deceptions!

19. *Who practised curious arts.* Luke is speaking, not only about magic and its tricks, but about the frivolous and useless studies, of which the majority of men are usually far too fond. For he uses περίεργα a word the Greeks use to describe whatever things do not contain any solid usefulness in themselves, but waste men's minds and efforts, diverting them through a variety of roundabout ways. Such is so-called judicial astrology, and all the divinations for the future that foolish men invent for themselves. But they burn their books, to deprive themselves and others of the means of going wrong in the future, and, by the fact that the very high value does not deter them from throwing the books away, they demonstrate, all the more clearly, how zealous their piety is. Therefore, while the confession that Luke has just described is a verbal one, so now this is a real one, if I may put it like that. Finally, since the Greeks use ἀργύριον for money of all kinds, it is not certain whether Luke means sesterces or denarii. However, because it is surely evident that the sum is mentioned by him, so that we may realize that the faithful firmly spurned wealth, I have no doubt that he means denarii, or some kind of coin of even greater value. In fact fifty thousand denarii are equivalent to about nine thousand French livres.

Mightily grew. The expression κατὰ κράτος, *mightily*, implies that the Word made no ordinary advance; as if he said that in those increases there was apparent an efficacy that was rare, and greater than usual. I take *growing* to refer to the number of men, as if he had said that the Church was increased by the gathering in of new disciples daily, because the teaching was being propagated widely. But I take the statement that *the Word was confirmed*, as applying to individuals, viz. that they made more and more progress in the obedience of the Gospel, and in godliness, and that their faith put down deeper roots.

21. *Purposed in the Spirit.* He understands that Paul made up his mind for this journey by the inspiration of the Spirit, so that we may know that the whole of his life was ordered according to the will of God. But the reasons why he had the Spirit superintending all his actions were that he both yielded himself to be ruled by God, and depended on His leading. And what follows a little later, that the

actual result of the journey disappointed his expectation, makes no difference. For God often rules His faithful people, while concealing the outcome from them. For He wishes to have them devoted to Himself to the extent that, when circumstances are obscure, and they cannot see ahead (*oculis clausis*), they follow what He has prescribed to them by His Spirit. Moreover we gather that he was thoroughly devoted to the churches, because, disregarding and neglecting his own convenience, he preferred to deprive himself of Timothy, the best and most faithful, the dearest, and, in fact, the most suitable companion of all, than to have no concern for the Macedonians.

And about that time there arose no small stir concerning the Way. For a certain man named Demetrius, a silversmith, which made silver shrines of Diana, brought no little business unto the craftsmen; whom he gathered together, with the workmen of like occupation, and said, Sirs, ye know that by this business we have our wealth. And ye see and hear, that not alone at Ephesus, but almost throughout all Asia, this Paul hath persuaded and turned away much people, saying that they be no gods, which are made with hands: and not only is there danger that this our trade come into disrepute; but also that the temple of the great goddess Diana be made of no account, and that she should even be deposed from her magnificence, whom all Asia and the world worshippeth. And when they heard this, they were filled with wrath, and cried out, saying, Great is Diana of the Ephesians. (23-28)

23, 24. *A tumult concerning the Way.* As far as the word *Way* is concerned, readers should be reminded that it is taken here for what Latin philosophers call *secta*, a school or sect, and Greek philosophers αἵρεσις, a school of thought. But because in the Church of God, where unity of faith ought to prevail, there is nothing more offensive, or even detestable, than for each one to make up his own mind as to what he may follow, I think that Luke avoided a word, which the godly quite rightly held in disrepute, and resorted to the Hebrew idiom, putting *way* for 'mode of life'.

But to turn to the main point, we see how wonderfully the Lord made use of His servant. He was hoping, when he was getting ready for his journey, that the Church would be peaceful when he departed, but, lo and behold, a tumult suddenly arises, where he feared it least. But in the case of Demetrius it is plain how injurious a plague avarice is. For one man, in the interests of his own private gain, does not hesitate to throw a great city into an upheaval with sedition. But the artisans, who are like torches set alight by him and spreading fire everywhere, are a warning to us, how easy it is to incite sordid men, men devoted to their bellies, to any sort of crime, especially if their living comes from an unrewarding occupation and their expectation of making money is snatched away.

Furthermore, we discern in this story a lively representation of our own time. Demetrius and his company raise a tumult, because, if the superstition, from which they have been accustomed to making their living, is taken away, their work will come to an end. Therefore they are fighting fiercely, as though for their lives, so that Demetrius may not be deprived of his rich spoil, and the rest of their daily bread. Today what zeal incites the Pope, the horned bishops, monks, and the whole dregs of the Papal clergy? Yes, and what madness urges them to oppose the Gospel so sharply? Indeed they boast that they are contending for the Catholic faith; and Demetrius certainly was not lacking a likely pretext, pleading the excuse of the worship of Diana. But the actual situation proclaims that they are fighting, not so much for altars, as for hearths, in other words to have well-heated kitchens. They calmly ignore horrible blasphemies against God, so long as these do not diminish their income. They are extremely energetic only in preserving superstitions, which bring grist to their mill.

Accordingly, with the warning of such examples, let us learn to choose the kind of life that is consistent with the teaching of Christ, so that eagerness for gain may not incite us to take up arms in an impious and wicked battle. But let those who, through ignorance or error, have fallen into some bad occupation, or have become entangled in some other vicious and impure way of life, nevertheless be on their guard against such rash sacrilege. But as far as godly teachers are concerned, let them learn by this example that they will never lack adversaries until the whole world procures peace by self-denial, and that, we know, will never be. Because Paul's teaching deprives Demetrius and the silversmiths of their livelihood, in a fury they leap to destroy it. And will those who oppose the Gospel not do the same? But there is not a man who has no occasion to fight; for all the desires of the flesh are hostile to God. Therefore it is bound to happen that there are as many enemies armed to resist Christ, as there are desires of the flesh holding sway in the world. Indeed it often happens that God bridles the wicked, so that they may not raise a tumult, or break out in open fury. However anyone who is not subjected to bearing the yoke of Christ, will always hold His Gospel in hatred. It must therefore be established that godly and faithful teachers will always have to deal with enemies in great numbers. Demetrius' avarice is perfectly obvious, yet at the same time we must realize that he was the fan of Satan, who was seeking to destroy Paul's teaching by all means, and found this convenient instrument. Now since we know that Satan is an implacable enemy of Christ and the truth, do we think that he will ever be without agents, at his instigation to rage with open violence, or attempt to overthrow the Gospel by secret stratagems, or spew out the venom of their hate, or at least give some evidence of hostility by grumbling and shouting?

25, 26. *By this business.* Here Demetrius vents his spite in a disgraceful manner. A man is entitled to pay a certain amount of attention to his own private source of income. But it is certainly a thoroughly disgraceful thing to disturb the public peace, to pervert human and divine right, to stoop to violence and slaughter, to make a serious attempt at destroying what is just and right, for his own interest. Demetrius admits that the heart of the matter is this, that Paul says that gods made by men's hands are not gods at all. He does not inquire whether that is true or not, but, blinded by his passion for money-making, he is driven to destroy the true teaching. The same blindness rushes him into violent remedies. Also, because the workmen are afraid that they will suffer poverty and hunger, they are just as violent in their haste. For the belly is deaf and blind, so that it permits no fairness. Accordingly each one of us ought to be all the more critical of himself, when his personal gain and advantage are in question, so that that cupidity, which drove those men to madness, may not remove all distinction between the just and the unjust, and the disgraceful and the honest.

27. *Not only is there danger of our trade coming into disrepute.* First of all, it is preposterous that the upshot is that Demetrius gives only a secondary place to religion, because there is nothing more absurd than to prefer the belly to a goddess. But it is also idle for him to be making the plea that the worship of Diana is endangered. For if he had suffered no loss through Paul's teaching, he would have stayed quietly at home; he himself would never have had any anxiety, or troubled others about the worship of Diana. Therefore what gave rise to such zeal and such a fever of activity except a personal blow? Indeed, because he saw that there would not be a sufficiently proper or likely reason for him and his men to fight, he takes pains to put a different complexion on it (*ascititio colore fucare*). Therefore, in order to conceal the infamy of the offence, he covers it with the plausible pretext of religion. Thus no matter how boldly the ungodly rise up against God, they nevertheless make impudent attempts to obtain respectable pretexts from all sides.[1] But God does not allow Himself to be mocked; on the contrary He drags them out of their subterfuges into the light. No other witness is needed to refute Demetrius' hypocrisy, because he convicts himself out of his own mouth, when

---

[1] Reading *hinc inde* with C.R. But if Tholuck's *inde* is read, then *from it* (religion). Tr.

he expresses his grief at his personal loss. Today the conduct of the Papists is similar. They have the effrontery to boast that they are the defenders of the Catholic faith, and the holy mother, the Church, but having begun in this way about their zeal, in the very presentation of the case they breathe out the smell of the kitchen with mouths agape. But if we have a mind to plead the cause of godliness clearly and earnestly, let us forget our own advantages, so that the glory of God may hold first place. For the prospect of profit so dulls our senses with its attractions, that, while wandering through all sorts of sinful things, we are nevertheless deluding ourselves, as long as our intention is to look to our own private interests.

Whom all Asia and the world. To Demetrius it seems intolerable for the majesty of Diana to fall to the ground, when the whole world esteems it and worships it. And it is a common evasion for all superstitious people to claim that a great number are in agreement. But the true religion requires a firmer support than the will of men. Today the only thing that holds back the simple and ignorant is the fact that they do not dare to abandon errors accepted by usage everywhere, because they imagine that what has satisfied many, albeit foolishly and thoughtlessly, must be regarded as legitimate. Accordingly they also do not hesitate to press the mere name of custom against God Himself. But the Lord lays down a far different rule for us, viz. that being content with His authority, the authority of Him alone, we have no regard for the opinion of men, or our own usage, or the custom of many nations.

And the city was filled with the confusion: and they rushed with one accord into the theatre, having seized Gaius and Aristarchus, men of Macedonia, Paul's companions in travel. And when Paul was minded to enter in unto the people, the disciples suffered him not. And certain also of the chief officers of Asia, being his friends, sent unto him, and besought him not to adventure himself[1] into the theatre. Some therefore cried one thing, and some another: for the assembly was in confusion; and the more part knew not wherefore they were come together. And they brought Alexander out of the multitude, the Jews putting him forward. And Alexander beckoned with the hand, and would have made a defence unto the people. But when they perceived that he was a Jew, all with one voice about the space of two hours cried out, Great is Diana of the Ephesians. (29-34)

29. Here Luke exposes the people's nature to view, as if it were painted in a picture. Like a fire sweeping over a thousand houses at once, so in a moment an uproar spread through the whole city; and

[1] Calvin, with Greek, reads *give himself.* Tr.

where such a storm is once raised, it is not easily assuaged. But since the servants of Christ cannot avoid this evil, they ought to be fortified with invincible steadfastness so that they may intrepidly hold out against popular uprisings, and not be thrown into confusion, as though by something new or unusual, when they see that people are out to make trouble. Thus Paul himself glories elsewhere that he carries on with unbroken courage through the midst of seditions (II Cor. 6.5). At the same time the Lord sustains the ministers of His Word with the best of consolation, and makes them steadfast with supreme confidence, when they are tossed about like this in the midst of many storms in heaving seas, when He testifies that He holds the helm of His Church, and not only that, but that He controls all whirlwinds and waves, so that He calms them as soon as He thinks fit. Therefore let us realize that we must sail as though on a storm-tossed sea; and, what is more, that we must put up with this bad reputation, as if we ourselves are stirring up the disturbances; and that nothing is to divert us from the right course of duty. Therefore, persisting in this way, we shall indeed be severely buffetted, but, at least, the Lord will not allow us to go under and suffer shipwreck. Besides, we see that, although sedition is a disorderly thing, the people nevertheless always move on to something worse, just as now the Ephesians seize Gaius and Aristarchus, and, shouting like madmen, reject Alexander. How does that come about, except that Satan takes possession of them and tyrannizes them, so that they prefer to support bad causes? There is also another reason, that a prior judgment, based upon a false accusation, fills their minds, so that they do not waste time in making inquiries about the situation.

30. *And when Paul wished.* One can discern Paul's firmness, that goes hand in hand with his modesty. Although he can keep safely out of sight, he is prepared to expose himself to danger. And yet he does not refuse to follow the advice of those, who were better informed about the state of affairs. If he had not been kept back, what he had intended to do, ought not to be put down to rashness. No sedition was being provoked through his fault; why should he not risk his life, especially when he does not despair of things turning out better? But when the brethren, and friends, with knowledge of the circumstances, advise against it, his modesty is praiseworthy, because he does not persist in his own plan.

33. *They brought out Alexander.* One may well believe that this Alexander was not sent out by the Jews, to present the nation's common cause, but because they wished to give him to the people to be put to death. However the name of *Jew*, made him such an object of hate, that they tumultuously reject whatever he was about to say

about the situation and their cause. Moreover it is not certain whether
he is the Alexander whom Paul mentions elsewhere (I Tim. 1.20;
II Tim. 4.14); yet it seems to me a likely conjecture. But if we do
believe that it is he, let us learn from this terrible example to walk
carefully, so that Satan may not drag us off into a similar defection.
For we see that a man who was on the point of martyrdom became
a perfidious and wicked apostate.

34. *Great is Diana of the Ephesians.* The confession, which was not
coming from the faith of the heart, was certainly noisy, but there was
nothing solid behind it. For what was the source of the divinity of
the great Diana, which they proclaim, except that, like madmen, they
furiously defend an error which they once imbibed? With the true
religion the method is different, that 'from the heart we believe unto
righteousness, and then confession with the mouth follows unto
salvation' (Rom. 10.10). In that lies the difference between the steadfastness and zeal of the martyrs, and the outrageous behaviour of mad
ravers and the insane stubbornness of all fanatics. And yet we are
disgracefully slothful if we are less frank and vigorous in the profession
of a sure faith, than they are with their offensive error. For we hear
what the Spirit of God lays down for us through David, 'I have believed, therefore I shall speak' (Ps. 116.10).

*And when the townclerk had quieted the multitude, he saith, Ye men of
Ephesus, what man is there who knoweth not how that the city of the
Ephesians is temple-keeper of the great Diana,*[1] *and of the image which
fell down from Jupiter? Seeing then that these things cannot be gainsaid,
ye ought to be quiet, and to do nothing rash. For ye have brought hither
these men, which are neither robbers of temples nor blasphemers of our
goddess. If therefore Demetrius, and the craftsmen that are with him,
have a matter against any man, the courts are open, and there are proconsuls: let them accuse one another. But if ye seek any thing about
other matters, it shall be settled in the regular assembly. For indeed we
are in danger to be accused concerning this day's riot, there being no
cause for it: and as touching it we shall not be able to give account of this
concourse. And when he had thus spoken, he dismissed the assembly.*
(35-40)

35. Here Luke tells that the tumult was ended, but in such a way
that superstition still held sway among the senseless people, and the
truth of God was not heard. For the clerk, as is the usual way with
politic men, thinks it enough if he can calm the excited crowd by any
means whatever. At the same time the actual cause is suppressed.
Without a doubt he was aware of Demetrius' spitefulness and saw

[1] Calvin reads *goddess Diana.* Tr.

that he took advantage of a religious pretext, and set the city in an uproar, for his personal advantage, but he does not touch a wound that was hidden from the ignorant. However, for the sake of putting a stop to the strife, he extols the spurious divinity of Diana, and affirms her superstitious cult. If Paul had been in the theatre at that moment he would have exposed himself to death a hundred times, rather than allow himself to be rescued at this price. For even if the clerk had not spoken like this at his command, yet there would have been perfidious dissimulation in public by a witness and herald of the heavenly doctrine. The clerk announces that the *image*, which the Ephesians were worshipping, fell from heaven, and that Paul, and his companions, did not use any insulting language against their goddess. Or could he (Paul) have said nothing, without approving of a trumped-up excuse by his very silence? But that was to surrender to idolatry. Therefore Luke had good reason for his earlier statement that Paul was kept back by the brethren from entering the theatre.

37, 38. *Men who are neither sacrilegious.* Certainly it is right and proper of him to deny that they are sacrilegious, but he goes on at once to give a wrong definition of a kind of sacrilege, to use insulting language against Diana. For since all superstition is profane and polluted it follows that all who transfer the honour due to God alone, to idols, are sacrilegious. But here it is the sagacity of the clerk, and carnal sagacity at that, that is being praised, and not his godliness. For all he was concerned about was to extinguish the fire of sedition. Therefore he finally draws to an end by saying that if Demetrius has any personal charge to make, the courts and magistrates are available; and that public matters must be dealt with in an assembly that is legally constituted, and not in a turmoil, in one that has met together at the command of the magistrates, and not in one that has hurriedly gathered at the random instigation and caprice of one man. He uses the plural *proconsuls*, not because Asia had more than one, but because deputies (*legati*) sometimes used to hold courts instead of proconsuls. He also subdues them by making them afraid, because an opportunity was given to the proconsul to give a rough handling to the city.

CHAPTER TWENTY

And after the uproar was ceased, Paul having sent for the disciples and exhorted them, took leave of them,[1] and departed for to go into Macedonia. And when he had gone through those parts, and had given them much exhortation, he came into Greece. And when he had spent three months there, and a plot was laid against him by the Jews, as he was about to set sail for Syria, he determined to return through Macedonia. And there accompanied him as far as Asia Sopater of Beroea, the son of Pyrrhus; and of the Thessalonians, Aristarchus and Secundus; and Gaius of Derbe, and Timothy; and of Asia, Tychicus and Trophimus. But these had gone before, and were waiting for us at Troas. And we sailed away from Philippi after the days of unleavened bread, and came unto them to Troas in five days; where we tarried seven days. (1-6)

1. In this chapter Luke narrates how Paul left Asia in order to go to Jerusalem, and crossed the sea again. But although everything written in this account deserves careful pondering, yet it does not require a lengthy explanation. It is apparent that the Church was saved by the wonderful power of God, when it was in the midst of those stormy waves. The Church at Ephesus was still young and feeble. Having once experienced an unexpected tumult the faithful could have been justifiably afraid of similar storms springing up from time to time. There is no doubt that Paul was reluctant to be parted from them, yet because greater need calls him elsewhere, he is forced to leave his recently begotten sons in a heaving sea, hardly yet clear of one shipwreck as they are. But as for them, although Paul's departure is a sad and bitter experience, yet they do not keep him back or detain him, in case they might do harm to other churches. So we see that they were not self-centred, but that they honoured the Kingdom of Christ by their care and devotion, so that they had regard for the brethren as well as for themselves, for their common advantage. This example ought to be carefully noted, so that we may take pains to help each other in this lamentable dispersion of ours. But if it ever happens that we are deprived of beneficial aids, let us not waver however, knowing that God grasps the helm of our ship. But we must observe that Paul does not leave without taking farewell of the brethren, but rather encourages them on his departure. Similarly

[1] After *the disciples* Calvin has *embraced them, and set out to go.* Vulg. (WW) agrees with Greek, which RV renders. Tr.

Luke goes on at once to say that Paul also exhorted the Macedonians at length, that is, in no cursory fashion, as if it were enough to remind them of their duty, but in the way he elsewhere orders it to be done (II Tim. 4.2), by urging even to the point of rudeness, and by thoroughly inculcating things that it is necessary to know, so that they might never fade from memory.

3-6. *A plot was laid for him.* God disciplined His servant in a variety of ways and incessant struggles, so that he might present to us an indefatigable example of steadfastness. As if it is not enough that he is exhausted by the effort and irksomeness of a long and difficult journey, there is also the added threat to his life from a plot. Let all the servants of Christ place this mirror before their eyes, so that irksome difficulties may never cause them to faint. However, when Paul turns his steps in another direction and avoids the ambush prepared for him, he is showing, at the same time, that we must have regard to our own lives to the extent that we do not rashly rush into the midst of dangers. Surely the companions who accompany him give no ordinary proof of their loyalty; and we see how precious his life was to the faithful, when several chosen associates, from different nations, undertake a hard, rough journey at great expense for his sake.

Luke says that Paul stayed at Philippi during *the days of unleavened bread,* because at that time there was a better opportunity for teaching. And since the abrogation of the Law was still unknown, he had to take care that the ignorant might not think him a despiser of God by disregarding the feast day. However it particularly appears to me as a special opportunity for him to teach, because the Jews were more attentive to learning on that occasion.

And upon the first day of the week, when we were gathered together to break bread, Paul discoursed with them, intending to depart on the morrow; and prolonged his speech until midnight. And there were many lights in the upper chamber, where we were gathered together. And there sat in the window a certain young man named Eutychus, borne down with deep sleep; and as Paul discoursed yet longer, being borne down by his sleep he fell down from the third story, and was taken up dead. And Paul went down, and fell on him, and embracing him said, Make ye no ado; for his life is in him. And when he was gone up, and had broken the bread, and eaten, and had talked with them a long while, even till break of day, so he departed. And they brought the lad alive, and were not a little comforted. But we, going before to the ship, set sail for Assos, there intending to take in Paul: for so had he appointed, intending himself to go by land. (7-13)

7. *On one day of the Sabbaths.*¹ He means either the first day of the week, the day after the Sabbath, or one particular Sabbath. And the latter would seem to me more likely for this reason, that according to custom that day was most suitable for holding a meeting. But since it is not unusual for the Evangelists to put 'one' instead of 'first' (Matt. 28.1; Luke 24.1; John 20.1), according to the Hebrew idiom, it will suit very well that they held their meeting on the day after the Sabbath. Moreover it would be too flat to take this to mean any day at all. For what is the point of mentioning the Sabbath except to note the suitableness and the choice of the time? It is also very likely that Paul waited for the Sabbath so that it would be easier for him to gather all the disciples into one place on the day before his departure. But the keenness of all of them is worth nothing, because it was no trouble to Paul to go on teaching until midnight, although he was getting ready for a journey, and the others did not grow tired of learning. For the only reason for prolonging his sermon was the eagerness and attention of his audience.

To break bread. Although the breaking of bread sometimes means a domestic feast in Hebrew, yet two reasons prompt me to take it in this verse as referring to the Holy Supper. For since it is easily inferred from what follows that a great crowd of people had been gathered together in that place, it is not consistent with that, that a supper could have been prepared in a private house. In the second place Luke will soon tell us that Paul took bread, not at supper-time, but after midnight in fact. In addition he says that he took the food, not for the sake of filling himself, but only to taste it.² Therefore I come to the conclusion that a solemn day, that was going to be more convenient for all, was appointed among them for celebrating the Holy Supper of the Lord. But in order to make good in some way the silence of rather a long absence, Paul draws out his sermon longer than usual. My statement about the great number of people is based on the fact that the upper room was a blaze of many lights; and that was certainly done, not to make an ostentatious display, but out of necessity. For when there is no need for something, it is ambition and vanity that make men extravagant. Moreover it was proper to have the whole place ablaze with lights, so that no suspicion of shameful or vicious behaviour might fall on that holy company. Add yet another conjecture, if the upper room had not been full, those who were present would not have allowed Eutychus to sit on the window. For it would have been a scandalous presumption, to spurn and reject

---

¹ Calvin gives a literal translation of the Greek Ἐν δὲ τῇ μιᾷ τῶν σαββάτων. Tr.

² v. 11. Greek, γευσάμενος; Calvin *degustasset*, both meaning *tasted*. Tr.

the heavenly teaching, by withdrawing to a window, when room was available elsewhere.

9. *When he was overpowered by sleep.* I see no reason why certain commentators condemn the young man's sleepiness so strongly and sharply, by saying that he was punished for his lethargy with death. For what is strange about his struggling with sleep at the dead of night and finally succumbing? And one may gather from the fact that he was attacked and overpowered by sleep against his will and contrary to his expectation, that he had not settled down to rest. It would have been a sign of laziness to try to get a suitable place for sleeping. But what else is his being overwhelmed by sleep, when sitting in the window, but innocently yielding to natural weakness; just as if a man may lose consciousness from fasting, or excessive fatigue? Drowsiness will be justifiably condemned in those who, being immersed in worldly cares, are scornful in their approach to the Word; in those who become sleepy as a result of stuffing themselves with food and wine; and in those who are alert in other matters but are careless in hearing the Word. But Luke clearly absolves Eutychus, when he says that just after midnight he sank into a deep sleep and fell down. Furthermore the Lord wished to awaken the faith of His own people not only by the sleep, but also by the death of this young man, so that they might receive Paul's teaching more eagerly, and keep it thoroughly imprinted on their minds. At first indeed there was a test that was by no means easy, but one that could have shaken even the firmest to the core. For who would think that Christ was in control of that company, when a wretched man belonging to it falls to an early death? Who would not rather think that this was a sign of God's curse? But by bringing in a remedy at once, the Lord freed their minds of all anxiety.

10. *He lay on him.* We know that when the apostles performed miracles they sometimes introduced certain outward ceremonies by which they might ascribe the glory to God as the Author. But I think that the only reason why Paul now laid himself on top of the young man was to stimulate himself to the effort of prayer. He acts just as if he were uniting himself with the young man. And perhaps it was done in imitation of Elisha, of whom the sacred history reports a similar thing (II Kings 4.34). Yet it was vehemence of compassion rather than emulation of the prophet that moved him. For that conjunction gives him a greater impetus to pray with all the feeling of his heart for the youth's life from the Lord. Similarly, when he embraces the body of the dead man, he is indicating by this gesture that he is offering it to God to be restored to life. And one may gather from the context that he did not give up his embrace, until he knew that life was given back to it.

Do not trouble yourselves. We must observe that the chief cause of
Paul's concern was that this sad event might not shake the faith of the
godly, and trouble their minds. At the same time the Lord ratified
the last sermon, that Paul delivered at Troas, as if with a seal impressed before their eyes. When he says that *his soul is in him*, he is
not denying that he was dead, because he would be obliterating the
glory of the miracle in that way, but the meaning is that life was
restored to him by the grace of God. I do not restrict the subsequent
statement that they felt greatly *comforted*, to the joy that they had at
the young man's recovery, but at the same time I include the confirmation of their faith, since God had given them such a remarkable
token of His love.

13. *We, having gone on board ship.* It is not certain why Paul preferred to make the journey by land, whether because sailing might be
difficult for him, or whether to visit the brethren in the passing. I
myself think that he avoided the sea on this occasion for the sake of
his health. But his consideration is to be commended, because he
spared his companions. For why did he send them away from himself, except to relieve them of trouble? So we see that they vied with
one another, in turn, in courtesy and acts of kindness. Those men
were ready and willing for service; on the other hand Paul, far from
being a hard taskmaster, without being asked, kindly relieved them
of the duties, which they were prepared to carry out; yes, and what is
more, he set aside his own advantage, and ordered what was going
to be for their comfort.

It is quite well known that the city of *Assos* is assigned to the Troad[1]
by the geographers. The same city was called Apollonia, according
to the evidence of Pliny. They say that it was a colony of the Ae-
tolians.

*And when he met us at Assos, we took him in, and came to Mitylene.
And sailing from thence, we came the following day over against Chios;
and the next day we touched at Samos; and the day after[2] we came to
Miletus. For Paul had determined to sail past Ephesus, that he might
not have to spend time in Asia; for he was hastening, if it were possible
for him, to be at Jerusalem the day of Pentecost. And from Miletus he
sent to Ephesus, and called to him the elders of the church. And when
they were come to him, he said unto them, Ye yourselves know, from
the first day that I set foot in Asia, after what manner I was with you
all the time, serving the Lord with all lowliness of mind, and with tears,
and with trials which befell me by the plots of the Jews: how that I*

[1] As well as the city, there was also the region of Troas, called the Troad. Tr.
[2] Calvin, as AV, reads *having tarried at Trogyllium.* Tr.

shrank not from declaring unto you anything that was profitable, and teaching you publicly, and from house to house, testifying both to Jews and to Greeks repentance toward God, and faith toward our Lord Jesus Christ. (14-21)

16, 17. *For Paul had determined.* There is no doubt that he had strong and important reasons for hurrying to Jerusalem, not because the sacredness of the day meant such a lot to him, but because strangers were in the habit of flocking to Jerusalem from all directions for the feast days. Since he hoped that he would do some effective work in such a great multitude, he did not wish to miss the opportunity. Let us therefore realize that worship according to the Law did not enter into the reason for his making such great haste, but that what he had in mind was the upbuilding of the Church, partly by reporting to the faithful that the Kingdom of Christ had been extended, partly by winning any who were still unfamiliar with Christ, partly by repelling the calumnies of impudent men. Yet we must observe that he is concerned for the rest of the churches at the same time. For in summoning the presbyters (*presbyteros*) of Ephesus to Miletus, he shows that he is not neglecting Asia. On the other hand their coming together when invited, is a sign not only of harmony, but also of modesty. For although there were many of them, yet they are not annoyed at obeying one apostle of Christ's, whom they knew to be distinguished by remarkable gifts. Moreover it will be quite clear from the context that those who are called *elders* (*seniores*) were not men who were of advanced years, but men who ruled over the Church. But it is usual in nearly all languages that those, who are placed in authority to rule over others, are called 'ancients' (*senes*) and 'fathers' (*patres*), even if their age does not always correspond.

18. *You know.* In this address Paul chiefly devotes himself to using his own example to encourage the pastors, whom he had appointed at Ephesus, to discharge their office faithfully. For this is the way that censure is properly given, and authority acquired for teaching, when the teacher does not give any instructions verbally, which he has not in actual fact carried out before. But there was no inconsistency in Paul commending his own virtues. Indeed there is nothing more intolerable in the servants of Christ than ambition and vanity, but since the modesty and humility of the holy man were rightly known to all, there was no fear of him incurring the suspicion of boasting, especially when, driven by necessity, he sets forth his faithfulness and diligence as an example to others. Certainly he gives a magnificent account of his own labours, patience, bravery and other virtues. But why does he do so? Certainly not to gain the applause of his listeners, but so

that his holy exhortation might be more sharp and penetrating, and be thoroughly imprinted on, and stick to, their minds. He also had another aim, that his integrity might afterwards have the effect of commending his teaching. And he appeals to eye-witnesses so that he might not appear to be speaking about unknown things. I mean by eye-witnesses, those who not only had knowledge of all the things, but also had a clear judgment, uncorrupted by any passions.

19. *Serving the Lord.* In the first place he recalls not only what great difficulties he sustained, but especially his humility, linked with the contempt of the world, and insults, and other afflictions; as if he said that he had not been received with honour or approbation, but that he had been among them under the contemptible form of the cross. On the other hand it is no light test, when we do not fail, although we see ourselves trampled by the cruel arrogance of the world.

However particular attention must be given to individual points. *Serving the Lord* is taken here, not for worshipping God in holiness and righteousness, something that is common to all the godly, but it means to carry out a public function. Therefore Paul does not speak as any private individual on his own, but as a minister who had been given to the Church. And so he testifies that he has discharged the apostleship committed to him, with humility and modesty, partly because, recognizing his own weakness, he lacked self-confidence, partly because, thinking upon the pre-eminence of his office, he thought of himself as far from equal to it, partly because he gladly submitted himself to endure the ignominy of the cross of Christ. For that humility is placed over against empty confidence as well as haughtiness.

In the second place he adds *tears*, which struggles, various attacks of Satan, the ferocity of ungodly men, the internal disorders of the Church and stumbling-blocks forced out of him. He finally adds that among *the plots of the Jews* he lived in a state of anxiety; and he admits that, although he did not succumb, he was agitated by them, as he was not made of iron. For he is not ashamed to confess his weakness.

But his aim is that those whom he is addressing may not succumb to similar troubles, and that they may carry out their duty reverently and punctiliously, free of all ambition, and not only that they calmly allow themselves to be despised by men, but also that they may be disheartened in themselves; because a man who smacks of any loftiness, will never be properly fit to obey Christ. And since a false show of virtue cannot last long, so that it may be clear that he has behaved like that, sincerely and from the heart, he publicly mentions his steadfastness during three years, in which he had kept the same even tenor. 'You know', he says 'what I was like throughout the whole time, right from the first day.' In a word, this is the true proof of the servants of Christ, that they are not moved according to the changes of the times, but remain self-consistent (*sui similes*) and always keep a straight course.

20. *I kept back nothing.* He commends his own faithfulness and diligence in teaching in three particulars, that he gave the disciples sound and thorough instruction so that he omitted nothing which made for their salvation, that, not satisfied with general preaching, he also took pains to be of service to individuals. In the third place he summarizes the whole of his teaching saying that he urged them to have faith in Christ, and to repent. Now, since he is portraying for us the model of a good and faithful teacher, the proper course for all, who wish to make their labour acceptable to the Lord, is to have the upbuilding of the Church set before their eyes; as he elsewhere orders Timothy to reflect upon the things that are beneficial, so that he may devote himself to teaching them (I Tim. 4.6ff). And of course Scripture, which must be the norm for testing every method of teaching, and, more than that, is the only method of teaching properly, contains no clever speculations, to give pleasure to men when they are at ease and leisure; but, according to the same witness, Paul, all of it is profitable for making the man of God complete (II Tim. 3.16). But Paul prescribes such zeal for edifying, so that a pastor may omit nothing, as far as he is concerned, that it is beneficial to know. For teachers, who keep their pupils at first principles, so that they never attain to knowledge of the truth, are bad teachers. And surely the Lord does not instruct us by half measures in His Word, but teaches wisdom that is perfect and complete in every way. That makes it plain that those, who not only conceal and encourage the ignorance of the people by their silence, but also take no notice of gross errors and impious superstitions, are impudent in their boasts that they are ministers of the Word. Indeed that sort of thing is to be found in the Papacy today, where a great many give out sparks of sound doctrine, but do not dare to scatter the darkness of ignorance, and, while a depraved fear of the flesh keeps them back, they make the excuse that the people are not capable of more solid teaching. Indeed I admit that everything cannot be taught at once, and we must imitate Paul's sensibleness in accommodating himself to the capacity of the ignorant. But what sort of moderation is this, when they allow the blind to fall into a pit, when they leave wretched souls under the tyranny of Antichrist, when they see that idolatry is rampant, the worship of God corrupted, His Law violated, and, in a word, all holy things desecrated, and they either pass over such abominable confusion in silence, or hint at it cautiously and obscurely, like men taking evasive action? Therefore we must pay attention to what Paul says when he

denies that he evaded telling all the things that were for the people's benefit, for we gather from that that a pure, candid, and straight-forward profession of sound teaching is required from the servants of Christ; and also that nothing is less becoming to them than insinuations that are indirect and wrapped up in a cunning disguise.

Publicly and from house to house. This is the second point, that he taught, not only all in the assembly, but individuals in their homes, as each man's need demanded. For Christ did not ordain pastors on the principle that they only teach the Church in a general way on the public platform, but that they also care for the individual sheep, bring back the wandering and scattered to the fold, bind up those broken and crippled (*luxatas*), heal the sick, support the frail and weak (Ezek. 34.2, 4); for general teaching will often have a cold reception, unless it is helped by advice given in private. Accordingly there is no excuse for the negligence of those who, after holding one meeting, live for the rest of the time free from care, as if they have discharged their duty. It is as if their voices were shut up in the sanctuary, since they become completely dumb as soon as they come out of it. Those who learn are also warned that, if they do indeed wish to be counted among the flock of Christ, they must admit the pastors, as often as they come to them, and that private warnings are not to be avoided. For those who do not think fit to hear the pastor's voice, except in the church building (*theatro*), and moreover cannot bear to be warned and reproved at home, no, and fiercely reject such a necessary function into the bargain, are bears rather than sheep.

21. *Testifying to the Jews.* Moving on to the third point he now gives a brief summary of his teaching, viz. that he urged all to faith and repentance, in accordance with the previous statement that the Gospel consisted of those two elements alone. From that we also gather what genuine edification of the Church properly consists of, and for that the pastors bear the burden of responsibility; and we learn what we must devote all our efforts to aim at, if we wish to make profitable progress in the school of God. We have already said that the Word of God is profaned when its readers occupy themselves with frivolous questions. But so that it may not be read in a random and erratic way, we must keep this twofold goal, that the apostle sets before us. For anyone turning aside to anything else, will only be walking in a circle, despite the great fuss he makes.

By the word *testifying* he expresses himself with greater emphasis, as if he had said that he commended by bearing witness, so that no room might be left for the excuse of ignorance. For he is alluding to the practice of the law courts, where testifying is introduced to remove all doubt. Similarly men must not only be taught, but also urged to embrace salvation in Christ, and yield themselves to God for newness of life.

And even if he asserts that he neglected nobody, yet he puts the Jews in the first place, because, just as the Lord had given them preference over the Gentiles with the position of honour, so it was proper for Christ and His grace to be offered to them, until they would break with Him completely.

Repentance towards God. The difference between *faith* and *repentance* must first of all be observed, for some wrongly and stupidly confuse them, saying that repentance is a part of faith. Indeed I admit that they cannot be separated, because God does not illuminate anybody with the Spirit of faith, without regenerating him to new life at the same time. Yet they need to be distinguished as Paul does in this verse. For repentance is a turning round (*conversio*) to God, when we compose ourselves and the whole of our lives to His obedience. On the other hand faith is the receiving of the grace which is presented to us in Christ. For the object of the whole of religion is that we may serve the Lord purely, devoting ourselves to holiness and righteousness, and, secondly, that we do not seek any part of our salvation from any other person than from Him, and that we do not search anywhere else than in Christ alone. Therefore the teaching of repentance contains the rule of godly living; it demands denial of ourselves, mortification of our flesh, and meditation on the heavenly life. But because we are all corrupt by nature, alienated from righteousness, and opposed to God Himself, secondly, because we avoid God whom we know to be hostile to us, there must necessarily be set before us a way of free reconciliation, as well as a way to obtain new life. Therefore unless faith is added, it is useless to speak about repentance. Yes, and what is more, teachers of repentance, who neglect faith and insist only on regulating life and on precepts about good works, are hardly to be distinguished from secular philosophers. They teach how men must live; but since they leave men in their own nature, no restoration from it to something better can be hoped for, until they summon lost men to the hope of salvation, until they restore the dead to life by the promised forgiveness of sins, until they show that by gracious adoption God embraces as His sons, those who were previously the slaves of Satan; until they teach that the Spirit of regeneration must be sought from the heavenly Father, and that godliness, righteousness and uprightness must be drawn from Him, the fountain of all blessings; and from these there follows invocation, which holds the chief place in the legitimate worship of God. Now we see that repentance and faith are tied together in an unbreakable connexion. For it is faith that makes God friendly to us, with the result that not only is He gracious to us, absolving us from the guilt that deserves death, by taking no account of our sins, but also that He washes away the filth of our flesh by His Spirit and restores us to His own image. He does not mention repentance first because it is superior to faith in every way, since a part of it springs from, and is the effect of, faith, but because the beginning of repentance is a preparation for faith. I mean by 'the beginning' the dissatisfaction with ourselves, which drives us, when we have been moved by a serious fear of the wrath of God, to seek for a remedy.

Faith in Christ. It is not without good reason that all through Scripture Christ is set before our eyes as the goal, and, to use the common expression, object of faith. For the Majesty of God in itself is too high for men to mount up to it. Therefore unless Christ the Mediator comes to meet us, all our senses fade away to nothing in the search for God. Secondly, seeing that He is the Judge of the world, without Christ the sight of Him cannot but terrify us to death. On the other hand God not only manifests Himself to us by His own image in Christ, but recreates us by His fatherly favour and restores us to life completely. For there is no part of our salvation, which may not be found in Christ. He has made expiation for our sins by the sacrifice of His death; He has borne the punishment to acquit us; He has made us clean by His blood; He has appeased the wrath of the Father by His own obedience; He has procured righteousness for us by His resurrection. Therefore it is no wonder that we have said that faith must be absolutely fixed upon the consideration of Christ.

And now, behold, I go bound in the spirit unto Jerusalem, not knowing the things that shall befall me there: save that the Holy Ghost testifieth unto me in every city, saying that bonds and afflictions abide me. But I hold not my life of any account, as dear unto myself, so that I may accomplish my course,[1] and the ministry which I received from the Lord Jesus, to testify the gospel of the grace of God. And now, behold, I know that ye all, among whom I went about preaching the kingdom,[2] shall see my face no more. Wherefore I testify unto you this day, that I am pure from the blood of all men. For I shrank not from declaring unto you the whole counsel of God. (22-27)

22. *And now behold I go.* He now explains more fully why he has been speaking about his own integrity, viz. because they were never going to see him again. But it was of very great importance that the example, which God had set before them to imitate, should always remain before their eyes, and the memory of it survive after his death. For we know how easily men depart from pure instruction.

---

[1] Calvin, as AV, has also, *with joy.* Tr.
[2] Calvin, as AV, adds *of God.* Tr.

Apart from that, although he denies that he knows what will happen to him at Jerusalem, yet because he had been warned by many predictions that bonds were waiting for him there, a little later he puts an end to the hope of his return, as if he were already prepared to die. And yet in speaking like that he is not being inconsistent. Indeed his introductory remarks have a deliberate note of uncertainty, so that he may soften what was going to be rather a bitter blow, yet he properly affirms that the way things will turn out is still unknown to him, because he had no definite and special revelation about the whole course of events.

Bound in the Spirit. Some explain that he was under obligation to the churches, who had imposed on him the task of carrying alms. However it rather seems to me that it is the inward power and influence of the Holy Spirit that is meant, not because he was possessed with enthusiasm (ἐνθουσιασμῷ), so that he was not in control of his mind, but because, having been made more certain of the will of God, he was freely or calmly following the secret leading or inspiration of the Spirit. Therefore the expression amounts to his saying, 'I cannot do anything else, if I do not wish to be an obstinate rebel against God, who draws me there, as if bound by His Spirit'. For in order to clear himself of rashness, he asserts that the Spirit is the Promoter and Guide of his journey. But one would wish that a great many fanatics, who boast that any product of their fancy is dictated to them by the Spirit, might know the Spirit as intimately as Paul. Yet he does not say that all his movements or impulses are from the Spirit, but he states that it happened in a particular set of circumstances as if it were an extraordinary thing. For men often foolishly and rashly undertake many things, and then persist with them obstinately, because they are ashamed of being fickle. But he means not only that he has good cause for undertaking a journey that the Spirit orders, but that it is absolutely unavoidable for him, because it is sinful to resist. Moreover let us learn by the example of the holy man, not to kick against the Spirit of God, but obediently to surrender ourselves to Him to direct us, so that He may move us according to His will, as if we were bound to Him, and so that we may not be dragged along by force. For if the reprobate, who are the slaves of Satan, are driven at his instigation, not only willingly but also eagerly, how much more should this willing slavery (ἐθελοδουλεία) be in the sons of God.

23. *Save that the Holy Spirit.* I do not take this to mean secret oracles, but predictions which he was hearing everywhere from prophets. But this statement is of more value for commending prophecies, than if the very men, who uttered them, were cited as witnesses. For a word of God has its authority established in this way,

when we acknowledge that His Spirit is the Author, even although men are its ministers. Now when the same Spirit who warns Paul in advance of bonds and afflictions, at the same time keeps him under obligation, so that he may not refuse to submit himself to Him, we are taught from that, that, whatever dangers threaten us, we are not absolved on that account from obeying the commandments of God, and following His calling. Therefore, those men are deceiving themselves in vain, who put a limit on acting correctly, in so far as it can be done without trouble, and who, by way of excuse, thrust forward inconveniences, injuries, and finally, the danger of death.

24. *But I do not care, and life itself is not precious to me.* All the godly, and especially ministers of the Word, ought to be composed in their minds like this, so that setting aside everything else, they may hasten to obey God in the right course of action. Certainly life is too remarkable a gift of God that it ought to be despised, seeing that in it we have been created after the image of God, so that we may meditate upon that blessed immortality, that is reserved for us in heaven, and that in it God now shows Himself a Father to us by many proofs. But because it has been arranged for us like a race-course, it is proper always to make haste to the winning-post, and to overcome obstacles, so that nothing may impede or delay us on the course. For it is a shameful thing for us to be so gripped by a blind love of living, that, because of life, we lose the reasons for living. And Paul's words bring that out. For he does not simply esteem his life as of no value, but he puts consideration of it out of his mind, so that he may finish his course, and complete his ministry, that he received from Christ. It is as if he said that he is not possessed by any desire to live, except to satisfy the call of God, and, for that reason, that the loss of life will not be a serious thing for him, provided that he is coming near, by death, to the goal of the function that God had prescribed for him.

But we must notice his words, *with joy*. For he means that there is no sadness or mourning when the faithful are deprived of life, but that they live and die to the Lord joyfully. For the joy of a good conscience lies hidden too deep for it to be driven out by external troubles or any fleshly grief; it is too lively in its exultation for it to be stifled.

We must also note the explanation of *course*, viz. that it is the *ministry received from the Lord*. Paul is certainly speaking about himself, but by his example he teaches that all, who do not have the Lord superintending their course, are wandering. The conclusion is that the calling of that one man is for each one of us the pattern for right living. And in fact the only way we may be sure that what we do is approved by the Lord, is if our lives are ordered according to His will. This certitude is particularly required in the ministers of the

Word, so that they may not undertake anything without Christ as the originator. And there is certainly no doubt that when Paul distinguishes his apostleship by that mark, as he is very often in the habit of doing, he is establishing its genuineness (*fidem*). He calls it *the gospel of the grace of God* from its effect or end. However it is a statement of rare commendation, that the grace and salvation of God are brought to us by the Gospel. For it is of supreme importance to us to know that in it God is found to be favourable.

25. *And now behold I know.* What he had hinted at rather cautiously he now states openly. But we have said that he deliberately deprived them of the hope of his return in order to imprint his exhortations more firmly on their memories. For we know how much force the last words of the departing and the dying have. He also wished them to heed this premonition lest in protracted uncertainty as to his coming their faith might collapse through weariness. Once again the teaching of the Gospel is called *the Kingdom of God*, for it lays the foundation of the Kingdom of God in this world, by the renewal of men in the image of God, until it is finally completed in the last resurrection.

26, 27. *For these reasons I call you to witness.* This amounts to the same thing as if he had said, 'I call you as witnesses', or 'I call you to witness[1] in the sight of God and the angels'. But he does this, not so much for his own sake, as, with greater authority, to prescribe for them a principle of their office. Furthermore this verse contains a brief summary of how to teach rightly and properly, and it exhorts teachers themselves, under a strong and severe penalty, to devote themselves diligently to their task. Therefore to what method of teaching must pastors adhere? In the first place, let them not use their own judgment to determine what is suitable to present in public and what to omit, but let them hand over the decision on that matter to God alone. In this way the door into the Church of God will not stand open for human fabrications. In the second place a mortal man will not arrogate to himself the presumption to tear to pieces or mutilate Scripture, to pick this or that as he pleases, to obscure some things, and suppress many things, but he will teach whatever is revealed in Scripture, although he will do so prudently and opportunely for the upbuilding of the people, yet simply and without any pretence, as befits a faithful and frank interpreter of God. I said that prudence must be shown, because we must always have regard to what is beneficial, provided that there is no cunning, in which many take an excessive pride, when they alter the Word of God to suit their own methods, and devise for us some vague philosophy or other, which is

1 *attestor* i.e. 'attest' but in the obsolete sense of 'call to witness'. Tr.

a mixture of the Gospel and their own fancies, because, of course, this concoction is more pleasing. From that we have free-will, from that the merits of works, from that the denial of God's providence and God's gracious election. But what I have just said deserves attention, that the *counsel of God*, which Paul mentions here, is included in His Word, and must not be sought anywhere else. For many things are hidden from us in this life, the full manifestation of which is deferred until that day, in which, with new eyes, we shall see God as He is, face to face. Therefore the men who make known the will of God are those who expound Scripture faithfully, and from it establish the people in faith, in the fear of the Lord, and in all godly practices. But, as I have just said that this sentence condemns those who, by their philosophical arguments, corrupt the purity of Scripture with their own leavening influences, in order not to teach anything out of step with the common understanding of men, and therefore offensive, so Paul thunders violently against those who, out of fear of the cross and persecutions, speak only enigmatically.

I am pure from the blood. I have no doubt that he referred to the passage in Ezekiel in which God declares that His prophet will be guilty of blood, unless he conscientiously urges the wicked to repent (Ezek. 3.18ff). For He places pastors in authority over His Church on this principle, that if anything perishes by their negligence an account is to be demanded from them; yes, and what is more, that, unless they show the way of salvation without deceit and ambiguities, the destruction of those who go astray is to be reckoned against them. But those who are not shaken out of their torpor by such a severe threat must be exceedingly dull. Therefore the epicurean impiety of the Papal clergy betrays itself all the more, when, despite their boasting magnificent titles, they think no more about rendering an account of so many perishing souls, than if no Judge were sitting in heaven; and their wickedness is no less disgusting in the eyes of the whole world, because, being intent only on devouring the sheep, they usurp the name of pastors. Moreover the Lord shows how precious He regards souls, when, because of their destruction, He exacts such a severe punishment for the laziness of pastors. Yet we see how small a value a great many set on their own salvation, when God is not reluctant to be actively associated in concern for it.

Take heed unto yourselves, and to all the flock, in the which the Holy Ghost hath made you bishops, to feed the church of God, which he purchased with his own blood. I know that after my departing grievous wolves shall enter in among you, not sparing the flock; and from among your own selves shall men arise, speaking perverse things, to draw away

the disciples after them. Wherefore watch ye, remembering that by the
space of three years I ceased not to admonish every one night and day
with tears. And now I commend you to God, and to the word of his
grace, which is able to build you up, and to give you the inheritance
among all them that are sanctified. (28-32)

28. *Therefore take heed.* He now directs his words to them, and
gives many reasons to show that they must be diligent and watchful,
and that he is so very anxious only because necessity demands it. The
first reason is that they know the faithfulness pledged (*obstrictam*
habeant fidem) to the flock, over which they are placed in authority.
The second is that they have been called to this office, not by mortal
man, but by the Holy Spirit. The third is that it is no ordinary honour
to rule the Church of God. The fourth is that the Lord bore witness
with clear proof, to the high regard which He has for the Church,
when He redeemed it with His own blood.

As far as the first is concerned he orders them to give heed not only
to the flock, but first of all to themselves. For a man who neglects his
own salvation will never be zealous in his concern about the salvation
of others; and a man, who shows no inclination for godliness, will
incite others to lead godly lives in vain. One should rather say that a
man who forgets about himself will not put out his devotion and
effort on the flock, although he himself is part of the flock. Therefore
in order that they may be anxious for the flock committed to them,
Paul warns them, as individuals, to keep themselves personally in the
fear of the Lord. For it was going to be in that way that they would
give the faithfulness due to the flock. For we have said that Paul concludes from their calling, that they are to devote their care to the
Church of God, over which they rule. It is as if he said, that they are
not their own masters, after they have been made pastors, but are
publicly bound to the whole flock.

The Holy Spirit has appointed you bishops (*episcopos*). By the very
name (bishops, overseers) he warns that it is as if they have been set on
a watch-tower, from which they keep watch for the common safety
of all. But Paul lays his main stress on the fact that they were not
ordained by men, but that the care of the Church has been committed
to their charge by God. Accordingly greater conscientiousness is
demanded from them, because there is going to be a difficult reckoning
before that supreme judgment-seat. For the more pre-eminent is the
authority of the Lord, whom we serve, the greater reverence do we
naturally offer Him, and the very reverence whets our zeal.

Further, although the Lord intended ministers of the Word to be
chosen, from the beginning, by the votes of men, nevertheless He

always arrogates the direction of the Church to Himself, not only so that we may acknowledge Him as its one and only governor, but also that we may know that the incomparable treasure of salvation comes only from Him. For He is cheated of His glory if we think that the Gospel is given to us either by chance, or by the will or activity of men. And Paul attributes this particular thing to the Spirit, through whom God governs His Church, and who is the secret witness to the calling of God to each man in his own conscience.

About the word *bishops* we must briefly note that Paul calls all the Ephesian presbyters this, without distinction. From that we gather that, according to the usage of Scripture, bishops do not differ from presbyters in any way. But through vice and corruption it came about that those who held the leading place in individual cities, began to be called 'bishops'. I say 'vice', not because it is a bad thing for any one man to be prominent in every college, but because it is an intolerable presumption, when men twist the words of Scripture to their own customs, and do not hesitate to change the language of the Holy Spirit.

To rule[1] *the church of God.* The Greek verb ποιμαίνειν means to *feed*; but, by an apt similitude, it is transferred to any sort of rule. But I have said that this is the third argument drawn from the excellence of the office. Similarly the self-same Paul elsewhere warns Timothy how he ought to behave himself in the household of God, which is the Church of the living God, the pillar and stay of the truth (I Tim. 3.15). It is as if he said that there is no place for laziness in such an arduous office; and that there is no excuse for those whom God appoints as stewards of His family, because it involves a higher degree of honour, if they do not match up to such great authority, that is, if they do not diligently devote themselves to their duties. Now if bishops are only created by God and by the Holy Spirit to feed the Church, the Papal hierarchy is ridiculous, in which bishops, proud of their empty title, make not even a pretence of undertaking the task of feeding.

Which he purchased. The fourth reason with which Paul urges the pastors to be diligent in the practice of their office is that the Lord has given no ordinary proof of His love towards the Church, by pouring out His own blood for its sake. That makes it plain how precious it is to Him. And surely there is nothing that ought to be more effective in spurring on pastors to devote themselves more eagerly to their duty than if they reflect that it is to themselves that the price of the blood of Christ has been entrusted. For it follows from this, that unless they are faithful in putting out their labour on the Church, not only are they made accountable for lost souls, but they are guilty of sacrilege, because they have profaned the sacred blood of the Son of

[1] Greek: ποιμαίνειν τὴν ἐκκλησίαν. Calvin: *ad regendam ecclesiam.* Tr.

God, and have made useless the redemption acquired by Him, as far as they are concerned. But it is a hideous and monstrous crime if, by our idleness, not only the death of Christ becomes worthless, but also the fruit of it is destroyed and perishes. But the Church is said to have been acquired by God so that we may know that He intends it to remain complete for Himself, because it is right that He have and hold those whom He has redeemed. Yet at the same time we must remember that the whole human race has been given over to Satan's possession, until Christ sets us free from his tyranny, and gathers us into the inheritance of the Father.

Still, because the expression used by Paul appears to be harsh, we must see what he means by saying that God procured the Church by *His blood*. For there is nothing more absurd than to suppose that God is corporeal or mortal. But by speaking like this he is commending the unity of the Person of Christ. For in view of the fact that there are separate natures in Christ, Scripture sometimes mentions separately what belongs to each in particular. But when it sets God before us, made manifest in the flesh, it does not separate His human nature from His deity. Yet because, on the other hand, the two natures are so united in Christ as to constitute one Person, what properly belongs to the one is sometimes improperly transferred to the other. For instance in this verse Paul attributes blood to God, because the man Jesus Christ, who shed His blood for us, was also God. This figure of speech was called the *communicatio idiomatum* by the Fathers, because the property of one nature is applied to the other. But I have said that in this way the unity of the Person of Christ is clearly expressed, so that we are not to think of Him as twofold, in the way that Nestorius once attempted to do. Yet we must not imagine the confusion of the two natures, such as Eutyches tried to introduce; or such as the Spanish dog, Servetus, has concocted at the present time, for to him the divinity of Christ is nothing else but an image (*spectrum*) of the human nature, which, he dreams, has always been shining in God.[1]

29. *For I know.* Now Paul exhorts the Ephesians to keep careful watch, because of necessity also, and that is the sharpest of goads. For he warns of the threat of serious attacks by *wolves*. Indeed it is, so to speak, the perpetual fate of the Church to be infested by wolves. Accordingly there is never any time to sleep. Indeed the more of them that break in, and the more harmful they be, the sharper the watch that pastors must keep. For sometimes God lightens some trouble, so that the flock may be fed quietly and at peace; and just as the sheep are fed more safely in the fields under a clear and serene sky, but, on the other hand, there is more danger in cloudy and dark

---

[1] See Calvin's *Institutes*, 2.14.8. Tr.

weather, so sometimes it is as if some fair weather is granted to the
Church of God, and after it comes a stormy time, which is more
suitable for the stratagems of wolves. Therefore Paul's meaning is that
there is need for greater vigilance than previously, because greater
dangers threaten.

But it is asked where Paul got this notion from? In the first place
there is no doubt that his presence had been very effective for keeping
wolves back, or driving them away; and indeed it is no wonder if the
power of the Spirit, which shines out in the ministers of Christ, puts
a curb on the ungodly, so that they do not dare to produce their own
poison; yes, and if that heavenly splendour scatters the great darkness
of Satan. Therefore since Paul knew that Satan's malice had been
restrained for a time by his own efforts, it is easy for him to foresee
what is going to happen after his departure. However, it is probable
that he was made more certain by the Lord, through the Spirit of
prophecy, so that others might then be warned through him, as we
see did actually happen. But be that as it may, whenever able and
faithful pastors depart, let us learn that we must be afraid of wolves,
when it is difficult for them to keep them away from the sheep-folds,
even with the strictest watch.

30. *And men shall arise from among yourselves.* It aggravates the
seriousness of the trouble that some of the wolves are among them,
and even hide under the title of 'pastors', waiting for the chance to do
harm. At the same time he also explains what must be feared from
those wolves, viz. the dispersal of the flock, when the Church is drawn
away from the unity of the faith and divided into sects. For all who
do not measure up to their office are not wolves, but are often hirelings,
a breed that does not do so much harm. But the corruption of doctrine
is a deadly disaster for the sheep.

Now in the third place the fountain and source of this evil is noted,
that they will wish *to draw away disciples after them.* Therefore ambition
is the mother of all heresies. For the purity of the Word of God
flourishes when pastors gain disciples for Christ with a common zeal;
because the state of the Church is sound only when He is the one
Master that is heard. Accordingly it is inevitable that both the teaching
of salvation is destroyed, and the safety of the flock goes for nothing,
when the passion for mastery prevails. But just as this verse teaches
that nearly all corruptions of doctrine flow from the pride of men,
when each one eagerly desires to be more prominent than is allowed,
so again we gather from the same source that it is hardly possible that
ambitious men will not turn aside from the proper purity and adulterate the Word of God. For since the pure handling of Scripture has
this for its aim, that Christ alone may be pre-eminent, and since, on

the other hand, men cannot arrogate anything to themselves without taking away just so much from the glory of Christ, it follows that those, who are devoted to themselves and strive after their own glory, which obscures Christ completely, are corrupters of the sound teaching. And the Lord Himself confirms that in John 7.18. Moreover by his use of the word *arise* he means that those wolves are now fostering destruction secretly, until they may break out when an opportunity is given them.

Apart from that this verse obviates very well a horrible stumbling-block that Satan presents to all generations for disturbing weak consciences. If external, professed enemies fight against the Gospel godly souls are less alarmed than if internal enemies appear from the midst of the bosom of the Church, and suddenly sound the trumpet, or treacherously stir up the people to defection. And yet God has disturbed His Church from the beginning, and still vexes it today, with this temptation. Accordingly let our faith be made secure by this bulwark, so that it may not give way, if at any time it happens that pastors assume the part of wolves. He states that they will be *grievous wolves*, to make them all the more fearful, secondly, that they will be the originators of perverse doctrine and will be so, in order to acquire disciples for themselves, because it is hardly possible that ambition will not adulterate the purity of the Gospel.

From this it is also apparent how worthless is the boasting of the Papists about a continuous succession. For since it is easy for us to show that those horned beasts are by no means what they wish to be regarded, when they have been completely refuted, they flee, nevertheless, to take refuge in this, that they have succeeded the apostles by a continuous chain. As if those fellows, whom Paul warns men to be on their guard against, did not also succeed them. Therefore although God often allows wolves to attack under the guise of pastors, either to prove the steadfastness of His own people, or by a just judgment, authority does not consist in name and position alone, and succession has no importance, unless faith and integrity are present at the same time. But if the Papists object that the name of wolves is not appropriate in their case, one word of Paul's will be like a Lydian stone, to settle the examination of the matter, *to draw away*, he says, *the disciples after them*. But what is the purpose of the whole of the Papal religion except that the caprice of men may bear rule instead of the Word of God? But Christ does not have disciples when He is not considered the only Master.

31. *Wherefore watch ye.* Again Paul urges them to diligence by his own example, although he links it at the same time with the fear of danger. It is as if he said that they need to show the greatest attentive-

ness in keeping watch, and indeed that weariness is intolerable in men who saw his unbroken endurance for three years. He also recalls his *tears*, which added great force to his exhortations.

His statement that he *admonished every one* can be referred to the ordinary people as well as to the presbyters. For, because he had made up his mind to make a general speech for the whole Church, he speaks as if the whole body were present. However, if anyone prefers to restrict it to the order of pastors, the meaning will be, not only that their zeal is fired by the present speech, but that it is right that so many exhortations, which for three years he had constantly pressed on them with tears, be fresh in their memories. However it seems to me more suitable that he is speaking about all.

32. *I commend you to God.* He interposes a prayer, and that ought not to appear incongruous in a moving speech. For he did not trouble himself about dividing his speech into parts like the rhetoricians, since no words would suffice for the vehemence of the feelings, with which he was inflamed. He had been dealing with great and difficult things, which went far beyond the ability of men. Therefore, turning to prayer, he breaks the thread of his sermon for a moment, although he is expressing a wish rather than a direct prayer. It is as if he had said that they are certainly not equal to such a great burden, but that he desires fresh help from heaven for them, so that relying on that they may emerge victorious over all temptations. But there is no doubt that, although he addresses the pastors only, he is nevertheless including the whole Church in this prayer. He commends them, first, to God, secondly, *to the Word of His grace.* Yet it is one and the same commendation, but Paul wished to describe the method by which the Lord is accustomed to preserve the salvation of His own, which Peter teaches is guarded by faith (I Pet. 1.5). And the method (*ratio*) of that protection depends on the Word, so that it might not be imperilled in the midst of so many dangers. But it is very important to know how God wishes to preserve us. For, because His Majesty is hidden from us, we look about in uncertainty, until He comes to us by His Word. Therefore as soon as He begins to save us, He brings forward His Word as the instrument for preserving our salvation. It is in that sense that he has added the epithet *of grace*, for in the Hebrew idiom the genitive describes an effect, so that believers might rest more securely on the Word, in which God reveals His favour. This explanation is plain and apt; for the interpretation of some people, that it refers to Christ, is far too forced.

Who is able to build you up. The participle δυνάμενος,[1] which Paul

---

[1] Greek: παρατίθεμαι ὑμᾶς τῷ θεῷ καὶ τῷ λόγῳ τῆς χάριτος αὐτοῦ τῷ δυναμένῳ κ.τ.λ. Tr.

uses, refers to *God* and not to *His Word*. Now this consolation is
added for this reason, that they may not despair out of an awareness
of their weaknesses. For as long as we are beset by the vices of the
flesh, we are like an unfinished building. Indeed all the godly must
be founded on Christ, but their faith is a very long way from being
perfect and complete. On the contrary, although the foundation
remains firm, certain parts of the building sometimes totter and fall.
Accordingly there is need, both of constant building, and, from time
to time, of fresh supports. At the same time Paul is also saying that
they must not lose hope, because the Lord does not wish to leave His
work incomplete; as he also teaches in Phil. 1.6, 'He, who began a
good work in you, will perfect it, until the day of the Lord Jesus'.
There is also a corresponding thought in Ps. 138.8, 'Thou wilt not
forsake the work of Thy hands'.

What he adds at once about the *inheritance* of life, refers to the actual
enjoyment of it. As soon as Christ has dawned upon us, we indeed
pass from death to life, and faith is the entrance into the Kingdom of
Heaven; and the Spirit of adoption has not been given to us in vain.
But here Paul promises the faithful a continuous increase of grace until
they see and possess the inheritance, to which they have been called,
and which is now laid up for them in heaven.

He mentions 'the power of God'[1], not as we are accustomed to
imagine it, without effect, but as something that is commonly described as 'active'. For the faithful ought to lay hold of it, so that they
may have it ready, like a shield, to hold before all the onslaughts of
Satan. Just as Scripture teaches that we have protection enough in
the power of God, so let us remember that the only ones who are
strong in the Lord, are those who renounce confidence in their own
free-will, and rest on Him, and Paul is quite right in asserting that He
alone can build up.

*I coveted no man's silver, or gold, or apparel. Ye yourselves know that
these hands ministered unto my necessities, and to them that were with
me. In all things I gave you an example, how that so labouring ye
ought to help the weak, and to remember the words of the Lord Jesus,
how he himself said, It is more blessed to give than to receive. And
when he had thus spoken, he kneeled down, and prayed with them all.
And they all wept sore,[2] and fell on Paul's neck, and kissed him, sorrow-
ing most of all for the word which he had spoken, that they should behold*

[1] For RV's 'Who is able to build you up', Calvin has *qui potens est superstruere.*
Tr.
[2] Calvin, as Greek and RV margin, *And there arose a great lamentation of all.*
Tr.

his face no more. And they brought him on his way unto the ship.
(33-38)

33. *Silver and gold.* As he has just been arguing how harmful a pest ambition is, so now he warns that they must beware of covetousness. And once again he puts forward his own example, because he had coveted no man's possessions. On the contrary he made his living by the work of his hands. This was not because it was sufficient for maintaining him, without any payment being made to him (*erogatione*), but because, devoting himself to manual work, he spared the churches, so that he might not burden them with any expense, as far as he could help. We must note, not only that he denies that he robbed, in the way that hungry men very often violently extort spoils, but that he says that he was innocent of every evil desire. From that we gather that nobody will be a good minister of the Word, without being, at the same time, one who puts little value on money. And we certainly see that there is nothing more common than that all, who are shamefully devoted to riches, corrupt the Word of God to please men. Elsewhere Paul severely condemns that fault in bishops (I Tim. 3.3).

34, 35. *Yes, you yourselves know.* He is not using these words to impose an absolute law, which all ministers of the Word must always, necessarily, keep, for he did not conduct himself so imperiously that he himself took away what the Lord granted to His servants. On the contrary in many places[1] he affirms his own right, for them, so that they may be maintained at public expense. Add to this that he allowed food and clothing to be supplied to himself by many churches. And in fact not only did he gladly accept wages for the work in hand, but when he was in need at Corinth he says that 'he robbed other churches' to relieve his poverty (II Cor. 11.8). Therefore he does not simply order pastors to make their living by manual labour, but immediately afterwards he makes it plain to what extent he urges them to follow his example, viz. to support the weak. Those Corinthians were not refusing him his due wages, but since false apostles commended themselves with free work, and tried to get the favour of the people in that way, Paul did not wish to give way to them in this respect, or to offer them the chance of putting him in a false light, as he himself reveals (I Cor. 9.15; II Cor. 11.12). He therefore warns them to be on their guard so that no stumbling-block may be given to the weak, and their faith may not be destroyed. For to *support the weak* amounts to the same thing as conceding something, by indulgence, to their ignorance, as in Rom. 14.1.

[1] E.g. I Cor. 9.14; cf. II Cor. 11.8; Gal. 6.6; Phil. 4.10, 16; I Tim. 5.17; and Matt. 10.10. Tr.

35. *To remember the words of the Lord.* This sentence is not to be found, word for word, anywhere else, but the Evangelists record others that are not unlike it, from which Paul could have elicited this one. In the second place we do know that not all of Christ's sayings were committed to writing. On the other hand He does repeat that general teaching about the despising of money, of which there is a genuine proof, when a man is readier *to give than to receive.* And Christ not only spoke about what was prudent, as if the liberal are blessed simply because they hold others in their debt by their benefits, and, on the other hand, it is a form of slavery to owe anything, but He was mindful of something deeper, that he who gives money to the poor is lending to the Lord (Prov. 19.17), that the faithful and honest stewards of God are those who share with their brethren the riches entrusted to themselves, that nothing brings men nearer to God than beneficence. These sayings about liberality are also to be read in the works of secular authors, and the majority of men admit that they are true, but they nod with a donkey's ears, as the proverb goes. For common life shows how few are convinced that there is nothing more desirable than to devote our goods to helping our brethren. That is why the disciples of Christ must meditate upon this felicity with greater zeal, so that by keeping away from someone else's property as far as they can, they may accustom themselves to giving, and to do so, not with a proud spirit, as if it is a wretched thing for them to be indebted to anyone, or out of a perverse ambition to lay others under obligation to them, but only to exercise themselves in the services of love, and, in this way, make the grace of their adoption manifest.

36. *He kneeled down.* The inward attitude certainly holds first place in prayer, but outward signs, kneeling, uncovering the head, lifting up the hands, have a twofold use. The first is that we may employ all our members for the glory and worship of God; secondly, that we are, so to speak, jolted out of our laziness by this help. There is also a third use in solemn and public prayer, because in this way the sons of God profess their piety, and they inflame each other with reverence of God. But just as the lifting up of the hands is a symbol of confidence and longing, so in order to show our humility, we fall down on our knees.

Finally, he seals the speech he has just made with a prayer, because it is only from the blessing of God that we can look for any success from teaching. Accordingly if we desire any reward for our trouble in teaching, warning and exhorting, let us always add this conclusion, in other words, let us end in prayer.

37, 38. *Great weeping.* It is no wonder that all the godly bestowed

extraordinary affection on this holy man. For it would have been a
mark of gross ingratitude to neglect him, when the Lord had equipped
him with so many outstanding gifts. But the main cause of their
weeping was, as Luke notes, that they were not going to see him any
more. For they had good reason for deploring their own situation,
and that of the whole Church in Asia, which they saw was going to
be deprived of an inestimable treasure.

Finally, when the Spirit, through the mouth of Luke, commends
their tears, as if they were witnesses of sincere godliness, he is condemning the thoughtlessness of those who demand from believers an
iron and inhuman firmness. For they falsely suppose that the feelings,
which God has implanted in us as natural, proceed only from a
defect. Accordingly the perfecting of believers does not depend on
their casting off all feelings, but on their yielding to them and con-
trolling them, only for proper reasons.

CHAPTER TWENTY-ONE

And when it came to pass that we were parted from them, and had set sail, we came with a straight course unto Cos, and the next day unto Rhodes, and from thence unto Patara: and having found a ship crossing over unto Phoenicia, we went aboard, and set sail. And when we had come in sight of Cyprus, leaving it on the left hand, we sailed unto Syria, and landed at Tyre: for there the ship was to unlade her burden. And having found the disciples, we tarried there seven days: and these said to Paul through the Spirit, that he should not set foot in Jerusalem. And when it came to pass that we had accomplished the days, we departed and went on our journey; and they all, with wives and children, brought us on our way, till we were out of the city: and kneeling down on the beach, we prayed, and bade each other farewell; and we went on board the ship, but they returned home again. (1-6)

1. Luke surveys the course of the voyage briefly, and he does so not only to give a faithful account, so that we may know what happened in each place, but so that readers may ponder, along with himself, the invincible and heroic bravery of Paul, who preferred to experience the upheavals from such long and tortuous and troublesome journeys, in order to labour for Christ, rather than be concerned for a quiet life for himself. His statement that they were *parted*, or pulled away, is not to be referred simply to spatial distance, but to the fact that the brethren stood on the shore as long as their eyes could follow the ship, in which Paul and his companions were sailing. He names the ports at which the ship called, so that we may know that the voyage was easy and calm. Readers should consult the geographical writers about the situation of the cities which he lists. It is enough for me to have pointed out Luke's intention.

4. *And having found the disciples.* Even if the number of believers was small, yet some seed of the Gospel had reached there, according to the predictions of the prophets, so that *Tyre* might not be altogether devoid of the blessing of God (Isa. 23.18). Here too, as in other places mentioned previously, Luke calls Christians *disciples*, so that we may know that the only ones counted in the flock of Christ, are those who have embraced His teaching by faith. For it is a useless and false profession to associate oneself with Christ, and not to grasp what He teaches or says. But let readers observe that the only reason why Paul stayed at Tyre for seven days was to encourage them. So we see

that, wherever he went, he did not neglect any opportunity of doing good.

They were saying through the Spirit, that is, with His approval of their speech, so that Paul might know that they are speaking by the Spirit of prophecy. It was certainly a great temptation not to complete the journey which he had undertaken, when the Holy Spirit was advising against it. Indeed, to be drawn back, as if by the hand of God, was a very plausible excuse for avoiding the cross, if consideration for his own personal safety had weighed with him. Yet he does not cease to carry on to the place where he knew he was called by the Lord.

However, the question arises here, How do the brethren advise, through the Spirit, against something, that Paul has testified that he is doing by the secret influence of the same Spirit? Or is the Spirit self-contradictory, so that he now sets Paul free, after holding him bound within? I reply that there are different gifts of the Spirit, so that it is no wonder that those who are strong in the gift of prophecy, are sometimes lacking in judgment or courage. The Lord revealed to those brethren, whom Luke mentions, what was to be; but at the same time, they do not know what is expedient, and what Paul's calling demands, because the measure of their gifts does not stretch so far. On the other hand the Lord deliberately intended His servant to be warned, partly that he might approach whatever he had to undergo better prepared by long meditation, partly that his perseverance might be plainer, when, having been informed of a sad outcome by the prophecies, he nevertheless willingly and knowingly hastens to suffer anything.

5. *With wives and children.* It was no ordinary testimony of love that they accompanied Paul out of the city even with their wives and children. And Luke has recorded this, partly for this purpose, that he might praise their loyalty in fitting terms, partly to show that Paul was given the honour, which he deserved. We also gather from this that nothing was further from his mind than looking to his own advantage, seeing that he was not deterred from his course by such great good will, which could have been a pleasant inducement to stay. We must also note the common habit of praying over more important matters, and that, having been informed about the danger, they are the more eager to pray.

And when we had finished the voyage from Tyre, we arrived at Ptolemais; and we saluted the brethren, and abode with them one day. And on the morrow we[1] departed, and came unto Caesarea: and entering into the house of Philip the evangelist, who was one of the seven, we abode

---
[1] Calvin adds, *who were with Paul.* Tr.

with him. Now this man had four daughters, virgins, which did pro-
phesy. And as we tarried there many days, there came down from
Judaea a certain prophet, named Agabus. And coming to us, and taking
Paul's girdle, he bound his own feet and hands, and said, Thus saith the
Holy Ghost, So shall the Jews at Jerusalem bind the man that owneth
this girdle, and shall deliver him into the hands of the Gentiles. And
when we heard these things, both we and they of that place besought him
not to go up to Jerusalem. Then Paul answered, What do ye, weeping
and breaking my heart? for I am ready not to be bound only, but also to
die at Jerusalem for the name of the Lord Jesus. And when he would not
be persuaded, we ceased, saying, The will of the Lord be done. (7-14)

7, 8. Luke briefly records that Paul was also received by the brethren
at *Ptolemais*. Now this was a city on the coast of Phoenicia, not far
from the borders of Judaea, and from there the journey to *Caesarea*
was a short one for Paul and his companions. But if they wish,
readers may find out more about the situation of the regions and the
cities from the geographical writers.

Moreover he says that at Caesarea they enjoyed the hospitality of
Philip, whom he calls an *evangelist*, although he was one of the seven
deacons, as is evident from chapter 6 (v. 5). From this it is easy to
gather that that diaconate was a temporary office (*temporale munus*),
because otherwise Philip would not have been free to leave Jerusalem
and move to Caesarea. But he is not set before us as a voluntary
deserter of office, but as one to whom a more important charge (*ex-
cellentior provincia*) has been committed. In my opinion *evangelists*
were half-way between apostles and teachers. For they used to discharge a function very close to that of the apostles, in that they preached
the Gospel everywhere, and were not appointed to a fixed station;
only their standing carried less honour. For in his description of the
order of the Church (Eph. 4.11) Paul puts them after the apostles, so
as to show that they were given a wider field for teaching than the
pastors, whose labour was devoted to definite places. Therefore
Philip exercised his diaconate at Jerusalem for a while, and after that
the Church considered him suitable to have the treasure of the Gospel
entrusted to him.

9. *Four daughters.* This has been added in commendation of Philip,
so that we might know that his house was very suitable, and that it
was famous and renowned by the blessing of God, for it was no
ordinary gift to have four daughters, all endowed with the Spirit of
prophecy. But God wished to give lustre to the beginnings of the
Gospel by this method of raising up men and women to predict
coming events. For very many years now prophecies had almost

ceased among the Jews, so that their minds might be more attentive
or more alert to hear the new voice of the Gospel. Therefore when
prophecy returned, as if by restoration, it was a sign of a more complete situation. Yet the reason why it ceased a little later, appears to
have been the same. For God sustained the people of old by various
predictions until, by His advent, Christ put an end to all prophecies.
Therefore it was fitting for the new reign of Christ to be distinguished
and adorned in this way, so that all might know that the promised
visitation of God was a present reality, and, on the other hand, it was
proper for it to flourish only for a short time, so that believers might
not always be in a state of uncertainty, or so that an opportunity
might not be given to those of a curious turn of mind to be looking
repeatedly for, or devising, something new. For we know that, when
that power had already been taken away, there were, nevertheless,
many fanatics who boasted that they were prophets. And it is also
possible that the perverseness of men deprived the Church of this gift.
But this one reason ought to be sufficient, that, by taking away prophecies, God bore witness that their end and fulfilment were present
in Christ.

Finally, it is not certain how those girls discharged the office of
prophesying, except that the Spirit of God ruled them in such a way
that He did not disturb the order that He Himself ordained. But since
He does not permit women to play a public part in the Church, one
may well believe that they prophesied at home, or in a private place,
outside the public meeting.

10, 11. *A certain prophet.* Although Luke does not say so explicitly,
yet I conclude that this is the *Agabus*, previously mentioned in chapter 11 (v. 28), who predicted that there would be a famine during the
reign of Claudius Caesar. But when Luke honours him with the title
of prophet, as he has just done in the case of Philip's four daughters,
he is hinting that it was no common gift, but a special one.

Now we must see why the threatening persecution was made known
once again, by Agabus. As far as Paul was concerned, he had already
been given more than enough warning. Therefore I have no doubt
that this confirmation was added for the sake of others, because the
Lord wished to make His servant's bonds famous everywhere, partly
so that all might know that he entered the fight of his own free-will,
partly so that they might learn that God had appointed him a champion
to fight for the Gospel. It was surely a useful example of invincible
steadfastness, when, knowingly and willingly, he offered himself to
the violence of his enemies. It is just as much to our advantage today
that his apostleship is confirmed by this voluntary, and equally steadfast devotedness of life.

The man who owns this girdle. It was common for the prophets to give a symbolic demonstration of what they were saying. But they did not confirm their prophecies with the use of signs at their own instigation, but at the command of the Spirit; as when Isaiah is ordered to go naked (Isa. 20.2); Jeremiah to bind a yoke on his neck, to sell and buy a field (Jer. 27.2; 32.7); Ezekiel, in fact, secretly to dig through the wall of his house, and carry his luggage out of it by night (Ezek. 12.7). These, and similar things could have appeared ludicrous to the mass of people, but the same Spirit who made symbols suit His words, used to touch the hearts of the godly within, as if they were already being confronted by the actual situation. So this spectacle, which Luke mentions, affected Paul's companions, just as if with their own eyes they were seeing him bound in earnest. Afterwards false prophets attempted to deceive the simple by this artifice, as Satan generally apes God, and his agents are jealous of the servants of God. Zedekiah made horns for himself with which he promised that Syria was to be pushed (I Kings 22.11). Hananiah broke Jeremiah's yoke, and created for the people a false hope of liberation (Jer. 28.2). God allowed the reprobate to be deceived by such delusions, in order to punish them for their unbelief. But since there was no underlying efficacy of the Spirit, their deception did no harm to the faithful. It is also worth while noting that Agabus does not present a spectacle in silence, but links it with the Word, by which he teaches the faithful the value and purpose of the ceremony.

12, 13. *Both we and the others besought him.* Because they all did not have the same revelation it is no wonder that there were conflicting opinions. For since those holy men knew that much depended on the life or death of one man, they did not wish him to be exposed to danger rashly, and their devotion is praiseworthy, because, by keeping Paul back, they wished to have regard to the common safety of the Church. But on the other hand Paul's determination deserves all the more praise, when he continues inflexible in the calling of God. For he was well aware of how much distress could result from his bonds. But yet, because he knows the will of God, which was the one and only rule in making up his mind, in order to follow it, he regards everything else as of no importance. And it is surely right for us to be so fixed to the will of God, that no advantage and no reason of any kind may shift us from simple obedience to Him.

When Paul takes the brethren to task because they are breaking his heart by their weeping, he makes it quite plain that he was not made of iron, but that he was moved, by love, to feel with them (*ad συμπάθειαν*). Therefore the tears of the godly were wounding his heart, but that tenderness did not turn him aside, for he continued to follow God with an even tenor. Therefore we ought to be gentle in our behaviour towards the brethren in such a way that God's will always has the upper hand. Now in his reply Paul once again declares that it is only by contempt of death that the servants of Christ will be prepared to discharge their duty, and that only those who will freely lay down their own lives as a testimony to the truth, will ever be properly disposed to live for the Lord.

14. *We acquiesced, saying.* If they had thought that in this way he was rushing to his death heedlessly, they would not have acquiesced like this. Therefore they give in, so as not to resist the Holy Spirit, by whom they understand that Paul is directed. For distress and grief drive out of their minds what they had previously heard from Paul's lips, that he is being drawn, as if by the bonds of the Spirit, but when they are again shown that this is what God wills, they do not consider it right for them to resist any longer. And all our feelings must be held in check by this bridle, that there is nothing so bitter or sad or hard that the will of God may not mitigate and soften. For as often as anything difficult or hard occurs, we show little honour to God, if this thought, that we must obey Him, does not have greater influence upon us.

And after these days we took up our baggage, and went up to Jerusalem. And there went with us also certain of the disciples from Caesarea, bringing with them one Mnason of Cyprus, an early disciple, with whom we should lodge. And when we were come to Jerusalem, the brethren received us gladly. And the day following Paul went in with us unto James; and all the elders were present. And when he had saluted them, he rehearsed one by one the things which God had wrought among the Gentiles by his ministry. And they, when they heard it, glorified God; and they said unto him, Thou seest, brother, how many thousands there are among the Jews of them which have believed; and they are all zealous for the law: and they have been informed concerning thee, that thou teachest all the Jews which are among the Gentiles to forsake Moses, telling them not to circumcise their children, neither to walk after the customs. What is it therefore?[1] they will certainly hear that thou art come. Do therefore this that we say to thee: We have four men which have a vow on them; these take, and purify thyself with them, and be at charges for them, that they may shave their heads: and all shall know that there is no truth in the things whereof they have been informed concerning thee[2]; but that thou thyself also walkest orderly, keeping

[1] Calvin adds, *the multitude must certainly come together, for they will hear.* Tr.
[2] Calvin reads, as RV margin, *those things whereof they were informed concerning thee, are nothing.* Tr.

the law. But as touching the Gentiles which have believed, we wrote, giving judgment that they should keep themselves from things sacrificed to idols, and from blood, and from what is strangled, and from fornication. (15-25)

15. *We took up our baggage.* Paul's companions make it clear that, when they attempted to call Paul back from danger, they were more concerned for the common safety of the Church, than each man for his own private life. For having accepted their rebuff, the upshot is that they do not avoid sharing the same danger; and yet there was the plausible excuse that they were bound by no law to be dragged to death through one man's obstinacy. And we are truly putting our feelings in subjection to God, when we are alarmed by no fear, but each one of us endeavours, as far as he can, to carry out what we know pleases Him. It is also more clearly evident what a strong flame of loyalty burnt in the others, who willingly attach themselves to him, and provide a host for him, when, nevertheless, they could have been justifiably afraid for themselves because of many troubles.

17. *The brethren received us gladly.* Luke mentions this in order to commend the fair-mindedness of the brethren, who had not relied on unfavourable rumours and misrepresentations. Although many spiteful and wicked men, one after the other, daily loaded Paul with odium, yet, because James and his colleagues were fully convinced of his integrity, they were not hostile to him. Therefore they now receive him as a servant of Christ in a brotherly and courteous fashion, and make it plain that his coming gives them pleasure. And we must pay diligent attention to this moderation, so as not to be too ready to believe vicious accusations, especially when those, who have given us some evidence of their uprightness, and whom we have found by experience to be serving the Lord faithfully, are burdened with charges that are doubtful, or unexamined. Because Satan knows that nothing will suit better for overthrowing the Kingdom of Christ than the disagreements and jealousies of the faithful, he does not cease spreading indirect rumours, which make them suspicious of each other. Therefore we must close our ears to accusations, so as not to believe anything about faithful ministers of Christ except on good information.

18. *All the presbyters were present.* One may gather from this verse what we have already found in chapter 15, that, as often as some serious business had to be transacted, the elders (*seniores*) were in the habit of meeting, so that their deliberation might be more orderly, without the crowd. We shall see a little later that the people were also admitted in their turn, but only after the elders had had a more intimate deliberation among themselves.

19. Paul certainly shows his modesty now, when he does not make himself responsible for the things that had been done, but gives the praise to God, and calls himself only the minister whose labour the Lord has used. Similarly we must confess that all that is splendid and praiseworthy is done, not by our own power, but to the extent that God works in us, especially, indeed, when it is a question of the up-building of the Church. Again, it is evident how far the elders were from envy, when they glorify God on account of the gratifying successes.

Apart from that, because the only apostle mentioned is *James*, one may conjecture that at that time they had gone to different regions for the sake of spreading the Gospel, as their office required. For the Lord had not assigned them a station at Jerusalem but He had ordered them to begin from there, and after that to go through Judaea, and, finally, other parts of the world. Furthermore, in chapter 15,[1] we refuted the error of those, who think that this James was one of the disciples, whom Paul included among the three pillars of the Church. But although he had the same commandment as the rest of his colleagues, yet I have no doubt that they came to such an agreement among themselves, that he would remain at Jerusalem, to which many foreigners were in the habit of flocking every day; for that amounted to the same thing as if he had published the Gospel far and wide in remote places.

20. *Thou seest, brother, how many thousands.* The speech has two parts. For, in the first place, the elders call to mind how many there are of the Jews who have been converted to Christ, who, since they are devoted to the Law, are badly disposed towards Paul, because they think that he is devoting himself entirely to the object of abolishing the Law. In the second place they urge him to clear himself by taking a solemn vow, so that no further suspicion might cling to him. They put the multitude of believers before him, so that he may give in to them more easily. For if there had been a few inflexible men he would not have been moved so much. Now he certainly cannot ignore an immense number of people and the whole body of the Church.

There is absolutely no doubt that that zeal for the Law was corrupt; and the presbyters certainly make it plain enough that it does not seem right to them. For although they do not condemn it openly, yet because they distinguish themselves from the attitude of those men, they are tacitly acknowledging them to be in the wrong. If zeal had been in accordance with knowledge, then it ought to have begun with themselves. But they are not fighting for the Law itself, and they are not pleading due reverence for it by way of an excuse, and

[1] Acts, 15.13. See page 44. Tr.

they are not approving of its so-called zealots. Therefore they are hinting that they have a different attitude of mind, and do not approve of the superstition of the people.

Nevertheless the opposite impression is given by their saying that Paul has been burdened with a bad reputation, false though it was. Secondly when they require him to make amends they seem to be supporting that zeal. I reply that, even if the rumour, which had offended the Jews, was true in some respect, yet it was stained by calumny. Paul was teaching the abrogation of the Law, so that in this way, nevertheless, its authority might not only remain intact, but also that it might be more sacred. For as we said in chapter 7¹ ceremonies would be empty things, if the effect (*effectus*) of them had not been exhibited in Christ. Therefore those who teach that they were abolished by the coming of Christ, far from being abusive of the Law, are rather confirming the truth of it. Close attention must be paid to two things in regard to ceremonies, the truth to which efficacy is linked, secondly, their outward use. Moreover the abrogation of the outward use which Christ brought, depends on the fact that He Himself is the true substance (*solidum corpus*), and that nothing was foreshadowed in earlier times, of which the fulness does not become visible in Him. It is a very different thing from defection from the Law, to show its proper aim, that, with figures coming to an end, their spiritual truth may always prevail. Accordingly we see that those, who were branding Paul with the charge of apostasy, although he was recalling the faithful from the external worship of the Law, were perverse and unjust in their interpretation. But their ordering Paul to make a public vow with the particular object of proving himself one who reverences the Law, has no other purpose except that he might testify that he does not abhor the Law, like an impious apostate, who would shake off the yoke of the Lord himself, and urge others to similar contumacy.

21. *Not to circumcise.* It was in fact so. For Paul was teaching that freedom has been procured for Jews and Gentiles without distinction. For these sentences of his apply to all. 'Circumcision is nothing' (I Cor. 7.19). Again, 'We are circumcised through baptism in Christ, not by a circumcision made with hands' (or rather, ἀχειροποιήτῳ, Col. 2.11). Again, 'Let nobody judge you in regard to food or drink, or the choice of feast-days, which are a shadow of the things to come, but the substance (*corpus*) belongs to Christ' (Col. 2.16, 17). Again, 'Whatever comes on the meat-market, and whatever is placed before you, eat, asking no question on the ground of conscience' (I Cor. 10.25, 27). Again, 'Do not be entangled again in the yoke of slavery'

¹ Generally, but in particular see on 7.1, 44, 51, Vol. I pages 172, 207, 212. Tr.

(Gal. 5.1). Since he had spoken everywhere in this way, without exception, he was setting the Jews free from the necessity of keeping the Law. And, so as not to spend too much time on this discussion, one passage will be sufficient, where he compares the Law to a tutor, under whose protection the old Church was, as if during its childhood, but says that, now that the grace of Christ has become known, it has grown up, so that it is free from ceremonies (Gal. 3.24ff). There he certainly includes the Jews along with the Gentiles. When he also says (Col. 2.14) that 'the written bond of the Law, which depended on ordinances, was cancelled by Christ and fastened to the cross', he sets the Jews, as well as the Gentiles, free from ceremonies, which he there calls 'ordinances'.

But there was no defection, such as those, who were ill-disposed to him, imagined, since he did not cast ceremonies aside absolutely, when teaching that the coming of Christ put an end to their observation. And the elders certainly were well aware of Paul's freedom. Therefore, although they have a proper grasp of the situation, they only wish it to be made known to the ignorant and inexperienced, that Paul had no intention at all of persuading the Jews to hold the Law in contempt. Therefore they pay no attention to the simple truth, but knowing what sort of opinion the common people held about Paul, based on malicious accusations, they desire to correct it. However I do not know whether this thing that they fiercely demanded of Paul was more harsh than fair. But it is clear from this how preposterously credulous[1] men are, when they listen to false accusations, and how an adverse opinion, once it is thoughtlessly adopted, sticks very tenaciously. There is no doubt that James and his colleagues tried to defend Paul's reputation, and to remove the lies which were damaging his good name. However they cannot prevent Paul from having a bad reputation; unless perhaps they were too slack to begin with, wishing to gratify their own fellow-countrymen, so that, afterwards, they were not their own masters.

22. *The multitude must certainly come together.* The verb is neutral (δεῖ), as if they said, 'It is inevitable that the multitude come together.' For it would have been absurd for an apostle, with such a great reputation, not to appear before the whole assembly of the faithful. For if he had avoided the light, and the eyes of the people, the sinister suspicion would have increased. At the same time we see how the elders conducted themselves with moderation, in fostering harmony, when they quickly anticipate the displeasure of the people; except that they are perhaps too indulgent to their weakness in requiring a vow from Paul. Finally, this moderation must be preserved in the Church,

---

[1] Reading *credulitas* with Tholuck, for C.R.'s *crudelitas*. Tr.

so that pastors may indeed be strong in authority, but not lord it proudly, and not despise the rest of the body. For the distinction of orders (*ordinum distinctio*), which is the bond of peace, ought not to provide any cause for disagreement.

23. *Do what we say to thee.* As I have just suggested, the elders appear to have fallen into foolish indulgence because of excessive love of their own nation. But a clear judgment on that matter depends on the circumstances, which are hidden from us today, but were obvious to them. Almost the whole body consisted of Jews, so that there would be no risk of causing offence to the Gentiles. For in other regions it was a cause of division that each man was devoted to his own custom, and wished to impose it as a law on others. In the second place, at Jerusalem they had many inducements to keep the ceremonies of the Law, so that there would be a greater excuse if they were rather slow in abandoning them. But even if that zeal was not without defect, yet correction, as it was difficult, could not have been such a sudden thing. We see that now, after a long time, this superstition has scarcely been torn out by the apostles. And because new disciples were daily entering upon the faith, the infirmity was being equally fostered in all. However it must not be denied that to obstinacy there was joined ignorance, which the presbyters nevertheless tolerated, in case they might do more serious harm with violent remedies. I leave it an open question whether they went too far.

Which have a vow on them. Although these four men may be reckoned in the number of the faithful, yet their vow was superstitious. From that it is plain that the apostles had a great deal of difficulty with that nation, which not only had become hardened by daily practice in the discipline of the Law, but also was naturally very obstinate and almost intractable. However, it is possible that those men were still novices, and therefore their faith was tender and not yet well formed. Accordingly the doctors were permitting them to fulfil the vow which they had rashly made in public, through ignorance. As far as Paul is concerned, since he did not submit to this vow because of his own conscience, but for the sake of those men, to whose error he was indulgent, his reason was different.

However, we must see whether this was one of the neutral ceremonies, which the faithful were free to observe or neglect. Indeed it seems to have had certain things mixed up with it, which had little in common with the profession of the faith. But since the object was an act of thanksgiving, as was said above in chapter 18 (v. 18), and nothing in the rite itself was in conflict with the faith of Christ, Paul did not hesitate to yield to such an extent, for the sake of bearing witness to his own religion (*religionis*). Therefore Paul is demonstrating what he states about himself elsewhere, that he associated himself with the adherents of the Law, as if he himself were also under obligation to the Law (I Cor. 9.20). In a word he became all things to all men, in order to win all (I Cor. 9.22); even to the altars, indeed, although he polluted himself with no sacrilege on the pretext of love. It would not have been just as permissible for him to go to a solemn sacrifice of expiation. But this part of the worship of God, which depended on a vow, he could discharge indifferently, provided it was not done for the sake of worshipping God (*religionis*), but only to encourage the weak. But neither had he any intention of worshipping God by this rite, nor was his conscience under any obligation, but he freely subjected himself to the weak brethren.

24. *Those things which they have heard concerning thee are nothing.* They seem to be inciting Paul to hypocrisy. For neither had the rumour sprung from nothing that he drew the Jews away from ceremonies, nor was he *walking* in observation of the Law. But we must keep in mind what I have said already, that it was enough for Paul and the elders, if they removed the calumny with which he was unjustly branded, viz. that he was an apostate from the Law; and, on the other hand, a better opportunity could have been given in a short time, that, by purifying himself, he might gradually call them back from their error. And it was certainly no help for Paul to be regarded for long as one who reverenced the Law, for at that time the disciples were generally of that sort. For in that way a thicker veil would have been drawn before their eyes to shut out the light of Christ. Accordingly, let us realize that Paul did not pretend, but sincerely professed that he had no hatred towards the Law, but, on the contrary, that his attitude towards it was one of reverence. They order him to pay the expenses along with[1] the men, because they were in the habit of contributing to a common fund, so that together they might offer the sacrifice.[2]

25. *But concerning those who have believed.* They add this lest any suspicion may dawn that they now wish to take away the liberty, which they had given to the Gentiles before, or to demand that they be burdened by some previous decision (*praeiudicio*). But at the same time they seem to be keeping the Jews under the yoke of slavery, from which they clearly release the Gentiles alone. I reply that, since the condition of all was equal, both had the same permission, as of right; but that no mention is made of the Jews, who were still so devoted to their own observances that they were unwilling that what was per-

---

[1] *cum ipsis.* Calvin misunderstands, but his text of v. 24 *super eos* is a more accurate translation of ἐφ᾽ αὐτοῖς, for 'Paul pays their expenses' (RSV). See a modern commentary. Tr.   [2] Cf. Num. 6.13-20 for the Nazirite's vow. Tr.

mitted, be allowed them. But the apostles stipulated for the Gentiles expressly, so that the Jews, according to their custom, might not reject as profane and impure those who were neither circumcised, nor reared in reverence of the Law. But, so that I may not load the paper with unnecessary repetition, let readers look in chapter 15 for what was said by way of explanation of this decree (Acts 15.20).

Then Paul took the men, and the next day purifying himself with them went into the temple, declaring the fulfilment of the days of purification, until the offering was offered for every one of them. And when the seven days were almost completed, the Jews from Asia, when they saw him in the temple, stirred up all the multitude, and laid hands on him, crying out, Men of Israel, help: This is the man, that teacheth all men everywhere against the people, and the law, and this place: and moreover he brought Greeks also into the temple, and hath defiled this holy place. For they had before seen with him in the city Trophimus the Ephesian, whom they supposed that Paul had brought into the temple. And all the city was moved, and the people ran together: and they laid hold on Paul, and dragged him out of the temple: and straightway the doors were shut. (26-30)

26. I have already rejected certain people's accusation that Paul was cunning, as if he presented something different from what was the real situation. However I do not deny that he was almost forced to concede this to the entreaties of the brethren. Therefore it is more plausible, and, as they say, more disputable, that he was too ready to submit, and yet I do not accept what some hold, that things turned out unhappily for Paul, because he assumed a new and unaccustomed role, and asserted, with less firmness than he usually did, the liberty procured by Christ. I certainly admit that foolish plans are often punished by God with an unfortunate outcome, but I do not see why this ought to be attributed to Paul, who, by voluntary subjection, was concerned to put himself alongside the ignorant, and those not properly instructed, in order to benefit them. Certainly he was not going to go through with that thing willingly, but because he preferred to yield to the brethren rather than persist in his own opinion. Moreover, once he was admitted, it might have been appropriate for him to pass over to moderating that zeal. Rather his considerateness (*humanitas*) deserves great praise, because, not only does he stoop courteously for the sake of the ignorant, ordinary people, but he also gratifies the foolishness of those men, who had undeservedly and unreasonably treated him with suspicion. He would have been justified in expostulating with them, because they had been so credulous of reports damaging to his reputation. When he abstains, he shows

wonderful tolerance. When he is so careful to win them over, he shows remarkable moderation. What is more, he could have been severer on James and his colleagues, because they had not exerted themselves more diligently to purge the people of error. For even if it is certain that they taught faithfully, yet it is possible that the sight of the temple, and the very seat of the Law, were hindrances to them in defending the use of liberty. But Paul, whether giving up his own right voluntarily, or thinking that they see better what is expedient, acquiesces in their plan.

But it does not need much to refute the false followers of Nicodemus (*Nicodemitae*), who, using Paul's example here, try to gloss over their treacherous dishonesty, while they pollute themselves with all the filthy things of the Papacy. They boast that they are conceding this to the weak brethren, as if Paul in fact allowed them to do anything at all, without distinction. If, as Jews, they were to undertake, according to the precept of the Law, to fulfil a vow to God among the Jews, one corrupted by no idolatry, then they would prove themselves to be like Paul. Now when they involve themselves in gross and undisguisedly impious superstitions, and do so out of a desire to avoid the cross, what sort of similarity do they imagine that to be?

27. *Who were from Asia.* It is certain that these men were hostile to the Christian Name. Accordingly, while Paul is intent on pacifying the faithful, he runs into the fury of enemies. And Asiatics are indeed rousers of the crowd, but the minds of all the people were gripped by such hatred of him, that frenzy swept through them all without difficulty. But this verse teaches us that we must not be too impatient, if ever hope disappoints us, and our plans, made with a proper and holy frame of mind, turn out unfavourably, so that our actions do not have a successful outcome.[1] We must not attempt anything except with a good conscience and according to the Spirit of God. But, if not even then does the situation go as we should like, let us be sustained by that inward feeling that we know that our effort is approved by God, although it is exposed to the insults and derision of men. And do not let us have any regrets about our gentleness, if ever the ungodly pay us back unjustly.

28. *Men of Israel, help.* They cry out as if they are in extreme danger, and call on all to bring help, as if their whole religion is in peril. That lets us see how inflamed they were with fierce hatred against Paul, simply because in warning that the full and genuine truth is found in Christ, he was teaching that an end has been put to

---

[1] This clause in Latin is a Second Edition addition, and obviously wrong: *ut actiones nostrae felicem habeant exitum.* The French has been followed: 'tellement que nos actions n'ayent pas toujours bonne issue'. Tr.

the figures of the Law. Now because they jump to a false supposition at the sight of *Trophimus*, they make it all the plainer, by this hasty and superficial judgment, how virulent they are. They accuse Paul of sacrilege. On what pretext? Because he brought an uncircumcised man into the temple. But on the basis of a false belief they have raised a most serious charge against an innocent man. The audacity of men, who are driven by a preconceived opinion, is usually preposterous like that. But let us learn from such examples to beware of uncontrolled passions, and not to give free rein to unfounded and prejudiced opinions, so as not to rush blindly in an assault upon the innocent.

30. *And the city was moved.* Here we see the irresponsible attitude (*levitatem*) of the common people, who already regard Paul as condemned before they have heard him. It is not to be wondered at that the city is in an uproar over a matter of piety; but it is a sign of perverted zeal and insane rashness that the people rise up against Paul, without examination of his case. For in this corrupt nature perverseness is added to foolishness; so that those, whom it would be difficult to move to right action with many exhortations, willingly, and with no trouble, fly to defend a bad cause. It is certainly a bitter situation that the whole world may be suddenly stirred up against us at the instigation of a few men, but since the Lord intends it to be so, let each one of us prepare himself by this and similar examples, to endure all disturbances.

And as they were seeking to kill him, tidings came up to the chief captain of the band, that all Jerusalem was in confusion. And forthwith he took soldiers and centurions, and ran down upon them: and they, when they saw the chief captain and the soldiers, left off beating Paul. Then the chief captain came near, and laid hold on him, and commanded him to be bound with two chains; and inquired who he was, and what he had done. And some shouted one thing, some another, among the crowd: and when he could not know the certainty for the uproar, he commanded him to be brought into the castle. And when he came upon the stairs, so it was, that he was borne of the soldiers for the violence of the crowd; for the multitude of the people followed after, crying out, Away with him. And as Paul was about to be brought into the castle, he saith unto the chief captain, May I say something unto thee? And he said, Dost thou know Greek? Art thou not then the Egyptian, which before these days stirred up to sedition and led out into the wilderness the four thousand men of the Assassins? But Paul said, I am a Jew, of Tarsus in Cilicia, a citizen of no mean city: and I beseech thee, give me leave to speak unto the people. And when he had given him leave, Paul, standing on

*the stairs, beckoned with the hand unto the people; and when there was
made a great silence, he spake unto them in the Hebrew language,
saying, (31-40)*

31. *As they were seeking to kill him.* Surely the power of Satan is
apparent in driving the people on to such a pitch of fury, that, behind
the closed doors of the temple, not being content with a moderate
punishment, they plot together for the death of Paul. We ought to
keep this thought before us, that the enemies of godliness are being
urged on by Satan, so that their raging may not disturb us, no matter
how furious and turbulent it may be. On the other side, the wonderful
goodness of God shines out, when He suddenly brings out the tribune
to save Paul's life. Indeed he himself has no such thought in his head,
but runs up to stop the tumult of the people. But the Lord gave clearer
proof of His providence by the fact that Paul's life was snatched out
of such immediate danger without any human plan. Thus He allows
the faithful not only to be afflicted but to be almost overwhelmed, so
that He might deliver them by a greater miracle from the midst of
death. Luke has improperly called him the *tribune of the cohort*,[1] since
each tribune was in command of one thousand soldiers, and that is
also clear from the context, where he says that *centurions* were taken
by the tribune.

32. *When they saw the tribune.* The men, whose fury neither the
majesty of God nor the sanctity of the temple was able to restrain,
are now quietened by fear of an unbeliever. That makes it obvious
that they were burning with savage cruelty rather than zeal. The
tribune makes it plain enough, by binding him with chains, that he
did not come in order to set him free. Unbelievers would have put
this down to fortune, but the Spirit has, so to speak, painted us a
picture of the providence of God ruling in the midst of men's con-
fusions and disturbances. But even if it is hard that God's holy minister
is treated so ignominiously, yet praise will have to be given to the
tribune's fairness, if he is compared with the Jews. He does put chains
on him, as if he were a vicious criminal, yet he has the patience to hear
the fettered man, whom they were flogging to death; and he only
thinks of any harsher punishment for him, when he knows something
about his case. Yes, and what is more, that was the best way of calming
down their ferocity, because they were expecting that Paul was going
to be punished on the spot.

34. *Some were shouting one thing, some another.* The agitated people
give complete vent to their madness. They fill the air with clashing

[1] A cohort consisted of 600 men, one tenth of a legion, and there were six
tribunes to a legion. Tr.

clamourings. At the same time they are at one in demanding the death of a man, who had been convicted of no crime. There is no doubt, however, that they were blinded by a kind of holy zeal. But a proper knowledge of the truth of their cause makes the true zealots of God like the martyrs, but violence betrays a diabolical madness.

Because a *fortress* is mentioned here, we should know that soldiers, who were posted for the defence of the city, had a place, which was walled and fortified all round, which they could defend like a stronghold, and from which they could hold off any attack, if any sedition were to break out. For it would not have been safe for them to be distributed here and there in many different quarters, with a population of doubtful loyalty (*fide*) and in a turbulent city. And we gather that the place was high up, because Luke says that, when they came to the stairs, Paul was carried by the soldiers. But whether the soldiers lifted Paul up in order to bring him into the station unharmed, or he was tossed like that by the violence and jostling of the crowd, this was no act of kindness or favour. But the more the ferocity of the persecutors burned, the clearer did God show His favour to His servant, in sparing his life, for fear that,[1] if he had been killed in the tumult, his death would be without its due reward.

37-40. *May I speak to you?* Because it is something that all the servants of God must do, Paul offered to defend his own case personally. For as far as we can we must take pains to make our integrity known to all, so that no discredit may redound upon the name of God from our bad name. But when the tribune asks whether Paul is not that *Egyptian* brigand, who, a little earlier, had incited a band of men to insurrection, let us learn that no matter how modestly and quietly ministers of Christ conduct themselves, and no matter how free from blame they are, yet they cannot avoid the insults of the world. Therefore we must take note of this, so that we may accustom ourselves to reproaches, and be prepared to be blamed for doing well.

When he asks about the *Egyptian*, he does not mean, as many wrongly suppose, Theudas the sorcerer (*magus*), whom Gamaliel mentions in chapter 5 (v. 36), and about whom Josephus has more to say in *Antiquities*, book 20. For to the fact that there (5.36) we find that only four hundred men were led away by Theudas, but here the tribune gives a figure of four thousand, and says that all of them were *assassins*, there must also be added the consideration that Theudas had raised that faction during the reign of Tiberius Caesar or even Caesar Augustus, but only a vague rumour of it remained, because a troop of cavalry had been sent out against it unexpectedly, and it had been destroyed.

---

[1] The final clauses are a loose Second Edition addition, omitted in French. Tr.

However Josephus appears to me to be wandering, because, first, he records that Cuspius Fadus was sent by Claudius, and then adds that Theudas was crushed by the same man, whereas I have previously shown that that former rebellion was stirred up, when Claudius was still a private citizen.[1] However, he also differs widely from Luke's account in regard to the number, since he says that about thirty thousand were enticed to the insurrection, unless perhaps we may interpret it like this, that, after he was put to flight by Felix, he escaped into the desert with four thousand men. For it would have been extremely absurd for the number to be increased tenfold, and similarly for an unwarlike crowd to be branded with the title of 'assassins'. For, according to the evidence of Josephus, that impostor deceived a simple and credulous mob with a false promise, boasting that he was a prophet of God, who was about to give the people a passage through the middle of the Jordan. But the same Josephus removes all doubt, when he relates that, when Felix was governor, a band of men was collected by an Egyptian prophet,[2] and led away to the Mount of Olives. Of these four hundred were slain, two hundred were captured, and the rest scattered. He was recounting a recent event. Finally, since the instigator of the insurrection had escaped, and the region was infested with brigands, when the tribune sees them all burning in their hatred against Paul like this, he has good reason for asking whether he is that Egyptian.

Luke does not tell of a longer conversation between the tribune and Paul. However it is probable that, since they both knew Greek, they had more to say to each other. As a result, Paul, who had completed his purification appointed by the Law, was given permission to speak to the people. For the tribune was never going to allow a man, who was polluted by crime, to make a public speech in such a suspect city.

[1] See on chapter 5.36, Vol. I p. 153. Tr.
[2] See a modern Commentary e.g. *The Acts of the Apostles* by R. B. Rackham (*Westminster Commentaries*, London), pp. 409f. Tr.

CHAPTER TWENTY-TWO

Brethren and fathers, hear ye the defence which I now make unto you. And when they heard that he spake unto them in the Hebrew language, they were the more quiet. And he saith, I am a Jew, born in Tarsus of Cilicia, but brought up in this city, at the feet of Gamaliel, instructed according to the strict manner of the law of our fathers, being zealous for God, even as ye all are this day: and I persecuted this Way unto the death, binding and delivering into prisons both men and women. As also the high priest doth bear me witness, and all the estate of the elders: from whom also I received letters unto the brethren, and journeyed to Damascus, to bring them also which were there unto Jerusalem in bonds, for to be punished. (1-5)

1. Even if one may gather from the beginning of the speech what Paul was aiming at, yet, because it was interrupted, one may not know for certain what he was going to say. However, what is reported here may be summarized as follows. Since he had been properly and faithfully instructed in the teaching of the Law, he was a loyal and conscientious worshipper of God in the eyes of the world. Secondly he was hostile to the Gospel of Christ, so that he was regarded by the priests as one of the outstanding defenders of the Law. In the third place he did not make a quick and casual move to the new sect, but it was when he was subdued and convicted by a heavenly oracle, that he gave his allegiance to Christ. In the fourth place he did not embrace things he knew nothing about, but God provided for him a reliable teacher, from whom he learnt everything accurately. Finally, when he returned to Jerusalem, and wished to be of service to his own fellow-countrymen, God did not allow him. So it was not by chance, or out of hatred of his own nation, but by the command of God that he carried the doctrine of salvation far away to foreign nations.

Men, brethren and fathers. It is a strange thing that he still gives so much honour to the enemies of the Gospel, who were given up for lost. For they had broken every bond of brotherly connexion, and, by suppressing the glory of God, had deprived themselves of every dignified description. But because Paul speaks here just as one of the people, he is sincere when he addresses the body itself so lovingly, and also the chief men with respect. And surely, because they had not yet made open renunciation, although they were unworthy of every honour, yet the grace of God's adoption, which Paul reverently acknowledged in them, was worthy of it. Therefore in calling them *brethren and fathers*, he is paying attention not so much to what they deserved, as to the standing to which God had raised them. And the whole speech is so ordered that he tries to satisfy them, frankly indeed, and without flattery, yet gently and quietly. Therefore let us learn to respect men, and give them honour, so that God's right may remain unimpaired for Him. That is why the pride of the Pope is the more detestable. Since he has made himself a high-priest, without any command of God's, and without any votes of assent from the Church, he not only arrogates to himself all titles of honour, but a tyranny, by which Christ is brought under his control; as if God, indeed, by exalting men, resigns His own right to them, and prostrates Himself on the ground.

2. *That he was speaking in Hebrew.* It is certainly a common thing, when many different tongues mingle together, that we are rather glad to hear men speaking in our own native language. But the Jews had another, special reason, because they had imagined that Paul was openly hostile to his own race, so that he also disliked the very language or that he was some vagabond, who had not even learnt the language of that nation, from which he was claiming to have sprung. Now, at the sound of their native speech, they begin to hope for something better.

Next, it is not certain whether Paul spoke in Hebrew or Syrian. For we know that after the exile the Jews had a language that was corrupt and degenerate, since they had obtained many words from the Chaldaeans and Syrians. However I myself conjecture that, because he was speaking to the common people as well as to the elders, he used the language[1] that was current everywhere.

3. *I am a Jew.* Since there was a general state of confusion among the Jews at that time, many vagabonds and idlers[2] used to pass themselves off as Jews, so as to have something to cover up their crimes. Therefore, in order to turn aside any suspicion of that sort from himself, Paul begins with his birth. He then says that he is well-known at Jerusalem, because he was educated there from boyhood. However this latter statement appears to have been made, not only for corroboration, but because it was of great importance that it also be known how well he had been instructed. None are bolder in causing trouble than ignorant men. Indeed at that time the government of the Church had so collapsed, that religion was not merely exposed to sectarian divisions, but was miserably torn to pieces. Therefore Paul names his own teacher, so that no one may think that

[1] *idiomate.* French: 'il a usé du langage'. Tr.
[2] *homines circumforanei.* See on 17.5, p. 96. Tr.

he abandoned the worship of their fathers, because he has had no
training and teaching, just as many whose character is not developed
by teaching, forget their own natural disposition and become degenerate. But Paul particularly mentions that he was well instructed
in the Law, so that the Jews may indeed know that it is not because
of ignorance, as usually very often happens, that he is causing a disturbance and thinking of them as monsters.

There is doubt as to whether this is the Gamaliel who was mentioned previously (5.34). However, disciples are said *to sit at the feet*,
because, since they are not yet endowed with a strong judgment, they
ought to be so docile and modest in their attitude, that they subject
their minds to their instructors and hang on their words. Thus Mary
is said to *sit at Jesus' feet*, when she listens to Him teaching (Luke 10.39).
But if this reverence is due to earthly teachers, how much more
appropriate is it to cast ourselves at the feet of Christ, so as to show
ourselves docile to Him as He speaks from His heavenly throne? This
speech also warns boys and youths of their duty not to be stubborn,
or inflated with a false confidence so that they are high and mighty
towards their teachers, but, with a quiet and gentle attitude, to allow
themselves to be directed by them.

Instructed in the law of our fathers. The Vulgate has translated it
literally: 'Educated according to the truth of the law of our fathers',
except that ἀκρίβεια is 'strict method' rather than 'truth'.[1] However
the question is raised, 'What does he mean by this excellent way (*ex-
quisita ratio*),[2] when they all had one and the same form of the Law?'
He seems to me to be distinguishing the purer form of knowledge
with which he had been imbued, from the general instruction, which
had departed rather far from the original sense of the Law. But
although the Law of the Lord was corrupted by many additions at
that time, even among the best teachers, yet because religion was
thoroughly adulterated among the multitude, Paul takes justifiable
pride in the fact that he was trained in the Law of their fathers properly
and diligently, or, what amounts to the same thing, strictly, so that
no one may think that he had received only a slight smattering like
any member of the crowd.

But because many who have received proper instruction are nevertheless full of an epicurean contempt of God, he testifies that he was

---

[1] Vulg.: *Eruditus iuxta veritatem paternae legis.* Calvin: *Institutus secundum
exactam rationem legis patriae.* Greek: πεπαιδευμένος κατὰ ἀκρίβειαν τοῦ πατρῴου
νόμου. Footnote, C.R. Calvin had included in the first Edition, but omitted from
second: 'However, because these things can be read distinctly, "Instructed
according to the strict form" i.e. "diligently", and secondly, "in the law of the
fathers", and the meaning is fuller, I gladly subscribe to Erasmus.' Tr.

[2] French: 'une façon exquise ou perfection'. Tr.

zealous for God; as if he said that a serious concern for piety was linked to learning (*doctrina*), so that he had no intention of trifling in sacred things, like worldly men, who deliberately mix everything together.

Finally, he makes himself like the rest of the Jews for that period of time, in that his zeal was thoughtless. However it can be put down to his credit that in those former days he worshipped God from the heart just as much as they are doing at the present time.

4, 5. *I persecuted this Way.* The second point is this, that he was hostile to the teaching of Christ, and, indeed, that he was more vehement than all the others in forcing his way in to attack it, until he was pulled back by the hand of God. He cites the *chief priest* and the *elders*, as witnesses of that action. Therefore no suspicion could have remained about such a sudden change. His statement that *letters* were given to him for the *brethren*, ought to be referred to the Jews, as if he had called them 'fellow-countrymen', but he intended to appease them with a more honourable title. For Paul bends his efforts to affirming his own genuine and legitimate origin from that nation, and, secondly, his desire for friendship (*coniunctionis*).

And it came to pass, that, as I made my journey, and drew nigh unto Damascus, about noon, suddenly there shone from heaven a great light round about me. And I fell unto the ground, and heard a voice saying unto me, Saul, Saul, why persecutest thou me? And I answered, Who art thou, Lord? And he said unto me, I am Jesus of Nazareth, whom thou persecutest. And they that were with me beheld indeed the light,[1] but they heard not the voice of him that spake to me. And I said, What shall I do, Lord? And the Lord said unto me, Arise, and go into Damascus; and there it shall be told thee of all things which are appointed for thee to do. And when I could not see for the glory of that light, being led by the hand of them that were with me, I came into Damascus. (6-11)

6. *And it came to pass.* Since I gave rather a full explanation of this story in chapter 9, I shall merely refer briefly to what I said there. But there is the peculiar difference in the present passage that Paul goes over his circumstances, to prove by them that he was converted by God. And this is the third part of his speech. Otherwise the change would not have been free from the mark of inconstancy, or rashness, or some other stigma of disgrace. For there is nothing more intolerable than to retreat from the path of duty (*pietatis*) once one has entered on it, and, in the second place, not to fulfil commands. Therefore in order that no one might have any suspicion about his

[1] Calvin, as AV, adds *and were afraid*. Tr.

conversion, Paul shows, by bringing many miracles to the people's attention, that God was responsible for it. Often at night lightning flashes out, produced from the hot vapours of the earth. But this was something far more unusual: about midday a light not only suddenly shone forth, but also surrounded him like a flash of lightning, so that he fell from his horse in terror, and lay on the ground. There is another miracle in the voice that called out from heaven. And there is still another in the fact that his comrades do not hear it as he does. Others finally follow; after he was sent to Damascus, the outcome corresponds to the oracle, because Ananias does come to meet him; and, again, his sight is restored to him in a moment.

7. *I fell to the ground.* As Paul was puffed up with pharisaic pride it was fitting for him to be thrown to the ground, and, as it were, deflated, so that he might hear Christ's voice. Indeed he would not have spurned God openly, and he would not have dared to ignore the heavenly oracle, yet his mind would never have been disposed to the obedience of faith, if he had continued untouched. He is therefore thrown down with violent force, so that he may learn to humble himself voluntarily. Moreover there is only a short reproof in Christ's words, to curb the ferocity and rage of this man. At the same time extraordinary consolation comes to us from this, that Christ, having assumed the part (*persona*) of all the godly, complains that He has suffered all the injuries that had been inflicted on them. But as nothing sweeter can be imagined for soothing the bitterness of persecution, than hearing that the Son of God suffers, not only along with us, but in us, so, on the other hand, the blood-thirsty enemies of the Gospel, who now scoff at the wretched Church, with stupid pride, will realize whom they have been wounding.

9. *Who were with me.* I have shown in the other passage that there is not the discrepancy, which appears to be in Luke's words (9.7). There Luke said that, while Paul's companions stood in astonishment, they heard the voice, but saw no one. Here, on the other hand, he says that they did not hear the voice of Him who was speaking with Paul, although they saw the light. Surely it is not absurd that they were aware of some indistinct voice, although they nevertheless did not distinguish it, like Paul himself, for Christ was wishing to curb and subdue him alone with His reproof. Therefore they do hear a voice, because a sound strikes their ears, so that they know that some-one is speaking from heaven. But they do not hear the voice of the person speaking with Paul, because they do not understand what Christ is saying. Also they see the splendour of the light encircling Paul, but they do not see anyone, who is sending out the voice from heaven.

10. *What shall I do, Lord?* This is the cry of a tamed man. And it is genuine conversion to the Lord, when, having laid aside all our ferocity, we freely put our necks under His yoke, and are ready to undertake whatever He commands. In addition it is the start of the right course of action to ask what God wants. For those who think of repentance without His Word, make a great fuss for nothing. Moreover in appointing Ananias to be Paul's teacher, Christ does not do so in order to affront him, or because He is reluctant to teach him, but in this way He wishes to commend and honour the external ministry of the Church. And in the person of one man, indeed, He has given a general warning that we are not to be unwilling to hear Him speaking by the tongue of men. What follows immediately after has the same object in view, that he was blind until, presenting himself as a learner, he might prove the humility of his faith. Certainly God does not blind all, whom He wishes to illuminate, but a general rule is laid down for all, that those who wish to be wise to Him, are to become fools in their own eyes.

And one Ananias, a devout man according to the law, well reported of by all the Jews that dwelt there, came unto me, and standing by me said unto me, Brother Saul, receive thy sight. And in that very hour I looked up on him.[1] And he said, The God of our fathers hath appointed thee to know his will, and to see the Righteous One, and to hear a voice from his mouth. For thou shalt be a witness for him unto all men of what thou hast seen and heard. And now why tarriest thou? arise, and be baptized, and wash away thy sins, calling on his name. (12-16)

12. *One Ananias.* Paul now passes on to the fourth point, viz. that, struck with amazement by the miracles, not only did he give his allegiance to Christ, but he was properly and soundly instructed in the teaching of the Gospel. I have already suggested that it was not by chance but by the guidance of Christ that Ananias met Paul. But in describing him as *devout according to the Law*, and saying that he was approved by the testimony of the whole nation, he anticipates the unfavourable opinion, which they could have conceived. As they abhorred the Gentiles, they would never have granted admittance to a teacher from them. Certainly they would have thoroughly detested an apostate from the Law. Therefore he asserts that he worshipped God 'according to the Law', and that his piety was known, and praised, among all the Jews, so that he ought not to be suspected. The phrase 'according to the Law', is clumsily connected by some to the following clause, that 'he was approved according to the Law'. Rather the religion of Ananias is in fact being distinguished from the

[1] Calvin reads: *I received my sight and saw him.* Tr.

superstitions of the Gentiles by this characteristic. However we must note that the Law is not mentioned to establish the merits of works, so that they may be set over against the grace of God, but the piety of Ananias is freed from all unfavourable suspicion in the eyes of the Jews. And it is apparent from the fact that he restored Paul's sight with one word, that he was sent by God, as I have already suggested.

14. *The God of our fathers.* Just as nothing is better fitted to incite us to move towards God eagerly, than the knowledge that God meets us by His gracious goodness, so that He may call us back from destruction to life, so Ananias begins from that. He says, 'God has appointed you to know His will'. For in this way Paul is warned that God had His eyes on Him, during the time he was wandering astray, and was completely hostile to his own salvation; and so God's predestination abolishes all the preparations, which sophists imagine, as if a man were to anticipate the grace of God by his own free-will.

In calling Him *the God of our fathers*, he renews the memory of the promises, so that the Jews may know that Paul's recent call is connected with them; and that those who make the transition to Christ are not abandoning the Law. Therefore by these words Paul confirms what he has previously asserted in person, that he has not deserted the God of Abraham, and the God who had already been worshipped by the Jews in times past, but that he is continuing in the ancient worship of the fathers, which he had learnt from the Law.

Accordingly, when it is a question of religion, let us learn by Paul's example, not to imagine some new God, as the Papists and Mohammedans have done, and all the heretics are in the habit of doing, but let us retain that God, who revealed Himself to the fathers long ago, not only by the Law but also by various oracles. This is the true antiquity, in which we must continue, and not the one in which the Papists take pride in vain, for they have made a new God for themselves, since they have departed from the proper fathers (*a legitimis patribus*). The same thing must be said about the Jews today, for, since their religion is alien from the Law and the Prophets, their God also must of necessity be fictitious and degenerate. For He who long ago was willing to be called 'the God of Abraham and the fathers', finally appeared in the Person of His Son, so that He is now called by the proper title of 'the Father of Christ'. Therefore he who rejects the Son, does not have the Father, who cannot be separated from Him.

But Ananias warns that it was due to the gracious election of God that the truth of the Gospel is now shining in Paul; and it follows from that, that it was not acquired by his own activity, and the experience of the event also made that plain. For no one was more stubborn than Paul, until Christ subdued him. But if we look for the cause and

origin, Ananias calls us back to the decision of God, by which he was
chosen; and surely it is a more valuable thing to know the will of
God than for men to attain to it by their own efforts. And Ananias'
assertion about Paul ought to be applied to all, that the treasure of
faith is not set before all indiscriminately, but is offered to the elect in
particular. Moreover it is clearer from the next clause what that will
of God is. For having spoken through His prophets in many places
and in many ways, God has now revealed His will fully, and Himself
completely, in His Son (Heb. 1.1).

And to see the Righteous One. Since nearly all the Greek manuscripts
agree on the masculine gender, I wonder why Erasmus preferred to
translate it in the neuter, 'what is righteous', for readers see that the
meaning is pointless and forced. Therefore I have no doubt that
righteous is used here for Christ; and in this way the connexion runs
smoothly, because immediately after there follows, 'to hear a voice
from his mouth'. And it is well known that the greatest longing that
all holy men had was to be allowed to enjoy the sight of Christ. That
gave rise to Simeon's confession, 'Now, O Lord, let they servant
depart in peace, because mine eyes have seen thy salvation' (Luke 2.29).
Christ Himself bears witness that godly kings and prophets had a
passionate desire for this vision (Luke 10.24). Therefore it is quite
rightly extolled as an extraordinary blessing of God. But because the
sight of the eyes, which we know to have been a deadly thing for
many, would be of little or no use, he adds 'the hearing of the voice'.

Ananias adds the purpose for which God has thought Paul worthy
of such a great honour, viz. that he might be a public witness to His
Son. And he prepares him in such a way, that he may not only learn
for himself privately, but he may be all the more eager to make
progress, in view of the fact that he is going to be a teacher of the
whole Church.

16. *And now why tarriest thou?* There is no doubt that Ananias
faithfully instructed Paul in the rudiments of the faith (*pietatis*). For
he would not have baptized him if he lacked true faith. But Luke
leaves out many things, and only gives a brief summary. Therefore
since Paul understands that the promised redemption has now been
procured in Christ, Ananias is quite right in saying that nothing
ought to cause his baptism to be delayed. But when he says, 'What
are you waiting for?', he is not rebuking Paul, and is not accusing him
of being slow, but he is further amplifying the grace of God by the
addition of baptism. We found a similar sentence in chapter 10
(v. 47), 'Can anyone prevent those people, who have been given the
Holy Spirit, just as we have, from being baptized with water?' And
when he adds, *Wash away your sins*, he is bringing out the force and

effect of baptism by these words, as if he had said, 'Wash away your sins by baptism.' But since in this way more appears to be attributed to the external and corruptible element than is proper, the question is asked, whether baptism is the cause of our cleansing. Certainly since the blood of Christ is the one and only expiation for sins, and since it was shed once for this purpose, and the Holy Spirit is cleansing us continually by the sprinkling of it through faith, the honour for this cannot be transferred to the symbol of water, without doing injury to Christ and the Holy Spirit. And experience shows how prone men are to this superstition. Therefore many godly men, for fear of putting their trust in the outward sign, weaken the power of baptism too much. But a proper balance must be preserved, so that the sacraments are kept in their proper place, in case they may obscure the glory of Christ, and yet not lack their own efficacy and value.

Accordingly we must hold, in the first place, that it is God alone who washes us from our sins by the blood of His Son, and that He acts by the secret power of the Spirit, in order that this washing may be effective in us. Therefore when it is a question of the remission of sins, we must look for no other originator of it than the Heavenly Father; we must imagine no other material cause than the blood of Christ. But when it comes to the formal cause the Holy Spirit indeed plays the leading role, but an inferior instrument is added, the preaching of the Gospel and baptism itself. Finally, even if God alone is acting by the inward power of His Spirit, yet that does not prevent Him from making use, as He pleases, of the instruments and means (*media*), which He knows to be suitable, not because He shuts up in the element something taken either from the Holy Spirit, or from the blood of Christ, but because He wishes the sign itself to be a prop for our weakness. Therefore since baptism helps our faith to receive remission of sins from the blood of Christ and that alone, it is called the laver (*lavacrum*) of the soul. So when he mentions washing Luke is not describing the cause, but is referring to Paul's understanding, for, by receiving the symbol, he grasped better that his sins were expiated. However we must also note this, that a bare form (*figuram*) is not set before us in baptism, but the giving of the reality (*rei exhibitionem*) is also connected to it at the same time, because God does not deceive us in His promises, but truly fulfills what He signifies under figures. However, on the other hand, we must be on our guard that the grace of God is not tied to the sacraments. For the external administration of baptism is of no value, except when it pleases God that it should be so. Another question, which can be raised, is also answered from this. For, since Paul had proof of the grace of God, his sins had already been forgiven. Therefore he was not merely washed by baptism, but obtained fresh confirmation of the grace which he had received.

Calling on the name of the Lord.[1] There is no doubt that he means Christ, not because the name of Christ alone is invoked in baptism, but because the Father commands us to seek from Christ (*ab ipso*)[2] all that is represented to us in baptism. And the operation of the Spirit has no other purpose except to make us sharers of Christ's death and resurrection. Therefore Christ is appointed to be the One prominent in baptism, but to the extent that He has been given to us by the Father, and in so far as He pours out His graces upon us through the Holy Spirit. The result is that invocation of the name of Christ includes in itself the Father and the Spirit. Accordingly Ananias does not mean that only the name of Christ must be uttered, but he is describing prayer by which the faithful testify that the effect of the outward sign is in the power of Christ alone. For the sacraments do not have any power of salvation shut up in themselves, or any effectiveness by themselves. Accordingly this clause is, so to speak, a correction of the preceding statement, because Ananias clearly directs Paul away from trust in the outward element, to Christ. It is well known how much the Papists differ from this example. They tie the cause of grace to their own exorcisms; and so far from being concerned to direct the wretched mass of the people to Christ, they rather drown Christ in baptism, and defile His sacred name with their exorcisms.

And it came to pass, that, when I had returned to Jerusalem, and while I prayed in the temple, I fell into a trance, and saw him saying unto me, Make haste, and get thee quickly out of Jerusalem: because they will not receive of thee testimony concerning me. And I said, Lord, they themselves know that I imprisoned and beat in every synagogue them that believed on thee: and when the blood of Stephen thy witness was shed, I also was standing by and consenting, and keeping the garments of them that slew him. And he said unto me, Depart: for I will send thee forth far hence unto the Gentiles. And they gave him audience unto this word; and they lifted up their voice, and said, Away with such a fellow from the earth: for it is not fit that he should live. (17-22)

17. *And it came to pass.* This would not have been the concluding section, if Paul's speech had not been cut short by their violent outcries. But from the preceding context it is easy to see what he had in mind. For he begins to deal with his own ministry to show that he did not go away from the Jews of his own accord, as if he deprived them of his services out of spite, but that he was drawn away to the Gentiles by the commandment of God, contrary to the expectation

[1] So Calvin; RV as Greek. Tr.   [2] French: 'en lui'. Tr.

and purpose of his own mind. For he had come to Jerusalem with the intention of sharing, with his own nation, the grace that had been entrusted to him. But the Lord cuts off the hope of success, and drives him out of there.

But there was a twofold stumbling-block that Paul wished to correct. For they used to think that the covenant of God was profaned if Gentiles were admitted into the Church along with them, indiscriminately; and nothing used to annoy this proud nation more than for others to be preferred to them, and even made equal to them. Paul's defence therefore consists in this, that as far as he was concerned, he was ready to devote himself to them, but that afterwards he was forced by the commandment of God to go over to the Gentiles, because He was not willing that he should remain inactive and useless at Jerusalem.

Erasmus' translation 'that I was transported outside myself'[1] is rendered literally in the Greek 'that I was in an ecstasy'. By that expression he wished to create confidence in the oracle. The circumstances of time and place also establish the same thing, because the Lord appeared to him when he was praying in the temple, and that was the best preparation for hearing the voice of God. As to the manner of the vision see what we touched upon round about the end of chapter 7 (7.56).

18. *Because they will not receive thy testimony.* Although the simple command of God ought to be more than sufficient for us to show obedience, yet in order that Paul might be readier to follow, Christ gives him a reason why He wishes him to leave Jerusalem, viz. because he would not do anything worth while there. But he had not been chosen to lie idle, or to accomplish nothing by his teaching. However this was a severe testing, and we may well believe that it filled the heart of the holy man with intense consternation. Paul had been charged earlier with the task of publishing the Gospel, so that his voice would sound through the whole world; now at the very beginning he is thwarted; yes, and what is more, his labour seems to be condemned by a special disgrace, when his testimony is rejected out of personal animosity, as men say. But it was necessary for the holy servant of God to be humbled like this, so that all teachers of the Gospel might learn by his example to devote themselves, wholly and completely, to obedience to Christ, so that when they are excluded from one place they may be ready to go over at once to some other place. And they are not to lose heart, or cease to do their duty, because they are undeservedly hated.

---

[1] Calvin follows this rendering, *ut raperer extra me.* Greek: γενέσθαι με ἐν ἐκστάσει. Tr.

19. *Lord they themselves know.* Paul makes it known by these words that he was not mentally disturbed or confused, but that he had assured confidence in the oracle. For without the shadow of a doubt he recognized Christ, whom he addresses by the name of *Lord.* However, Paul objects that it is scarcely possible for them not to be disturbed by the spectacle of the sudden change that they find in him; and from that he concludes that he will not be unsuccessful. At all events that is what he was thinking; but Christ gives the definite reply that He has chosen him for another field of service, and takes away the groundless hope that he has conceived concerning the Jews. But the question is raised whether it was right for Paul to bring forward these objections to Christ. For it is just as if he contends that what Christ said would not happen, probably would. I reply that God allows His saints to unburden their feelings on His bosom in an intimate way, especially when all that they are seeking is the confirmation of their faith. If anyone relies on his own wisdom, or stubbornly rejects what God orders, his arrogance will be justifiably condemned. But God thinks His faithful people worthy of the unique privilege that they may humbly put before Him things that could call them back or detain them, when they are eager to obey, so that, freer and readier, they may commit themselves wholly to God. We find an example of it here, for after Paul has been instructed to please the Lord in this way, he does not reply, and does not make any further assertion, but content with that one objection, and desisting from it, he prepares himself for the journey, which he had appeared to be avoiding. At the same time the untameable obstinacy of the Jews is exposed by the fact that they remain unmoved by so many miracles. Such a reproach no doubt drove them into a fury.

22. *Away with such a fellow from the earth.* Here Luke tells how Paul's speech was interrupted by an uproar. For not only do they overwhelm him with their shouting, but they demand his death; which makes it perfectly plain how frenzied their pride is. The Jews used to have such pride in themselves that not only did they despise the whole world in comparison with themselves, but they fought more passionately for their own dignity than for the Law itself, as if the whole of religion turned on this point, that the descendants of Abraham excelled over all other mortals. So they are now driven violently against Paul, because he had said that he was sent as the apostle to the Gentiles, as if God's own generosity laid Him under obligation to put up with contempt of His deity in impious and ungrateful men, whom he honoured above all others with extraordinary gifts. And it is no wonder that there was so much ferocity in the Jews at that time, when today they are completely trampled upon (*attriti*)

and accustomed to extreme insults, and yet do not cease to be swollen with a servile pride. But those are the consequences of rejection, until God gathers together the remnant, according to Paul's prophecy (Rom. 11.5).

And as they cried out, and threw off their garments, and cast dust into the air, the chief captain commanded him to be brought into the castle, bidding that he should be examined by scourging, that he might know for what cause they so shouted against him. And when they had tied him up with the thongs, Paul said unto the centurion that stood by, Is it lawful for you to scourge a man that is a Roman, and uncondemned? And when the centurion heard it, he went to the chief captain, and told him, saying, What art thou about to do? for this man is a Roman. And the chief captain came, and said unto him, Tell me, art thou a Roman? And he said, Yea. And the chief captain answered, With a great sum obtained I this citizenship. And Paul said, But I am a Roman born. They then which were about to examine him straightway departed from him: and the chief captain also was afraid, when he knew that he was a Roman, and because he had bound him. But on the morrow, desiring to know the certainty, wherefore he was accused of the Jews, he loosed him, and commanded the chief priests and all the council to come together, and brought Paul down, and set him before them. (23-30)

24. *The tribune commanded.* The tribune acted prudently and correctly in removing Paul from the people's sight, since his presence might provoke still further minds that were already inflamed more than enough. For in this way he takes care of the life of the holy man, and partly calms the madness of the people. But he does appear to be acting unjustly when he orders the scourging of a man, concerning whom he has heard no definite charge. And yet there was some excuse for this injustice, because it was probable that the whole of the people conspired, and not without good cause, for the head of one man. Therefore a strong presumption on his part was the cause of such a harsh examination. But it should be noted that it is the practice of astute (*politicis*) men to be fair judges, in so far as it is to their own interest, but if something to their advantage calls elsewhere, they turn aside in any direction. At the same time it is enough for them to gloss over this crooked behaviour with the title of 'prudence', because they maintain that general principle that the world cannot be governed without a show of justice. But when it comes to individual cases that astuteness, which I have mentioned, has the upper hand, so that what is advantageous carries weight rather than what is fair and right.

25. *A man that is a Roman.* In the first place Paul brings forward the right to the privileges of citizenship, and then pleads a general

right in his defence. But although the second point was the more
important, viz. that it is not right for a man to be scourged without a
hearing, yet it would have been useless if the centurion had not been
more disturbed about the honour of the Roman Empire. For at that
time there was no greater crime than the violation of the liberty of
the Roman people. The laws of Valerius, Porcius, Sempronius, and
others like them, forbade anyone to inflict punishment on the body
of a Roman citizen without the command of the people. The privilege was so sacred that they considered it not only a capital, but also
an inexpiable offence, for a Roman citizen to be beaten. Therefore
Paul escaped because of a privilege, rather than common justice; but
he did not hesitate to use, in a good cause, this shield of citizenship to
ward off the injury that was prepared for him. But it must be realized
that he asserted the right of citizenship in this way, so that the tribune
might be convinced; because the tribune would not have been rash
enough to believe what he said, without making an investigation.
Moreover it was not difficult for a man, who was quite well known,
to bring forward witnesses. But in chapter 16 we gave the reason
why, at Philippi, he submitted in silence to the punishment of flogging,
which he now forestalls by his own announcement; it was because he
would not have been heard when the people were in an uproar (16.37).
Now he takes the opportunity, because he is dealing with Roman
soldiers, who were conducting themselves with more moderation and
dignity.

26. *This man is a Roman.* Somebody may wonder that the man,
who was in charge of holding the examination, was so credulous that
he makes a firm assertion, as if about something of which he had
certain knowledge. For if he was bound to give credence to Paul's
statement, then any criminal could have avoided punishment by this
artifice. But this was their method of acting: a man who was asserting
that he was a Roman citizen, was punished, unless he produced
someone who knew him, or proved legally that he was a citizen; for
it was a capital offence to lay false claim to the right of citizenship.
Accordingly the centurion refers the matter to the tribune, as if it
were in doubt, but the tribune, as we have said, immediately hastens
to investigate. But even if Luke does not tell what evidence Paul
used to prove himself a Roman citizen, yet there is no doubt that the
tribune obtained full knowledge of the truth, before he untied him.

28. *With a great sum I obtained.* The tribune makes this objection
in order to refute him, as if he said that the right of citizenship is not
such a common thing, and is not open to all. He says, 'How can it
be that an obscure fellow of the Cilician people like you acquired
this honour, which cost me a great deal of money?' When Paul

replies that he was *born* (a Roman citizen), he, who had never seen the city, and, furthermore, whose father had perhaps never gone near it, there is no reason for that to upset anyone. For those who are acquainted with Roman history know that certain men in the provinces were granted citizenship, if they deserved well of the State either in war or in other important affairs, and requested this reward for themselves from the proconsuls; so there is nothing absurd about a man having been born a Roman citizen, although, being a native of a remote province, he yet might never have set foot in Italy.

However it is asked how the fact that the tribune was afraid because he had bound a Roman citizen, agrees with the fact that he nevertheless only removed his bonds on the next day. It is possible that he put it off to the following day so as not to give any sign of fear. However I think that the reason for the tribune's fear was that Paul had been bound, in order to be scourged, at his command, and that was a violation both of the body of a Roman citizen, and common liberty; but I also think that confinement in prison was permitted.

CHAPTER TWENTY-THREE

And Paul, looking stedfastly on the council, said, Brethren, I have lived before God in all good conscience until this day. And the high priest Ananias commanded them that stood by him to smite him on the mouth. Then said Paul unto him, God shall smite thee, thou whited wall: and sittest thou to judge me according to the law, and commandest me to be smitten contrary to the law? And they that stood by said, Revilest thou God's high priest? And Paul said, I wist not, brethren, that he was high priest: for it is written, Thou shalt not speak evil of a ruler of thy people. (1-5)

1. *And Paul looking stedfastly.* Paul begins by testifying to his *good conscience,* so that the whole crowd may understand that it is unjust to charge him with such an atrocious offence, as if he had attempted to overthrow the worship of God. Certainly it is possible for a man, who at other times will not be one to despise either God or religion, to go wrong through ignorance; but Paul merely wished to soothe their irritated minds at the outset with this plea, in order to get a hearing for himself. For he would never have been allowed to defend himself, so long as the opinion, that he was an impious apostate, had stuck fast in the minds of the priests. Therefore before he enters upon his defence, he removes that charge, not only to gain favour for himself because of his devotion to godliness, but also to anticipate calumnies, or at least to refute the unjust prejudices about himself, by which, he saw, the whole crowd was infected and corrupted. It is not known what else he was going to say. But this preface teaches that no one can handle the teaching of godliness properly, unless the fear of God rules, and holds first place, in him. Now, indeed, although he gives the priests a less honourable title than he did a little earlier on the steps of the fortress, nevertheless he still bestows on them the honour of the name of *brethren,* not because they deserve it, but to testify that the cause of their breach is not due to his fault.

2. *But the high priest.* Luke's narrative does not appear to agree with the accepted history. For this is what Josephus records about the high priests of that time. When Quadratus, proconsul of Syria, dismissed Cumanus from the procuratorship of Judaea, and ordered him to defend himself before Caesar, he sent Ananias the high priest bound along with him. He does not mention who was appointed in Ananias' place, but it is probable that the honour was conferred on

Jonathan, who, he says, was later killed by the deception and treachery of Felix, the governor who succeeded Cumanus. For Felix had been admonished rather often by him, and, when he took badly with the persistence of the man, he arranged with a certain Doras to incite assassins to kill him in secret. Then, according to the evidence of the same Josephus, King Agrippa conferred the priesthood on Ishmael the son of Phabi. But when he was sent to Rome by the people to intercede in a certain matter (*deprecationis cuiusdam causa*), and was kept there by Poppaea, the wife of Nero, Agrippa substituted in his place Josephus Chabus, the son of Simon. But having soon grown sick of this man also, he appointed Ananus, the son of Ananus, high priest. Moreover he narrates that this last event took place at the time when, after the death of Festus, Albinus was on his way to succeed in his place. But I do not see why some men give the name of Ananias to this Ananus. Certainly there is some plausibility about this, because he is said to have been a Sadducee, and also, bold and arrogant, since he exposed James, the brother of the Lord, to stoning without any lawful authority. But if Josephus is to be believed, he could not have been the Ananias, whom Luke mentions here, for he was appointed the Priest, only when several years had already passed after Felix had left the province. Another conjecture comes into my mind. For throughout the whole of that period of time there flourished a certain Ananias, a high priest, who, apart from the official title, played almost the leading role in the order; and because Josephus leaves some of the period between the first Ananias and Ishmael blank it is possible that that man held the office of high priest in that interval of time. But even if that was not the case, it is established from Josephus that Ananias, who died when the city was besieged, was equal in dignity to the high priests, who held office during the reigns of Claudius Caesar and Nero. Yes, and what is more, his authority is honoured, just as if the supreme control was in his hands, although others bore the insignia of office. Again, he is called ἀρχιερεύς, 'chief priest' indiscriminately, just like those who were possessed of the highest office in the priesthood. Now let readers decide whether the word ἀρχιερεύς, does not mean 'of the first rank' (*primarium*) in this verse also, as it often does in other passages, rather than 'the highest' (*summum*). For throughout their writings the evangelists call priests according to the order of Aaron, ἀρχιερεῖς, 'chief priests', to distinguish them from the Levites, who belonged to an inferior order of the priesthood. In addition, that Ananias, who was regarded as a vigorous and judicious character, could have discharged the duties of the high priest in his absence. Finally, the things that we have reported from Josephus are to be found, partly in *Antiquities*, book 20, chapters 3 to 8, and partly in *The Wars of the Jews*, book 2.

He commanded them to strike him. We see that extraordinary madness was raging in this crowd. For when the high priest was possessed by that violent impulse to order Paul to be struck for no reason, there is not the shadow of a doubt that he did it with the consent of them all; and, what is more, to try to win the favour of the madmen. The Lord permits the ungodly to be agitated by Satan in this way, so that they lose all appearance of calmness and self-control. On the other hand, hypocrites would desire to give some show of moderation; and there is no doubt that here the high priest tried to show a gravity that became his part. But the Lord plucked this mask from him, so that he did not even maintain the moderation of the ordinary man in the street, but gave vent to his fierce and violent temper like a beast.

At the same time we see what disgraceful and horrible laxity there was in the Church at that time. When Ananias, the president of the Council, ought to have been a restraining influence on the others by his gravity, he forgot all moderation, and incites them to violence and cruelty. Therefore no respect for discipline prevailed then, but disorderly and uncivilized behaviour reigned. And it is not to be wondered at; for they had alienated themselves from God; they had cast Christ aside as the supreme laughing-stock; the whole of religion in their midst was mercenary and corrupt (*venalis*). Therefore they were bound to rush into a furious madness, which would be detestable even among worldly men, so that they might suffer for their ungodliness in their own disgrace.

3. *God shall smite thee.* Paul cannot pass over that insult in silence, without at least expostulating with the high priest in grave terms, and threatening him with God's punishment. For it is not a curse, as the Greek context makes plain enough, but rather a reproof coupled with the announcement of a punishment. Someone may object that Paul has not preserved the humility, which Christ enjoins on His own, in commanding them, when they have been struck on the left cheek, at the same time to offer the right one also (Matt. 5.39). But there is an easy solution, that by those words Christ does not demand silence from His people, which may encourage the boldness and impudence of the wicked, but only puts a bridle on their minds, so that they may not be impatient in bearing an injury that they have received. Christ wishes His people to be prepared to suffer a second injury as well as one they have already received, and in this way He curbs all desire for revenge. This is a true and brief definition of endurance, which is becoming to all the faithful, so that they may not boil over in anger, and match injury with injury (*ne certent maleficiis*), but strive to overcome evil with goodness. But this does not prevent them

from complaining about injuries done to them, convicting the ungodly of their guilt, and summoning them to the judgment-seat of
God, provided that they do so calm of mind, and, secondly, without
ill-will and hatred, just as here Paul appeals to God's judgment, so
that the high priest may not pride himself in his tyranny. Therefore
he accuses him of violating the Law, by means of which he claims to
hold his power, and from that he concludes that he will not get off
unpunished. If anyone gives way to impatience, and merely murmurs,
he will not be without blame. But if a clear and serious accusation
comes from a composed mind, then it does not go beyond the limits
laid down by Christ. If anyone objects that reviling is mixed up with
it, I reply that we must always observe what sort of attitude of mind
produces the words. Christ pronounces a man, who merely said *Raca*
to his brother, guilty of the council, but He subjects the man who
said *Thou fool* to a severer sentence (Matt. 5.22). But if the opportunity
for censuring presents itself we must often speak in sterner terms.
From that one deduces that Christ's intention was only to protect
His own, first from all indignation, secondly, from being abusive.
Therefore let there be no desire to revile, and in that way it will be
lawful, not only to take note of foolishness in our brothers, but also
to describe their crimes for their own sakes when the need arises.
Thus Paul did not speak for his own sake, in order to avenge the high
priest's insult with abusive language; but, because he was a minister
of the Word of God, he did not wish to pass over in silence an outrageous act, that deserved a grave and earnest rebuke, especially since
it would be a beneficial thing to drag out the gross hypocrisy of
Ananias from its hiding-place into the light of day. Therefore, whenever we have to deal with impudent men, if we desire to present a
good case well, we must take care that no emotion of anger surge up
in us, and that no desire for revenge stimulate us to be abusive. However if the spirit of gentleness rules in us, we shall be free to deal with
impious men, as if out of the mouth of God, in accordance with their
deserts; yet in such a way that it is apparent that we are prophets
rather than people who thoughtlessly blurt out anything with uncontrolled passion.

4. *Those standing by said.* It is clear from this that they all suffered
from the same fanaticism. For why do they not rather find fault with
Ananias, when they saw that he forgot all moderation, and broke out
in violence and blows in a barbarous manner? For that was also contributing to their common disgrace. But it is the practice of hypocrites that, while they are extremely severe critics of others, they blandly
close their eyes to their own faults. Secondly, this pride goes hand in
hand with tyranny, so that those who bear rule wish their subjects to

have absolutely no freedom, while they allow themselves anything they like. So today in the Papacy the more that their impure clergy indulge themselves in licence, and the more unconcernedly they lead wanton lives, and contaminate the whole world with their enormities, the more rigidly do they suppress the people, and keep their tongues silent. Therefore, if anyone dares to mutter, a tiny expression of liberty raises enormous outcries, as if it were an abominable sacrilege.

5. *I do not know, brethren.* Those to whom this excuse of Paul's seems artless (*figura carere*), are not paying sufficient attention to the counter-objections which refute their error. They say that Paul did not know the high priest, because he had been away for a long time; as if in fact he had no idea that the man, who presided over the assembly, derived his power from his official standing as high priest. And certainly Ananias was not so insignificant, that Paul was ignorant of his rank. But Paul's words put the matter beyond argument, when he rebukes him, because he makes the Law his excuse for occupying the judge's bench, and proceeds contrary to the Law, without any moderation. Therefore Paul knew what rank he held, when he said that he made wrong use of his power.

Others think up a more subtle fabrication, that here he is not speaking about the man, but about the office and the public personage. But in the first place, this explanation is forced, because if Paul respected the priesthood, then he ought to have paid more honour to the man who possessed it. Then surely, since the dignity of the priesthood had been abolished by the advent of Christ, and so much unseemly profanation followed, one cannot believe that Paul bestowed customary honour on men, who were at that time lording it, without any right, under the title, of 'high priest', as if their entire and legitimate power still prevailed.

Therefore I myself agree with Augustine, and have no doubt that this excuse is ironical; and the fact that plain speaking befits ministers of the Truth does not stand in the way of that. For while irony is of two kinds, one that is concealed by the artifice of deception, the other that is a figurative description of a matter that is under discussion, so that it may sting more sharply, there is nothing in this second kind that is unworthy of the servants of Christ. Therefore the meaning of his words is, 'I, brethren, recognize nothing priestly about this man.' He also adds a proof-text from Exod. 22.28, where, although Moses is referring particularly to judges, yet the meaning is extended to any lawful order. Therefore every office of dignity, which has been instituted for the preservation of the civil order (*politiae*) ought to be respected scrupulously, and held in honour. For whoever rises in rebellion against the magistrate, and those endowed with authority or official standing, is striving after anarchy. But a passion of that sort tends to the disruption of order, yes, and what is more, deals a shattering blow to humanity itself (*humanitatem ipsam concutit*). Therefore Paul clears himself of this charge, but in such a way as to deny that Ananias, who has corrupted and ruined the whole order of the Church, is to be regarded as a priest of God.

But here the question arises whether we must obey a ruler, although he exercises tyranny. For if a man, who discharges his office badly, is not to be stripped of honour, Paul has sinned in robbing the high priest of his honour. I reply that there is a certain distinction between civil magistrates and leaders (*praesules*) of the Church. For although the administration of earthly or civil sovereignty is disorderly and corrupt, yet the Lord wishes submission to it to remain unaffected. But when the spiritual rule degenerates the consciences of the godly are released from obedience to an unjust domination, especially if impious and profane enemies of holiness make a false pretence to the title of the priesthood to destroy the doctrine of salvation, and arrogate to themselves a lordship by which God Himself is reduced to order. Thus today it is not only permissible but also necessary for the faithful to shake off the yoke of the Pope, since they can only obey his laws if they revolt from God.

But when Paul perceived that the one part were Sadducees, and the other Pharisees, he cried out in the council, Brethren, I am a Pharisee, a son of Pharisees[1]: touching the hope and resurrection of the dead I am called in question.[2] And when he had so said, there arose a dissension between the Pharisees and Sadducees: and the assembly was divided. For the Sadducees say that there is no resurrection, neither angel, nor spirit: but the Pharisees confess both. And there arose a great clamour: and some of the scribes of the Pharisees' part stood up, and strove, saying, We find no evil in this man: and what if a spirit hath spoken to him, or an angel?[3] (6-9)

6. *But when Paul perceived.* Paul's stratagem, which Luke reports, seems out of keeping with a servant of Christ. For the astuteness, which he used, was closely related to a feint, that was not far removed from lying. He says that the circumstances of his case turn on the resurrection of the dead. But we know that the issue was about other matters, that he abrogated the ceremonies, and admitted the Gentiles to the covenant of salvation. I reply that even if those things are true, yet he did not lie. For he does not deny that he was accused of other

[1] Calvin, as RV margin, reads *a Pharisee*. Tr.
[2] Calvin, as RV margin, reads *being judged*. Tr.
[3] Calvin, as RV margin, reads also, *let us not fight against God*. Tr.

things, and he does not resolve the dispute on this one issue, but truly acknowledges that the Sadducees are hostile to him, because he affirms the resurrection of the dead. He knew that those, who had conspired against him, suffered from internal disagreements. Certainly his own conscience was perfectly clear, and it would have been easy for him to present a good case to fair judges. However, because he sees that they are in an uproar and clamouring against him, and that no opening is being allowed for his defence, he sets his enemies to fight among themselves. It is also made clear from that, that they are being carried away by ignorance and blind zeal. Therefore we must note that Paul began by wishing to explain his whole situation frankly and sincerely, and that he did not cunningly avoid a clean and honest confession, such as the servants of Christ should have given. But we must also observe that, because an opening was barred, and no hearing was granted to him, he used an extreme remedy to make it plain that his adversaries were being swept off their feet by a blind hatred. For the outcome shows that men who are gripped, and driven astray, by mutual disagreements, are not moved by reason and judgment. If anyone nowadays obscures the light of sound doctrine, and uses Paul's example as an excuse for his own cunning, he is easily refuted. For it is one thing to look to one's personal interests, at the expense of the truth, but another to bring professed enemies of Christ from attacking Him, to fighting among themselves.

Further, we see that, although the ungodly disagree among themselves, they forget their own struggles, when they have to wage war against the Gospel. For Satan, the father of dissensions, manages to make his own followers agree on this one thing, that they are at one in mind and purpose for extinguishing godliness. Similarly today we see that the factions, that are aflame in the Papacy, are quiet so long as they are at one in their eagerness to suppress the Gospel. Accordingly the disciples of Christ ought to be the more determined to foster the truth, so that, united, they may offer better resistance. We also gather from this what kind of peace Scripture commends to us. Christ says that 'the peacemakers are the sons of God' (Matt. 5.9). And that is true to the extent that they do what they possibly can, so that all may agree together as brothers under the Lord. But that does not prevent us from rousing up the wicked, under the auspices of the same Lord, as if by the sound of the trumpet, so that, like the Midianites, they may destroy each other (Judges 7.22); provided that honest zeal and the wisdom of the Spirit direct us to do so.

One part were Sadducees. Here again we see, as in a mirror, what a sorry state of disorder and ruin the Church presented then. Faith is the soul of the Church; nothing is more characteristic of faith than agreement, and nothing is more contrary to it than sects. But that was bound to happen when the Word of God was set aside, and everyone attracted disciples to his own ideas. For there is no other holy bond of unity than the simple and genuine truth of God. As soon as it is departed from, it is no wonder if men are drawn in different directions like lacerated limbs. Therefore corruption of the Law was the origin of sects among the Jews. Similarly the Lord has avenged the profanation of His Word in the Papacy with a similar punishment, when it was corrupted by various human fabrications. Accordingly we must be the more afraid of a more horrible and lamentable break-up threatening us, who make pretence to the Gospel, than the one which there was in the Papacy; and certain signs of it are apparent. And it is no wonder when our ingratitude provokes the wrath of God in so many ways. But no matter how the face of the Church is marred by many spots and blemishes, even no matter what kind of deformity befalls it in the future, this may be a help and consolation to us; just as God was concerned in those days to snatch the Church out of destruction in a marvellous way, so, by His grace, some seed will always be left. Certainly it is not possible that some despair may not occasionally steal over the minds of the godly, when things are in so much disorder, but let us quickly learn to advance this shield, that the Lord, who preserved His Church among the Jews in such a thick fog of errors, in such a great heap of superstitions, in the unbridled licence of sects, will never allow it to suffer total destruction in the world. The same thing happened in the Papacy. For when the worship of God was overthrown in it, the doctrine of salvation suppressed, the Kingdom of Christ driven out, and ungodliness held sway openly, God nevertheless saved a hidden remnant, and some wheat always lay concealed under the chaff. It is very useful to compare these two examples. Today when we inveigh against the Papacy its hired advocates retort that nothing is more absurd than the supposition that the Church of God has been completely extinguished for many generations; as if we really supposed that no people survived for God, when those, who ought to have maintained the pure worship of God, fell away and deserted Him. Indeed we do complain that the Church was corrupted by those tyrants; that the temple of God was profaned, so that it was scarcely different from a pigsty; that Christ's flock was scattered, and His sheepfold destroyed; and, finally, that the Church was hidden from human eyes, although the Lord nevertheless knew His elect, even if they were scattered, and cherished them in secret under His wings. How foolish the Papists really are in boasting about titles of honour, is apparent from the fact that it was not the mass of the ordinary people, or a few private individuals but the priests themselves, who long ago split the Jewish Church by fatal disagreements. Accordingly there is no reason for us to hesitate to be firm in resisting the arrogance of the Pope and all his men, with whom we have the same struggle as the prophets and apostles had with the priests of their day. But just as reverence of the Church did not prevent the holy men from attacking the impious tyranny of bad priests, so we ought not to be frightened by the worthless disguises, by which the Papists deceitfully commend themselves, while, nevertheless, they have given up the doctrine of godliness.

It is quite certain that at that time the people were divided into three sects, but Luke omits the Essenes and mentions only the Pharisees and Sadducees, because it suited his purpose to do so. Now the commonly accepted opinion about the names is that the Pharisees were so named from 'separation', because they removed themselves from the rest of the flock, on account of a false sanctity, and that the Sadducees took their name from 'righteousness', as if they were צְדוּקִים (zaddukim),[1] 'righteous men'. However, as I have acknowledged elsewhere, I rather agree with those who hold the opinion that the Pharisees derived their name from 'interpreting'. For פָּרוֹשׁ means 'exposition', and from that there also comes the name for 'interpreters', פָּרוֹשִׁים.[2] On the other hand we know that the Pharisees were not content with the genuine teaching of the Law and the Prophets, and with it mixed up fabrications of their own, which, they boasted, had been handed down from the fathers.

8. *For the Sadducees say.* Although Luke gives three points on which those sects disagreed, yet a little later he limits them to two, because the nature (*ratio*) of angels and spirits is the same. Therefore he says that the Pharisees confessed both, viz. that resurrection awaits the dead, and that human and angelic spirits are immortal. And Luke here makes it clear in what sense the apostle professed himself a Pharisee, that he subscribed, not to all their made-up ideas, but only to the resurrection of the dead. We know how severe Christ is in his censure of their worst errors. Therefore an exception had to be added, so that no one might think that Paul associated himself with them in every respect. Now, because the Sadducees used to deny the

---

[1] There is confusion in the Latin texts here. C.R. has transliterated *zedukim* for צְדוּקִים, an incorrect form. Tholuck has צַדּוּקִים (*zaddukim*) the correct form for Sadducees. 'Righteous men' would be צַדִּיקִים. Derivation from צַדִּיק 'righteous' is generally rejected now, because of the ו, in favour of derivation from צָדוֹק (*Zadok*). Tr.

[2] This means 'separated ones'. The Hebrew פָּרַשׁ means (1) 'to separate', (2) 'to define', 'make clear'. Tr.

resurrection of the dead, that is no reason for us to think that they were completely like the Epicureans. For they used to confess that the world is governed by the providence of God, and that each man is rewarded according to his works. In that respect they were a little sounder than the Epicureans. But it was too stupid and crazy of them to include rewards and punishments of sins in this life. For to say nothing of Scripture, experience clearly shows that the good and the bad are either afflicted by many troubles, or treated kindly and indulgently, without any distinction between them; and indeed that the ungodly often lead a life of pleasure, while the worshippers of God are wretchedly tormented, as Ps. 73.4 has it. Therefore anyone who measures the judgment of God according as the present circumstances of men are favourable or adverse, is bound in the end to forfeit his faith to an Epicurean contempt of God. Now it is brute-like stupidity to be satisfied with the life that is changing and transitory, and not to have a taste for what is above the earth. Accordingly that error must be all the more avoided, just as if it were a detestable monster. For even if godliness does have the promises of earthly life also, yet, because we are most wretched if our hope is confined to this world, the sons of God ought to begin, like recruits, with this, that they raise their eyes to heaven, and meditate continually upon the glory of the final resurrection.

Neither angel nor spirit. This part of the verse is explained in three ways. Many make it refer to the Holy Spirit, and that appears to be quite inappropriate. For although an excuse can nevertheless be made for the Sadducees in connexion with other errors, yet, because Scripture so often presses the name of the Spirit of God upon our attention, I am hardly led to believe that they denied what the Pharisees believed only slightly and vaguely. For the belief of the latter (*horum*) about the Holy Spirit was not clear, so that they recognized the particular Person (*hypostasin*) of the Spirit in the being (*essentia*) of God.

Some think that *angel and spirit* are synonymous, as if the same thing is referred to twice. But what was the use of repeating something that is not obscure? Evidently they have been misled by the phrase that comes next, in which Luke appears to make no distinction. But the reason has already been given,[1] that, since angels and the souls of men have the same nature and substance, they are placed in the same order. Therefore I have no doubt that Luke's true meaning is that the Sadducees denied any knowledge of angels, and secondly, of spirits of any kind.

Now when Paul declares that he is a Pharisee in this aspect of doctrine, he openly condemns all the fanatics, who labour under a

---

[1] At the beginning of verse 8. Tr.

similar error today. For there are certain profane and ignorant men who fondly imagine that angels and devils are nothing but good and bad inspirations; and so as not to be without an excuse, they say that all that Scripture teaches about good and bad angels sprang from the heathen, when it is rather the case that the belief, that is accepted throughout the world, took its origin from the heavenly teaching, but by their fables the heathen corrupted the teaching, that they received from the patriarchs. As far as the souls of men are concerned, because even today certain good-for-nothing fellows suppose that souls vanish at death until the resurrection day, their madness is similarly refuted by Luke's testimony.

9. *There arose a great clamour.* The dissension, which Luke mentioned a little earlier, is now described more fully, viz. that not only did they hold divergent opinions, but they strove with a tumult of shouting. Accordingly στάσις means something more than 'dissension'. Moreover this verse teaches what evil disagreements carry along with them. For, because they generally take their origin from ambition, men then easily leap into contention, and soon afterwards obstinacy makes itself felt. When it comes to that the case can no longer be brought to a decision, because there is no room left for either judgment or moderation. Those who were cursing Paul suddenly begin to defend him. That would have been quite in order, if they were doing it with judgment; but because they are set against the Sadducees, they are inflamed with hatred of them and their eyes are closed to Paul's case. Accordingly we must be on our guard against the heat of quarrels, for it throws everything into confusion and disorder.

What if a spirit. This certainly ought to be taken as applying to the Holy Spirit. But nothing could have been said more respectfully or modestly. For as soon as it is established that any teaching has originated from heaven, all, who do not embrace it, are impiously resisting God. But what brought about such a sudden change, where the scribes regarded Paul as a prophet, when they would have been ready to kill him by their own hands, and when they had condemned him by their prejudice, until the quarrel with the Sadducees broke out? Moreover, just as they cut their throats, as if with their own swords, by these words, so God wished them to be warnings to us not to despise oracles that have issued from heaven. Again, however, we see that those who are not seriously intent on listening to what God says, are in a state of suspense and doubt, and vacillate as often as anything is made known, because they are not worthy to grasp the certain truth. Accordingly if we desire to have our studies directed by the spirit of discretion, let us apply ourselves to learning.

And when there arose a great dissension, the chief captain, fearing lest Paul should be torn in pieces by them, commanded the soldiers to go down and take him by force from among them, and bring him into the castle. And the night following the Lord stood by him, and said, Be of good cheer[1]: for as thou hast testified concerning me at Jerusalem, so must thou bear witness also at Rome. And when it was day, the Jews banded together, and bound themselves under a curse, saying that they would neither eat nor drink till they had killed Paul. And they were more than forty which made this conspiracy. And they came to the chief priests and the elders, and said, We have bound ourselves under a great curse, to taste nothing until we have killed Paul. Now therefore do ye with the council signify to the chief captain that he bring him down unto you,[2] as though ye would judge of his case more exactly: and we, or ever he come near, are ready to slay him. But Paul's sister's son heard of their lying in wait, and he came and entered into the castle, and told Paul. (10-16)

10. Again we see what an atrocious evil contention is. Once it has fermented, it produces such violent emotions that even the wisest of men lose control of themselves. Accordingly as soon as it shows any sign of beginning, let us endeavour to counter it quickly, so that the remedy may not be too late in the end for checking it when it is at its height, because no fire spreads so quickly. But as the tribune had been appointed as the minister of God's providence to save Paul's life, once again he snatches him out of the jaws of death by his soldiers. For even if the tribune hastens so diligently to his aid, for no other purpose except to prevent more serious tumults and slaughter, yet from heaven the Lord provides help for His servant, and guides blind hands to him.

11. *And the following night.* Luke tells that Paul was encouraged by an oracle, so that, when things were in such an upheaval, he might stand with unbroken spirit against terrible attacks. It was surely impossible for him not to have been dismayed by many anxieties, and at the same time tormented about the future. Therefore the oracle was not unnecessary. Indeed the preceding events, by which he had been reminded that he was the object of God's care, ought to have been enough to nourish and sustain his hope, so that he would not give way. Yet in great dangers Satan immediately presents new terrors, by which he may obscure, if he cannot blot out completely, as if with clouds, the promises of God in the hearts of the godly. Because of that the memory of those promises needs

---

[1] Calvin, as RV margin, adds *Paul.* Tr.
[2] Calvin, as RV margin, adds *tomorrow.* Tr.

to be renewed so that faith, helped by fresh supports, may continue more firmly.

But the main point is that Paul is to bear himself with confidence, because he is going to be a witness for Christ at Rome also. But this seems to be cold and empty comfort. It is as if He said, 'Do not be afraid, because a far harder situation is awaiting you.' For, according to the flesh, it would have been preferable to die once and for all, getting it over quickly, than to languish in chains for a long period of time. The Lord does not promise him freedom, not even a favourable outcome. He is merely protracting for a long time the troubles, which already press upon him more than enough. But from this we gather better how very important in itself is this confidence, that in our afflictions God cares for us, although He may not put out His hand at once to help us. Therefore let us learn even in the very worst afflictions to rest on the Word of God alone, and let us never be disheartened as long as He revives us by the testimony of His fatherly love. But because oracles are not sent from heaven now, and the Lord Himself does not appear by visions, we must meditate upon His innumerable promises, by which He affirms that He will always be near us. If it is to our advantage for an angel to come down to us, the Lord will not deny this kind of confirmation even now. Meanwhile we must pay this honour to the Word, that, content with it alone, we patiently anticipate the help, which it promises to us. Besides, some people got no benefit from hearing angels sent from heaven. But, on the other hand, it is not in vain that the Lord seals the promises given by Him on the hearts of believers by His Spirit. Meanwhile, just as He does not inculcate them for nothing, so let our faith exercise itself diligently in continually recalling them to mind. For if Paul's faith needed to be encouraged by fresh help, there is not one of us who does not require far more supports. At the same time our minds must be equipped with endurance, so that they may get over the long, involved circuits of troubles.

12. *And when it was day.* Luke shows by these circumstances how necessary it was for Paul to have his confidence renewed and reinvigorated, so as not to be afraid in very great and unexpected danger. For when he had been warned about such desperate fury on the part of his enemies, he might have been quite convinced that it was all over with him.

This vow (*devotio*), that Luke mentions, was a kind of curse. The reason for a vow was to make it impossible for them to change their plan, or retract what they had agreed upon. Indeed a tacit curse always underlies an oath, if anyone swears falsely or perjures himself, but sometimes, in order to lay themselves under a greater obligation, men adopt specific forms of anathema, and solemnly vow fearful things for themselves, which may produce unaccustomed terror.

Apart from that this incident teaches that hypocrites have such blood-thirsty zeal, that they do not think about what is lawful for them, but they heedlessly rush wherever their passion drives them. Let us grant that Paul was an impious scoundrel deserving to die, yet who had given permission to private individuals to punish him? Now if anyone had asked why they hated Paul so much, they certainly had a ready answer, that he was an apostate and a schismatic. But that was merely a foolish judgment of his case, one based on a vague rumour, and one that had rashly taken possession of their minds. Today the same blindness and the same stupidity incite the Papists to think that nothing is forbidden them in destroying us. Hypocrisy blinds them so that like men set free from the laws of God and men, they are pushed by their zeal now to treachery, now to various deceptions, now to monstrous cruelty, and finally to dare to do anything they like.

Moreover in this incident we see how great the rashness of the ungodly is. Using a curse they swear that they will take no food, until they have killed Paul, as if his life really were in their hands. Therefore those madmen are usurping for themselves what the Lord so often in Scripture arrogates to Himself alone, that He is the Arbiter of life and death of the men whom He has created (Deut. 32.39). Besides, we do not find two or three partners in this act of madness, but more than forty. From that we also learn what a great propensity men have for wrongful action, when they combine in crowds like this.

Moreover when Satan violently drives them headlong to their own destruction, how disgraceful is our sloth, in scarcely moving a finger to maintain the glory of God?[1] Indeed moderation must be preserved, so that we do not attempt anything except by the commandment of God, but when God expressly calls us, there is no excuse for inactivity.

14. *And they came to the chief priests.* By their approval of such an infamous and impious conspiracy the priests prove that they are neither touched by any fear of God, nor endowed with any humane feeling. Not only do they approve of the suggestion made about killing the man by an ambush, but they are prepared to take part in fraudulent practice, in order to deliver into the hands of murderers the man, whom they wish destroyed by any means whatever. For what else were they doing in dragging a man out of the hands of a judge to a violent death, but raving like brigands in the very court of justice? The priests would certainly never have approved such a preposterous

[1] Reading *pro asserenda Dei gloria* with Tholuck, for C.R.'s *afferenda*. Tr.

plan as this, if there had been a trace of a proper and godly attitude in them, yes, and humane feeling as well. Moreover, it was not owing to them that they did not bring a great disaster both on the whole people and themselves. But the Lord publicly exposed their hopeless impiety, which they were hiding under the disguise of their official standing, and He did it in the following way.

16. *Paul's sister's son.* Here we see that God counters the plan of the ungodly as though by a flanking attack. Indeed He allows them to devise many schemes and He even allows their wicked enterprises to proceed, but in the end He shows, in the nick of time, that He is laughing out of heaven at all the things that men are busy about on earth. Solomon says, 'There is no wisdom, there is no counsel, against the Lord' (Prov. 21.30). To that corresponds this word of Isaiah's, 'Devise your plan, and it will be destroyed; speak a word and it will not stand' (Isa. 8.10). That is set before us in the present story, as in a mirror, for our consideration. The matter is almost accomplished that Paul should come forth on the following day to be slain, like a victim devoted to a sacrifice. But the Lord shows that his life is faithfully guarded and protected, so that anything that men endeavour to do is in vain. As for ourselves, let us not doubt that He extends His providence, evidence of which He showed on that occasion, to protect us; because the promise remains unshakable, 'Not a hair of your head will be lost' etc. (Luke 21.18).

In addition it is worth while noting that He is often in the habit of acting by unexpected means to save His own, in order to exercise our faith better. Who would have thought that the ambush was to be discovered by a lad, when the conspirators thought that they were the only ones who knew about it? Therefore although no ordinary way of obtaining deliverance is apparent to us, let us learn to lean on the Lord, who will find a way through impassable places.

And Paul called unto him one of the centurions, and said, Bring this young man unto the chief captain: for he hath something to tell him. So he took him, and brought him to the chief captain, and saith, Paul the prisoner called me unto him, and asked me to bring this young man unto thee, who hath something to say to thee. And the chief captain took him by the hand, and going aside, asked him privately, What is that thou hast to tell me? And he said, The Jews have agreed to ask thee to bring down Paul to-morrow unto the council, as though thou wouldest[1] inquire somewhat more exactly concerning him. Do not thou therefore yield unto them: for there lie in wait for him of them more than forty men, which have bound themselves under a curse, neither to eat nor to drink

[1] Calvin, as RV margin, reads, *they would.* Tr.

239

till they have slain him: and now are they ready, looking for the promise from thee. So the chief captain let the young man go, charging him, Tell no man that thou hast signified these things to me. And he called unto him two of the centurions, and said, Make ready two hundred soldiers to go as far as Caesarea, and horsemen threescore and ten, and spearmen two hundred, at the third hour of the night: and he bade them provide beasts, that they might set Paul thereon, and bring him safe unto Felix the governor. (17-24)

17. *And Paul called.* Paul was certainly not so eager for life, that he would not have gladly hastened to die, if the Lord had wished him to do so. But since he knows that he serves Christ on this condition, that he lives to Him just as much as he dies to Him, he does not disregard the danger that has been made known to him. And indeed he has no doubt whatever that God is the Guardian of his life, but he does not wait until He puts out His hand from heaven to perform a miracle. On the contrary he uses the remedy presented to him, having no doubt that it is ordained for him by God. All the ministers of Christ must act in this way, so that, provided with invincible perseverance, as far as their calling demands, they do not fear dangers, and yet do not yield themselves to death with heedless temerity. Let them quietly call upon the Lord in the midst of difficulties, and yet do not let them despise the aids that come to hand. Otherwise they will be insulting God, not only by being deaf to His promises, but also by rejecting the means of liberation set before them by God.

19. *Took him by the hand.* We ought to ascribe it to the grace of God that the tribune showed such courtesy and kindness to the youth, that he took him by the hand and led him aside, that he heard him willingly and patiently. For God promised that He would give favour to His people in the eyes of the Egyptians (Exod. 3.21); He is accustomed to softening hearts of iron, taming fierce spirits, and making those, whom He has decided to use to help His own people, considerate in every way. For the soldier could have cast aside an unknown youth, just as he could have rejected the pleas of Paul himself. Therefore the Lord, who has the hearts of men in His power, moved this worldly man (*profanum hominem*) to listen to him. It was also an advantage that he knew beforehand how fiercely they were raving against Paul, so that he might be more willing to help the man in his wretchedness and abandonment. Finally, let those who are in positions of authority over men, learn from this example, what a great virtue considerateness is. If he had been a difficult man to approach, then, through ignorance, he would have given Paul to the Jews to be killed. Thus magistrates often rush into many serious

offences, because of their pride, simply because they do not deign to receive warnings from others.

23. *He called two centurions.* Here indeed the providence of God is seen still more clearly. For even if the tribune's plan is to seek to avert a public disturbance, of which account would have had to be given before the governor, yet he executes God's plan in delivering Paul. For soldiers had to be collected, the city stripped of its garrison, and the expedition demanded some expense. Therefore we must reflect upon the prudence of the tribune, so that faith may lift up its eyes to heaven, and perceive that God is directing the heart of this worldly man by a secret inspiration, and that He also is the leader for the journey for Paul and the soldiers, so that he may reach Caesarea in safety.

The third hour of the night was the end of the first watch. Therefore it amounts to the same thing as if the tribune commands the soldiers to be ready at the second watch.

Luke gives the name *spearmen (lanciarios)* to javelin-carrying soldiers, who, being armed more lightly, used to be stationed on the wings, whereas the soldiers belonging to the legions were better suited for standing and fighting (*statariae militiae*).

> *And he wrote a letter after this form:* Claudius Lysias unto the most excellent governor Felix, greeting. This man was seized by the Jews, and was about to be slain of them, when I came upon them with the soldiers and rescued him, having learned that he was a Roman. And desiring to know the cause wherefore they accused him, I brought him down unto their council: whom I found to be accused about questions of their law, but to have nothing laid to his charge worthy of death or of bonds. And when it was shewn to me that there would be a plot against the man, I sent him to thee forthwith, charging his accusers also to speak against him before thee.[1] *So the soldiers, as it was commanded them, took Paul, and brought him by night to Antipatris. But on the morrow they left the horsemen to go with him, and returned to the castle; and they, when they came to Caesarea, and delivered the letter to the governor, presented Paul also before him. And when he had read it, he asked of what province he was; and when he understood that he was of Cilicia, I will hear thy cause, said he, when thine accusers also are come: and he commanded him to be kept in Herod's palace.* (25-35)

25. *He wrote a letter.* In the first place, readers, who are not conversant with the historical narratives, must be briefly informed that this *Felix* was the brother of Pallas, who, since he was Caesar's freed-

---

[1] Calvin adds, with RV margin, *Farewell.* Tr.

man, was the equal of the highest and leading men of the city in wealth and power. Yes, and the Senate voted him the insignia of a praetor, not without descriptions, shameful and disgusting in their flattery. Therefore since his freedmen took advantage of Claudius' foolishness to rule the Roman Empire as they liked, but especially Narcissus and Pallas, it is no wonder if the latter imposed his brother on Judaea. But the substance of the letter has this purpose in view, that the tribune may help Paul by the judgment that he has already formed, and that he may give advance warning to Felix about the unjust activity of the opposing side,[1] and discredit them, so that they may have no power to do him harm.

27. *This man was seized.* When he says that a man, who was a Roman, was violently beaten, and almost killed by the Jews, he does so with hatred towards the Jews, but with kindness towards Paul. In the second place he commends him by his right to obtain the privileges of citizenship, so that he may be treated more gently. Moreover that commendation was not elicited by entreaties or flatteries, and it was not obtained by money. How then shall we maintain that it happened that the tribune showed such kindness to an obscure man, and one hateful to all, for nothing, except that the Lord appointed him the defender of His servant? Therefore we see that He controls the tongues and the hands of unbelievers for the benefit of His own.

29. *Whom I found.* Here he absolves Paul of an offence, according to the capacity of his judgment of course. But let us note that it is an unenlightened (*profanum*) man who is speaking. For among the people of God the crime of corrupting the teaching of godliness with perverse and impious doctrines deserves just as severe a penalty as violating fairness and justice among men by some injury or wrong. Certainly the Romans would not have allowed their superstitions or their man-made cults of their gods to be overthrown, but since the Law of God meant nothing to them, and what is more, since they wished to have it abolished, it was not an offence in their eyes to abrogate faith in Moses and the Prophets, or to disturb the Church with false doctrines. It was therefore a law that governors were not to make investigations about this matter, but the provincials would continue to have their own religion, so that if anything were perpetrated against it, the Roman magistrates would not be responsible for punishment. That is the reason why the tribune does not consider it an offence or crime, that they have carried out an investigation about the Law. But wrongly using this as a pretext ignorant men wish themselves and others to be granted the freedom to stir up

---

[1] French: 'so that the governor might not give his whole attention to their false report'. Tr.

trouble. The Lord has something quite different to say, for He punishes violation of His worship more severely than any injuries inflicted on men. And surely there is nothing more absurd than to let committers of sacrilege get off with impunity, when thefts are punished. Finally, as the tribune has no interest in the Jewish religion, so the false accusations, which the Jews had gladly heaped on Paul, are removed.

30. *And when it was shown to me.* Here in the second part of the letter the tribune casts odium back on Paul's adversaries, because they attempted to kill him by means of an ambush. From that one also concludes that they are in the wrong in creating trouble for Paul, and showing such great hostility to his life. For if they had proceeded against him justly, believing in the goodness of their cause, they would have committed him to trial. Now when they have recourse to murder, it is apparent that they have not a leg to stand on (*ratione destitui*).[1]

32. *On the following day.* Although Luke did not mention previously that the soldiers were ordered to return from the journey, yet it is certain that Paul was escorted only to that place, where the tribune expected him to be safe; for he had left secretly at night. And the tribune knew that, with part of the journey completed, there was no further cause to fear, because their enemies would have no hope of overtaking them. But he also knew that it was not safe to send part of the garrison too far away.

[1] French: 'they do not have reason or right on their side'. Tr.

CHAPTER TWENTY-FOUR

And after five days the high priest Ananias came down with certain elders, and with an orator, one Tertullus; and they informed the governor against Paul. And when he was called, Tertullus began to accuse him, saying, Seeing that by thee we enjoy much peace, and that by thy providence evils are corrected for this nation, we accept it in all ways and in all places, most excellent Felix, with all thankfulness. But, that I be not further tedious unto thee, I intreat thee to hear us of thy clemency a few words. For we have found this man a pestilent fellow, and a mover of insurrections among all the Jews throughout the world, and a ringleader of the sect of the Nazarenes: who moreover assayed to profane the temple: on whom also we laid hold: (and we would have judged him according to our law. But the chief captain Lysias came, and with great violence took him away out of our hands, commanding his accusers to come before thee.)[1] From whom thou wilt be able, by examining him thyself, to take knowledge of all these things, whereof we accuse him. And the Jews also joined in the charge, affirming that these things were so. (1-9)

1. The fact that Ananias came down to Caesarea in order to complain against Paul, gives greater credibility to the conjecture, which I brought forward previously concerning his priesthood,[2] for such an expedition was beneath the dignity of the high priest. Therefore somebody else was the high priest (*summus*) at that time; but Ananias being a priest 'of the first rank' (*primarius*), since he held government, and was an active man, it was in order for him to undertake this mission. Indeed he brings a train along with him, and from the venerable college of elders (*ex venerando seniorum collegio*) at that, so that by the very spectacle they presented the governor may be moved to condemn Paul. But since Paul made no use of skill in speaking, there was no need, at any rate, for a hired orator to contend with him in eloquent words. Besides, they were superior, both in authoritative standing, and numerically, so that it would be easy for them to overwhelm a wretched man, who was without any aid whatever. It was therefore a sign of a bad conscience for men, able by dint of great experience of affairs, versed in public questions, and experts in forensic cases, to bring an orator along with them. Eloquence, I

[1] vv. 6c-8a. Calvin includes this Western reading given in RV margin. Tr.
[2] See page 226.

admit, is certainly a gift of God, but in this case they merely desired to make a pretence of it, to deceive the judge. But Luke tells us this so that we may know that the Jews omitted nothing, by which they might get the better of Paul, and not only destroy his innocence, but shake his defence by terrifying and confusing him. And so let us reflect that it happened by the wonderful grace of God that Paul held out, undaunted, against such severe assaults. Accordingly if it ever comes about that a godly man, all alone, is beset by a great number of enemies, let this story come to his mind, and let him take fresh courage, after his fear. Similarly David encourages us by his example, 'If a host surrounds me in their tents, I shall not be afraid, because Thou art with me' (Ps. 27.3).

2. *Since we enjoy much peace.* Tertullus' preface has nothing to do with the case, because he praises Felix's prudence and virtues in order to gain his favour for himself. The beginning is therefore an affected piece of flattery. Not that I agree with the opinion of those who criticize Tertullus because he mollifies the judge, and wins him over to his side, with flatteries. For it is not always inconsistent with a proper and legitimate manner of pleading to praise the judge; and this could be argued for and against, as it is commonly said. But I condemn only what is clearly vicious. For this orator ingratiates himself indirectly with false praises, in order to becloud the real question at issue. For why does he speak about peace and a well-ordered state, except that Felix, thinking that the safety of Judaea depends upon the condemnation of Paul, may not investigate the case? Besides it is clear from Josephus how avariciously, cruelly and capriciously Felix behaved in that province. The shameful and tragic murder of the high priest, Jonathan, because he had dared to oppose his dissoluteness and tyranny, had already preceded this. And, finally, about that time, Claudius Caesar was forced by the importunate complaints of the whole nation, to substitute Festus in his place, and recall him to defend himself. Therefore we see how disgracefully and brazenly this orator lied. But because all Paul's adversaries are in agreement, we see that, blinded by hatred and malice, they treacherously betray the common state of their native land, and are indifferent to it, so long as Paul is given up to death.

Where Erasmus translates 'many things are done properly', the Vulgate seems to come closer to Luke's intention, for it reads 'things are being successfully achieved' (κατορθώματα *fieri*), which amounts to the same thing as 'reforms' or 'improvements'.[1] Therefore Tertullus

---

[1] Erasmus: *multa recte gerantur.* Calvin: *multa restituantur.* Vulg.: *multa corrigantur.* Greek: διορθωμάτων γινομένων ('reforms are being carried out'), but a great many MSS have κατορθωμάτων. Tr.

commends Felix's activity because he purged Judaea of many corruptions, and changed many things for the better which otherwise were going to ruin, and Tertullus clearly did so, in order that Felix may be the more eager to gain for himself, by the death of one man, the favour of a nation, which, he knew, was otherwise hostile to him.

5. *For we have found this man.* Tertullus has a double aim. In the first place he strives to get Paul handed over to the Jews, since they have the right to make a judicial inquiry into questions concerning the worship of God and the Law of Moses. Should this, however, be denied, he brings forward a capital charge, that Paul stirred up sedition among the common people. For they were aware that no crime was more offensive to the Romans; and therefore they particularly burdened Paul with the disgrace of it. And Tertullus dilates upon that point when he says that Paul stirs up the Jews all over the world. But it is strange why he adds that he is a leader of *the sect of the Nazarenes* (*Nazaraeorum*[1]), because we know that the Jews regarded that as praiseworthy rather than blameworthy. But I do not think that he means those who used to consecrate themselves to God according to a legitimate and ancient rite of the Law, but those turbulent assassins, who also took a praiseworthy name and boasted that they were zealots. That faction emerged round about that time, and indeed one gathers from Josephus' history that they were already active then. Others think that the word *Nazarenes* (*Nazarenos*) is used here for Christians, and I am quite willing to accept that. But if the first explanation is acceptable, he cunningly alleges that Paul belongs to a sect hateful to the Romans. For since those zealots wished to be regarded as excelling others in upholding the Law, under the pretext of zeal they were, so to speak, raising the standard to inflame the minds of the common people. At the same time those good men, zealots for their own liberty, do not spare the chief defenders of it, so long as they may involve Paul in the hatred of them. Apart from this case, they would have applauded the Nazarenes, whom I have mentioned, as spirited defenders of the Law. Now, as if their contagion defiles the whole world, they besmear Paul, disgracing him completely, by associating him with them. In addition they are impudently making a false accusation against Paul, for no one was suspecting him of that sort of thing. Therefore they are as wrong as they are malicious in putting on him a charge, that was picked up, as it were, from the street, and conceived without any justification. But as we have said elsewhere hypocrites barge their way in, heedlessly and indifferently, like this, thinking that they can do anything they like, so long as they make a pretence of zeal.

[1] *Nazaraeus* means (a) a Nazirite, (b) a Nazarene. Tr.

6, 7. Who also attempted to profane the temple. This was a trivial, almost frivolous charge, in the eyes of the Roman governor, who would have desired the temple to have been destroyed completely. But because nothing was better suited for raising tumults than profanation of the temple, he cunningly accuses Paul of that; as if he said that it was not his fault that the city was not in an uproar, and that he showed that he would have been the instigator of a most serious conflagration, if he had not been prevented. At the same time he also includes that other matter, that, because Paul had outraged religion, the investigation of such a case is, strictly speaking, the concern of the Jews. And at this point he makes a complaint about the tribune, Lysias, because he had forcibly deprived them of their right. He therefore tries to make the governor restore to them what the tribune had taken away. This is not without cunning also, because Tertullus discredits the tribune who had behaved towards Paul more humanely than the priests wished, and he raises suspicion against him in an indirect way, because he does not dare to accuse him openly. But the question is raised whether they could have expected the governor to grant them so much, since at that time the Roman magistrates alone made investigations about cases involving the death penalty. I reply that here they are making pretence to fairness, as if they were intending to treat Paul more gently than he deserved. For although they had no power to sentence a man to death, yet they were allowed to inflict ordinary punishment, like beating with rods. At the same time Tertullus does not cease to accuse him before the governor for the death penalty.

8. Having made an examination. It is a fair request that the judge is not to pass judgment before he has found out about the case, and that he is to condemn Paul only when he is legally convicted. But how do they dare to litigate on these terms when they are so well aware of being in the wrong? I reply that they had witnesses available, and that the decision to present them for examination lies with them alone. However there was another object. For they were hoping that it would be easy for them to persuade Felix with such bombastic words to hand over the accused, as if he were condemned, to them, to do with him as they liked. In a word, they think that, the more fiercely they insult him by boasting about themselves, and the more elated they are with self-confidence, in that way they will be victorious, because every avenue will be closed for the accused to make a defence. Perverters of the law confidently boast like that, that they are bringing forward a proved case, in order to pull the wool over the judges' eyes.

And when the governor had beckoned unto him to speak, Paul answered,

247

Forasmuch as I know that thou hast been of many years a judge unto this nation, I do cheerfully¹ make my defence: seeing that thou canst take knowledge, that it is not more than twelve days since I went up to worship at Jerusalem: and neither in the temple did they find me disputing with any man or stirring up a crowd, nor in the synagogues, nor in the city. Neither can they prove to thee the things whereof they now accuse me. But this I confess unto thee, that after the Way which they call a sect,² so serve³ I the God of our fathers, believing all things which are according to the law, and which are written in the prophets: having hope toward God, which these also themselves look for, that there shall be a resurrection both of the just and unjust. Herein do I also exercise myself to have a conscience void of offence toward God and men alway. Now after many years I came to bring alms to my nation, and offerings: amidst which they found me purified in the temple, with no crowd, nor yet with tumult: but there were certain Jews from Asia—who ought to have been here before thee, and to make accusation, if they had aught against me. Or else let these men themselves say what wrong-doing they found, when I stood before the council, except it be for this one voice, that I cried standing among them, Touching the resurrection of the dead I am called in question before you this day. (10-21: Calvin 10-22)

10. *Paul answered.* The character of Paul's defence does not depend on quality, but in fact he is denying the charges laid against him; not because he was ashamed of the Gospel, or avoided the cross, but because there was no opportunity for a fuller confession of faith at that time. Therefore since his accuser had not referred to the cause of the Gospel, Paul omits it, and simply replies to the false accusations made against him. But before he comes to that, he prefaces his remarks by saying that he pleads his case before Felix *the more cheerfully*, because he has ruled over Judaea for a long time; and clearly he does so because any new governor, through ignorance, would perhaps have been overwhelmed by such a severe accusation. And it is a sincere and frank method of defence to oppose words with the truth (*rem*). However Paul seems to infer wrongly that because Felix has been governor for several years already, he can find out about the time of his arrival. I reply that this is said because it is consistent with his acting with greater moderation. It is as if he said, 'Because you have been used to their customs for a long time now, I have less fear of them deceiving you.' For inexperience has the habit of making judges too credulous, and drives them to make preposterous haste.

¹ Calvin, with RV margin, reads, *the more cheerfully*. Tr.
² Calvin, with Greek and RV margin, reads, *heresy*. Tr.
³ Calvin, with RV margin, reads, *worship*. Tr.

11. *To worship.* In the first place it is certain that he came for other reasons, and afterwards he will acknowledge that the principal one was to bring alms for the assistance of the needy brethren. But he is easily excused, because there was no need for him to give any reason for his coming. He merely wished, in passing, to clear himself of violating religion. Accordingly, although there was another purpose for undertaking the expedition, it is always true that he came with no other intention except to profess himself a worshipper of God, and also to endorse the sacredness of the temple by his worship. There is another, more perplexing, question, how he says that he came in order to worship, when the religion of the temple had already been abolished, and all distinction in the temple taken away. Here I also reply that, although he does not explain his purpose, yet he does not make any false pretension. For worship in the temple was not forbidden to believers in Christ, so long as they did not attach sacredness to the place, but lifted up pure hands freely and with no distinction of places (I Tim. 2.8). When Paul had come to Jerusalem, he was at liberty to enter the temple in order to give evidence of his piety, and there engage in the customary rites of the worship of God, because he was undefiled by superstition as long as he undertook no expiations contrary to the Gospel. Yet religion did not impel him to come to Jerusalem as the Law laid down, as if the sanctuary were the face (*facies*) of God, as it had been in the past; yet he did not shrink from outward worship, which men looked upon as evidence of piety.

12, 13. *Disputing with any man.* Paul had no need to deny any of these things, if he had done them; because he could have maintained that it was in order to do them. He had been one of the scribes, who held discussions every day; and they were certainly not prohibited by law or custom from gathering together in bands for the purpose of teaching. Yes, and what is more, for that purpose synagogues were distributed at different places throughout the city, and in these they held their meetings. In addition he knew that it had been done both by Christ and the apostles. It was even easy to turn back on his adversaries the accusation they made against him, for this was a daily practice of theirs. But, because the only thing to be done at the moment, is to disprove the misrepresentations of his enemies, and refute the attacks made on him, rashly and without cause, by persistent men, he does not argue about legal right (*de iure*), as men say, but only about fact (*de facto*). In particular he devotes his attention to dispelling the smoke of that false charge, that had accused him of stirring up the crowd. He therefore concludes that he has been accused falsely and unjustly, because his enemies will never prove the things that they have brought forward for investigation. It ought to have carried enough weight to acquit him, that he, to whom not even the slightest suspicion adhered, was burdened with monstrous lies.

14. *But I confess.* Because they had charged Paul with impiety and profanation of the temple, he now clears himself of both, so that Felix may understand that his adversaries are driven by malevolence and nothing else. For even if a religion, which is being alleged as an excuse, is false and absurd, yet zeal for it often meets with good-will among men, who are not particularly interested in it. Accordingly there was a real fear that, if Felix had suspected Paul of anything sinister, he would not only overlook the zeal of the priests, but also grant their requests. Accordingly Paul puts an end to this aspect of the accusation also, and in such a way indeed, that he does not mention the faith of the Gospel, because, as we have said, that was not yet the opportune time for confessing it.

But why does he confess that he worships God according to the *Way that they call a heresy?* Some think that this was added like a concession, because his enemies were putting down to a bad intention (*in malam partem trahebant*), what ought to have been attributed to decision and right choice; as if Paul had said that the form of religion, which he was following, was indeed called a heresy, but without justification. But since at that time neither the Jews nor the Gentiles looked upon that name with disfavour, it is unlikely that he defends himself before an unenlightened man about something that was considered everywhere praiseworthy rather than blameworthy. When Christians are talking with each other, the Spirit of God directs that heretics be regarded as detestable, and teaches that they must be on their guard against heresies, because they cause destruction and the breaking-up of the Church. Therefore it is something that is not to be tolerated in the people of God, whose safety consists in the unity of faith. But because the Jews at that time openly boasted of their sects, that excuse, which we have just mentioned, was unnecessary. Therefore the remaining solution is either that he means that he is a Pharisee, or that he calls the Jewish religion, or the profession of the Gospel, a heresy, without any bad connotation, because they were distinct from every practice and custom of the Gentiles. Since he confessed previously that he was a Pharisee, there will be nothing absurd if we say that he repeats the same thing now, especially when he mentions the resurrection of the dead a little later on. But because this first point contains only the confession of worship of the God of the fathers, it rather seems to me that the Jewish religion, in general, is meant, or the Christian faith which flowed from it.[1] Paul was a Roman citizen; nevertheless, as he was of Jewish descent, he confesses that he is con-

---

[1] The last clause is a Second Edition addition. Tr.

tinuing in the religion that he had learnt from the fathers. And the adverb of comparison relates to this, for it points to something well-known, viz. the kind of worship to which the Jews were devoted. He expressly mentions *the God of the fathers* because a man who was a Roman citizen was not allowed to make the transition to the doctrine of the Law, if he was not Jewish in origin. He is also reproaching his adversaries, by whom he is so cruelly attacked, when both sides nevertheless agree in the worship of the One God. He says, 'I worship God according to the custom handed down by our forefathers, just as they do.' And it is no barrier that he had departed from the ceremonies of the Law, and was content with the spiritual worship of God. For Paul thinks it enough for him to remove the stigma of impiety, which had been put on him falsely. Therefore the Papists are ridiculous in thinking that any sort of antiquity has Paul's assent and approval. They say, 'We worship the God of the fathers along with Paul, as custom has been delivered to us from hand to hand.' As if, even with the Papists themselves as the judges in fact, it were enough for the Turks and the Jews to put forward the same shield against the faith of Christ. But in fact the apostle did not by any means propose to found religion simply on the authority of ancestors, and preserve his piety by that defence, which was going to be common to all the superstitions of the Gentiles. He merely wished to silence his adversaries. At the same time he was taking it for granted that the fathers, from whom the Jewish religion had originated, were honest and true worshippers of God, so that genuine Jews could justly boast that the God of their fathers, whom they were worshipping, was the one and only Maker of heaven and earth, and that the national gods of all the rest of the world were empty figments.

Believing all things. This is a brief explanation of the preceding part of the sentence. For, since he had not made the simple assertion that he worshipped God, but had added the adverb *so* (οὕτως), he now explains how he worships God. It is evident from that that he takes great care not to associate himself with the adventitious superstitions, which reigned among the Jews. It is as if any one of us today replies to the Papists that he worships the God whom they profess, but in the way that we have been taught from the Law and the Gospel. Let us learn from this that it is only by faith, which is the one and only foundation of piety, that God is worshipped correctly, so that our devotional acts are pleasing to Him. For in order to prove himself a servant of God, Paul does not plead the excuse of bare ceremonies, but plainly asserts that he believes. Apart from that this verse contains the useful doctrine that the one and only foundation of correct and orthodox faith is to subject oneself to Scripture, and reverently embrace its teaching. Moreover, here Paul divides Scripture into the Law and the Prophets, to prove more clearly that he does not hold anything different from the universal agreement of the Church.

15. *Having hope toward God.* The connexion in the speech must be noted. For after professing that he believes in Scripture, he now adds the hope of the future resurrection, in order that it may be plain that it is conceived not from the carnal understanding, or from the opinion of men, but from the Word of God. Reverence for Scripture therefore takes the leading place, so that its authority may keep us under obligation, and it is the beginning of faith. Secondly, there follows the knowledge of those things that God reveals in it, and to that knowledge is linked certain hope. But the fact that he associates himself with those men, is put down to a sounder motive, although there is no doubt that by this artifice he does try to strip them of their pretences and put them in a clear light before Felix; and that will again be evident from the conclusion of his defence. Finally, the general resurrection is asserted here against certain fanatics, who restrict it to the members of Christ. But as Paul says in this verse that all will rise again, so Christ clearly refers to all, without distinction, in His word, 'some to judgment, some to life' (John 5.29).

16. *Herein do I exercise myself.* There is no sharper stimulus to the desire to lead an upright and holy life, than the hope of the final resurrection, as Scripture reminds us in many passages. Thus everywhere else when Paul wishes to give effective encouragement to the faithful, he reminds them of it (Phil. 3.20). Accordingly he has good cause for saying here that, relying on this faith, he has taken pains to live purely before God, and to practise uprightness among men. And surely a bad conscience is as good as a thousand witnesses to convict men of stupidity, so that they may conclude with certainty that they do not seriously believe the truth of eternal life, when they do not desire to attain it.

He describes *conscience* as ἀπρόσκοπον, as if, one might say, 'without any hindrances', when the servants of God exert themselves to remove obstacles which impede their course. But he gives two aspects of *conscience.* For there is a certain inward, mental awareness that has regard to God alone. From that the faithfulness and integrity, which we cultivate among men, afterwards proceed. Finally, when he says that he constantly pursued both piety in honouring God, and uprightness among men, he is pointing out that those who hope for the final resurrection never tire of doing good. For the adverb *always* indicates perseverance in a consistent course.

17, 18. *Now after many years.* The meaning is that he had not been at Jerusalem for a long time, but had been occupied in other countries far away, and after a long interval of time he had now come to bring alms and offer a sacrifice of thanksgiving to God. That also makes plain the inhumanity as well as the ingratitude of those men, because, when he should have won the good-will of the whole nation in every way, they recompense him with an unjust reward. The verse in fact explains the previous one, where mention was made of worshipping. For it is certain that Paul did not come with the express purpose of offering a sacrifice in the temple, because his plan to do so only began to take shape after his arrival. Finally, when he says that he was discovered in the temple when doing this, and indeed, first, after a solemn purification had intervened, and, secondly, peaceful and raising no tumult of any sort, he is once again turning aside both charges from himself. For the purification was evidence that the temple was not profaned by him; secondly, since he behaved quietly, without a crowd of men, there was no suggestion of a tumult.

19-22.[1] *Certain from Asia.* The sentence is defective; yet there is no doubt about the meaning, that it was rather those Asiatics, about whose absence he complains, who raised a tumult without cause. It is as if he said, 'You, who heap so many charges on me, cannot affirm what the true state of affairs is, but at the governor's judgment-seat present a rumour that you have rashly believed.' But those who bear the blame for all the mischief, and who fanned the flames, are not present. After Paul has turned back the charge on others, now, as if he has recovered his confidence, he challenges his adversaries, who are present, to be free to make it known if they have definite information against him. However I disagree with Erasmus and the Vulgate in regard to the participle στάντος, for they translate it in the present tense[2]; and they explain συνέδριον of the governor's court of justice, which seems to me to be different from Paul's intention. For in my opinion he means that in their *council* (συνεδρίῳ) he was prepared to give an account of everything; but that on that occasion they knew nothing of which they could accuse him, because they grew violent only at one statement that he made, that he was being judged concerning the resurrection of the dead, i.e. the only reason why he endured all this trouble was that he hoped for the resurrection. From that it is apparent that a fresh accusation is now being made without any justification, because, if he had committed any offence, they would not have kept quiet about it then. Indeed it is probable that afterwards other disputations were held between the two sides, and

---

[1] Calvin begins v. 19 at 'Certain from Asia', and numbers RV's 20 and 21, 21 and 22. Tr.

[2] Greek: τί εὗρον ἀδίκημα στάντος μου ἐπὶ τοῦ συνεδρίου. Vulg.: *cum stem in concilio.* Calvin: *si quid deprehenderunt in me iniquitatis, cum steti in synedrio.* Tr.

they came to closer grips as if engaged in hand to hand fighting, because we shall see elsewhere that there was a contention about Christ[1]; but Luke merely intended to show that Paul had cleared himself of the false calumnies of his accusers.

> *But Felix, having more exact knowledge concerning the Way, deferred them, saying, When Lysias the chief captain shall come down, I will determine your matter. And he gave order to the centurion that he should be kept in charge, and should have indulgence; and not to forbid any of his friends to minister unto him. But after certain days, Felix came with Drusilla, his wife, which was a Jewess, and sent for Paul, and heard him concerning the faith in Christ Jesus. And as he reasoned of righteousness, and temperance, and the judgment to come, Felix was terrified, and answered, Go thy way for this time; and when I have a convenient season, I will call thee unto me. He hoped withal that money would be given him of Paul[2]: wherefore also he sent for him the oftener, and communed with him. But when two years were fulfilled, Felix was succeeded by Porcius Festus; and desiring to gain favour with the Jews, Felix left Paul in bonds. (22-27; Calvin 23-28)*

22. *But when he heard these things.* It is apparent that, although Felix gave no decision on the case, he sensed that Paul was being charged through no fault of his own, but by the ill-will of the priests. For when Luke narrates that the action was deferred until the arrival of Lysias, he inserts at the same time, as if instead of a reason, that the governor had precise knowledge about the things pertaining to *the Way.* By these words I think is meant either that long experience had already made him familiar with the practice of the priests, and how they were accustomed to behaving; or that he perceived, from the things that had been said on both sides, how trivial the accusation was. And that is confirmed by the more considerate and more indulgent treatment given to Paul himself. For he commits him to the charge of a centurion, so that he may have, so to speak, greater freedom in custody. Others prefer to read these words in a single connexion, as part of what Felix says (*in persona Felicis*), 'When Lysias comes, who knows more about this case, then I shall pronounce judgment'. But they draw out such a forced meaning from a reason that is hardly strong enough. They deny that the word *Way* is ever found for the teaching of the Law without an addition. But I do not explain it of the Law, but of the sects, of which no foreigners were ignorant. Certainly nobody had any doubt that the Pharisees maintained the

[1] See on 25.19, p. 266. Tr.
[2] Calvin, as RV margin, adds, *that he might loose him.* Tr.

immortality of souls. Therefore since this situation was universally well-known, it is no wonder if Felix absolves Paul of blame. Moreover it would be hard to take *Way* for knowledge of what happened. Certainly I do not see how it is appropriate for the governor to attribute greater knowledge of the Law to Lysias. But Paul's innocence is made clear from the fact that an unbelieving man prejudged it in such a way, that he allowed him to be visited by his friends, and helped by their services, as if he was taken out of the class of fettered prisoners. We also gather from this verse that Paul was not forsaken by his companions and the rest of the Church. For what was the point of his friends being granted access to him, unless they were at hand, showed their concern, and desired to perform acts of kindness to him? Therefore let us learn from this example that, as long as we have freedom, and the opportunity is given to us, we must not defraud the martyrs of Christ of any kind of comfort, while they suffer for the sake of the Gospel.

24. (Calvin 25.) *Felix with Drusilla.* I have already said something about the avarice and corruptions of Felix. Now as far as his wife Drusilla is concerned, readers must be reminded that she was the daughter of Agrippa the Elder, of whose loathsome death Luke gave an account in chapter 12. She had been betrothed to Epiphanus, son of the King of Antioch. But when the young man refused to submit to the Jewish rites, as he had promised that he would do, her brother Agrippa the Younger, of whom mention will be made in the next chapter, gave her, after their father's death, to be the wife of Azizus, King of the Emesenes; and she was seduced from her life with him by the flatteries of Felix. For, captivated by her matchless beauty, Felix instigated a certain Jew, called Simon, a native of Cyprus, to allure and entice her to a new marriage. The upshot therefore was that the lustful woman broke her marriage vow (*fide*) and married an uncircumcised man, contrary to the Law. But although she had defiled herself by a profane marriage yet it is easy to conjecture from this verse that the feeling for religion, that she had imbibed from infancy, had not been completely obliterated from her mind. For Felix would neither have desired to hear Paul, nor deigned to speak with him, except to please his wife. Certainly Luke does not say so explicitly, but in naming Drusilla he gives enough of a hint that Paul was called to speak about the Gospel for her sake. However apostates of that sort are tickled by a certain curiosity rather than moved by a sincere desire to learn.

Heard him concerning the faith. This confession of Paul's is evidence that he did not keep quiet about Christ before, because he was afraid for his life, or to keep himself out of the vexation of the cross, but because the time was not yet ripe for a hearing. When he had been summoned as a prisoner before the judgment-seat, he was bound to reply to the charges brought against him, so that afterwards he might profess the faith of Christ, free and unimpeded. Therefore when he now sees a door open for him to speak, he neither fears the hatred of the governor, nor is terrified of danger, so as to disguise cunningly the fact that he is a Christian. Therefore we see that he was endowed with unbroken steadfastness, as well as prudence and judgment; and that he never deliberately concealed the light of the Gospel, but only made choice of the time.

Now here it is worth while noting the marvellous purpose of God, who sometimes wishes the Gospel to be presented to the reprobate, not in order that they may benefit from it, but so that they may be rendered the more inexcusable. It would have been better for Felix and Drusilla never to have heard a word about Christ, because they did not get off unpunished for rejecting, or contemptuously neglecting, the grace of salvation presented to them. Moreover we must note that some people, because of the seed of godliness implanted in them at birth, long for the Gospel, but as soon as they hear it they either loathe it or cannot bear it. At the same time no matter what result the preaching of the Gospel has, whether it gives life to men or kills them, it is a good and sweet savour to God (II Cor. 2.15).

25. (Calvin 26.) *And as he reasoned.* Felix was hoping to derive pleasure from Paul's conversation, just as men who are eager for new things, gladly feast their ears on wordy arguments. At the same time he wanted to gratify his wife's desire without any trouble to himself. Now he is forced to realize the efficacy of the Word of God, an efficacy of which he had had no conception, and which drives away all his pleasures. Paul is in chains as he speaks of the judgment of God. The man, who had power of life and death over him, is trembling all over, as if he were standing before his own judge; and the only relief he finds is if he removes him out of his sight.

In the first place let us learn from this what a great influence the Spirit of God exercised not only in Paul's heart but also in his tongue. Because he is aware that he must speak in the name of Christ, he does not adopt a submissive attitude, but, as if from a higher level, he carries out splendidly the mission enjoined on him, and, forgetting that he is a prisoner, bound in chains, he exercises the judgment of heaven in the name of Christ. Now, in the fact that the heart of Felix is so disturbed by the words of a man who is a captive, the majesty of the Spirit indeed reveals itself, the majesty which Christ extols, 'When the Spirit comes, He will judge the world' etc. (John 16.8); and there is also revealed that power of prophesying, which the same Paul

praises in I Cor. 14.24. Similarly, there is fulfilled what he says elsewhere, that the Word of God has not been bound along with him
(II Tim. 2.9), for not only did he declare it freely and boldly, but it
penetrated effectually into the hearts of men, of men proud in their
greatness at that, as if lightning flashed out of heaven.

Again, we must note that although the judgment of God strikes the
reprobate, yet they are not restored to penitence, merely by terror of
it. Indeed when he hears that God will be the Judge of the world,
Felix is disturbed but at the same time he avoids the judgment-seat,
of which he is afraid, so that this is a false sorrow, which does not work
salvation. Therefore penitence requires fear, both to create a voluntary
hatred of sin, and to make a man stand before God, so that he may
willingly bear to be judged by His Word. And it is a sign of true
success, when a sinner seeks for medicine from the place at which he
was wounded. Moreover this verse teaches that men are examined
to the root of their being, only when their faults, about which they
are troubled, are brought out into the open, and their consciences
are recalled to the judgment that is to come. For when Paul discussed
righteousness and self-control, he touched Felix sharply on a sore point,
since he was both a lustful man, leading a thoroughly riotous and
dissolute life, and a man given over to injustice.

26. (Calvin 27.) *Hoping that money.* Although Paul's integrity was
obvious to Felix, so that he felt ashamed to condemn him for payment
by the Jews, yet, since he was an avaricious man, given to corrupt
practices, he was not willing to acquit him for nothing. That is why
he sent for Paul again and again, to speak to him in flattering terms,
and raise his hopes of obtaining his freedom. For mercenary judges
ingratiate themselves like that, when they wish to open up the way
for corrupt methods. From this we gather that the fear, which seized
Felix when he heard Paul's discussion, vanished, seeing that hope of
gain gives him a compelling urge to call the man, whom he had been
forced to remove from his presence because of his alarm. How did
Felix expect money from a man who was penniless and destitute?
For a handful of booty would not have satisfied that abyss. As those
who have justice for sale are sharp and shrewd, I have no doubt that,
when he saw the Jews pressing so vigorously for Paul to be destroyed,
he got a vague inkling into him, viz. that he was no ordinary man,
but one whom many held in the highest esteem. Accordingly he had
no doubt that many of his friends would gladly meet the cost of
releasing him.

27. (Calvin 28.) *But when two years were fulfilled.* Since Paul knew
that the mercenary judge would show favour to him on handing over
money, and he had plenty time to collect it, it is probable that he not

only spared the brethren, but also shrank in horror from that sort of trafficking, by which the sanctity of the civil order is shamefully defiled. Now, although governors, on departing from a province, are in the habit of releasing from captivity prisoners, whom they know to be guilty of no crime, Felix took the opposite course, to gain favour. The Jews had often complained of his disgraceful money-making, of his plundering, cruelty and lax government. Wearied by so many complaints, Claudius Caesar withdrew him from Judaea. In order to have the Jews less hostile to himself, he leaves Paul *in bonds*. In this way he substitutes the innocent servant of God, like an expiatory victim,[1] for his own crimes, to appease the priests.

---

[1] *catharma*, i.e. Greek κάθαρμα, also περικάθαρμα, off-scouring, expiatory victim, outcast. Cf. Calvin's Commentary on I Cor. 4.13. Tr.

CHAPTER TWENTY-FIVE

Festus therefore, having come into the province, after three days went up to Jerusalem from Caesarea. And the chief priests and the principal men of the Jews informed him against Paul; and they besought him, asking favour against him, that he would send for him to Jerusalem; laying wait to kill him on the way. Howbeit Festus answered, that Paul was kept in charge at Caesarea, and that he himself was about to depart thither shortly. Let them therefore, saith he, which are of power[1] among you, go down with me, and if there is anything amiss in the man, let them accuse him. And when he had tarried among them not more than eight or ten days,[2] he went down unto Caesarea; and on the morrow he sat on the judgment-seat, and commanded Paul to be brought. And when he was come, the Jews which had come down from Jerusalem stood round about him, bringing against him many and grievous charges, which they could not prove; while Paul said in his defence, Neither against the law of the Jews, nor against the temple, nor against Caesar, have I sinned at all. (1-8)

1-4. *Festus therefore.* Here there is described for us the second action, in which Paul underwent just as severe and difficult a struggle as in the first. Because he had been left in prison Festus could have suspected that the case was an intricate one, and as a result could have prejudged it unfairly. But another aspect of the situation brought a more serious danger. We know that new governors, seeking to win the favour of provincials, are in the habit of granting them many things on their arrival. One might therefore well believe that the death of Paul would not be unacceptable to Festus, as a preliminary way of grasping at favour. Therefore the faith of the holy man is assailed and tested all over again, as if the promise of God, on which he had rested so far, had been empty. But the grace of God reveals itself all the more clearly in liberating him, because, contrary to expectation, he is snatched out of the jaws of death.

The Jews forestall the governor with their false accusations. However they do not yet demand his punishment, but only ask that he be not dragged into an alien court to plead his case. They demand fawningly and by way of a great favour something that was, on the face of it, fair. How then does it come about that they do not get what they want, except that God puts a restraint on the mind of Festus,

[1] Calvin reads, *who can.* Tr.   [2] Calvin reads, *more than ten days.* Tr.

so that he firmly denies what he is afterwards ready to grant? But just as the Lord then held his mind in check by the secret bridle of His providence, so when He allowed him to be willing, He tied his hands so that he would not be free to carry out his intention. Let this confidence sustain us in dangers, and at the same time move us to call upon God; and let it calm our minds that, by opposing His hand and breaking such a strong conspiracy, the Lord gave lasting proof of His power to protect the faithful.

5. *Therefore let those among you who can.* The Greek (οἱ οὖν δυνατοί) is literally, 'those who are able', or 'possible'; but he means those for whom it will be convenient. And it is easy to conjecture that they pled the irksomeness and the expense, and begged the governor not to tire out so many of their leading men, especially some who were very old, by an unnecessary journey, rather, what was no trouble to him, to order Paul to be brought by a few guards. Therefore so that they may not complain that they are being incommoded, he relieves them of this necessity, and allows them to choose those whom they wish out of their company. At the same time he makes it plain enough that he does not give credence to their accusations, and declares openly that he will be an unbiased judge, who will only act according to the truth of the case.

6. There are different readings of the next verse in the Greek also. For some manuscripts have the rendering of the Vulgate, *not more than eight or ten days.* If that reading is acceptable the meaning will be that the governor came to Caesarea a little later, so that on the pretext of a longer delay the Jews might not be too persistent in their pressure upon him. The other reading,[1] which is the more usual one in the Greek manuscripts, will have a different meaning, that, although he was going to be long enough at Jerusalem to investigate the case, yet he did not give in to the requests of those who wished Paul to be dragged there by force. From that the likely conjecture may be made that he was already informed about their ambush.

7, 8. *Many and grievous charges.* As long as Paul had lived under the Law his integrity had been known and renowned. Then, after his conversion to Christ, he had been a remarkable exemplar of a blameless life. Yet we see that he submits to many insults and severe misrepresentations. But the situation of the servants of Christ is nearly always like that. Therefore they ought to be the more courageous so that they may advance firmly through bad and good repute, and so that it may not be strange to them to be blamed when they have done well. In the meantime they must take care not only that their own consciences are clear before God, but also that they are equipped with

---

[1] As Calvin, *diebus amplius quam decem*, 'more than ten days'. Tr.

a proper defence before men, when the opportune moment is given. For Paul does not neglect his own advantage, but wisely opposes their false charges with the defence of his own innocence. However let us note that the ungodly can never be restrained from slandering good men and reviling them impudently. For they reproduce the nature of Satan, by whose spirit they are moved. Therefore the command given to us to silence the wicked, ought not to be taken as if everyone who leads an upright life will be immune from all undeserved detraction, but that our life is to reply for us, and remove all the stains made by false infamy. Thus we see that although Paul's adversaries had a favourable judge, yet they slandered him in vain, since he affirmed his innocence by his deeds. And yet it is very likely that they did not lack false witnesses, and were not slow in suborning them, but because the Lord inspires His servant with unconquerable power, so that he scatters their empty clouds with the splendour of his upright life, they are refuted and shamed, and finally leave the court with the disgrace of laying false charges (*calumniae*).[1] Finally, Paul's defence shows the particular false charges, which the Jews used to attack Paul. The first charge was lack of reverence towards God, because he overthrew the Law and polluted the temple; the second was rebellion against Caesar and the Roman Empire, because he caused disturbances everywhere. He was given help to remove both by the extraordinary grace of God, who makes the innocence of His own shine like the dawn.

But Festus, desiring to gain favour with the Jews, answered Paul, and said, Wilt thou go up to Jerusalem, and there be judged of these things before me? But Paul said, I am standing before Caesar's judgment-seat, where I ought to be judged: to the Jews have I done no wrong, as thou also very well knowest. If then I am a wrong-doer, and have committed anything worthy of death, I refuse not to die: but if none of those things is true,[2] whereof these accuse me, no man can give me up unto them. I appeal unto Caesar. Then Festus, when he had conferred with the council, answered, Thou hast appealed unto Caesar[3]: unto Caesar shalt thou go. (9-12)

9. *But Festus desiring.* Whether Festus had learnt something about their ambush, and it is easy to conjecture that he had, or whether he was completely ignorant of it, nevertheless he deals with Paul unfairly. And we see how all, who are not led by the Spirit of God, are swayed towards all corruption. For Festus does not intentionally

---

[1] Reading *cum infamia calumniae* with C.R., for Tholuck's *cum infamiae calumnia*. French: 'with the mark of infamy, as calumniators'. Tr.

[2] Calvin has simply, with AV and Greek, *if there be none of these things*. Tr.

[3] Calvin, as AV and RV margin, *Hast thou appealed unto Caesar?* Tr.

treat Paul as of no consequence, or hate him, but ambition, perhaps also the passion for gain,[1] has the upper hand, so that, to please the opposing side, he exposes him unjustly to the danger of death. For it is probable that he was attracted by the suggestion of a reward also, with the result that he was so ready to gratify the priests. However it is strange how he gives Paul the choice, and does not rather order him, by virtue of his authority, to be led away against his will. Certainly we gather that he was held back by fear of infringing his right to obtain the privileges of a Roman citizen, and that was a very odious offence. However he deceitfully desires to persuade Paul not to refuse to be tried at Jerusalem. For he knew quite well, what did happen, that a Roman citizen had the right to appeal, with the result that he himself would not be allowed to proceed further. All the same it was not his fault that he did not abandon Paul to vicious brigands to be killed.[2]

10. *I am standing before Caesar's judgment-seat.* Because Paul sees that he has been betrayed to the Jews by the governor's ambition, he brings forward his right to the privileges of Roman citizenship. If he had received justice and fairness, he would have submitted humbly. Now because the judge does not do his duty of his own accord, necessity forces the holy man to defend himself with the assistance of the law. And by this means the Lord delivers him once again, just when he had almost been delivered to his enemies to be slain. But in demanding that his case be dealt with at *Caesar's judgment-seat*, he is not submitting the teaching of the Gospel to the investigation of an unbelieving and ungodly man, but, being prepared to give an account of his faith everywhere, he avoids a court in which he could no longer expect fairness. Moreover, although Roman citizens still had their privilege intact, yet the procedure had been changed at that time, since the Caesars had transferred judicial investigation from the people to themselves, as if they were the best vindicators and protectors of public liberty.

No injury to the Jews. Since those who have bad consciences, and no confidence in their case, usually have recourse to rather evasive objections, Paul turns aside that reputation from himself. And surely ministers of Christ ought to be just as concerned to bear witness to their innocence as to save their lives. If Paul had said emphatically that he would not defend himself, his enemies would have triumphed, and he would have been taunted with the diffidence due to a bad

---

[1] This clause and sentence following are Second Edition additions. Tr.

[2] *Interea per eum non stetit, quominus sceleratis latronibus mactandum obiiceret.* French: 'Cependant il n'a pas tenu a luy qu'il ne l'abandonnait a des meschans brigans pour estre meurtre.' Tr.

conscience, to the disgrace of the Gospel. But now when he cites the governor as a witness to his integrity and does not refuse punishment, if he is found to have done any wrong, he denies the opportunity for all misrepresentations. Therefore he shows that he is not snatching at a way of escape by shifting his ground, but is seeking an asylum, where he may defend himself properly, and where he may ward off injury without hindrance, seeing that his accusers have so far contended with him showing nothing but dishonesty and impudence, and now, avoiding a judicial investigation, they endeavour to drag him off to be executed. And he certainly does not disguise the fact that it is unjust of the governor to act in collusion with his accusers, and at the same time he checks his cupidity, as if by applying a bridle, so that he does not dare proceed further.

11. *I appeal unto Caesar.* After acknowledging that he is not to escape if any blame were to be found in him, he freely makes use of human aids. Accordingly if ever a similar need overtakes us, we ought not to have any scruples about seeking help from the laws and the political order. Because not for nothing is it written that the magistrates are appointed by God to give approval to those who are good (Rom. 13.3). Certainly Paul had no fear of litigating under an unbelieving judge, for an appellant is raising a new action. Let us therefore realize that God, who has instituted courts of law (*iudicia*) also allows His own the legitimate use of them. Therefore those interpreters are wrong who suppose that the Corinthians are absolutely condemned by Paul, because they invoke the help of the magistrate for the defence of their right, whereas he is there reproving an obvious fault, viz. that they could not put up with any injury, and, in their eagerness to go to law, they exposed the Gospel to a great deal of reproach (I Cor. 6.1).

12. *Festus, when he had conferred.* Governors had the practice of having some leading citizens in their train, to assist in the trial of cases, so that they might pronounce judgment only in accordance with the will of the council. Moreover Festus seems to have spoken with some irritation in using the question form, '*Hast thou appealed to Caesar?*' This is apparently because he was indignant that the freedom to do a favour was snatched away from him. However I leave that un-decided, because it is not very important, and depends on mere conjecture.

Now when certain days were passed, Agrippa the king and Bernice arrived at Caesarea, and saluted Festus. And as they tarried there many days, Festus laid Paul's case before the king, saying, There is a certain man left a prisoner by Felix: about whom, when I was at Jerusalem, the chief priests and the elders of the Jews informed me, asking for sentence against him. To whom I answered, that it is not the custom of the Romans to give up any man,[1] before that the accused have the accusers face to face, and have had opportunity to make his defence concerning the matter laid against him. When therefore they were come together here, I made no delay, but on the next day sat down on the judgment-seat, and commanded the man to be brought. Concerning whom, when the accusers stood up, they brought no charge of such evil things as I supposed; but had certain questions against him of their own religion,[2] and of one Jesus, who was dead, whom Paul affirmed to be alive. And I, being perplexed how to inquire concerning these things, asked whether he would go to Jerusalem, and there be judged of these matters. But when Paul had appealed to be kept for the decision of the emperor,[3] I commanded him to be kept till I should send him to Caesar. (13-21)

13. *And when certain days.* The purpose of recounting this long narrative here is that we may know that, although the hearing of the case had been broken off, Paul's imprisonment was nevertheless notorious, and that in the meantime he was brought out of prison to profess his faith, and speak about the Gospel, before a distinguished audience. In the second place it tells us that, although he was treated with contempt, yet he was not regarded as a criminal, so that his bad name might not detract from the glory of Christ in any way; on the contrary, that, when he was in prison he had greater liberty to promulgate the Gospel as a herald, than if he had been living free in a private house.

Agrippa the king and Bernice. It is certain that this *Agrippa* was the son of Agrippa the Elder, whose loathsome and abominable death was narrated in chapter 12. But although, after the death of his father, this man had been appointed King of Chalcis in place of his father's brother, later on he obtained a larger tetrarchy. The *Bernice*, who is mentioned, was his full sister. She had been married at first to her uncle, Herod, King of Chalcis, and lived as a widow for some time after his death, but not a very virtuous or chaste one, for she was suspected of being excessively familiar with her brother Agrippa. And indeed, to put an end to the reproach of incest, she married Polemon, King of Cilicia. Again however she gave herself up to lust rather than propriety, and divorced him. The historians nowhere record that she was her brother's wife. And in his *Life* Josephus assigned her a domi-

[1] Calvin, with RV margin, has the Western addition, *to die.* Tr.
[2] Calvin, with RV margin, reads *superstition.* Tr.
[3] Calvin's text reads *Augusti.* Tr.

nion of her own in part of Galilee. It is therefore credible that, since they had become hardened in their disgraceful conduct, they lived together, defying rumour, and yet at the same time that they abstained from marriage in case an incestuous marriage might betray, and also increase, their crime. And there is nothing strange about the king arriving to greet the governor out of respect, seeing that he reigned only on sufferance, and depended on the pleasure and favour of the Roman Emperor, and these had to be retained and fostered through the governor.

14-16. *Since they were staying there for many days.* Accordingly when some time had passed, and they were at a loss for something to talk about, as men with nothing to do are in the habit of looking here and there for a subject of conversation, mention was made of Paul. For Luke meant to hint at that when he said that, when a few days had slipped away through idleness, Festus told the king about a certain prisoner. But although here he both censures the malice of the priests, and pretends to a wonderful fairness on his own part, yet a little later, by clearing the man actually accused, he condemns himself without knowing it, when he admits that it was the case of a man appealing so as not to be dragged to Jerusalem. Finally, in praising the Romans Festus is giving judges guidance about what they ought to do. But if nature declared to profane men that all favour, which crushes the innocent, must be prohibited by judges, those judges who are enlightened by the Word of God, ought to be all the more alert and on their guard against corruption of every kind.

18, 19. *They brought no charge.* It is strange why Festus says that no charge, such as he expected, was laid against Paul, when he had been accused of sedition. But again we may conjecture, in fact know clearly, from this, that the false accusations were so empty, that they ought not to have come into a court of law, being more like the insults shouted by some hothead. Accordingly he says that the essence of the case depends on questions of the Law. Therefore we see that he distinguishes between crimes, which were usually punished by the laws of men, and the controversy which was raised between Paul and the Jews. He did so, not because religion ought to be violated with impunity, or the impudence of those who corrupt the worship of God with their own fabrications, to be tolerated, but because the Law of Moses meant nothing to a Roman. That is why he speaks so contemptuously when he says that they contended about *their own superstition*: although the word δεισιδαιμονία is used in a good sense as well as a bad by the Greeks, because, of course, the chosen (*electicii*)[1] cults

---

[1] French: 'because everywhere people had accepted the cults (*les services*) of false gods, which they had invented as they liked'. Tr.

of false gods were accepted everywhere. But still, he means that it is of no importance to him what the religion of the Jews is like. And it is no wonder that a heathen man, who has not learnt that the rule of godliness is to be sought from the mouth of God, is unable to distinguish between the pure worship of God and superstitions. Accordingly there is all the greater need for us to keep hold of that distinguishing mark, that there is no godliness except what is based on the knowledge of faith, so that we may not grope about in the darkness. In addition the Romans were made drunk by so many favourable successes that they thought that they were more acceptable to God than all other peoples, just as today the Turks scoff at the teaching of Christ because of their many victories. Indeed it was a deplorable indignity that a man, who was an unbeliever and an idolater, was sitting as judge and mediator among Jews, and was going to pass judgment concerning the sacred oracles of God according to his ignorance. But the entire blame stuck fast to Paul's adversaries, who cared nothing for the majesty of God, so long as they gratified their own madness. Nevertheless all that remained for Paul to do was to put an end to the reproaches that were made against him unjustly. Thus today even if the internal disputes, with which Christians contend bitterly among themselves, bring dishonour on the sacred name of Christ and His Gospel in the eyes of Turks and Jews, yet it will be undeserved to put the blame on the defenders of the sacred teaching, who are forced to descend into the arena.

Of one Jesus. There is no doubt that Paul spoke seriously, and with the earnestness it deserved, about the resurrection of Christ, but, because of his own pride, Festus did not think it a fitting subject to which to turn his mind. Certainly he does not mock openly at Paul, but he makes it plain enough how heedless he was, when he heard him speaking about Christ. We perceive from that how little effect preaching has, indeed how it has no effect at all, unless the Spirit of the Lord affects hearts inwardly; for the ungodly take no notice of all that is said, just as if someone were telling fairy-tales. Accordingly there is no cause for the heedlessness of many today to disturb us, when Paul accomplished nothing with Festus.

Finally this verse makes it evident that during the hearing of the case many disputations (*sermones*), which Luke has not mentioned, were held between the two sides.[1] For so far he had said nothing about Christ, and yet this later narrative shows that Paul had serious discussion with the Jews about His death and resurrection; and he could not have done that without dealing with the main points of the Gospel. I therefore conjecture that Paul spoke in such a way, that

[1] See also p. 254. Tr.

when he had refuted the false accusations of the Jews, with which they had tried to burden him before the governor, as though finding an opportunity, he then began to talk more freely about Christ.

And Agrippa said unto Festus, I also could¹ wish to hear the man myself. Tomorrow, saith he, thou shalt hear him. So on the morrow, when Agrippa was come, and Bernice, with great pomp, and they were entered into the place of hearing, with the chief captains, and the principal men of the city, at the command of Festus Paul was brought in. And Festus saith, King Agrippa, and all men which are here present with us, ye behold this man, about whom all the multitude of the Jews made suit to me, both at Jerusalem and here, crying that he ought not to live any longer. But I found that he had committed nothing worthy of death: and as he himself appealed to the emperor I determined to send him. Of whom I have no certain thing to write unto my lord. Wherefore I have brought him forth before you, and specially before thee, king Agrippa, that, after examination had, I may have somewhat to write. For it seemeth to me unreasonable, in sending a prisoner, not withal to signify the charges against him. (22-27)

22. *I also was wishing.* One may conjecture from this that, while Agrippa was eager to hear Paul, he nevertheless felt ashamed to acknowledge his desire, so that Festus might not think that he came for any other reason than a courtesy visit. And indeed it is possible that it was not only curiosity that stimulated his desire to hear Paul, but that he was hoping to benefit from his discourse. Yet it is easy to gather how cold his desire was, from the fact that he allowed many days to slip past, in which he showed no sign of his need, and this was undoubtedly because he was more inured to earthly goods, which he considered preferable. And he did not dare or care to say a word before Festus invited him without being asked. Thus the holy minister of Christ is brought forward as a spectacle so that a worldly man may cheer his guest, except that Festus does wish to be instructed by the advice of Agrippa and his companions, so that he may give proof of his diligence to Caesar. But the situation was transformed to serve another purpose by the secret providence of God. For there is no doubt that a report was spread far and wide, that had a great effect in encouraging the godly. And it is also possible that some of his listeners were moved, and received the seed of faith, which afterwards brought forth fruit in its own good time. Finally, although not one of them embraced Christ sincerely and from the heart, yet it was no ordinary outcome that, with the malice of his enemies exposed, the ignorant were quietened, so that they were not inflamed with such great

¹ Calvin, with RV margin, reads *was wishing*. Tr.

hatred against the Gospel; that impiety was put to shame, and the
faithful gathered fresh vigour, and were more and more confirmed in
the Gospel.

23. *And on the next day.* Agrippa and his sister do not come as humble
disciples of Christ, but bring a *pomp* and splendour that would close
their ears and blind their eyes. And one may well believe that arrogance of mind was the exact counterpart of that magnificent show.
It is therefore no wonder if they were not won over to obedience to
Christ. However it seems that Luke mentioned the magnificence so
that we may know that, in a great gathering, and before the most
select witnesses, who carried great influence, Paul was given the
opportunity and the freedom, not only to plead his case, as if a prisoner
defending himself, but also to promulgate the Gospel. For he appears
in the role of teacher, and nothing else, so that he may give lustre to the
name of Christ. The truth of God therefore broke out from his bonds,
and soon spread everywhere by a free and unimpeded course, yes, and
what is more, has flowed even to us.

By the word φαντασία Luke means what we usually call 'outward
show' (*apparentia*); but apparel (*cultus*) of a different kind must be
brought to the spiritual marriage of Christ.

26. *So that, when an examination has been made.* We do not know
whether the governor wishes by this artifice of personally absolving
Paul, to coax him to give up his appeal. For it was a likely thing that
he could easily be induced to lay fear aside and intrust himself wholly
to the investigation of a just judge, especially if Agrippa were to add
his favourable judgment. Whatever his purpose was in doing it, he
condemns himself of injustice out of his own mouth, because he did
not discharge an innocent man, whom he is now ashamed to send to
Caesar without any written charge. This also happened by the
wonderful providence of God, that the Jews themselves made a prior
judgment in Paul's favour. Perhaps the governor cunningly tries to
elicit what the king and the leading citizens of Caesarea think, so that,
if it turns out that Paul is acquitted, he may unload the odium on them.
For he was unwilling to have the priests hostile to himself, when the
majority of the citizens of Jerusalem depended on them; and the best
and shortest way of writing to Caesar was to insert the judgment of
Agrippa. But the Lord, whose property it is to govern events contrary
to what men expect, had something else in mind, that, with the clouds
of misrepresentations dispelled, Paul might have greater freedom to
declare the true teaching.

CHAPTER TWENTY-SIX

And Agrippa said unto Paul, Thou art permitted to speak for thyself.
Then Paul stretched forth his hand, and made his defence: I think myself
happy, king Agrippa, that I am to make my defence before thee this day
touching all the things whereof I am accused by the Jews: especially
because thou art expert in all customs and questions which are among
the Jews: wherefore I beseech thee to hear me patiently. My manner of
life then from my youth up, which was from the beginning among mine
own nation, and at Jerusalem, know all the Jews; having knowledge of
me from the first, if they be willing to testify, how that after the straitest sect
of our religion I lived a Pharisee. And now I stand here to be judged
for the hope of the promise made of God unto our fathers; unto which
promise our twelve tribes, earnestly serving¹ God night and day, hope
to attain. And concerning this hope I am accused by the Jews, O king!
Why is it judged incredible with you, if God doth raise the dead? (1-8)

2, 3. We have mentioned the purpose for which Paul was brought
before that gathering, viz. so that Festus might write to Caesar in
accordance with the advice of Agrippa and the others. He therefore
does not use the simple or usual form of defence, but rather adapts his
speech to teaching. Luke certainly records an expression of apology,
but one that suits quite well where an account is being given of teaching. Moreover because Paul knew from experience that Festus was
indifferent to, and despised, anything taken from the Law and the
Prophets, he turns to the king, who, he hoped, would be more attentive, as he was no stranger to the Jewish religion. And because he
had so far been pouring out words on deaf ears, he now rejoices because
he has a man, who, because of his knowledge and experience, may
judge properly. But as he praises Agrippa's experience, because he is
a legitimate judge of the matters in question, so, on the other hand,
he asks that he may be willing to hear him patiently, for, otherwise,
neglect and aversion would be less excusable in him.

By *questions* he means the points of doctrine which were in the
habit of being dealt with among the scribes, who used to investigate
religion rather minutely. By the word *customs* he means the rites
which were common to the whole nation. The point therefore is that
king Agrippa was ignorant of neither the teaching nor the ceremonies
of the Law.

¹ Calvin, with RV margin, has *worshipping*. Tr.

269

As I have already mentioned in passing that conclusion, *wherefore I beseech thee to hear me patiently*, means that the more progress a man has made in the knowledge of Scripture, the more attentive he ought to be, when an inquiry is being made about religion; for what we understand causes us less trouble. Indeed it is right for us to be so concerned about the worship of God, that we are not reluctant to hear what is said by way of explanation of it; especially when we are already imbued with the principles, so that judgment may be easy for us, if we are willing to give our attention to it.

4, 5. *My manner of life then.* He does not enter into the circumstances of the case yet. But because he had been falsely disgraced, and burdened with many charges, he begins by asserting his innocence, so that king Agrippa might not be hostile to his cause because of hatred of his person. For we know that, once a sinister suspicion has taken possession of the minds of men, all the senses are kept closed, so to speak, so that they admit nothing. Therefore Paul starts off by driving away the clouds of a wrong opinion, clouds which had been gathered and made thicker from false rumours, so that he may gain a hearing for himself among men whose ears are clear and well cleaned. We see from this that Paul was compelled by the necessity of the case to commend the life that he had led previously. But he does not spend much time on that aspect, but immediately makes a transition for himself to the resurrection of the dead, in reminding them that he was a *Pharisee*. I take *the strictest sect* to be said, not with regard to a holier life, but because a more genuine sincerity of doctrine existed in it, and greater learning was conspicuous in it. For they used to pride themselves in possessing a secret understanding of Scripture. As far as the Sadducees were concerned, although they boasted that they were literalists (*literales*), they had surely put out the light of Scripture, and had lapsed into disgraceful and crass ignorance. The Essenes, content with a life of austerity, did not trouble themselves very much about the study of doctrine. And it is no objection that Christ inveighs against the Pharisees in particular, as the worst of all corrupters of Scripture (Matt. 23.13). For their claiming for themselves the right to interpret Scripture according to a secret and hidden sense (*ex arcano et recondito sensu*), was the source of that presumption to change and innovate, which made the Lord burn with anger. But Paul makes no mention of those fabrications, which they had rashly devised, and were urging with tyrannical severity, for his intention was to speak only about the resurrection of the dead. For although they had corrupted the Law in many of its aspects, yet it was right that the influence of that sect in the protection of the true faith should be valued more than that of others, which had departed further from the original purity. Moreover Paul is speaking only about the opinion of the multitude, which regarded the outward show of more minute knowledge.

6. *For the hope of the promise.* He now passes on to the case, viz. that he suffers on account of the principal point of the whole faith. But even if he seems to have spoken in general terms about the resurrection, yet one may gather from the context that he began from a more fundamental principle, and that he included those circumstances which belonged properly to the faith of the Gospel. He complains that he was *accused by the Jews*, because he affirmed *the hope of the promise made to the fathers*. Therefore the beginning, and indeed the chief point, of the defence, was that the covenant, that God had made with the fathers, is made to apply to eternal salvation. Accordingly this was the substance of the argument, that the religion of the Jews was of no value, unless their attention was directed to heaven, and they similarly turned their gaze on Christ, the source of new life. They were boasting that the Lord chose them alone out of all the peoples of the earth. But their adoption was useless, unless they looked to the inheritance of the Kingdom of God relying on the promised Mediator. Therefore one ought to understand much more than Luke explicitly records. And his narrative surely has only one purpose, that we may know what subjects Paul touched on; nevertheless he does not mention what they were or what words he used. At the same time we may gather from the brief summary the matters that belong to this disputation, which was carried out freely and frankly before Agrippa, when the opportunity was given to speak quietly.

7. *To which our twelve tribes.* He complains before Agrippa that the circumstances of the Church have declined so far, that the priests are fighting against the common hope of the faithful. It is as if he said, 'Look at those of our nation who worship God punctiliously, and devote nights and days to the offices of piety. What is the object of their sighing out their prayers, except that at last they may attain to everlasting life? But that is precisely the goal of all my teaching, because, when the grace of redemption is presented, at the same time the gate of the Kingdom of Heaven is opened. And when I preach that the Author of salvation has been raised up from the dead, I am offering the firstfruits of blessed immortality in His Person.' Thus the first confirmation of his teaching was taken from the Word of God, when he publicly cited the promise made to the fathers. Now in the second place he adds the agreement of the Church. And this is the proper way to affirm the doctrines of the faith, the authority of God taking the lead, and the approval of the Church coming after. At the same time, however, we must wisely distinguish the true

Church, as Paul teaches here by his own example. For although he knew that the priests were bringing the charge of a sham Church (*ecclesiae larvam*) against him,[1] yet he fearlessly declares that the sincere worshippers of God are on his side, and he is content with their support (*patrocinio*). For when he mentions the *twelve tribes* he is not lumping together all who were physically descended from Jacob, but he means only those who were maintaining a true zeal for godliness. For it would not have been fitting to commend the nation itself, without distinction, for fear of God, when it was flourishing only in a small number.

The Papists are wrong in both respects, because they both bury the Word of God under the opinions of men, and distinguish a motley and worthless rabble of ignorant or infamous men, with the title of the 'Catholic Church', without any excuse or shame. But in order that we may show that we are in agreement with the true Church, the proper thing is to begin with the prophets and the apostles; then to them there must be added those whose godliness is known and attested. If the Pope and his clergy disagree with us there is no need for us to be greatly concerned. But the true religious attitude is proved by constancy and fervency[2]; and that was of extraordinary value, especially at that time when the Jews were being afflicted most miserably.

8. *Why is it judged incredible?* I have no doubt that he affirmed what he said about the resurrection and the heavenly life with both reasons and Scriptural proof-texts. But he is justified in calling back those, whom he is addressing, to the power of God, so that they may not form an opinion on the matter according to the measure of their own understanding. For there is nothing more difficult to bring home to men than the future renewal of bodies, when they have been reduced to nothing. Therefore because the mystery is far too deep for the human mind, let the faithful remember that in this connexion they must ponder how widely the immense power of God extends, and not what they themselves may understand, as the same Paul warns in Phil. 3.21. For when he says that our humble body must be transformed to the glorious Body of Christ, immediately afterwards he adds, 'according to the effective power (*efficaciam*), by which He can subject all things to Himself'. But men, who do not wish God's arm to be stretched out further than their understanding may reach, are

---

[1] French: 'que les sacriteurs proposassent contre luy le nom d'Église': 'that the priests brought the name of "Church" against him'. Tr.

[2] *affectus religionis.* French: 'Nevertheless St Paul gives proof of the true religious attitude (*affection*) by continuance and ardour; which was a singular virtue, especially at that time, when the Jews were severely afflicted.' Tr.

usually grudging and unjust towards God; therefore they desire, as far as they can, to restrict the magnitude of His works, which surpass heaven and earth, to their own narrow minds. But Paul, on the contrary, commands us to consider what God can do, so that, having been raised above the world, we may learn to grasp the faith of the resurrection, not according to the weak capacity of our mind, but according to His omnipotence.

I verily thought with myself, that I ought to do many things contrary to the name of Jesus of Nazareth. And this I also did in Jerusalem: and I both shut up many of the saints in prisons, having received authority from the chief priests, and when they were put to death, I gave my vote against them. And punishing them oftentimes in all the synagogues, I strove to make[1] them blaspheme; and being exceedingly mad against them, I persecuted them even unto foreign cities. Whereupon as I journeyed to Damascus with the authority and commission of the chief priests, at midday, O king, I saw on the way a light from heaven, above the brightness of the sun, shining round about me and them that journeyed with me. And when we were all fallen to the earth, I heard a voice saying unto me in the Hebrew language, Saul, Saul, why persecutest thou me? It is hard for thee to kick against the goad.[2] And I said, Who art thou, Lord? And the Lord said, I am Jesus whom thou persecutest. But arise, and stand upon thy feet: for to this end have I appeared unto thee, to appoint thee a minister and a witness both of the things wherein thou hast seen me, and of the things wherein I will appear unto thee; delivering thee from the people, and from the Gentiles, unto whom I send thee, to open their eyes, that they may turn from darkness to light, and from the power of Satan unto God, that they may receive remission of sins and an inheritance[3] among them that are sanctified by faith in me. (9-18)

9. *And I indeed.* If Paul had not said more than Luke has so far recounted, his speech would have been disconnected; and that goes to prove what I have already said, that, when he had mentioned the covenant of God, he dealt with the office and the grace of Christ, as the situation demanded. On the other hand he repeats the story of his conversion, not only to remove the reproach of fickleness from himself, but also to testify that he was called by God, and was even urged to action by a commandment from heaven. For, seeing that he was suddenly transformed from a wolf to a sheep against his own will, such a violent change is most effective for gaining confidence in his teaching. Accordingly he dilates upon his eagerness to inflict injury,

[1] Calvin, with RV margin, reads *compelled them to.* Tr.
[2] Calvin, with RV margin, reads *goads.* Tr.
[3] Calvin, with RV margin, reads *a lot.* Tr.

which drove him against the members of Christ, and the pertinacity to which he yielded himself completely. If he had been imbued with the faith of Christ from his earliest childhood, or having been instructed by some man he had embraced it of his own free-will and with no resistance, his call would indeed have been certain to him personally, but it would not have been so illustrious in the eyes of others. But now, when this man, who was burning with stubborn, inflexible fury, who was not prompted by any motive, and not persuaded by any mortal man, underwent a change of heart (*novam mentem induerit*), it is clear that he was subdued by the hand of God. Therefore that contrast has great importance, because he recalls that he was inflated with perverse self-confidence, so that he thought that he would be the one to conquer Christ; and he wished to teach by it that it was not by any means in accordance with the inclination of his own mind that he became a disciple of Christ. The name *Jesus of Nazareth* is taken here for the entire public profession of the Gospel, which Paul had determined to stamp out by stupidly undertaking a war against God in this way.

10. *And this I also did in Jerusalem.* He shows by actual deeds how great was the violence of the zeal which carried him away to attack Christ, until a stronger force drew him back and turned his steps in the opposite direction. Moreover he had his adversaries as witnesses of that vehemence, so that it might be established without any doubt that he was changed suddenly. This task would certainly not have been given to him by the priests, if he had not acted vigorously in inflicting cruelty; and he had to be very bold in order to satisfy their fury. But we must observe that Paul was not ashamed to confess how gravely he had sinned against God, so long as it resulted in the glory of Christ. It was certainly a shameful thing to him that, carried away by blind zeal, he compelled those, who wished to serve God, to utter impious blasphemies, that he caused a variety of troubles for good and sincere people, that he voted for the shedding of innocent blood, and, finally, that he raised his horns against heaven, until he was thrown to the ground. But he does not spare his own character, but freely makes known his own disgrace, so long as the mercy of God may be revealed more clearly out of it. Accordingly no sinister suspicion could have clung to his speech, when, without regard for himself, and without being asked, he brings accusation against himself on account of things, by which he had obtained the praise and approbation of the whole people. Therefore he also condemns his mad zeal which others honoured. That makes it plain how disgusting is the vanity of those who are ashamed to make a simple confession, if they have committed any offence through ignorance or error. For although they do not

exactly excuse themselves, yet they try to minimize or gloss over things, for which they ought to have asked for pardon with sorrow and tears. But when Paul could have retained the reputation of being a prudent man, he testifies that he was a maniac. For that participle[1] which Luke uses means that he *compelled* many *to blaspheme*. We know from this that even among the very first believers there were many worthless persons, who, having professed themselves disciples of Christ, afterwards, weakened by fear or floggings, not only denied Him but also reviled His sacred name; although the actual denial in itself contains a horrible blasphemy.

13. *At midday, O king.* The object of telling this is that king Agrippa may understand that it was no empty apparition, and that it was not such an ecstatic experience as deprived him of his sanity and powers of judgment. For although he was overcome by fear and fell to the ground, yet he hears a voice distinctly, he asks who is speaking, he understands the reply that is given; and these are signs of a mind in good order. It follows from this that he did not undergo a change by accident, but obeyed the heavenly oracle loyally and conscientiously, so as not to continue to rebel against God deliberately.

16. *But arise and stand.* Christ threw Paul to the ground in order to humble him; He now raises him up and bids him be of good courage. And we too are daily cast down by His voice with the object of our being taught to be modest. But those whom He casts down He soon afterwards kindly raises up. And it is no ordinary consolation when Christ says that He has appeared to him, not as an avenger, to exact punishment for his mad behaviour, for the floggings that he had inflicted unjustly and cruelly, for the blood-thirsty sentences on, or the trouble caused to, the saints, for impious opposition to the Gospel, but as a gracious Lord, who wishes to make use of his services, and indeed thinks him worthy of an honourable ministry. For He appoints him a witness of the things which he has seen, and of the things which he is to see afterwards. This was already a memorable vision, for it had taught him that Christ reigns in heaven, so that he might no longer impudently despise Him, but understand that He is the Son of God, and the promised Redeemer. He did have other revelations later on, as he records in II Cor. 12.1.

17. *Delivering thee from the people.* Here he is armed against all the fears which were awaiting him, and at the same time prepared for bearing the cross. However when He goes on at once to add that Paul will go to enlighten the blind, to reconcile to God those who had been alienated from Him, and restore the lost to salvation, it is strange

---

[1] The Greek verb is in the aorist, ἠνάγκαζον βλασφημεῖν. Tholuck however quotes the following participle, ἐμμαινόμενος, 'raging madly against'. Tr.

why He does not also promise that it will happen that all, who have such extraordinary blessings bestowed upon them, will, in their turn, receive him joyfully and favourably. But here the ingratitude of the world is hinted at, because it repays the ministers of eternal life with precisely the opposite reward, just as madmen hostilely attack their doctors. And Paul is warned that wherever he goes, the majority of those, whom he will be eager to benefit, will be hostile to him, and plot his destruction. On the other hand Paul clearly explains that he was appointed a witness to the Gentiles as well as the Jews, so that he may not be blamed for making the Gospel common to both without distinction. For the Jews had conceived such virulent hatred towards him, because they were indignant that the Gentiles were made equal to them. But even if they were pretending to behave like that out of zeal, so that the covenant, which God had made with the descendants of Abraham, might not be profaned by being transferred to outsiders, yet sheer self-seeking was driving them, because they wished a superior position for themselves alone, with all the rest reduced to order. Finally, in the person of one man all godly teachers are given encouragement to do their duty, so that the ill-will of men may not keep them back from continuing to offer the grace of God to wretched men, unworthy though they may be.

18. *To open their eyes.* Paul seems to be putting himself on too high a level in arrogating to himself what properly belongs to God. For we know that the eyes of the mind are enlightened only by the Holy Spirit. We know that Christ is the one and only Liberator, who snatches us out of the tyranny of Satan. We know that it is God alone, who, having destroyed our sins, admits us into the lot of the saints. But it is a common thing for God to transfer to His ministers the honour due to Himself alone, not in order to take anything away from Himself, but to commend the efficacy of His Spirit, which He puts forth in them. For He does not send them to work so that they may be dead instruments, or as if they were play-actors, but so that He may work powerfully with their assistance. But the effectiveness of their preaching depends on the secret power of Him, who 'works all things in all men' (I Cor. 12.6), and who alone 'gives the increase' (I Cor. 3.7). Therefore teachers are sent, not to strew their words uselessly on the air, or to beat men's ears merely with empty sound, but to bring life-giving light to the blind, to transform men's hearts into the righteousness of God, and to confirm the grace of salvation, which has been procured by the death of Christ. But they do not carry out any of these things, except in so far as God works through them, so that their labour may not be in vain, with the result that all the praise remains with Him alone, as the effect comes from Him.

Accordingly we must note that, as often as Scripture gives such honour and praise to the outward ministry, it must not be separated from the Spirit, who gives life to it just as the soul quickens the body. For in other passages it teaches how human activity achieves nothing,[1] and, what is more, confers nothing, by itself. For it is their responsibility to 'plant' and 'water', but it lies with God alone to 'give the increase' (I Cor. 3.6f).

But because their own ignorance and ill-will stand in the way of a great many, so that they do not obtain from the Gospel the fruit that they ought to get, we must note this description, which briefly and splendidly sets that incomparable treasure before our eyes. Therefore this is the goal of the Gospel, that, delivered from mental blindness, we may become sharers of the heavenly light, that, snatched out of the dominion of Satan, we may be turned to God, that, having received the free forgiveness of sins, we may obtain a share in the eternal inheritance among the saints. All who desire to make proper progress in the Gospel ought to have their senses turned intently towards it. For what good will the constant preaching of it be to us, if we shall not understand its true use?

And at the same time the complete means of our salvation is described for us. All assert that they are eager for salvation, but few give heed to how God wishes to save them. Therefore this verse, which describes the method beautifully, is like a key for opening the gate of heaven. Moreover we must realize that the whole human race is by its nature deprived of those blessings, which Christ declares we obtain by the faith of His Gospel. Thus it follows that all are blind, because they are enlightened by faith; that all are the slaves of Satan, because they are freed from his tyranny by faith; that all are hostile to God and liable to eternal death, because they receive the remission of sins by faith. Accordingly there is nothing more wretched for us than to be without Christ and His faith. It is also apparent from that how no room may be left for free-will and human merits.

Now let us look at each of the aspects. Illumination is referred to knowledge of God, because all our sharp-sightedness is mere vanity and thick darkness, until He shines on us by His truth. The following phrase, to be *turned from darkness to light*, goes further, for that happens when we are 'renewed in the spirit of our mind' (Eph. 4.23). Therefore, in my opinion, there is a close connexion between this clause and the next one, to be turned *from the power of Satan unto God*. For that renewal, which Paul explains more fully in Eph. 2.10,[2] is described

---

[1] Following C.R.: *quam nihil per se efficiat hominum industria: imo quam nihil per se conferat.* Tholuck omits all from *quam* to *imo.* Tr.

[2] Tholuck also quotes Eph. 4.23. Tr.

by different figures of speech. Next comes *remission of sins,* by which God freely reconciles us to Himself, so that we may have no doubt that He will be reconciled (*placatum*) and well-disposed to us. Finally, he ends with the completion of all things, viz. the inheritance of eternal life. Some read 'among those sanctified by faith',[1] connecting 'by faith' to this alone; but this is wrong, because it covers the whole series of clauses (*complexum*) in this verse. Therefore the meaning is that it is *by faith* that we come to possess all the blessings, which are offered through the Gospel. But faith is properly directed to Christ, because in Him are included all the aspects of our salvation; and the Gospel tells us not to seek them anywhere else but in Him.

> *Wherefore, O king Agrippa, I was not disobedient unto the heavenly vision: but declared both to them of Damascus first, and at Jerusalem, and throughout all the country of Judaea, and also to the Gentiles, that they should repent and turn to God, doing works worthy of repentance. For this cause the Jews seized me in the temple, and assayed to kill me. Having therefore obtained the help that is from God, I stand unto this day testifying both to small and great, saying nothing but what the prophets and Moses did say should come; how that the Christ must suffer, and how that he first by the resurrection of the dead should proclaim light both to the people and to the Gentiles.* (19-23)

19, 20. He now gives a brief reminder of what his purpose was in relating the story of his conversion, that is, to testify to Agrippa and the rest that he holds God responsible for all those things, which the Jews were condemning as sacrilege and apostasy. He addresses Agrippa by name, because he knew that Festus and the Romans would have absolutely no idea what the *heavenly vision* meant. Now it is apparent that in the actual substance of his teaching there is nothing in disagreement with, or far removed from, the Law and the Prophets; and, as a result, greater credence is given to the oracle, by which Paul was ordered to teach only what was in accordance with Scripture.

To *repentance* there is added *turning to God,* not as something different, but so that we may know what repenting[2] means, just as, also, on the other hand, corruption and depravity are nothing else but alienation from God. But because repentance is an inward thing, and depends on the disposition of the heart, Paul, in the second place, demands works to prove it, and this is in accordance with the exhortation of John the Baptist, 'Bring forth fruits worthy of repentance' (Matt. 3.8).

---

[1] Calvin's text reads *et sortem inter sanctificatos, per fidem, quae est in me.* Tr.
[2] Calvin uses *resipiscere* 'to come to one's self' for 'to repent'. His text of v. 20 reads, *ut resipiscerent et converterentur ad Deum.* Vulg.: *ut paenitentiam agerent.* Tr.

Since the Gospel of Christ now calls all to repentance it follows that all are naturally vicious and corrupt, and need to be changed. This verse similarly teaches that those, who separate the grace of Christ from repentance, are stupidly perverting the Gospel.

21. *They tried to kill me.* Here he complains about the injustice of his enemies, so that it may be apparent from it that they are pleading a bad case with a bad conscience. For if Paul had committed any offence, they were at liberty to take legal proceedings against him, and in doing so would have had the greater advantage, because they carried far more influence and authority. Therefore the fury, into which they fly,[1] proves that they have no grounds.

Paul's statement that he was saved by *the help of God*, effectively confirms his teaching. For why does it happen that He deigns to stretch out His hand to bring help to him, except that He acknowledges His minister, and wishes to defend the cause of which He approves? Moreover he ought to have been encouraged by God's help to continue in his office so much the more steadfastly; for it would have been the mark of an ungrateful man to withdraw from Him, who was bringing him help. We are also taught by this example that, as often as we are snatched out of dangers, the Lord is not prolonging our lives so that we may fritter them away through idleness, but so that we may discharge our office with alacrity for the glory of Him, who has preserved us for Himself. And yet Paul had not forgotten what he owed to the tribune. But here he commends the help of God, to show that it was inevitable that he would do nothing else but devote the remaining course of his life to Him, who had delivered him, although his deliverance actually took place by the agency and work of a man.

22. *Testifying both to small.* We have said elsewhere that *testifying* is more than teaching, for it is as if a solemn contestation were taking place between God and men, to establish the majesty of the Gospel.

But he says that he is a witness to *great and small*, so that king Agrippa may realize that this also applies to himself, and that, although the teaching of salvation is presented to all the lowest of men, that does not prevent it from also ascending to the highest of kings. For Christ gathers all men together into His bosom in the same embrace, so that those, who were previously lying in the dirt, and are now raised to such great honour, may glory in His gracious goodness, and those, who really have been placed in a position of high esteem, may freely humble themselves, and not be annoyed to have brethren drawn from the contemptible, lowest rabble, and thus become the sons of God. Similarly in Rom. 1.14 he mentions that he 'is a debtor both to the

---

[1] *ad quam prosiliunt.* French: 'which transports them'. Tr.

wise and to the foolish', so that confidence in their own wisdom
might not prevent the Romans from submitting to his teaching. Let
us learn from this that a teacher has no authority to choose his audience,
and that it is insulting to God as well as defrauding men of their right,
for teachers to restrict their labour to the great, whom God associates
with the small. It would be silly to limit this to men's ages. Therefore
I have no doubt that the restriction between the illustrious and the
ignoble is removed, because Paul neither respected the superiority of
the former, nor despised the insignificance of the latter, but proved
himself a faithful teacher to both without distinction.

Saying nothing but. In the first place it is worth while noting that in
order to produce suitable witnesses of the first rank for his teaching,
Paul does not take them from men, but cites Moses and the prophets,
to whom the Lord had given undoubted authority. And this is certainly one principle of sound teaching, to mention only what is
agreed to have come from the mouth of God. In the second place it
is worth while noting that the principal points of the argument were
these which Luke now mentions briefly, that it was Christ's special
function to atone for the sins of the world by His death, to obtain
righteousness and life for men by His resurrection, but the results of
His death and resurrection are common to both Jews and Gentiles.
But since no clear and, as they say, literal evidence of His death and
resurrection exists in the Law, there is no doubt that they had teaching
handed down from the fathers, from which they learnt to refer all
figures to Christ. As for the prophets, who were plainer in their predictions about Christ, just as they drew only from that fountain, so
they convinced their own generation that they were teaching nothing
new or different from Moses. But now Paul either did not complete
his defence, or produced clearer testimonies of all those things, in
which he had acknowledged that Moses and the prophets were his
sources (*autores*).

23. *First from the resurrection.* The resurrection of certain others did
indeed precede His in time, namely, if we accept that the saints, who
are mentioned by the Evangelists (Matt. 27.52 only), came forth from
their graves before Christ, something that corresponds to the taking
up of Enoch and Elijah (Gen. 5.24; II Kings 2.11). But here he calls
Him *first*, as elsewhere he calls Him, 'the firstfruits' of those who rise
again (I Cor. 15.23). Therefore this word describes the cause rather
than order in time, because in rising again Christ came forth as the
conqueror of death and the Lord of life, to reign forever, and make
His own sharers in His blessed immortality.

The word *light* includes everything that makes for full happiness,
just as by *darkness* Scripture everywhere means death and misery of

every kind. And I have no doubt that Paul alluded to these sayings by the prophets. 'The people who were walking in darkness have seen a great light' (Isa. 9.2). Again, 'Behold, darkness will cover the earth, and thick darkness the peoples, but the Lord will be seen upon thee' (Isa. 60.2). Again, 'Behold, to those who are in darkness light will appear' (Isa. 42.16). Again, 'I have given thee for a light to the Gentiles' (Isa. 42.6; 49.6). And it is plain from a great many oracles that the light of life must be diffused more widely from Judaea to the Gentiles.

And as he thus made his defence, Festus saith with a loud voice, Paul, thou art mad; thy much learning doth turn thee to madness. But Paul saith, I am not mad, most excellent Festus; but speak forth words of truth and soberness. For the king knoweth of these things, unto whom also I speak freely: for I am persuaded that none of these things is hidden from him; for this hath not been done in a corner. King Agrippa, believest thou the prophets? I know that thou believest. And Agrippa said unto Paul, With but little persuasion thou wouldest fain make me a Christian.[1] *And Paul said, I would to God, that whether with little or with much, not thou only, but also all that hear me this day, might become such as I am, except these bonds. And*[2] *the king rose up, and the governor, and Bernice, and they that sat with them: and when they had withdrawn, they spake one to another, saying, This man doeth nothing worthy of death or of bonds. And Agrippa said unto Festus, This man might have been set at liberty, if he had not appealed unto Caesar.* (24-32)

24. *Festus with a loud voice.* This outburst of Festus shows how much progress the truth of God makes with the reprobate, viz. when, no matter how well and clearly it is presented, it is nevertheless trampled upon by their pride. For he attributes to madness the things which Paul had dealt with out of the Law and the Prophets, although they had no relation to raving, but, on the contrary, were based on the soundest reason, and he does so, not because he sees anything absurd in them, but because he repudiates anything that he does not understand. There was nothing more foolish or pointless than the superstitions of the Gentiles, with the result that their high priests were justifiably ashamed to mention their mysteries, the absurdities of which were ridiculous in the extreme. Festus admits that there is profound *learning* in Paul's speech. Yet, at the same time, because the Gospel is concealed from unbelievers, whose minds Satan has blinded

[1] Calvin, as RV margin, reads, *In a little thou persuadest me to become a Christian.* Tr.

[2] Calvin, with RV margin adds the Western reading, *when he had thus spoken.* Tr.

(II Cor. 4.3f), he thinks that Paul is a fanatic, who is entangled in a confusion of obscurities. Accordingly, although he cannot ridicule and disparage him openly, yet, far from being moved, he regards Paul as a man who is raving, and insanely inquisitive. As a result of this he cannot bear to pay attention, in case he may involve himself in the same madness. Similarly many today run away from the Word of God, so that they may not lose themselves in a labyrinth; and they think that we are foolish, and nuisances to ourselves and others by starting arguments about secret things. Accordingly, let us be warned by this example and ask the Lord, when the light of His teaching is disclosed to us, at the same time to let us experience the taste of it, so that its obscurity may not make it tasteless to us, and pride and disgust finally erupt in blasphemy.

25. *I am not mad.* Paul is not angry, and he does not criticize Festus' blasphemous utterance too severely, but, on the contrary, addresses him respectfully. For there was no occasion for a sterner reproof, and the ignorance of the man had to be pardoned, since he did not rebel against God deliberately. He also respects the personage; for although he might not deserve honour, yet he had the authority of a governor. However he does not let his blasphemy pass on that account, but he maintains the glory of the Word of God; from that we also see that he put aside regard for himself and was concerned only about the teaching. For he does not boast about his own acuteness, or contend or strive on behalf of his own prudence, but is content with this one defence, that he teaches only what is true and reasonable. Moreover the *truth* is set over against all sorts of impostures and fallacies; reasonableness over against empty speculations or subtle and thorny questions,[1] which are merely the seeds of contentions. Certainly Paul replies to Festus' error, but one may gather from this what the right method of teaching is, viz. one that is not only free from all fallacies, but does not fill the minds of men with futile questions; one that is not indulgent to foolish curiosity, and does not encourage an immoderate itching to know more than is proper, but is moderate and aims at genuine edification.

26, 27. *For the king knoweth of these things.* He turns to Agrippa, from whom he could expect more. And in the first place, indeed, he says that he knows the story of these events, but immediately calls him back to the Law and the Prophets. For there was not much use in his knowing what had taken place, if he did not realize that the things, which had been foretold about the Christ, have been fulfilled in the person of Jesus, who was crucified. But when Paul says that he has no doubt about Agrippa's faith, he does so, not so much in order

---

[1] French: 'subtilitez entortillées', 'involved subtleties'. Tr.

to praise him, as to free Scripture from all controversy, so that he may not be forced to waste time on the very fundamental principles. The meaning therefore is that Scripture is self-authentic (αὐτόπιστον),[1] so that a Jew has no right to detract from its authority even in the slightest. Yet Paul does not flatter him. For although he did not reverence Scripture as a godly man should, yet from childhood he had imbibed this basic principle, so that he was convinced of it, that Scripture contains nothing but the oracles of God. Similarly even if the great mass of men do not bother very much about the Word of God, yet they know in a general and confused way that it is the Word of God, so that reverence for God (religio) at least holds them back from rejecting or despising it.

28. *And Agrippa said unto Paul.* The apostle accomplished at least this, that he wrested an involuntary confession out of king Agrippa, just as those who cannot resist the truth any longer are in the habit of nodding, or at any rate giving some sign of assent. Agrippa indeed means that he will not be a Christian willingly, and what is more, has no intention of becoming one, yet that he is unable to resist, but is somehow being drawn in spite of himself. That goes to show how great the stubbornness of human nature is, until it is reduced to obedience by the Spirit of God.

Interpreters give different explanations of the phrase ἐν ὀλίγῳ. Valla thought that it ought to be translated like this, 'You are very near to making me a Christian'. Erasmus renders it, 'in a small degree' (*modica ex parte*). The Vulgate has the simpler reading, 'in a little', because, in rendering it word for word, it has left readers free to make up their own minds. And it certainly can be made to apply to time well, as if Agrippa had said, 'You will make me a Christian all at once, or in a single moment.' If anyone objects that Paul's reply does not fit in with that, there is an easy solution.[2] For since his words were ambiguous Paul skilfully referred what had been said about time to the situation (*rem*). Therefore when Agrippa meant that he was almost made a Christian in a short time, Paul added that he wished that both he and his companions might ascend from small beginnings to higher levels of progress. Yet it is quite suitable to take ἐν ὀλίγῳ as amounting to the same thing as 'almost'. But this reply is evidence of how greatly the holy man's breast was inflamed with zeal for increasing the glory of Christ, when, patiently carrying the fetters put on him by the governor, he desires that the governor be rescued from the deadly snares of the devil, and to make both him and the others

---

[1] French: 'hors de toute doute', 'beyond all doubt'. Tr.

[2] C.R. footnote. The First Edition had added, 'for it is probable that Agrippa spoke in Syriac'. Tr.

sharers and partners in the same grace as himself, at the same time being content with his own irksome and ignominious lot. It must be observed that he does not make a simple wish, but wishes *by God*, as it is His part to draw us to the Son, because outward teaching will always be coldly received, unless His Spirit is teaching within.

29. *Except these bonds.* It is certain that Paul did not find his *bonds* so burdensome and wretched, for he often glories in them, and mentions them openly in order to honour them as the badge of his ambassadorship (cf. Phil. 1.7, 13, 14, 16); but he is concerned about those, for whom he is praying for faith without trouble and the cross. For men who were not yet believing in Christ, were far from that attitude of mind, where they would be prepared to fight for the Gospel. And certainly all the godly ought to be endowed with this gentleness of spirit, that they bear their cross quietly, but that on the other hand they desire to treat others kindly, and, as far as they can, to be eager to relieve them of all trouble, yet without being envious of their quiet and joyful lot. This considerateness and moderation are far removed from the severity of those, who seek to obtain comfort from calling down their own misfortunes on others.

31, 32. *They spoke to one another.* Paul's acquittal by their unanimous decision resulted in no ordinary glory for the Gospel. And when Festus agrees with the rest he is condemning himself, as it was he who had forced Paul into such an impasse by his injustice, in treacherously surrendering his life to the ambush of his enemies on the pretext of changing the place (25.9f). But even if the appeal seems to be harmful to the holy man, yet, because it had been the one and only way for him to escape death, he remains calm, and does not make a fuss to extricate himself from that noose, not only because a decision had already been made in the case (*res iam non erat integra*), but because he had been warned in a vision that God was calling him to Rome also (23.11).

CHAPTER TWENTY-SEVEN

And when it was determined that we should sail for Italy, they delivered Paul and certain other prisoners to a centurion named Julius, of the Augustan band. And embarking in a ship of Adramyttium, which was about to sail[1] unto the places on the coast of Asia, we put to sea, Aristarchus, a Macedonian of Thessalonica, being with us. And the next day we touched at Sidon: and Julius treated Paul kindly, and gave him leave to go unto his friends and refresh himself.[2] And putting to sea from thence, we sailed under the lee of Cyprus, because the winds were contrary. And when we had sailed across the sea which is off Cilicia and Pamphylia, we came to Myra, a city of Lycia. And there the centurion found a ship of Alexandria sailing for Italy; and he put us therein. And when we had sailed slowly many days, and were come with difficulty over against Cnidus, the wind not further suffering us, we sailed under the lee of Crete, over against Salmone; and with difficulty coasting along it we came unto a certain place called Fair Havens; nigh whereunto was the city of Lasea. (1-8)

1. Luke's chief purpose in giving us an account of Paul's voyage is that we may know that he was led to Rome in a wonderful way by the hand of God, and that on the actual journey the glory of God was clearly evident in many ways in his sayings and doings, and confirmed his apostleship more and more. He is certainly handed over to be transported along with other *prisoners*, but afterwards the Lord makes a wide distinction between him and the wretches and criminals, who were fettered along with him. Yes, and a little later, we shall see that the tribune releases him, and looks upon him as a free man among prisoners.

I have no knowledge of the *cohort*, which Luke calls the *Augustan*, unless perhaps it was what used to be called 'a praetorian cohort' before the rule of the Caesars.

But Luke says expressly that they were put on a ship belonging to *Adramyttium*, because they were going to sail near the coast of Asia; for Adramyttium is a city of Aeolia. But I am not certain from which port they set sail,[3] because the direct course would not have been in the direction of *Sidon*, unless the maps (*topographicae tabulae*) are

---

[1] Calvin, as RV margin, reads, *we launched, meaning to sail.* Tr.

[2] Calvin, as RV margin, reads *receive attention.* Tr.

[3] C.R. footnote. The First Edition then reads, 'except that it is a probable

greatly in error.[1] It is a probable conjecture that they were brought
to that place, either because a ship was not to be found anywhere else,
or because they had to take aboard the prisoners, who have been
mentioned, from that region.

2. *Continuing with us.* Luke appears to be praising the constancy
of one man in order to censure others. For a great many companions
had followed him to Jerusalem, but we see that only two of them are
now left. But because it is possible that good reasons kept the others
back, or even that Paul refused their services, I affirm nothing either
way. In fact it is not absurd that Luke had a special reason for commending this man in comparison with others, although he was nevertheless one out of many. Surely it is quite likely that he was a wealthy
man, who was able to bear the expense of being away from his home
for three years. For we read earlier that many of the leading families
of Thessalonica embraced Christ (17.11); but Luke recounted that
Aristarchus and Secundus accompanied Paul to Asia in order to show
honour to him (20.4). Therefore let it suffice to grasp what is certain
and useful to know, that an example of holy patience is set before us,
because Aristarchus is not wearied by any irksomeness or trouble, but
of his own accord submits to the same lot as Paul, and, after he had
shared his imprisonment for two years, is now crossing the sea, in
order to look after him in Rome also; not without the disapproval and
reproaches of many, apart from the loss of his home and possessions,
and the inconveniences of so much expense.

3, 4. *Gave him leave to go to his friends.* Paul could have found a
hiding-place in this large city by the sea. But he was held bound by
the oracle so that he would not withdraw from God's call. In the
second place, because the centurion had been so considerate as to
entrust him to friends to be cared for, when he could have left him in
the stench of the ship, he should not, and could not, have had regard
to his own life to the peril of that man's without infamous treachery.
But we must not act in such a way that the consideration, which some
kindly person shows us, may be to his detriment through our fault.
Let readers find out from geographical works the course of the voyage
which Luke records. I would only remind them that all that is said
has this object in view, that we may know that the voyage was difficult and stormy after they left the port of Sidon until they came near
Malta, and that afterwards the sailors struggled with contrary winds
for a long time, until a fiercer storm prevailed, which finally ended in
shipwreck, as we shall see.

conjecture that they made a longer journey by land beyond Sidon', and then
goes on to, 'either because a ship ...'. Tr.
[1] French: 'if our present-day maps are good'. Tr.

And when much time was spent, and the voyage was now dangerous, because the Fast was now already gone by, Paul admonished them, and said unto them, Sirs, I perceive that the voyage will be with injury and much loss, not only of the lading and the ship, but also of our lives. But the centurion gave more heed to the master and to the owner of the ship, than to those things which were spoken by Paul. And because the haven was not commodious to winter in, the more part advised to put to sea from thence, if by any means they could reach Phoenix, and winter there; which is a haven of Crete, looking north-east and south-east.[1] And when the south wind blew softly, supposing that they had obtained their purpose, they weighed anchor and sailed along Crete, close in shore. But after no long time there beat down from it a tempestuous wind, which is called Euraquilo[2]: and when the ship was caught, and could not face the wind, we gave way to it, and were driven. And running under the lee of a small island called Cauda,[3] we were able, with difficulty, to secure the boat: and when they had hoisted it up, they used helps, undergirding the ship; and, fearing lest they should be cast upon the Syrtis, they lowered the gear, and so were driven. And as we laboured exceedingly with the storm, the next day they began to throw the freight overboard; and the third day they cast out with their own[4] hands the tackling of the ship. And when neither sun nor stars shone upon us for many days, and no small tempest lay on us, all hope that we should be saved was now taken away. (9-20)

9. *Sailing was now dangerous.* He means not only that the winds were then contrary, but that it was also an unsuitable time of year, and he then brings that out more clearly by saying that the *fast* was past; for I think that that clause was added by way of explanation to indicate the end of autumn. And it does not matter that the centurion and the rest of the passengers, and the sailors, knew nothing about that annual time of fasting, which Luke indicates, for he describes the seasons of the year according to the custom of the Jews. Moreover there is no doubt that it was the autumn fast. However I do not agree with the opinion of those who think that it was one of the four fasts, which the Jews instituted for themselves after their exile to Babylon (Zech. 8.19; 7.5). For Luke would not simply have cited the third one, without adding some distinguishing mark, since it was no more celebrated than the rest, inasmuch as it was appointed on

---

[1] Calvin, as Vulg., reads, *looking to Africus and to Chorus* (the south west and north west winds). Cf. AV, 'lieth toward the south west and north west'. Opposite directions are given depending on whether the Greek κατά is read as 'against' or 'down'. Tr.

[2] Calvin, as AV, reads *Euroclydon.*   [3] Calvin, as RV margin reads, *Clauda.*

[4] Calvin, as AV, reads *we cast out with our.* Tr.

account of the death of Gedaliah and the destruction of the rest of the people (II Kings 25.25). In the second place I do not know whether that custom was retained by the people after the return from exile. It is more likely that the Feast of the Atonement is meant, in which the Lord commanded the people to afflict their souls for seven days[1]; beginning, in fact, on the tenth day of the seventh month (Lev. 16.29), to which part of September and part of October now correspond. Therefore since they had already moved into October, *sailing* is said, with good reason, to have been *dangerous* at that time.

But if you refer it to lack of food, as some do, I do not see what sense can be made of it. For there was still an abundance of wheat in the ship, so that they ought not to have gone hungry from necessity. Moreover why would he say that the time of a voluntary fast was completed? In addition it will be plain from what follows after that they were warned by Paul to stop, because winter was approaching, the severity of which normally closes the sea. For although he was quite sure that God would be in control of the ship, yet he was not willing that He be tempted by making rash haste.

11. *But the centurion.* The centurion is not blamed because he listened to the captain and the owner rather than Paul. In fact what should he have done? For although he deferred very much to Paul's advice in other matters, yet he knew that he had no skill in navigation. Therefore, like a prudent and modest man, he allows himself to be guided by those who were trained and experienced. And necessity itself was almost forcing him to do so, for the harbour was unsuitable to winter in. But the captain was not advising that the ship be taken out on the high seas, but that they go to a neighbouring port, which was almost within sight. In this way a suitable place for spending the winter was being procured with little trouble. However Luke does not record this for nothing, but so that we may know that right from the start Paul was provided with the assistance of the Spirit, so that he saw better than the masters themselves what were the proper things to do. We do not know whether he was informed by an oracle or by secret inspiration to give this advice. This indeed is certain that it had a great effect in commending him later on.

Further, when he says (v. 13) that they *sailed along the coast of Crete* until they were swept away in the opposite direction, our friend Beza rightly finds fault with deluded translators in making the name of a city out of the adverb ἆσσον.[2]

---

[1] So Calvin; but there is no reference to 'seven days' in the relevant texts, Lev. 16.29-34; 23.27-32; Num. 29.7-11; Exod. 30.10. Tr.

[2] 'nearer', RV *close in shore.* Cf. Vulg.: *cum sustilissent de Asson.* Calvin: *cum transgressi essent propius.* Tr.

15. *When the ship was caught.* Here Luke tells that what normally happens in a moment of extreme danger did happen, that they allowed themselves to be driven by the winds. At first when they progressed for a certain distance, and the sailors thought that their plans and desires were being realized, there is no doubt that they scoffed at Paul's advice, in the way that foolhardy men have of being insolent as long as fortune smiles on them. Now, having been *caught*, they suffer punishment for their audacity far too late, yes, and more than that, having been driven near an island they are just as afraid of the ship breaking up, as they previously were of its overturning. And Luke diligently notes down all these things, from which we may gather that the storm was so violent and severe, and persisted so long, that death was threatening them continually. At the same time he also makes it clear that they made strenuous use of all remedies, which could ward off shipwreck, and did not spare the cargo and the tackle; and from that we learn that they were driven by a lively sense of danger to take desperate means. And Luke adds that finally, when they had tried everything, they despaired of their safety. Certainly the thick dark sky was like some tomb; and there is no doubt that in this way the Lord wished to give greater commendation to, and make more remarkable, the favour of deliverance, which followed a little later. In the meantime He allowed His servant to suffer with the others, until he thought that he was destined to die. For He did not appear to him by an angel, before it must look as if it was all over with him. Accordingly not only was his body tossed about in the midst of the storms, but his soul was also shaken by severe and violent temptations. Nevertheless the actual outcome shows that he stood firm by faith and did not give way. Luke indeed does not record his prayers, but because he himself afterwards states that *an angel of the God*, whom he was serving, appeared to him, it is likely that, while the others were cursing heaven and earth, he directed his prayers above, and so was calm, and waited with mind composed for what God chose to do. And Luke's statement that the *hope of being saved was taken away* ought not to be referred to his outlook (*ad eius sensum*), but only to human media, as if he had said that things were in such a state of confusion that they were beyond deliverance by men.

And when they had been long without food, then Paul stood forth in the midst of them, and said, Sirs, ye should have hearkened unto me, and not have set sail from Crete, and have gotten this injury and loss. And now I exhort you to be of good cheer: for there shall be no loss of life among you, but only of the ship. For there stood by me this night an angel of the God whose I am, whom also I serve, saying, Fear not, Paul; thou

must stand before Caesar: and lo, God hath granted thee all them that
sail with thee. Wherefore, sirs, be of good cheer: for I believe God, that
it shall be even so as it hath been spoken unto me. Howbeit we must
be cast upon a certain island. But when the fourteenth night was come,
as we were driven to and fro in the sea of Adria, about midnight the
sailors surmised that they were drawing near to some country; and they
sounded, and found twenty fathoms: and after a little space, they
sounded again, and found fifteen fathoms. And fearing lest haply we
should be cast ashore on rocky ground, they let go four anchors from the
stern, and wished for the day. And as the sailors were seeking to flee out
of the ship, and had lowered the boat into the sea, under colour as though
they would lay out anchors from the foreship, Paul said to the centurion
and to the soldiers, Except these abide in the ship, ye cannot be saved.
Then the soldiers cut away the ropes of the boats and let her fall off. (21-32)

21, 22. *And when they had been long without food.* Although Luke
does not explicitly state how the sailors and soldiers behaved, yet he
distinguishes Paul from them clearly enough, by telling that he *stood*
in the midst of them, in order to raise their fallen spirits. For only a man
who is himself an example of steadfastness and fortitude is qualified
to encourage. Moreover Paul put off this exhortation until they
were all lying almost at death's door. It is easy to gather from the
way that unbelievers usually behave that at first they were in a state
of violent and uncontrolled uproar. In the midst of their shouting
and clamouring a moderate voice would never have been heard. Now,
when, worn out by their wailing and commotion, they sit down like
men thunderstruck, Paul addresses them. Therefore it was necessary
for them to flag, as if half-dead, before they would be calm for a little
while, and listen quietly and in silence to someone giving good advice.
However, Paul appears to be speaking out of season when he casts
their foolishness in their teeth, because they were not willing to
comply with his advice when all was going well, when they knew
that he had no experience of ships, and he himself was also well
aware of his ignorance. But if we consider how reluctant men are to
be persuaded, and brought to their senses, this reproach was particularly beneficial. No persuasion of Paul's would move them, unless it
was made plain to them that things had turned out unfortunately for
them because they had taken no notice of him in the first place.
Certainly reproof, that carries no comfort, is cruel. But if it is seasoned
with an added remedy, it is now an actual part of the medicine. Thus
after Paul got the attention of those on board, and taught from what
actually happened, that they ought to trust him, he exhorts them to be
of good courage and promises them safety. But it is a sign of extra-

ordinary confidence when he says that they ought to have obeyed him. Therefore he proves by these words that he had not uttered anything rashly, but that he passed on to them what God had commanded. For even if we read of no special revelation having been given to him then, yet he was conscious of the secret direction of the Spirit, so that he, who had the Spirit of God guiding him, could confidently assume the role of an admonisher. That makes all the plainer what I have just mentioned, that Paul arouses the passengers by starting off in this way, so that they may listen more attentively to what he is about to say. Otherwise it would have been ridiculous for a man suffering shipwreck to promise deliverance to those sharing the same calamity as himself.

23. *For there stood by me.* So that he might not be accused of rashness, because he promised safety to all so fearlessly, he brings God in as witness and source. But there is no doubt that he had definite confidence in the vision, so that he had no fear of Satan's deceptions. For, because that father of lies often makes a fool of men by pretending to give revelations, God never appeared to His servants, either by Himself or by His angels, without removing every scruple of doubt by clear signs, and, secondly, without providing them with a spirit of discernment, so that there might be no opportunity for deceptions.

Finally, Paul clearly honours the name of His God before unenlightened men, not only that they may learn that the true God is worshipped in Judaea, but also that they may know that Paul himself is a worshipper of Him. For they all know why he had been put in prison. Now, when angels come down to him from heaven, it is easy to gather that his cause is approved by God. Therefore in these words there is an underlying commendation of the Gospel. At the same time we see that Paul triumphs in his bonds, when he is the minister of salvation and the interpreter of God to so many men.

24. *Fear not, Paul.* He deliberately devotes himself to claiming the glory of their deliverance for God alone, so that the superstitious men may not wrongly transfer it to their own idols, and in this way he invites them to the right faith. But it is evident how great the perverseness of men is, from the fact that they close their ears to sound and wholesome advice, and immediately forget the grace of God, although it was made known to them in an intimate way; yes, and what is more, they do not see it and notice it when it appears before their very eyes. But however ungrateful the majority were, yet the disclosure of this oracle was not without effect. Yes indeed, for it was a good thing in itself that those, who gave themselves up to deceptions (*in fallaciis*)[1] too much, were rendered inexcusable. On the other

---

[1] French: 'en tromperies et abus', 'deceitful things and corrupt practices'. Tr.

hand his confession that he *must stand before Caesar* aimed at strengthening the godly more, for by it they were reminded that he came forth as a witness definitely chosen by God to affirm the teaching of the Gospel, and saved by Him for that purpose.

He has granted thee all the souls. Luke seems to suggest that Paul prayed, not only for himself, but for the others, that God would snatch them all out of shipwreck. And it is surely likely that, since he was aware of the common danger, he was not so full of concern for his own life that he neglected the rest, whom he saw involved in the same danger as himself.[1] Yet it may be that the Lord of His own accord anticipated his prayers. And it is certainly no new thing for His blessing to be extended to the unworthy, who are bound up with the faithful in some social connexion. Thus the Lord would have spared Sodom if ten righteous men had been found in it (Gen. 18.32).

Here the question is asked, 'To what extent does the integrity of the saints benefit the ungodly?' In the first place we must remove the superstition of the Papists, who, when they hear that the bad are blessed for the sake of the godly, imagine that the latter are mediators, who obtain salvation for the world by their own merits. But they are foolish and preposterous twice over, because they refer these descriptions, that belong to the living, to the dead, and hope that God will be favourable to themselves simply by His consideration of the dead, and therefore they adopt them as their patrons. I pass over the fact that they obscure the gracious goodness of God by extolling the merits of the saints. Now to answer the question raised, it must be considered briefly in this way. Since the good and bad are mixed up together, adverse and favourable things befall them both, without distinction, and yet it sometimes happens that, when the Lord spares His own, He preserves the ungodly for a time along with them. In the second place there are many reasons why He blesses the wicked and reprobate for the sake of the faithful. 'He blessed Potiphar's house for Joseph's sake' (Gen. 39.5), in order to move his heart to show kindness to that holy man. He showed His favour towards Paul by saving many men unharmed, in order that He might bear witness to his godliness and that, as a result, the majesty of the Gospel might shine forth. Finally, we must grasp that all the blessings, that God lavishes on the ungodly, finally make for their destruction, just as, on the other hand, the punishments, which the faithful suffer in common with the reprobate, are to their advantage. In the meantime it is a remarkable pledge of God's love towards us that He makes some drops of His kindness flow from us to others.

---

[1] This clause is a Second Edition addition, and this explains the use of *discrimen* ('danger') twice in the sentence. Tr.

25. *For I believe God.* Paul again emphasizes what gives him such great confidence that he is undaunted in affirming that, in spite of the innumerable raging abysses of the sea, they will all come to port; it is because God has promised that it will be so. These words bring out the nature of faith, when a mutual relation is established between it and the Word of God, so that it may sustain men's minds against the attacks of temptations. But not only does he encourage those on board to believe by his own example, but, as it were, he undertakes the functions of a sponsor, in order to gain their confidence in the oracle.

The immediately subsequent statement about *an island* is a later sign, by which it may be all the clearer, after the episode has come to an end, that there was no uncertainty about this voyage; otherwise it was of no interest to those on board to know the way they were to escape. Therefore we see that God distinguishes the safety, that He has promised, so that it cannot appear to happen by chance. Yet at the same time we must observe that God keeps them in a state of suspense, partly to exercise the faith of His servant, partly that all may know that Paul learnt from the Holy Spirit something that no human mind could have comprehended as yet. Nevertheless Luke's context shows that they did not even believe what he said in that connexion. For the sailors' suspicion that they were approaching some mainland[1] did not agree with the promise of landing on an island. Therefore we see that, forced by experience, in the end they scarcely thought that he was telling the truth.

30. *And as the sailors were seeking.* Now the grace of the Holy Spirit also shone forth in Paul in the way that he prudently warned that the sailors must be kept back from escaping. For why does the centurion, or someone else from the crew, not rather detect their ruse, except that Paul is to be the minister of their deliverance right to the end? But it is strange that he says that the rest of the passengers cannot be saved unless the sailors are kept on board; as if it was really in their power to nullify God's promise. I reply that here Paul is not dealing with the power of God absolutely, in order to separate it from freewill and intervening means. And God certainly does not commend His power to the faithful in order that they may give themselves up to laziness and inactivity, with contempt for intervening means, or rashly rush into danger, when there is a definite reason for taking care. God had promised Hezekiah the deliverance of the besieged city (Isa. 37.35). If he had opened the gates to his enemies, would Isaiah not have declared at once, 'You are destroying both yourself and the

---

[1] *regionem mediterraneam*, lit. 'a region with land far from the sea'. *mediterraneam* was added in the Second Edition. Greek, χώρα 'a region'. Tr.

city'? Yet it does not follow on that account that the hand of God
is tied to means and aids; but when God ordains this or that method
of acting, He holds the minds of men in check, so that they may not
leap over the bounds appointed for themselves.

> *And while the day was coming on, Paul besought them all to take some
> food, saying, This day is the fourteenth day that ye wait and continue
> fasting, having taken nothing. Wherefore I beseech you to take some
> food: for this is for your safety: for there shall not a hair perish from the
> head of any of you. And when he had said this, and had taken bread, he
> gave thanks to God in the presence of all: and he brake it, and began to
> eat. Then were they all of good cheer, and themselves also took food.
> And we were in all in the ship two hundred threescore and sixteen souls.
> And when they had eaten enough, they lightened the ship, throwing out
> the wheat into the sea. And when it was day, they knew not the land:
> but they perceived a certain bay with a beach, and they took counsel
> whether they could drive the ship upon it. And casting off the anchors,
> they left them in the sea, at the same time loosing the bands of the rudders;
> and hoisting up the foresail to the wind, they made for the beach. But
> lighting upon a place where two seas met, they ran the vessel aground;
> and the foreship struck and remained unmoveable, but the stern began
> to break up by the violence of the waves. And the soldiers' counsel was
> to kill the prisoners, lest any of them should swim out, and escape. But
> the centurion, desiring to save Paul, stayed them from their purpose; and
> commanded that they which could swim should cast themselves over-
> board, and get first to the land: and the rest, some on planks, and some
> on other things from the ship. And so it came to pass, that they all
> escaped safe to the land. (33-44)*

33, 34. *And while the day was coming on.* No matter what the
soldiers may have in mind, Paul's faith does not waver, but he rests
securely on the promise given to him. For not only does he encourage
them to take food, like the man who was reported as saying, in utter
hopelessness, 'Soldiers, break your fast, for we shall dine in the underworld today',[1] but, holding fast to his prediction, he bids them be of
good courage. The power of faith reveals itself, when it arms us to
endure, and intrepidly sustains and repels the assaults, which Satan
makes against it in his endeavours to shake it.

But his statement that they *fasted* continuously *for fourteen days,*
could appear absurd. Some individual will be found, who may endure fasting longer, but one can hardly believe it of such a great
crowd. The reply is easy, that unaccustomed abstinence from food is

---

[1] Cf. Calvin's Commentary on I Corinthians 15.32. Tr.

improperly called 'fasting', because they had never been revived by a proper meal for the whole of that time, as those who are in trouble and sorrow are almost nauseated by food. But because despair was the cause of their distaste, he again affirms that they will survive, provided that they recover their spirits. For a faithful minister of the Word ought not only to make promises publicly known, but at the same time to add advice, so that men may follow the call of God, and not remain idle and listless. Moreover, what the words mean is this, 'God has determined to save you. This assurance ought to encourage you, and make you eager not to neglect yourselves.'

35. *When he had taken bread.* In order to encourage them better by his own example, he takes *bread* and *eats.* Luke says that he *gave thanks,* not only because that was his daily custom, but because it was of great value as evidence of his confidence. Indeed there is no doubt that in taking food Paul was being careful to do what he was enjoining on the others. But now not only does he bear witness to his own gratitude, and not only does he ask God to bless the food which he is about to eat, but he boldly calls on God, the source of life, that those wretched men, who were in the grip of despair, might be given some element of good hope. And at least he accomplished this, that the men, who, through fear, had forgotten to look after themselves, recovered their spirits, and took food.

37. *And all were . . . souls.* The number of men is reported, in the first place, so that it may be all the clearer that not one of the crowd perished. For Luke does not tell how many escaped by swimming to the shore, but how many were then in the ship. The number is given, in the second place, so that the miracle may be made the more remarkable. For it could scarcely have come about by human means that of two hundred and seventy-six every single man would escape from shipwreck to land, for, apart from the sailors, it is likely that few were experienced swimmers. But even if their strength was revived a little by the food that they had taken, yet they had been so weakened by a long spell of weariness and despair, that it was a wonder that they were able to move their arms easily. Moreover we must ponder what a great state of confusion they were in, when it scarcely happens that twenty or thirty men swim in a dangerous situation like that, without colliding with, or drowning, each other. Therefore God plainly stretched out His hand, seeing that the full number of those who had cast themselves into the sea, was accounted for on the shore.

38. *When they had eaten enough.* This incident shows that at last they were roused by Paul's words. It had not yet grown light, so that they could know whether there was any harbour in the neighbourhood. However they throw what is left of the *wheat* into the sea, in

order to lighten the ship. They would not have done that, unless Paul's authority carried more weight with them now than it did before. But as all unbelievers are fickle, that persuasion soon vanished easily from their minds.

41. *They ran the ship aground.* At that moment indeed God could have appeared to have been making sport of Paul, and Paul himself to have been talking nonsense and cajoling his companions in shipwreck with an empty hope. But God soon shattered that error by a more favourable outcome. Of course, when the ship was wrecked and broken, it was fitting for the spirits of all of them to be so broken and weakened, that their despair might increase the glory of the miracle. For God usually regulates what He is doing in such a way that He confronts us with an outward appearance of difficulty, with many obstacles presenting themselves. In this way He sharpens our senses to pay better attention, so that at last we may learn that, although the whole world is in opposition, nothing prevents Him from emerging victorious. That is the reason why He preferred to pull Paul and the others, who were shipwrecked, from the broken ship, rather than bring it intact to the shore.

42. *Moreover the soldiers' advice was.* The soldiers' ingratitude was far too cruel. Although they owed their lives to Paul on two or three occasions, they plan to kill him, when the proper thing would have been to spare the others for his sake. Safety had been brought to them by him just as if by an angel of God; they had heard salutary advice from his lips; that very day he had revived them when they were half dead with fear. Now they do not hesitate cruelly to destroy the man by whom they had been delivered so often and in so many ways. Accordingly, if it falls out that we are repaid unjustly for our good deeds, that is no reason why the ingratitude of men ought to disturb us, for it is an exceedingly common disease. But they are not only ungrateful to Paul, the minister of their life, but at the same time they display shameful unbelief and forgetfulness of God's grace. Shortly before they had accepted that oracle, that their souls were granted to Paul (v. 24); now, when they wish to be saved by putting him to death, what else are they trying to do but oppose God, so that they may escape from death in a way that is contrary to His will? Therefore they have now forgotten the grace, which they had been forced to taste in the utmost despair, and they have no longer any taste for it, after a haven appears near. But it is fitting that we ponder the wonderful purpose of God, both in saving Paul, and in fulfilling His promise, when He brings to land the very men, to whom no thanks were due for the fact that the promise was not nullified. His goodness is usually very often in conflict with the malice of men like that. Yet He is

merciful to the ungodly in such a way that, while He puts off their punishment to a suitable time, He does not absolve them of guilt; yes, and what is more, He makes up for such a great delay, that is due to His tolerance, with the severity of the punishment.

CHAPTER TWENTY-EIGHT

And when we were escaped, then we knew that the island was called Melita. And the barbarians shewed us no common kindness: for they kindled a fire, and received us all, because of the present rain, and because of the cold. But when Paul had gathered a bundle of sticks, and laid them on the fire, a viper came out by reason of the heat, and fastened on his hand. And when the barbarians saw the beast hanging from his hand, they said one to another, No doubt this man is a murderer, whom, though he hath escaped from the sea, yet Justice hath not suffered to live. Howbeit he shook off the beast into the fire, and took no harm. But they expected that he would have swollen, or fallen down dead suddenly: but when they were long in expectation, and beheld nothing amiss come to him, they changed their minds, and said that he was a god. (1-6)

1, 2. At the beginning of the chapter we are presented with the sad spectacle of so many men, soaking wet, filthy with the spume and dirt of the sea, and also stiff with cold, crawling with difficulty ashore. For it was just as if they had been pushed out of the sea for a different kind of death.

Luke then narrates that the *barbarians* received them kindly, that a fire was kindled so that they might dry their clothes, and warm their limbs, powerless with the cold, and, finally, that they were given shelter from the rain. Therefore Paul shows his gratitude by praising these acts of kindness; and such great generosity towards strangers deserves to be praised, when examples of it are rare in the world. But although ordinary human nature forces some feeling of pity from the barbarians in such necessity, yet there is no doubt that God moved the minds of the Maltese to sympathy so that His promise might be firmly fulfilled, for it could have appeared to have been shattered if the shipwreck had proved fatal to anyone.

3. *A viper out of the heat.* The event had now proved that Paul was a true and undoubted prophet of God. Now in order to make him as outstanding on the land as he had recently been on the sea, God sets the seal to His earlier oracles with a fresh miracle; and in this way He confirms his apostleship among the Maltese. And although not many derived any benefit from it, nevertheless the majesty of the Gospel was resplendent even among unbelievers. It was also a great confirmation of the oracles among the passengers and crew, for they had not reverenced them enough. And the *viper* certainly did not come

out of the bundle of sticks by chance, but, according to His secret purpose, the Lord directed it to bite Paul, because He saw that it would be for the glory of His Gospel.

4. *When the barbarians saw.* Everywhere, and in every generation, it was the accepted opinion that those who suffered rather severely were involved in some dreadful crime. And there was, in fact, some justification for that opinion, yes, and one might say that it sprang from a proper sense of piety. For in order to make the world inexcusable, God wished it to be impressed on the minds of all that troubles and adversities, but extraordinary disasters in particular, are examples of His wrath and just vengeance on sins. Therefore whenever some memorable calamity occurs, at the same time it comes into men's minds that God is deeply offended, when He exercises judgment so severely and harshly. And in fact impiety never prevailed to such an extent that all did not retain this principle, that in order to show that He is the Judge of the world, God inflicts conspicuous punishments on the wicked.

But at this point an error has also nearly always crept in, that men condemned as wrongdoers all, without exception, whom they saw being treated rather severely. But even if God does always punish sins with adversities, yet in this present life He does not take vengeance strictly according to what each one deserves; and sometimes the afflictions of the godly are not so much punishments as tests of their faith and exercises in endurance. Therefore those, who make a general rule for themselves to judge every single individual according to prosperous or adverse circumstances, are mistaken. That was the point of the debate between Job and his friends; when they thought that a man, whom God afflicted, was reprobate and hateful to God, he, however, took the opposite view, that the godly are sometimes humbled by affliction.

Therefore in order not to talk nonsense in this connexion, we must beware of two things. The first is that we do not make a blind and hasty judgment about unknown men based on their lot alone. For seeing that God afflicts the good and bad indiscriminately, yes, and even spares the reprobate and scourges His own with greater severity, in order to make a proper judgment, we must begin from something other than punishments, viz. we must inquire about life and deeds. If any adulterer, or blasphemer, or perjurer, or robber, if anyone given over to lust, if any defrauder, if any blood-thirsty person is punished, God is pointing out His judgment as if with His finger. If no offence is apparent to us, the best thing is for us to suspend judgment about punishment. The other caution is to wait for the final outcome. For God's purpose is not plain to us as soon as He begins to strike; on the contrary a different outcome finally makes it plain that those, who seem to be sharing in the same punishment in the eyes of men, are quite different in the sight of God. If anyone objects that it is not for nothing that the Law repeats so often that all afflictions, private and public, are the scourges of God, I certainly admit that that is true, but yet I deny that it prevents God from sparing those, whom He wishes, for a time, although they may be the worst of all, and, on the other hand, from inflicting severer punishment on others whose fault is insignificant. At the same time it is not for us to make something that happens often (ἐπὶ τὸ πολύ), permanent.

Now we see how the Maltese were mistaken, viz. because, without inquiring about Paul's life, they judge him to be a criminal, merely because the viper bit him; and secondly, because they make a hasty judgment without waiting for the final outcome. At the same time we must note that those who try to pluck out of their hearts all awareness of God's judgment are detestable monsters, since that awareness is innate in all of us, and dwells in the minds of even ignorant and savage men. In accusing Paul of *murder* rather than any other crime, they are following the view that murder has always been the most abominable of crimes.

Vengeance does not allow to live. They conclude that he is a criminal, because vengeance pursues him after he has emerged from the sea. But they imagined that, seated by Jupiter's throne, was an avenging goddess, to whom the name Diké (Δίκη; *Justice*) was commonly applied. Certainly they did so in a confused way, as men ignorant of the pure religion; and yet not without a tolerable meaning, as if they depicted God as the Judge of the world. Apart from that, by this word the wrath of the Godhead (*numinis*) is distinguished from fortune; and so the judgment of God is affirmed over against all blind, chance events. For the Maltese understood it to be a striking sign of heavenly vengeance that Paul, although just saved, cannot be saved.

5. *He shook off the viper.* In shaking off the viper he reveals his composure of mind. For we know how greatly fear disturbs and unnerves a man; yet you are not to understand that Paul was devoid of all fear. For faith does not make us unfeeling, as fanatics, who are safe beyond the firing range (*in umbra et extra teli iactum*), imagine. But although faith does not remove the awareness of calamities, yet it does temper it, so that alarm may not unduly strip the godly of their courage, with the result that they always maintain their confidence. Thus, although Paul understood that the viper was dangerous, yet he was not afraid of its deadly bite to the extent of being alarmed, because he relied on the promise given to him, and also because he was ready to die if necessary.

6. *They changed their minds and said.* Such an astonishing and un-expected change ought to have moved the Maltese in earnest, to give glory to the mercy of God, as they had previously given it to ven-geance. But as human reason always wrongly rushes to extremes, they suddenly make Paul a god instead of a vicious murderer; but if it was necessary to choose one or the other, it was better to be re-garded a murderer rather than a god. And Paul would certainly have preferred not only to be condemned for one crime, but also to be loaded with infamy of every kind, and be plunged into the depths of the underworld, rather than appropriate the glory of God to himself; and all those, who had heard him preaching in the midst of the storms, were quite well aware of that. However, it is possible that later on, after they received instruction, the Maltese realized that God was responsible for the miracle.

Moreover let us learn from this episode to look with composed and quiet minds for a happy outcome to melancholy events, which at first seem to make for the diminution of the glory of God. Which of us would not have been violently alarmed by this spectacle, which gave the ungodly weapons for damaging and dishonouring the glory of the Gospel with any abuses and insults they liked. However we see that God quickly set it to rights. Let us therefore have no doubt that, after He has allowed His own to be beclouded by stumbling-blocks (*scandalis*), He will bring forward a timely remedy, and turn their darkness into light. At the same time let us remember to beware of the judgment of the flesh. And because men always lose control of themselves, let us ask the Lord for a spirit of moderation to keep us properly balanced.

Further, let us learn from this how prone the world is to supersti-tion. Yes, and what is more, we are almost born with this perverse attitude of gladly embellishing created things with the spoils stripped from God. Accordingly it is no wonder if new errors have repeatedly appeared in all generations, when each one of us, from his mother's womb, is wonderfully adept at devising idols. But so that the chance of an excuse may not be sought from this incident, it bears witness that the source of superstition lies in the fact that men are ungrateful to God and transfer His glory to another person or thing.

Now in the neighbourhood of that place were lands belonging to the chief man of the island, named Publius; who received us, and enter-tained us three days courteously. And it was so, that the father of Publius lay sick of fever and dysentery: unto whom Paul entered in, and prayed, and laying his hands on him healed him. And when this was done, the rest also which had diseases in the island came and were

cured: who also honoured us with many honours; and when we sailed,
they put on board such things as we needed. And after three months we
set sail in a ship of Alexandria, which had wintered in the island, whose
sign was The Twin Brothers.[1] *And touching at Syracuse, we tarried*
there three days. And from thence we made a circuit, and arrived at
Rhegium: and after one day a south wind sprang up, and on the second
day we came to Puteoli: where we found brethren, and were intreated to
tarry with them seven days: and so we came to Rome. (7-14)

7. *But in those places.* Because *Publius* is a Roman name, I rather
suspect that the man, who is mentioned here, was a Roman citizen
rather than an islander. For Greeks and other foreigners, apart from
insignificant men, were not in the habit of borrowing names from the
Latins. And it is possible that one of the leading men of Rome was
visiting his estates at that time, and is called *the chief man of the island*,
not because he stayed there, but because no one would equal him in
wealth and abundance of possessions.

But it is hardly possible that the whole crowd of Greeks was given
hospitality for three days. I rather suspect that when he received the
centurion, he also showed honour to Paul and his companions,
because the miracle had prompted him to believe that Paul was a man
pleasing to God. However, be that as it may, his hospitality did not
go unrewarded. For a little later the Lord restored his father to health
from a grave and dangerous illness by the hand of Paul. And in this
way He wished to make it plain how much the kindness, which is
shown to the wretched and needy, is pleasing to Him. Although
those who are given some help are often ungrateful and forgetful of
kindness, or they lack the means to make recompense, yet God Himself abundantly repays whatever has been expended on men at His
command; but sometimes he has appointed some of His servants to
the kind and hospitable, to bring a blessing with them. It was already
a great honour that Publius had received Christ as a guest in the person
of Paul. However the crowning feature was that Paul came endowed
with the gift of healing, so that he was able not only to repay him in
his turn, but also to give far more than he had received. We do not
know whether he then imbibed the rudiments of the faith, as miracles
generally make the ignorant and the unbelieving docile.

Luke points out the nature of the disease, the better to commend
the grace of God. For since the cure of dysentery is difficult and slow,
especially when fever goes along with it, the old man at death's door
was not restored to health so suddenly, by the laying on of hands
alone and prayers, without the power of God.

[1] Calvin, as AV, reads *Castor and Pollux*. Tr.

8. *And had laid his hands upon him.* By *praying* Paul makes it plain that he is not the one responsible for the miracle, but only the minister, so that God may not be defrauded of His glory. He also confirms that by the outward sign. For as we have seen earlier in other passages,[1] the *laying on of hands* was nothing else but a solemn rite of presentation. Accordingly when Paul presented the man to God with his own hands, he showed that he was humbly asking for his life from God. By this example not only is a warning given to those, who are strong in the extraordinary graces of God, that they must take very great care not to obscure the glory of God by extolling themselves, but also we are all taught in general that gratitude must be shown to the ministers of God in such a way that the glory remains with Him alone. Paul is certainly said to have healed a man suffering from dysentery, but the added details bring out that this blessing was given by God through him.

9. Luke's subsequent statement that other sick people on the island were also healed, does not extend to all; but he means only that the power of God, which had appeared clearly enough already, was demonstrated by many examples, to confirm Paul's apostleship. But there is no doubt that Paul took pains to heal their souls just as much as their bodies. However Luke does not record what sort of reward followed, except that the barbarians gave him and his companions provisions and necessities for the voyage, when they sailed out of the port. At the same time we must note that although Paul had it in his power to slip away and escape in many ways, yet God's will for him was voluntary fetters instead, because he had been summoned so often by a heavenly oracle as a witness before Nero's judgment-seat (cf. 23.11; 27.24). In the second place he knew that if he did run away, the way would be closed to him for spreading the Gospel in the future, so that he would lie useless in some out-of-the-way place for the whole of his life.

11. *In a ship of Alexandria.* Luke means by these words that the first ship was either sunk, or so broken and wrecked that it was useless afterwards. That helps us to understand how serious the shipwreck was.

But he clearly says that the *ship of Alexandria*, in which they were conveyed to Rome, had the *sign* of *Castor and Pollux*, so that we may know that Paul was not given the choice to sail with people like himself, but was forced to board a ship that was dedicated to two idols. The ancient poets imagined that Castor and Pollux were the offspring of Jupiter and Leda, as a result of which they were also called in Greek Διόσκουροι, the word which Luke uses in this verse, as if you might

[1] See on 13.3; also 6.6; 8.17, 18; and 19.6. Tr.

say, 'the sons of Jupiter'. In the second place they said that they are the Gemini in the zodiac. Another superstition also prevailed among sailors that the same two are the fiery exhalations which appear in tempests. Therefore long ago they were supposed to be gods of the sea, and invoked, as Nicholas, Clement and the like are today. Moreover, as ancient errors are retained in the Papacy merely with changes of names, today they do honour to those exhalations under the name of Saint Hermes or Saint Ermus. Since, on the one hand, if only a single exhalation appears it is a gloomy presentiment, and, on the other hand, two of them, according to Pliny, are salutary, and tokens of a prosperous voyage, the Alexandrian sailors placed the figurehead of both Castor and Pollux on their ship, so that they might be favourable to them. Therefore as far as they are concerned, the ship was polluted by an impious sacrilege, but because Paul did not freely choose it for himself, he contracted no defilement from it.

Certainly since an idol is nothing, it cannot corrupt the things created by God; and that means that the faithful may use them lawfully and unconditionally. And we must be utterly convinced of this, that all the filthy things, with which Satan, in his deceitful ways, tries to defile God's created things, are washed away only by a pure conscience, while the ungodly and the impious, with their unclean touch, contaminate things that are pure in themselves. In a word, the boarding of this ship no more defiled Paul than did the sight of the altars at Athens, because, being pure, and free from all superstition, he knew quite well that all the sacred things of the heathen were mere illusions. Finally, the men could have entertained no suspicion that he had any sympathy with that profane error. For if he had been obliged to make any show of worshipping Castor and Pollux, he would have preferred to die a hundred times. Therefore he boarded the ship freely, because he had no fear of a stumbling-block. Yet there is no doubt that he did so with pain and sorrow, because he saw the honour due to God being paid to useless images. Therefore we must include this among the things exercising him, that those, whom he had to conduct him on the voyage, were men, who thought that they were under the control of idols, and had committed their ship to their care and protection.

12-14. *When we had come to Syracuse.* Luke gives an account of the remaining course of the voyage, that they landed first in Sicily, and then made an indirect crossing to Italy, because of the swell of the sea. But while the port which Luke names here is the most famous one in Sicily, it is farther from the coast of Italy than the port of Messina, opposite which is *Rhegium*, mentioned by Luke. And Rhegium is in the territory of the Brutians, just as *Puteoli* is a city of Campania.

Finally, we gather from the fact that the brethren kept Paul at

Puteoli for seven days, how kindly and indulgently the centurion
dealt with him. And indeed I have no doubt that the holy man gave
him a promise that he would always report back at an agreed time.
On the other hand the centurion was so convinced of his integrity
that he had no fear of being deceived. Moreover we conclude from
this verse that the seed of the Gospel was scattered abroad by then,
seeing that there was also some body of the Church at Puteoli.

*And from thence the brethren, when they heard of us, came to meet us as
far as The Market of Appius, and The Three Taverns; whom when
Paul saw, he thanked God, and took courage. And when we entered
into Rome,[1] Paul was suffered to abide by himself with the soldier that
guarded him. And it came to pass, that after three days he called together
those that were the chief of the Jews: and when they were come together,
he said unto them, I, brethren, though I had done nothing against the
people, or the customs of our fathers, yet was delivered prisoner from
Jerusalem into the hands of the Romans: who, when they had examined me, desired to set me at liberty, because there was no cause of
death in me. But when the Jews spake against it, I was constrained to
appeal unto Caesar; not that I had aught to accuse my nation of. For
this cause therefore did I intreat[2] you to see and to speak with me: for
because of the hope of Israel I am bound with this chain.* (15-20)

15. *When the brethren heard.* God now encouraged Paul by this
meeting with the brethren, to hasten more eagerly to his defence of
the Gospel. On the other hand the zeal and godly concern of the
brethren are revealed in the fact that they inquire about Paul's arrival,
and go out to meet him. For at that time profession of the Christian
faith not only produced hatred, but could also have endangered their
lives. And it was not merely a matter of a few men running a personal
risk, because the odium was falling upon the whole Church. But
nothing mattered more to them than their duty, in which they
could not have failed without shamefully branding themselves with
cowardice and ingratitude. For it would have been a dreadful thing
to neglect such a great apostle of Christ, especially when he was
suffering for the common salvation. But since he had already written
to them, and had offered his services to them without being asked, it
would have been unworthy of them not to repay him with brotherly
good-will in turn. Therefore by this act of kindness the brethren bore
witness to their own loyalty to Christ; and Paul's eagerness was the

[1] Calvin adds, with RV margin and AV, the Western reading, *the centurion
delivered the prisoners to the captain of the guard, but Paul, etc.* Tr.
[2] Calvin, with RV margin and AV, reads *call for you, to see and to speak with
you.* Tr.

more inflamed because he saw the reward for his steadfastness provided for him. For although he was endowed with invincible fortitude,
so that he did not depend on the help of men, yet God, who is in the
habit of strengthening His own by human means, gave him fresh
vigour in this way. Afterwards, when he was abandoned in prison,
as he complains elsewhere (II Tim. 4.16), nevertheless he did not
despair, but waged war under the auspices of Christ just as bravely
and intrepidly, as if he had led huge forces into battle along with him.
But at that time also the memory of this meeting was of value for
encouraging him, when he reflected that in Rome there were many
loyal, but weak, brethren, to whom he had been sent to sustain them.
But, to return to his present circumstances, there is no reason for us
to wonder that Paul took heart at the sight of the brethren, because
he hoped that the confession of his faith would be very fruitful. For
as often as God shows His servants some success for their labour, He
incites them, as if by applying a goad, to continue more eagerly in the
work.

16. *The centurion handed over the prisoners.* Luke means that Paul
was given more than the rest, for his circumstances were different and
special. For he was allowed to live in a private house, with one guard
to whom he was bound, while the others were confined in the public
prison. For the commander of the praetorian guard knew from
Festus' official report that Paul had no part in any crime. And it is
likely that the centurion faithfully reported things that had the effect
of procuring favour for him. However let us realize that God, from
heaven, mitigated the imprisonment of His servant, not only to lessen
his troubles, but also so that the faithful might have freer access to
him. For He did not wish the treasure of his faith to be held confined
within the walls of a prison, but to be kept free and open, to enrich
many on all sides. Yet Paul was not given the freedom of house
custody in such a way that he did not always carry a chain. Luke
calls the commander of the praetorian guard στρατοπεδάρχης, 'chief of
the camp', for it is well known from the histories that that office
belonged to him.

17. *And after three days.* Paul's meekness was certainly a wonderful
thing; because, despite the fact that he had been harassed and insulted
so much by his own nation, he nevertheless takes pains to appease the
Jews, who are at Rome, and excuses himself to them, so that they
might not hate his cause, because they hear that the priests are hostile
to him. Certainly he would not have lacked a justifiable excuse in the
eyes of men, if he neglected the Jews and turned to the Gentiles. For
although he had constantly tried for several years and in many places
to bring them to Christ, they had become more and more exasperated;

and yet he had neglected nothing to mitigate their fury, in Asia, or in Greece, or, finally, in Jerusalem. Therefore everybody would have rightly pardoned him if he had left in peace men whose hopeless stubbornness he had experienced so often. But because he knew that the Father gave his Master to be a minister to the Jews (Rom. 15.8), to fulfil the promises by which God had adopted the seed of Abraham as a people for Himself, keeping that call of God's in mind, he is never wearied. He saw that he must remain at Rome. Since he was granted freedom to teach, he did not wish them to be deprived of the fruit of his labour. In the second place he did not wish them to be driven by hatred of his cause to disturb the Church, since the least opportunity was likely to lead to great destruction. Therefore Paul meant to take care, so that they might not conform to their usual madness and be the torches to start a very bad fire.

I had done nothing against the people. These two things could have stirred up ill-will against him among the Jews: (1) that he had harmed the public good of his nation, as some deserters, by their treachery, had further increased their servitude, already more than cruel enough; or (2) that he had violated the worship of God. For even if the Jews had departed from the standards of the fathers, and religion among them was spoiled and corrupted by many errors, yet they had great respect for the very name of the Law and the worship of the temple. Moreover Paul does not deny that he freely set aside the ceremonies to which the Jews were superstitiously attached, but he turns away from himself the charge of defection, of which he could have been suspected. Therefore understand those institutions of the fathers, by which, according to their belief, the sons of Abraham and the disciples of Moses ought to have been distinguished from the rest of the nations. And certainly in cleaving so conscientiously to Christ, who is the soul and perfection of the Law, so far was he from detracting anything from the institutions of the fathers, that he observed them more thoroughly than anyone else.

19. *I was forced to appeal.* This *appeal* was full of offence, because the justice and liberty of the Jewish nation, who desired to live by their own laws, seemed to be set aside rather harshly; and, secondly, because his defence carried with it the disgracing and damaging of the whole of the people. He therefore removes this objection also, because he was forced by the stubbornness of his enemies to have recourse to this asylum. For the necessity of circumstances excuses him, because no other means of escaping death was left to him. But having presented his excuse for something that was past and done with, he also promises, for the future, that he will plead his case in such a way as not to attack the Jews.

20. *Because of the hope of Israel.* We ought to understand much more than Luke expresses by this single phrase, as we gather from the reply, in which the Jews mention *the sect*, obviously repeating something he said that Luke leaves out. Therefore Paul spoke about Christ to make it clear that neither the Law nor the temple was any use to the Jews without Him, because the covenant of adoption was confirmed, and the promise of salvation fulfilled, in Him. Indeed they were in no doubt that the restoration of the kingdom depended on the coming of the Messiah, and at that time their ruined and hopeless circumstances further increased their hope and desire for Him. Accordingly Paul is justified in saying that he is *bound with a chain because of the hope of Israel.* We also learn from this that it is only those who direct their gaze to Christ and His spiritual Kingdom, who have the proper hope; for when he places the hope of the godly in Christ, he definitely excludes all other hopes.

And they said unto him, We neither received letters from Judaea concerning thee, nor did any of the brethren come hither and report or speak any harm of thee. But we desire to hear of thee what thou thinkest: for as concerning this sect, it is known to us that everywhere it is spoken against. And when they had appointed him a day, they came to him into his lodging in great number; to whom he expounded the matter, testifying the kingdom of God, and persuading them concerning Jesus, both from the law of Moses and from the prophets, from morning till evening. And some believed the things which were spoken, and some disbelieved. (21-24)

21, 22. *We neither received letters.* The priests and scribes had not kept silent because they had become more mellow towards Paul, or to spare him. Rather, their silence had been caused either by contempt, or despair, because they had no easy means of crushing him, when he was far away, and to them transportation to Italy could have seemed like the grave. For at home they lorded it securely, as well as proudly, so long as nobody caused them trouble. Moreover, even if the Jews are not exactly above reproach in coming to listen, they do show some desire to learn, when they do not refuse to hear him defend that teaching, which is opposed everywhere. For many close the way for themselves by this prior decision, that they cannot bear to hear what is repudiated by general consent, but assent to the opinion of others for the condemnation of teaching about which they know nothing. At the same time they are not blameless, as I have said, because they bring up the opposition, in order to stir up ill-will, or introduce unfavourable suspicion; as if Isaiah had not foretold that God would be *a stone of offence* to all the people (Isa. 8.14).

23. It is uncertain whether, on the *appointed day*, Paul argued un-interrupted, or whether they debated with each other, except that one may conjecture from the circumstances of time, that Paul did not speak without a break, for he could scarcely have made a speech *from morning to evening*. Accordingly I have no doubt that after the apostle gave a brief exposition of the substance of the Gospel, he gave an opportunity to his listeners to ask questions in their turn, and then replied to the questions put to him.

But we must note the essential features of the speech, which Luke makes twofold. In the first place Paul taught what was the nature of the Kingdom of God among them, and particularly of the supreme happiness and glory promised them, which the Prophets everywhere praise so much. For since most of them had dreams of the Kingdom of God having a transitory state in the world, and wrongly made it consist in ease, pleasures and an abundance of present goods, it was necessary for the right definition to be established, so that they might know that the Kingdom of God is spiritual, and that the beginning of it was newness of life, and the end, blessed immortality and the glory of heaven.

In the second place Paul strongly urged them to receive Christ, the source of the promised happiness. And once again this second point had two parts. For it could not have been dealt with profitably and thoroughly, without an explanation of the office of the promised Redeemer; and secondly, without showing that He has already been revealed, and that the Son of Mary is the One for whom the fathers had hoped.

Indeed the principle was accepted among all the Jews that the Messiah would come to restore all things to the order of perfection. But Paul gave attention to another aspect which was not so well known, that the Messiah was promised to make atonement for the sins of the world by the sacrifice of His death, to reconcile God to men, to procure eternal righteousness, to regenerate men by His Spirit and fashion them according to the image of God, and, finally, to make His faithful ones heirs with Him of the life of heaven; and that all these things have been fulfilled in the Person of Jesus Christ, crucified. He could not have dealt with those things without calling the Jews from their gross and earthly notions to heaven, and, at the same time, removing the stumbling-block of the cross, since he taught that there was no other way for us to be reconciled with God.

And let us note that according to Luke's evidence Paul took all that he taught about Christ from the Law and the Prophets. For the true religion differs from all spurious ones in the fact that it has the Word of God, and nothing else, for its rule. Also the Church of God differs from all unenlightened sects in the fact that it listens only to what He says, and is governed by His command. Now indeed we see from this how the Old Testament agrees with the Gospel in establishing faith in Christ. In the second place we see that double use of Scripture, which the same Paul commends elsewhere (II Tim. 3.16; Titus 1.9), viz. that it is effective for instructing those willing to learn, as well as rebutting the stubbornness of those who oppose the truth. Therefore let those who wish to be wise and prudent, and to teach others properly, set this restriction before them, that they do not produce anything except from the pure fountain of Scripture. It is quite different with the philosophers, who fight with nothing but reasons, because there is no genuine authority among them; and the Papists are wrong in their excessive emulation of them, for, setting aside the oracles of God, they fall back only on the inventions of the human brain, that is, on mere foolishness.

24. *Some believed.* Luke records that in the end the outcome of the disputation was that by no means did they all derive equal benefit from the same teaching. We know that the apostle was endowed with such grace of the Spirit that he ought to have moved stones; yet, by arguing a great deal for a long time, and also by testifying, he did not manage to win them all to Christ. Accordingly do not let us wonder if today the unbelief of many resists the clear teaching of the Gospel; and many remain inflexible, although the truth of Christ is just as plain to them as the sun shining at noon. Moreover men who had come willingly to Paul, as if with a mind to learn, go away from him blind and stupid. If there was such obstinacy in willing listeners, is there any wonder if men, who are swollen with pride and bitterness, and deliberately avoid the light, reject Christ with a bitter mind?

And when they agreed not among themselves, they departed, after that Paul had spoken one word, Well spake the Holy Ghost by Isaiah the prophet unto your fathers, saying, Go thou unto this people, and say, By hearing ye shall hear, and shall in no wise understand; And seeing ye shall see, and shall in no wise perceive: For this people's heart is waxed gross, And their ears are dull of hearing, And their eyes they have closed; Lest haply they should perceive with their eyes, And hear with their ears, And understand with their heart, and should turn again, And I should heal them. Be it known therefore unto you, that this salvation of God is sent unto the Gentiles: they will also hear. (And when he had said these words the Jews departed, having much disputing among themselves.[1]) And he[2] abode two whole years in his own hired dwelling,

[1] v. 29. RV margin. Tr.
[2] Calvin, with RV margin, reads, *Paul.* Tr.

and received all that went in unto him, preaching the kingdom of God, and teaching the things concerning the Lord Jesus Christ with all boldness, none forbidding him. (23-31)

25. *And when they disagreed among themselves.* The malice and perverseness of unbelievers has this effect, that Christ, who is our peace, and the one and only bond of sacred unity, is the occasion of disagreement, and makes those, who previously enjoyed friendly relations with each other, fight among themselves. For just look! When the Jews meet together to hear Paul, they all think the same thing, and say the same thing; they all profess their devotion to the Law of Moses. When they have heard the teaching of reconciliation, dissension appears among them, so that they are split into opposing factions. However we must not think that the disagreement begins with the preaching of the Gospel, but the animosity which was lying hidden before in their malicious hearts, finally emerges then; just as the shining of the sun does not introduce new colours, but clearly reveals the difference, which was hidden by the darkness. Therefore since God enlightens His elect especially, and faith is not common to all, let us remember that when Christ has been publicly presented, it is bound to happen that men part from one another. But let us then bear in mind that Simeon's prophecy about Him is being fulfilled, that He is a target for contradiction,[1] so 'that the thoughts out of many hearts may be revealed' (Luke 2.34, 35), and that disbelief, which is rebellion against God, is the mother of disagreement.

After Paul had said. At first he tried to win them gently and quietly. Now, when their obstinacy has been revealed, he makes a sharper attack, and gives a grave warning of the judgment of God. For rebels whose pride cannot be subdued by plain teaching, must be handled in this way. We must maintain the same procedure, gently directing the docile and the quiet, but summoning the inflexible to the judgment-seat of God. When he represents the Holy Spirit as speaking rather than the prophet, that is a valuable thing for creating confidence in the oracle. For since God demands that He alone be heard, teaching can have authority only if we know that it has come from Him, and did not originate in the minds of men. In the second place, he hints that it is not the stubbornness of only one generation that is being pointed out there, but that the oracle of the Spirit is extended to the future.

26. *Go to this people, etc.* This is a famous passage, because it is quoted six times in the New Testament. But because it is introduced

[1] *contradictionis scopum*; cf. Vulg. *in signum cui contradicetur.* RV 'for a sign which is spoken against'. Tr.

in other contexts for a different object, we must grasp why Paul makes it apply to the present situation. It was because he wished to use it like a hammer to smash the hardness of the ungodly; and, on the other hand, to encourage the believers, who were still frail and tender, so that they might not be upset by the unbelief of the others. Therefore the point is that what the prophet had foretold is being fulfilled, and so there is no cause for the reprobate to be pleased with themselves, or for believers to be terrified as if by something new and unusual. But although it is certain that the blindness, which the prophet mentions, had already begun in his day, yet John (12.40) reminds us that it referred properly to the Kingdom of Christ. Therefore Paul suitably adapts it to that contempt of the Gospel, which he saw. It is as if he had said, 'Nothing is happening that the Holy Spirit has not already predicted long ago through the mouth of Isaiah.'

Although this passage is applied in different ways, not only by the Evangelists, but also by Paul himself, the appearance of contradiction is easily removed. Matthew, Mark and Luke say that this prophecy was fulfilled when Christ spoke enigmatically to the people, and did not reveal the mysteries of the Kingdom of Heaven to them (Mark 4.11 and pars.). For then the voice of God beat upon the ears of the unbelieving, but they got no benefit from it. John (12.37) says what amounts to much the same thing, that the Jews were not persuaded to believe by many miracles, so that this same testimony of the prophet might be fulfilled. Therefore those four agree in this, that the just judgment of God brought it about that in hearing, the reprobate did not hear, and in seeing, did not see. Paul is now calling to mind what the prophet has testified about the Jews, so that no one might wonder at their blindness. Moreover in Rom. 11.5-8, he goes a step higher, saying that the cause of this blindness is that the Lord gives the light of faith only to a remnant, whom He has chosen by grace. And it is indeed certain that the rejection of the teaching of salvation by the reprobate is due to their ill-will, and therefore the blame remains with themselves. But this cause, mentioned here, does not prevent the secret election of God from distinguishing between men, so that those, who have been ordained to life, believe, but the others continue to be senseless. I shall not dwell on the words of the prophet too long now, since I have explained them elsewhere. In fact Paul has not carefully repeated the exact words of the prophet himself, but rather has adapted his words to his own purpose. Therefore, whereas the prophet attributed their blindness to the secret judgment of God, he ascribes it to their ill-will. For the prophet is ordered to close the eyes of his listeners; here Paul reproaches the unbelievers of his own day because they have shut their own eyes. However he distinctly states both things, that God is responsible for their blindness, and yet they have closed their own eyes and are blind of their own accord, since these two agree with each other very well, as I have said elsewhere.

In the last clause where it is said, 'Lest they perceive with their eyes, or hear with their ears, or understand with their heart', God is showing how very clear His teaching is, viz. that it is abundantly sufficient for the enlightening of all the senses, except in so far as men maliciously bring darkness on themselves. Paul also teaches that in II Cor. 4.3, where he says that his Gospel is open,[1] so that none are blinded in its light, except those who are destined for destruction, whose eyes Satan has closed.

27. *Lest they should turn again, and I should heal them.* We gather from this that the Word of God is not declared to all so that they may return to soundness of mind, but the spoken words ring in the ears of many without the effective power of the Spirit, only so that they may be rendered inexcusable. But here the pride of the flesh rashly cries out against God; just as we see many protesting that it is in vain, yes even absurd, for men to be called, unless they possess the ability to obey. For even if the reason why God appears to the blind, and speaks to the deaf, is hidden from us, yet His will alone, which is the rule of all justice, ought to be like a thousand reasons to us. In conclusion, we must note what a salutary effect the Word of God has, viz. the conversion of men, which is not only the beginning of health, but a kind of resurrection from death to life.

28. *Be it known therefore.* So that the Jews may not accuse him later on of defection, because he leaves the holy race of Abraham and betakes himself to the profane Gentiles, he declares what the prophets had asserted so often, that the salvation, of which they were the proper, or at least primary heirs, must be transferred to outsiders. However, his statement that *salvation has been sent to the Gentiles* means, in the second place, of course, after it has been rejected by the Jews, something that we have already dealt with at greater length in 13.46. The meaning therefore is that there is no cause for the Jews to complain that the Gentiles are being admitted to the vacant possession, when they have abandoned it.

Also, in saying that *the Gentiles will hear*, he does not make faith common to every individual, without exception. For he knew well enough from experience how many of the Gentiles also impiously resisted God. But he sets all the Gentiles, who were believers, over against the unbelieving Jews, to provoke them to jealousy, as it is put in the Song of Moses (Deut. 32.21). At the same time he is pointing

[1] Reading *apertus*, with Tholuck, cf. RV 'the manifestation of the truth', v. 2. C.R. has *opertus*, agreeing with Vulg. and RV 'veiled', of v. 4. Tr.

313

out that the teaching, which they are rejecting, will not be unprofitable among others.

29. *Having much disputing among themselves.* There is no doubt that he irritated the ungodly more, because he quoted the prophecy against them. For so far from being subdued by the reproofs, they whipped themselves up to a more violent fury. The reason why they had a dispute when they left Paul was that the majority did not wish to give their assent. But since there was a two-sided argument it is plain that some had embraced what Paul had said, so that they did not hesitate boldly to defend and affirm what they had believed.

Finally, it will be in vain for anyone to object from this that the Gospel of Christ causes contentions, when it is obvious that these spring only from the stubbornness of men. And indeed, in order to enjoy peace with God, it is necessary for us to wage war with those who treat Him with contempt.

30. *Received all.* The holy apostle gave a remarkable example of steadfastness, in making himself available so unreservedly to all who wished to hear him. He was certainly not unaware of how much ill-will he stirred up for himself, and that it was to his best advantage, if he were to appease the hatred of the opposing faction by keeping silent. For a cautious man, wishing to watch out for himself, should not have behaved like that. But because he remembered that he was just as much an apostle of Christ and a herald of the Gospel in prison, as if he were unfettered and free, he considered that it was not right to hold himself back from anyone, who was prepared to learn, in case he might neglect an opportunity presented to him by God. And so the sacred calling of God meant more to him than concern for his own life. But so that we may know that he submitted to danger of his own free-will, Luke expressly commends his *boldness* a little further on, as if he said that he set fear aside and faithfully obeyed the command of God, and was not terrified by any difficulties, but continued to devote his efforts to all whom he met.

31. *Preaching the Kingdom of God.* He does not separate *the Kingdom of God* and *the things concerning Christ*, as if they were different, but adds the second phrase rather by way of explanation, so that we may know that the Kingdom of God is founded on, and consists in, the knowledge of the redemption procured by Christ. Therefore Paul taught that men are outside the Kingdom of God as strangers and exiles, until their sins are atoned for, they are reconciled to God and they are renewed in holiness of life by the Spirit. But he also taught that in fact the Kingdom of God is set up and flourishes, only when Christ the Mediator unites men to the Father, both pardoned by the free remission of sins, and born again to righteousness, so that, while

they begin the heavenly life on earth, they may always desire to reach heaven, where they will have the complete and full enjoyment of glory.

Luke also makes known the remarkable blessing of God, that Paul was granted so much freedom. For that did not come about by the connivance or indifference of those who could have prevented him, seeing that they detested religion, but because the Lord closed their eyes. Accordingly Paul himself has every right to glory that the Word of God was not bound with his chains (II Tim. 2.9).

INDEX OF SCRIPTURE REFERENCES